ALL ROADS LEAD TO THE TEXT

ALL ROADS LEAD TO THE TEXT

Eight Methods of Inquiry into the Bible

A Template for Model Exegesis
with Exegetical Examples Employing
Logos Bible Software

Dean B. Deppe

WILLIAM B. EERDMANS PUBLISHING COMPANY
GRAND RAPIDS, MICHIGAN/CAMBRIDGE, U.K.

Published 2011 by

Wm. B. Eerdmans Publishing Co.

2140 Oak Industrial Drive N.E., Grand Rapids, Michigan 49505 /

P.O. Box 163, Cambridge CB3 9PU U.K.

Printed in the United States of America

17 16 15 14 13 12 11   7 6 5 4 3 2 1

Library of Congress Cataloging-in-Publication Data

Deppe, Dean B.

  All roads lead to the Text: eight methods of inquiry into the Bible:
  a template for model exegesis with exegetical examples employing
  Logos Bible Software / Dean Deppe.
        p.   cm.
  Includes bibliographical references.
  ISBN 978-0-8028-6594-6 (pbk.: alk. paper)
  1. Bible — Criticism, interpretation, etc. — Data processing.   I. Title.

  BS534.8.D47   2011
  220.60285 — dc23

                                                              2011022671

www.eerdmans.com

Contents

ABBREVIATIONS   viii

INTRODUCTION: A Sample Exegetical Method   xii

1. The Infrared Lens of Literary Analysis:
   Form and Genre Criticism   1

   A. *Pericope Delimitation*   1

   B. *The Identification of Genre*   7

   C. *The Identification of Literary Techniques*   25

      STUDY AND DISCUSSION QUESTIONS   35

2. The Grammatical Route:
   Using an Exegetical Microscope   38

   A. *Textual Criticism*   38

   B. *Word Study*   43

   C. *Analysis of Phrases*   51

   D. *Clausal Analysis*   57

   E. *Examining Word Order*   71

   F. *English Translations*   75

      STUDY AND DISCUSSION QUESTIONS   85

3. The Structural Analysis Route:
   Employing a Skeleton Snapshot   89

   A. *The Structure of Various Biblical Books*   89

   B. *Grammatical and Literary Structure*   105

   C. *Clausal Outlines*   115

      STUDY AND DISCUSSION QUESTIONS   127

4. The Literary Context Route:
   Employing a Wide-Angled Lens   131

   A. *The Context Surrounding the Pericope*   131

   B. *Redactionary Activity*   141

      STUDY AND DISCUSSION QUESTIONS   154

5. The Cultural and Historical Background Route:
   Using a Telescopic Lens   158

   A. *Historical and Cultural Elements*   158

   B. *The Old Testament as Background*   171

   C. *Basic Background Information for Biblical Books*   178

      STUDY AND DISCUSSION QUESTIONS   190

6. The History of Interpretation Route:
   Using a Motion Picture Exegetical Camera   194

   A. *The Major Commentators*   194

   B. *Different Periods in Church History*   213

      STUDY AND DISCUSSION QUESTIONS   224

7. The Theological Exegesis Route:
   Developing the Finished Photo   228

   A. *A Theological Analysis of the Biblical Text*   229

   B. *An Investigation of the Reader's Presuppositions*   245

   C. *Exploring the Canonical Meaning*   249

      STUDY AND DISCUSSION QUESTIONS   259

8. Exploring Spiritual Exegesis:
   Using an Exegetical X-Ray Camera   262

   A. *The Insufficiencies of the Historical-Critical Method*   263

   B. *The Dangers of Spiritual Exegesis*   267

   C. *The Disciplines of Spiritual Exegesis*   268

   STUDY AND DISCUSSION QUESTIONS   292

   Conclusion   294

   APPENDIX I: Genres   296

   I. *A Morphology of Genre*   296

   II. *Canonical Examples of Controversy Dialogues*   333

   III. *Principles of Interpretation for the Main Genre Types*   345

   APPENDIX II: Literary Techniques   353

   Literary Devices As Organizational Techniques   353

   A GLOSSARY OF LITERARY TECHNIQUES AND
   GRAMMATICAL TERMS   364

   SELECT BIBLIOGRAPHY   369

   INDEX OF NAMES   376

   INDEX OF SCRIPTURE AND OTHER ANCIENT LITERATURE   381

Abbreviations

1QS	*Rule of the Community*
AB	Anchor Bible
ABD	*Anchor Bible Dictionary.* New York, 1986.
ABR	*Australian Biblical Review*
ABRL	Anchor Bible Reference Library
adj ptc	adjectival participle
adv ptc	adverbial participle
AGJU	Arbeiten zur Geschichte des antiken Judentums und des Urchristentums
AnBib	Analecta biblica
ANRW	*Aufstieg und Niedergang der römischen Welt.* Berlin, 1972–
Ant.	Josephus, *Jewish Antiquities*
art inf	articular infinitive
ASV	American Standard Version
AUSS	Andrews University Seminary Studies
BDAG	W. Bauer, F. W. Danker, W. F. Arndt, F. W. Gingrich, *A Greek-English Lexicon of the New Testament and Other Early Christian Literature.* 3rd ed. Chicago, 2000.
BDF	F. Blass, A. Debrunner, R. W. Funk, *A Greek Grammar of the New Testament and Other Christian Literature.* Chicago, 1961.
BETL	Bibliotheca ephemeridum theologicarum lovaniensium
BRS	Biblical Resource Series
BT	*Bible Translator*
BTB	*Biblical Theology Bulletin*

BZAW	Beihefte zur Zeitschrift für die alttestamentliche Wissenschaft
CBQ	*Catholic Biblical Quarterly*
CD	Cairo Genizah copy of the *Damascus Document*
comple inf	complementary infinitive
CRINT	Compendia rerum iudaicarum ad Novum Testamentum
CTJ	*Calvin Theological Journal*
CTM	*Concordia Theological Monthly*
CTR	*Criswell Theological Review*
CurTM	*Currents in Theology and Mission*
dir obj	direct object
ErIsr	*Eretz-Israel*
ESV	English Standard Version
Exp	*The Expositor*
ExpTim	*Expository Times*
FOTL	The Forms of the Old Testament Literature
GBS	Guides to Biblical Scholarship
GNB	Good News Bible
HNTC	Harper's New Testament Commentaries
hort subjun	hortatory subjunctive
HSM	Harvard Semitic Monographs
HTR	*Harvard Theological Review*
HUCA	*Hebrew Union College Annual*
ICC	International Critical Commentary
imper	imperative
indir quest	indirect question
inf	infinitive
Int	*Interpretation*
ISV	International Standard Version
JAOS	*Journal of the American Oriental Society*
JBL	*Journal of Biblical Literature*
JETS	*Journal of the Evangelical Theological Society*
JQR	*Jewish Quarterly Review*
JSJSup	Journal for the Study of Judaism Supplement
JSNT	*Journal for the Study of the New Testament*
JSNTSup	Journal for the Study of the New Testament: Supplement Series
JSOT	*Journal for the Study of the Old Testament*
JSOTSup	Journal for the Study of the Old Testament: Supplement Series

KJV	King James Version
LB	*Linguistica Biblica*
LEC	Library of Early Christianity
LXX	Septuagint
NAB	New American Bible
NAC	New American Commentary
NASB	New American Standard Bible
NCB	New Century Bible
NCV	New Century Version
NEB	New English Bible
Neot	*Neotestamentica*
NET	New English Translation
NIB	*The New Interpreter's Bible.* Nashville, 1994-2004.
NICNT	New International Commentary on the New Testament
NIGTC	New International Greek Testament Commentary
NIV	New International Version
NJB	New Jerusalem Bible
NKJV	New King James Version
NLT	New Living Translation
NovT	*Novum Testamentum*
NovTSup	*Novum Testamentum Supplements*
NRSV	New Revised Standard Version
NTS	*New Testament Studies*
NTTS	New Testament Tools and Studies
OTL	Old Testament Library
PG	Patrologia graeca. Paris, 1857-86.
prep phrase	prepositional phrase
ptc	participle
rel clause	relative clause
ResQ	*Restoration Quarterly*
RevExp	*Review and Expositor*
RSV	Revised Standard Version
RTR	*Reformed Theological Review*
Sanh	Tractate *Sanhedrin*
SBLDS	Society of Biblical Literature Dissertartion Series
SBLSBS	Society of Biblical Literature Sources for Biblical Study
SBLSP	*Society of Biblical Literature Seminar Papers*
SBT	Studies in Biblical Theology
SE	*Studia evangelica*

SJT	*Scottish Journal of Theology*
SNTSMS	Society for New Testament Studies Monograph Series
ST	*Studia theologica*
STRev	*Sewanee Theological Review*
supple comple	Supplementary participle with complementary usage; cf. Daniel B. Wallace, *Greek Grammar Beyond the Basics*, 646.
SwJT	*Southwestern Journal of Theology*
TDNT	*Theological Dictionary of the New Testament*. Grand Rapids, 1964-1976.
temp	temporal
TEV	Today's English Version
TJ	*Trinity Journal*
TNIV	Today's New International Version
TynBul	*Tyndale Bulletin*
TZ	*Theologische Zeitschrift*
VCSup	Supplements to Vigiliae christianae
VT	*Vetus Testamentum*
WBC	Word Biblical Commentary
WTJ	*Westminster TheologicaL Journal*
YLT	Young's Literal Translation
ZAW	*Zeitschrift für die alttestamentliche Wissenschaft*
ZNW	*Zeitschrift für die neutestamentliche Wissenschaft*

Introduction

The notorious quip "all roads lead to Rome" demonstrates the centrality of that city within ancient culture. In the same manner, the text is the destination of every method of biblical investigation, so that each road of exegesis should lead us to the identical results. The following template for investigating the text proposes that the exegete journey down several distinctive roads but that the destination will remain the same, i.e., a clearer and more profitable understanding of the meaning of the biblical text.

We advocate using eight methods or paths of inquiry. These include:

1. The literary study of genre, various literary techniques (*inclusio,* chiasm, parallelism, repetition etc.), and figures of speech (alliteration, anthropomorphism, irony, etc.);
2. The grammatical study of words, phrases, and clauses that result in various translations of the Bible;
3. The structural analysis of the relationship between clauses and sentences in a paragraph until the arrangement of a passage becomes clearly visible;
4. An analysis of the context both preceding and following a particular pericope so that the flow of an author's thought is perceived;
5. An investigation of the cultural and historical background of a particular text and the book of the Bible within which it resides;
6. A history of interpretation of the text through the church fathers, the Reformation, and the modern critical period;
7. Theological exegesis which concentrates upon the theological themes

and content in a passage as well as analyzing the reader's presuppositions in interpreting the text;

8. Employing the spiritual disciplines of a practicing faith perspective, personalizing the text, praying Scripture, picturing concepts through meditation, listening prophetically, paradigm building through mirroring, and imaginative application.

Some students of the text prefer to begin with the smallest unit and work to the largest. First they study words, then phrases, clauses, sentences, paragraphs, books, the whole Bible, and finally the cultural world behind the biblical text. Others prefer the opposite approach to first envision the big picture and gradually work down to an investigation of the details. Our method leaves these options to the individual; any road can be walked down first or last. Since each path leads to the text, the procedural order is negotiable. However, it is crucial that each path is investigated.

Instead of supplying a philosophical and theoretical grounding for each of these methodologies, we will concentrate on an exploration of examples to enlighten the biblical text. This approach separates this book from others on the subject of hermeneutics and biblical methodology. These case studies of various biblical passages are intended to demonstrate the value of each road of investigation. Therefore readers can begin at any chapter which piques their attention, since each exegetical road should lead in the same direction. Students today want immediate payoff for their research, so the use of examples will concentrate both on exegesis and application. After accumulating exegetical data through the use of each of these eight methods, the reader is ready to arrive at the theme of the passage and employ his or her results in a Bible study or sermon. Computer-generated exegesis is becoming an important component of the study of the Bible, so in several of the exegetical examples we will demonstrate how the use of Logos Bible Software can be employed to facilitate our study of the text.[1] In our analysis of

---

1. I will employ the terms Libronix and Logos as synonyms. Logos 4 appeared in 2009 to replace Libronix 3. Although they appear on your computer with separate icons, they perform similar features. Because both programs are in use, I will explain when different procedures are necessary to get results in the two editions of this software system. John H. Hayes and Carl R. Holladay, *Biblical Exegesis: A Beginner's Handbook,* 3rd ed. (Louisville: Westminster John Knox, 2007), include in the Appendix an analysis on "Using Electronic Technologies in Exegesis," but this field changes so quickly that Logos 4 is not mentioned. Information on this computer program and training videos can be found at www.logos.com. Click the icon "Training" at the top of the home page and then choose "Tutorial Videos."

the text, we will normally employ the New International Version as our English translation unless otherwise noted.[2] After each chapter we include a list of questions for continued study and application as well as for use in small group Bible studies.

All exegesis, of course, contains certain presuppositions. This involves what we normally call hermeneutics. Following W. Randolph Tate,[3] we define exegesis as the process of examining a text to ascertain what its first readers would have understood it to mean. Interpretation (exposition or contextualization), on the other hand, is the task of explaining or drawing out the implications of that understanding for contemporary readers and hearers. Finally, if one combines exegesis and exposition with an examination of the hermeneut's presuppositional repertoire, then we are speaking about hermeneutics. In these eight exegetical journeys which we will undertake, the following ten principles of interpretation will be assumed.

1. Exegesis must concern itself not only with the content but also with the form of the text, both what is said (content) and how it is said (genre, form).

2. Exegesis involves both semantics, the study of the language of a text, and pragmatics, the study of the circumstances surrounding the text. In the same vein, Peter Cotterell and Max Turner[4] talk about text (actual words), co-text (relationships between the words), and context (historical and sociological setting).

3. Exegesis must always analyze a text within various descriptions of context: historical, ideological, and literary.

4. Context does not merely help us understand meaning; it virtually creates meaning. The most likely meaning is that one which causes the least interruption to the context.

5. Meaning is determined on the basis of the congruence of the semantic field (the number of possible meanings at the time of writing) and the context (revealing which of the possible meanings takes priority in the particular passage).

6. The locus of meaning is discovered in the interplay of the three worlds

2. Sometimes the 2011 NIV is employed to avoid exclusively male language. In addition we will employ the NRSV version of the Apocrypha.

3. W. Randolph Tate, *Biblical Interpretation: An Integrated Approach* (Peabody: Hendrickson, 1991), p. xv.

4. Peter Cotterell and Max Turner, *Linguistics and Biblical Interpretation* (Downers Grove: InterVarsity, 1989), pp. 15-19.

of author, text, and reader. As Grant Osborne maintains, "There is a dialogue, indeed a trialogue, between author, text, and reader, leading to the meaning of the text."[5] Or put another way, "Meaning resides in the conversation between the text and reader with the world behind the text informing that conversation."[6]

7. Any proper hermeneutics must study the text both diachronically and synchronically.

8. Exegesis must never be swallowed up in application, but must necessarily precede it.[7]

9. All readers of the text have their own theological, cultural, philosophical, and psychological presuppositions which must be recognized and acknowledged if faulty exegetical conclusions are going to be eliminated. During the process of interpretation, the text will legitimate, deny, clarify, or modify our assumptions.

10. The exegete must not only interpret the text but must allow the text to interpret him or her as well (the hermeneutical circle).

A Sample Exegetical Method

Already we have employed one image in order to picture a proper exegetical method: we will travel down various roads trusting that we will arrive at the same destination. A second image requires the use of various camera lenses to examine the text. Each lens offers a distinctive picture of the exegetical scenery.

Literary analysis involves the employment of an infrared lens to investigate what cannot always be seen in natural light. We focus upon authorial indications of the extent of the paragraph, the type of genre employed along with the expectations involved for an interpretation of that particular genre, and the literary and rhetorical devices that the author places in the text to hint at its meaning. Then, for grammatical exegesis, we employ an exegetical microscope which scrutinizes the details of a passage from words, to phrases, to clauses until we arrive at various translations of the text. Third, we take a skeleton snapshot of the text so that we can envision the structure of the pas-

---

5. Grant R. Osborne, *The Hermeneutical Spiral: A Comprehensive Introduction to Biblical Interpretation* (Downers Grove: InterVarsity, 1991), p. 380.

6. Tate, *Biblical Interpretation*, p. xx.

7. Tate, *Biblical Interpretation*, p. 3.

sage through developing a clausal outline. Then we avail ourselves of a <u>wide-angled lens</u> to probe the context of the pericope. We peer before and after the passage to examine how our particular field of study fits into the larger purpose of the document before us. Next we utilize a <u>telescopic lens</u> and explore the world behind the text by inspecting the cultural and historical background. This includes a study of intertextuality so that we explore how the Old Testament background shapes the meaning of a New Testament text. Sixth, we roll out the <u>motion picture camera</u> to study the various periods of church history and to investigate how an examination of the major commentaries benefits our exegesis.

Next to last, we develop the <u>finished photo</u> through a theological analysis of the text and an exploration of the canonical meaning. Finally, we do not want to forget to explore the world in front of the text by an investigation of the reader's presuppositions and various spiritual exercises and disciplines that enable us to apply the text to contemporary life. This <u>x-ray</u> of our personality, presuppositions, and spiritual makeup certifies that we are not deceiving ourselves and that this whole process is not just an intellectual exercise completely separated from our life experience. These exegetical camera shots form a <u>sample album of proofs</u> that offer snapshots of the text from various angles. Step by step we will employ these various lenses attached to our exegetical camera to offer a complete picture of the text. Let us begin!

CHAPTER 1

The Infrared Lens of Literary Analysis

Form and Genre Criticism

Just as the human eye cannot see "everything that's out there," so our exegetical eye has not always been trained to perceive indications of when a passage begins and ends, the particular genre of a section of Scripture, or literary devices that subtly offer the meaning of the text. Through a series of biblical examples in this chapter the reader will develop literary skills in discerning clues to the delimitation of a pericope, distinguishing the genre and its principles of interpretation, and identifying the literary techniques employed by the author such as *inclusio* and chiasm as well as understanding their significance for exegesis.

A. Pericope Delimitation

PROCEDURE

Perceptive readers can establish the limits of a pericope under study by noting a number of "tells" in the text. Transition devices like statements of introduction or conclusion are certainly the most obvious as, for example, the use of disjunctive clauses in Hebrew. In narratives, a change in the setting, time frame, or characters regularly introduces a new section. Literarily, the substitution of alternative genres as well as the presence of repetitive grammatical features signal a new beginning. Finally, the reader should always attempt to perceive an alteration of theme.

EXAMPLES

1. Matthew 1:18–2:23: The Fulfillment of Five OT Texts

Discerning readers of the text are on the alert to spot literary devices like repetition as an indicator of pericope delimiters. For instance, in Matt 1:18–2:23 one discovers the repetition of five OT texts as fulfilled prophecies (Matt 1:23; 2:6, 15, 18, 23) indicating five short paragraphs that call attention to Jesus as the fulfillment of prophecy. This section is preceded by a genealogy of Jesus where the Greek verb ἐγέννησεν ("begot, fathered") is repeated 39 times with a change to the passive form ἐγεννήθη in 1:16b in order to climax the genealogy with Jesus. In our section the genre changes to a narrative of Joseph's three dreams (1:20-21; 2:13, 19-20) interspersed with the violence of Herod, who attempts to manipulate the magi into revealing the location of this new king (2:4, 7-8) and who finally viciously massacres innocent children to protect his throne (2:16).

Throughout this pericope the five OT texts stand out prominently, highlighting each subsection, so that Jesus' name as Immanuel (Isa 7:14 at 1:23), his birth in the city of David (Mic 5:2 in 2:6), his exodus out of Egypt (Hos 11:1 in 2:15), the lament over the slain children (Jer 31:15 in 2:18), and Jesus' identification with Nazareth (Isa 11:1 in 2:23) all become fulfilled OT prophecies in the history of salvation. This division is captured by several English versions such as the NRSV and the ESV, which divide Matt 1:18–2:23 into five distinct sections. Logos Bible Software contains a helpful tool to visualize the structuring of pericopes. Under the "Tools" menu and the "Passage Analysis" bar, choose "Compare Pericopes" at the bottom of the screen. Then you can choose which Bible versions you want to compare and easily visualize the pericope delimitation of the various translations. Through discerning the literary devices of repetition and a change in genre, we have discovered how Matthew structures Jesus' birth narrative as his prologue to the Gospel. The fulfillment of OT prophecies is crucial to the message that Matthew intends to deliver to his audience.

2. 1 John 1:6–2:2: Three Pairs of Conditional Sentences

Although chapter divisions were intended to clarify the major break points in the narrative, frequently these markers misconstrue the extent of the passage which the author intended. For example, the first chapter of 1 John concludes with a negative statement whose positive counterpart was regretfully placed in chapter 2 by Stephen Langton around the year 1205. The chapter now ends, "If we claim we have not sinned, we make him out to be a liar." To end a Bible study or homily with the thought that we have characterized God as a liar would certainly not edify the audience. This negative truth must be balanced with the greater and more gracious statement in 1 John 2:1, "But if anybody does sin, we have one who speaks to the Father in our defense — Jesus Christ, the Righteous One." Certainly John intended to extend this passage to 2:2, where the reader can focus on Jesus Christ, the defense lawyer who pleads our case so that we are proclaimed righteous.

A search in Logos Bible Software of ἐάν clauses in 1 John reveals that 1 John 1:6–2:2 consists of six conditional (ἐάν) clauses in a row which alternate between positive and negative "if" statements (1 John 1:6-7; 1:8-9; 1:10–2:2). Therefore, on three successive occasions a negative confession of sin is trumped each time by a positive affirmation of God's loving character and a corresponding human righteousness. Rather than claiming fellowship with God while we daily live a contrary lifestyle of deceit, we walk in the light and continually experience the cleansing of Christ (1:6-7). Instead of boasting of a life without sin, we confess our shortcomings with integrity because we are convinced that God is faithful and just (John 1:8-9). Finally, in the third pair we no longer introspectively search for sinless perfection within ourselves, but instead focus on the atoning sacrifice of Jesus Christ. If we analyze the pericope correctly, the positive character of Christ's work shines through brightly. The correct delineation of a passage through the identification of literary repetitions enables proper exegesis.

3. John 2:24–3:21: A Positive or Negative Interpretation of Nicodemus?

As a child, whenever we read around the family dinner table Jesus' conversation with Nicodemus in John 3, I pictured Nicodemus as a model Christian who was born again of water and the Spirit. But if we examine pericope markers in the Gospel of John, we perceive that John was already preparing for the arrival of Nicodemus in John 2:24 when he declares that "Jesus would not entrust himself to them . . . for he knew what was in a man." The man Jesus would not entrust himself to is Nicodemus.

Throughout the Gospel John portrays Nicodemus on a journey from a frightened but searching representative of the Jewish aristocracy (John 3:1; 7:50), to a secret disciple who remains within the synagogue (19:38-39), to one who speaks out for Jesus (7:51) and finally comes out of the closet to publicly stand with Jesus in his suffering and death (19:39-40). Two characters in the story, Joseph of Arimathea and Nicodemus, represent all secret disciples who must journey into the light and become a model for a group of John's readers who, according to 12:42-43, "would not confess their faith for fear they would be put out of the synagogue, for they loved the praise from men more than praise from God."

Not only did our family begin the story at the wrong place, we always concluded at John 3:15-16, where Nicodemus seems to disappear. But the imagery of night in 3:2 is balanced by the metaphor of light in 3:19-21, which explains that "Light has come into the world, but people loved darkness instead of light because their deeds were evil." The Pharisees represented here by Nicodemus love darkness rather than light and must be replaced in the kingdom of God by other leaders who are born again. The delimitation of the pericope determines the meaning of the incident. Nicodemus is not yet born of the Spirit in John 3.

4. John 9:1–10:21: The Extent of the Blind Man Pericope

The chapter division at John 10 likewise prohibits many readers from a correct understanding of the Parable of the Sheep Pen in John 10:1-6. Contrary to the chapter division, the story of the healing of the blind man in John 9 is not concluded until John 10:21, "Can a demon open the eyes of the blind?" In John 10:22 a new section is introduced by the arrival of the Feast of Dedication, whereas John 7:1–10:21 concentrates on the Feast of Booths, just as Jesus fulfils the Passover feast in John 6 and the Sabbath in chapter 5. Therefore the Parable of the Shepherd and His Flock (10:1-6) must be an application of the healing of the blind man.

Throughout chapter 9 the blind man's confession of faith gradually deepens as he envisions Jesus more clearly. In the first scene the person who healed him is merely labeled "the man they call Jesus" (John 9:11); then he becomes "a prophet" (9:17) and the "godly one" who is "without sin" (9:25, 31). Only after the blind man is thrown out of the synagogue (9:34) does he have new eyes to see Jesus as the transcendent Son of Man (9:35) and ultimately as God himself who alone deserves worship (9:38). Picturing Jesus as divine is the pinnacle of Johannine Christology.

With this as background, Jesus speaks a parable (10:1-6) where God as the watchman of Israel opens the gate of the sheepfold only to the true shepherd, Jesus Christ. Then Jesus as shepherd walks ahead of his sheep and out of the sheepfold the ones who hear his voice (10:3). In other words, ⌐ ⌐ is directing his sheep out of the synagogue just as the blind man was thrown out of the synagogue. Only outside of the synagogue could Christians without fear of reprisal and persecution proclaim that Jesus is God.

This split between Christianity and Judaism was a very traumatic and difficult experience for all involved. Culturally it seemed to the Christians that they were being thrown out of their house of worship by their former brethren, but in reality John is saying that Jesus himself is leading them out. The disciples remain blind to Jesus' true identity until they renounce being secret disciples and proclaim, as Thomas does in the climactic pericope of the book (20:28), that Jesus is "my Lord and my God." The commitment demanded of a disciple is the radical confession of Jesus as God himself, a confession more important than any allegiance to a group of people, even if they are your own family and heritage. The cost of discipleship is great. Yet this theological conclusion only becomes clear when we ignore the chapter divisions and read John 9:1–10:21 as one unit.

5. Markan Intercalations

The evangelist Mark loves to sandwich two narratives together (also called a Markan Intercalation) in order to equip the reader to understand properly the purpose of an event. By positioning the cleansing of the temple within the story of the cursing of the fig tree (Mark 11:12-26), Jesus proclaims that the time of temple worship is ended just as the fig tree is destroyed from its roots. Traditionally, we have entitled Jesus' action as a temple cleansing, but for Mark the event is a prophetic action of the destruction of the temple. Jesus shuts down the temple activities for a short period of time by prohibiting the selling of sacrificial animals and not allowing anyone to carry merchandise through the temple courts (11:15-16). Just as the season for figs has passed (11:13) and no one will eat fruit from the fig tree again (11:14), so the temple will be destroyed and no longer serve as the life fount of Israel. Mark clarifies this theological interpretation by encapsulating the temple action with the cursing of the fig tree. Together these two events constitute a single pericope for Mark.

At first glance Jesus' family and the Jewish teachers of the law don't seem to have much in common. However, Mark sandwiches the two groups together in 3:20-33 with Jesus' family proclaiming that Jesus is insanely out of his mind and the Pharisees claiming that he casts out demons by the devil himself. His family arrives to retrieve him from this new fanatic lifestyle (3:20-21), and the scribes conclude that Jesus is possessed by Beelzebul, the prince of the demons (3:22-30). Jesus' family end up outside the circle of disciples (3:31-33), just like the Jewish leaders. By framing this passage with the calling of the twelve disciples in 3:13-19 and the description of Jesus' true family in 3:34-35, the Gospel of Mark powerfully demonstrates that those expecting to be inside the kingdom (blood relation and religious leaders) may in reality be outside. Again the two stories must be read together. The reader discerns the extent of the pericope through the presence of a literary device.

6. Vocatives in the Epistle of James

Frequently, a direct address (like "brothers and sisters") introduces a new section. Performing a morphological search of the vocative in a book like the Epistle of James yields a series of meaningful transitions. Those who prefer visual indicators can employ the visual filter in Logos Bible Software and place a visual marker around all the vocatives in the text. To perform this procedure, click the "File" menu, go to "Visual Filters," specify a "morph" search rather than a basic or Bible search, and choose "Logos Greek Morphology" in the fourth option on the search line. Now place a @ symbol in the first box and choose "Noun" and "Vocative" and then in the formatting box highlight the text with something obvious like a double box or a yellow glow. Then, in all your Bibles, the vocative will stand out. A second option is to perform a morphological search of all vocatives. You can even search an English Bible like the NIV with Logos Greek Morphology and repeat the above procedure so that all the vocative nouns in the New Testament will appear. Simply scroll down to the Epistle of James and you will discover the vocatives in this book.

Performing this procedure we discover that Jas 1:2, 16, 19; 2:1, 14; 4:13; 5:1, 7, 12, 19 employ vocatives like "my brethren" (ἀδελφοί μου) and "my beloved brethren" (ἀδελφοί μου ἀγαπητοί) to introduce new sections. These addresses divide the Epistle of James into distinct sections. Since this book could be entitled "The Paraenesis of James," I like to divide the exhortations into the sub-genres of extended paraenesis (1:2-15; 1:16-18; 1:19-27), treatises or diatribes based upon one theme (2:1-13, 14-26; 3:1-12), prophetic denunciations (4:13–5:6), and general paraenesis crafted into a primitive church order (5:7-11; 5:12-18; 5:19-20).[1] The perceptive reader will pay close attention to this literary device in discerning the structure of documents.

7. Repeated Phrases in 1 Corinthians

Finally, sometimes the author himself directly reveals that a new section is beginning. Notice in 1 Corinthians how Paul clearly lets the reader know the next theme by means of certain phrases such as "now about food sacrificed to idols" (8:1), or "now about spiritual gifts" (12:1), or "now about the collection for God's people" (16:1). In this case the chapter divisions have picked up the intended transitions in the text (but notice 7:25 and 16:12). Paul is directly responding to issues for which the church at Corinth sought his advice and discernment (see 7:1), and these form the sections of 1 Corinthians 7–16. Although in this case the author clearly specifies his transition points, frequently the reader must perceptively detect the literary devices that reveal the author's directives.

B. The Identification of Genre

The determination of genre is crucial to detecting the meaning of a literary text, since like an infrared lens it offers a photo that we do not always observe in normal light. Dan Via defines genre as the "hidden or unconscious structure" of the whole that is "beyond the text from which the latter draws its meaning."[2] Genres trigger different expectations and thus demand divergent reading strategies.

In reading the daily newspaper, I am sure you peruse sections of the paper differently without even realizing it. You expect trustworthy facts and true-to-reality reporting when you study the front page news, while you place a filter over your mind while digesting editorials because you recognize the writing as only someone's opinion. You would never scrutinize the horoscopes as if they were tomorrow's weather page. Certainly, you would not understand the stock market reports as if they were the events of science fic-

---

1. See Dean B. Deppe, *The Sayings of Jesus in the Epistle of James* (Chelsea, MI: Book-crafters, 1989), pp. 58-59. Consult Appendix I, IE4 (pp. 328-29), for explanations of these subgenres.

2. Dan O. Via, Jr., *Kerygma and Comedy in the New Testament: A Structuralist Approach to Hermeneutic* (Philadelphia: Fortress, 1985), p. 15.

tion. When you read the comics, you expect to laugh or else you are disappointed, which certainly varies greatly from your response to the obituaries. You would never fill in the crossword puzzle as a secret code to tomorrow's sports page scores.

Just as we interpret each genre of the newspaper uniquely, so the biblical literature contains divergent rules of interpretation for each genre. Branson Woodard and Michael Travers explain that

> Generic conventions are closely related to meaning; they are not gratuitous decorations minimally relevant to the meaning of a work. . . . In the Old Testament narratives the theological truth is communicated in the chronological development of the events of the story; the reader does not just understand the truth — he experiences it. In Old Testament poetry the truth is expressed in the emotional intensity of a speaker's particular situation, prompting the reader to empathize with the speaker, not just to understand him.[3]

Different genres produce meaning in various ways. Whereas we normally consider the immediate context first for a proper interpretation, in wisdom literature the context frequently plays no role at all. We approach most literature expecting a literal interpretation, but in apocalyptic literature symbolic explanations take priority. A lengthy specification of genre including its division into subgenre, principles of interpretation, and specified examples within the biblical text is given in Appendix I.

Walter Russell[4] advises preachers that the genre characteristics of the biblical passage should also impact the form of the sermon. A narrative passage would not fit a doctrinal sermon with three points since OT narratives do not attempt to teach a theological doctrine in a direct manner. The book of Proverbs is best preached topically around a string of proverbs with similar content, since the context of wisdom literature usually is not significant. If the forms of sermons violate the genre qualities of the passages under consideration, they will either detract from the biblical message or distort the meaning of the passage. These insights make genre identification important for both exegetes and practitioners.

---

3. Branson L. Woodard, Jr. and Michael E. Travers, "Literary Forms and Interpretation," in *Cracking Old Testament Codes: A Guide to Interpreting Literary Genres of the Old Testament,* ed. D. Brent Sandy and Ronald L. Giese, Jr. (Nashville: Broadman and Holman, 1995), pp. 29-43.

4. Walter B. Russell III, "Literary Forms in the Hands of Preachers and Teachers," in Sandy and Giese, p. 291.

With each biblical text that is discussed, we will specify its literary form (narrative, lament, parable, controversy dialogue, miracle story, apocalyptic literature, etc.) and research the particular laws of interpretation as exemplified in Appendix I, Section III (pp. 340-47). We will follow the canonical order in the examples below to demonstrate the significance for interpretation of the genres of OT narrative, psalms, controversy dialogue, miracle story, epistle, and hymn.

EXAMPLES

1. Principles for Interpreting Narratives
and the Succession of David's Throne

Since narratives are extremely common in biblical literature, familiarity with the principles of interpretation is vitally important. The succession of Solomon to David's throne is a fascinating series of events that examines the lives of David's four sons, Amnon, Absalom, Adonijah, and Solomon. The central question raised as the book of Kings begins is, "Who will sit on David's throne?" as evidenced by the repetition of the phrase "sitting on the throne" at 1 Kgs 1:13, 17, 20, 24, 27, 30, 35, 46, 48. Finally at 2:12 the narrative concludes, "So Solomon sat on the throne of his father David, and his rule was firmly established." Throughout what has come to be entitled "the Succession Narrative" in 2 Samuel 9–20 and 1 Kings 1–2, possible heirs to the throne rise to the forefront of the narrative. When David flees Jerusalem, Saul's grandson Mephibosheth exclaims, "Today the house of Israel will restore to me the kingdom of my father" (2 Sam 16:3). Will Saul's family again take the throne? On the other hand, Solomon's older brothers Amnon, Absalom, and Adonijah all deserve the throne because of birthright. What disqualifies them?

This early exemplar of Israel's scribal literature provides a window into the theological presuppositions of Israel's writers of salvation history. Narratives record what happened, but not necessarily what should have happened or what ought to happen. The Succession Narrative is filled with lust, violence, deceit, ambition, and selfishness, but no direct evaluation of this behavior is offered. Within biblical narratives readers are not normally informed at the conclusion whether what happened was good or bad. Therefore in the Succession Narrative the Lord's hand is directly visible only in 2 Sam. 11:27; 12:24; and 17:14. The writer certainly had a definite theological standpoint but exercised immense restraint in expressing it, as is typical of narratives. Therefore, a number of interpretations have been suggested.

Especially popular today are political interpretations. Roger Whybray, for instance, contends that the Succession Narrative is "a work written to rally support for the Solomonic regime by legitimizing Solomon's posi‐tion."[5] On the other hand, Lienhard Delekat attempts to demonstrate that "the respect in which David was held was unjustified and that Solomon's rule was illegitimate, not divinely appointed."[6] He contends that the faults of each king are exalted so that David is pictured as an adulterer, a deficient military commander, and an incapable judge, whereas Solomon is described as a murderer and usurper of the throne. This would explain David's inactivity during the Ammonite war, his callousness at the death of Uriah (2 Sam 11:25), his orders to kill Shimei, and the editor's omission that Ahithophel was the grandfather of Bathsheba.[7] However, the opposite poles expressed in these two contrary interpretations argue against a political apologetic in these chapters. As Gillian Keys concludes, "The author is interested in the humanity of David — in his private affairs, rather than his public life. Indeed the writer is not interested in conveying a picture of 'David the king', but of David the Man — the personality behind the throne."[8]

In discussing historical narratives, John Van Seters explains, "History writing examines the causes of present conditions and circumstances. In antiquity these causes are primarily moral — who is responsible for a certain state of affairs?"[9] Both David and Solomon exhibit political greatness in

5. Roger N. Whybray, *The Succession Narrative: A Study of II Samuel 9–20 and 1 Kings 1 and 2*. SBT, 2nd ser. 9 (London: SCM, 1968), p. 54. See also Leonhard Rost, *Die Überlieferung von der Thronnachfolge Davids* (Stuttgart: Kohlhammer, 1926); Eng. trans. *The Succession to the Throne of David* (Sheffield: Almond, 1982); and P. Kyle McCarter Jr., "Plots, True or False: The Succession Narrative as Court Apologetic," *Int* 35 (1981): 355-67, an entire issue dealing with this topic.

6. L. Delekat, "Tendenz und Theologie der David-Salomo-Erzählung," in *Das ferne und nahe Wort*, ed. F. Maass. BZAW 105 (Berlin: Töpelmann, 1967), pp. 26-36; quoted in Gillian Keys, *The Wages of Sin: A Reppraisal of the Succession Narrative*. JSOTSup 221 (Sheffield: Sheffield Academic, 1996), p. 22.

7. Taken from Keys, *The Wages of Sin*, p. 22.

8. Keys, *The Wages of Sin*, p. 149.

9. John Van Seters, *In Search of History: Historiography in the Ancient World and the Origins of Biblical History* (New Haven: Yale University Press, 1983), p. 5. Even Whybray, *The Succession Narrative*, pp. 49-50, who favors a political interpretation, admits that "An Old Testament narrative which carried no moral or religious lesson whatever would be most unusual."

their early careers, but a deterioration of character is emphasized as their reigns conclude. The author of the Succession Narrative is interested in the character of the ruler. Amnon, Absalom, and Adonijah are eliminated as heirs to the throne because of their character faults. Yahweh will not choose a ruler who is captivated by lust like Amnon. In 2 Sam 13:1-2 Amnon is literally sick with lust and as a result rapes Tamar (13:14), leading her brother Absalom to murder him out of revenge (13:28).

Neither will God select a leader who is captivated by personal ambition and selfish greed. Whereas David waited patiently until God bestowed the throne upon him, Absalom initiates a plot to overthrow God's anointed. He pretends compassion to steal away the hearts of the people (2 Sam 15:6), but his decision to travel in a chariot with fifty warriors running ahead of him (15:1) conceals "an implicit claim to royal status"[10] (see 1 Sam 8:11). Absalom decides upon Hebron (2 Sam 15:7) as a fitting rallying point for the rebellion, since there David was crowned king over Judah (2:3-4) and eventually king over all Israel (5:1). The author buries this negative evaluation in the story line, but if one understands the parameters of OT narrative, the text shouts forth a refrain.[11] Finally, immediately following Absalom's death we are told about his erecting a monument to himself (18:18), which offers a suggestive summary of his entire life. Personal ambition and selfish greed cannot inherit the kingdom of God.

Finally, Adonijah becomes the legal heir to the throne with the deaths of Amnon and Absalom. The book of Kings begins with this description of Adonijah: "He was also very handsome and was born next after Absalom" (1 Kgs 1:6). But physical beauty and priority of birth never qualify one for leadership. Remember that David was the youngest of the eight sons of Jesse, and from the lists of 2 Sam 3:2-5 and 5:14-16 Solomon appears to be the tenth of seventeen sons. Saul was chosen king because he stood a head taller than anyone else (1 Sam 9:2), but the Spirit of God deserted him (16:14) because of his disobedient spirit (15:11, 19, 23, 26). Adonijah imitates the actions of foolish Absalom and states according to 1 Kgs 1:5, "'I will be king.' So he got chariots and horses ready, with fifty men to run ahead of him." Although fifty soldiers comprised a standard military unit (Exod 18:21; Deut 1:15), Adonijah will not take charge of Israel because he is not chosen by God.

When God chose David through Samuel, the Lord laid down his divine principle for the selection of a ruler: "Man looks at the outward appearance,

---

10. A. A. Anderson, *2 Samuel*. WBC 11 (Dallas: Word, 1989), p. 194.

11. Only at 2 Sam 17:14 does the narrative specifically reveal that the Lord determined to bring disaster on Absalom.

but the LORD looks at the heart" (1 Sam 16:7). David, in fact, is later described as "faithful and righteous and upright in heart" (1 Kgs 3:6). Similarly, when Bathsheba gives birth to Solomon, the narrative reports, "The LORD loved him" (2 Sam 12:24). Further evidence of God's favor derives from the similarity between the name of Solomon and shalom (שְׁלֹמֹה; שָׁלוֹם). As Hans Wilhelm Hertzberg asserts, "The child is thus described from the start as a child of God's grace, a most important statement in the context of the succession texts."[12] In addition, Solomon's alternative name Jedidiah (12:25) suggests an echo of David's name and therefore provided assurance that the Lord loved Solomon with the same intensity he loved David. Finally, 1 Kgs 8:20 provides a fitting commentary to the story: "The LORD has kept the promise he made: I have succeeded David my father and now I sit on the throne of Israel, just as the LORD promised." In each case the evaluation is not political but moral and religious. Notice the contrast between the success of David in 1 Sam 18:14 ("In everything he did he had great success because the LORD was with him") and the negative evaluation of 2 Sam 11:27 ("But the thing David had done displeased the LORD"). Similarly, the narrator contrasts the obedient beginning of Solomon's reign (1 Kgs 3:3: Solomon loved the Lord; 3:14: he walked in all God's ways) with his "love" and "walking" at the conclusion (11:1: he loved many foreign women; 11:5, 10: he walked after many foreign gods). The evaluation is hidden in the details of the story.

In the final analysis, God is the hero of all the biblical narratives. This is even true of a book like Esther, where the name of God is completely omitted. Although Yahweh does not function as an upfront character, the divine presence is behind the scenes like the director of a film orchestrating all the events. Providentially, the perfect timing of Esther's rise to power "for such a time as this" (Esth 4:14) must be recognized as a divine initiative. This same scenario is expressed in the history of the monarchy, as Gillian Keys explains: "The narrator of SN (i.e. Succession Narrative) saw Yahweh as the unseen power providentially at work behind the scenes of human history — 'the ultimate force.'"[13] God does not choose according to human standards of beauty, age, wealth, and education. As Walter Brueggemann maintains, "David is a model for the last becoming first, and the story should only be told when we intend to make that subversive claim."[14] In the narrative describing

12. Hans Wilhelm Hertzberg, *I and II Samuel.* OTL (Philadelphia: Westminster, 1964), p. 317.

13. Keys, *The Wages of Sin*, p. 176.

14. Walter Brueggemann, *David's Truth in Israel's Imagination and Memory* (Philadelphia: Fortress, 1985), p. 23.

his rise to power, David does not usurp the throne, but patiently endures Saul's pursuits from one location to another until the Lord gives him the throne (1 Samuel 16–2 Sam 5:5). Likewise, the Succession Narrative offers the reader an excellent example of what to expect when reading a biblical narrative. The more we learn about genre, the better our ability to interpret the Scriptures.

2. Psalms 42–43: Belong Together

Suppose you are preaching on Psalm 42. In your slow meditative reading of this psalm, you notice that verses 5 and 11 are identical in the NIV: "Why are you downcast, O my soul? Why so disturbed within me? Put your hope in God, for I will yet praise him, my Savior and my God." You conclude that this must be an important thematic chorus in the psalm. But you go one step further and search the phrase, "Why are you downcast?" You discover that the same verse is repeated in Ps 43:5. Therefore, Psalms 42 and 43 must be read together so that the text for your sermon includes both psalms.

This delimitation of a section would furthermore change the theme of your sermon, since the conclusion is now praise rather than lament. The second stanza in Ps 42:10 ends on a lament, "My bones suffer mortal agony as my foes taunt me, saying to me all day long, 'Where is your God?'" However, the third stanza in Ps 43:4 concludes with "I will praise you with the harp, O God, my God." The appropriate ending of the text is a song of assurance, not a personal lament. This modification of genre will necessarily produce a flow from lament to assurance in the message of the preacher. Therefore the determination of the genre is important to the overall theme of the passage as well as your sermon.

3. Psalm 108 Alters the Genre of Psalms 57 and 60

Suppose that in your personal reading of the Psalms, you are impressed with the chorus in Ps 57:5, 11: "Be exalted, O God, above the heavens; let your glory be over all the earth." As a preacher you want to proclaim the thought of God's glory encompassing the entire earth and the accompanying response of exalting the Lord. Unfortunately, the first four verses of Psalm 57 are a personal lament, whereas you want to orate a triumphant message of praise and thanksgiving on Sunday. So you perform a search in Logos Bible

Software on the phrase "your glory be over all the earth." You discover that Psalm 108 omits the lament of Ps 57:1-4 and instead attaches Ps 60:5-12 to 57:7-11. Now a personal lament (Psalm 57) and a communal complaint (Psalm 60[15]) have been transformed into the genre of community thanksgiving. Psalm 108:1-5 exalts in God, whose glory covers the whole earth, and Ps 108:6-13 provides an example that God not only reigns over places in Israel like Ephraim and Judah (v. 8) but also unexpected territory like Edom and Philistia (v. 9). Through a close monitoring of the genre, you have discovered a passage that will appropriately fit your Sunday message.

4. Controversy Dialogues on the Sabbath in Mark 2:23-28 and 3:1-6

The normal reader of the text will unfortunately miss the intention of Mark if she stops at the chapter division and does not conclude this section of material at 3:6. Mark has placed together five pericopes of the same genre entitled controversy dialogues or pronouncement sayings[16] (2:1–3:6), which demonstrate that the kingdom of God arrives in the midst of conflict. In the healing of the paralytic in 2:1-12, the kingdom promise of forgiveness of sins becomes not just a future expectation but a present reality administered by Jesus. Although the eschatological future becomes a kingdom reality, ironically Jesus and the community are accused of blasphemy. In the calling of Levi, the marginalized are welcomed to a feast with the Messiah (2:13-17) that becomes a preliminary manifestation of the eschatological banquet. However, the religious establishment is upset because of the ceremonial contamination that table fellowship with tax collectors and sinners brings. In the third controversy over fasting (2:18-22), Jesus is introduced as the bridegroom who ushers in the joy of the eschatological wedding feast, but in the process Jesus and his disciples are accused of being unspiritual since the devout discipline of fasting is not held in high esteem. This section concludes with two controversies about the Sabbath, which the chapter division separates. Through Jesus' ministry Sabbath rest (2:23-28) and wholeness and healing (3:1-5) become realized in history, but paradoxically these realities only produce a death plot against Jesus (3:6).

---

15. See Erhard S. Gerstenberger, *Psalms, Part 1*. FOTL 15 (Grand Rapids: Eerdmans, 1988), pp. 229, 239.

16. See Appendix I, Section II (pp. 333-44) for an exhaustive list of the controversy dialogues in Mark.

These five controversy dialogues are organized into a chiastic structure, which is another indication that this entire section must be read together:[17]

A   (2:1-12) Forgiving sins (the paralytic is healed)
> B   (2:13-17) Impurity through eating with sinners (Jesus eats at Levi's house)
> > C   (2:18-22) Fasting and the new age
> B′   (2:23-28) Sabbath eating rituals (picking grain to eat on the Sabbath)
A′   (3:1-6) Sabbath healings (the man with the withered hand is cured)

Functioning as bookends, the first and last controversy dialogues are constructed from both a miracle story (healing of a paralytic and withered hand) and a controversy (forgiveness of sins and healing on the Sabbath). At the center of the five controversies as well as at the middle point of this specific controversy dialogue (double saying in 2:18-19, reference to the crucifixion in 2:20, double saying in 2:21-22) stands a reference in 2:20 to Jesus' crucifixion ("when the bridegroom will be taken from them"). The kingdom of God will only arrive through suffering and death. Determining where a section begins and ends opens the eyes of the reader to the theological intention of the author. But sometimes chapter divisions blockade these insights. A recognition of the genre of controversy dialogue enables the interpreter to overcome this faulty chapter division.

5. Miracle Stories in Matthew 8–9

More than all the other Synoptic Gospel writers, Matthew creatively organizes Jesus' teaching so that Jesus' word ministry in the Sermon on the Mount (Matthew 5–7) is followed by Jesus' deed ministry in the miracle stories of chapters 8–9. Normally, exegetes consider an individual miracle story as a pericope, but Matthew establishes a pattern in these chapters so that the delimitation of a passage becomes three miracle stories and a call to discipleship.

Whereas Mark as the first Gospel writer includes several of these mira-

---

17. See Johanna Dewey, "The Literary Structure of the Controversy Stories in Mark 2:1–3:6," *JBL* 92 (1973): 394-401; and *Markan Public Debate*. SBLDS 48 (Chico: Scholars, 1980), pp. 111-15.

cles in his section of five controversy dialogues (Mark 2:1–3:6), Matthew groups together the material into three sets of three miracle stories followed by a call to discipleship. Therefore, the purpose of the Matthean miracle narratives is not to demonstrate the compassion of Jesus, or to illustrate Jesus' signs of the kingdom, or to extend an evangelistic call to faith, or even to emphasize Christology, but to deepen discipleship. A call to discipleship emphatically concludes each of the three sections delineated by Matthew.

1. Matt 8:1-22: Healings of the leper, a centurion's paralyzed servant, and Peter's mother-in-law lead to a discipleship call (8:18-22) to leave parents and follow Jesus without expecting the security of a home.
2. Matt 8:23–9:17: Stories describing the stilling of a storm, the exorcism of the Gadarene demoniacs, and the healing of a paralytic lead to the discipleship call of Matthew and the discipline of fasting in the church age (9:9-17).
3. Matt 9:18-38: Healing accounts of Jairus's dead daughter and the woman with a hemorrhage, two blind men, and the mute demoniac lead to a discipleship call (9:35-38) to summon dedicated workers for the coming harvest.

Through the retelling of Jesus' miracle stories Matthew strives to deepen the Christian commitment of his audience. Therefore, to reenact Matthew's purpose in narrating the miracle stories, present-day preachers should choose these longer passages culminating in discipleship narratives rather than deciding upon a shorter preaching text that would only encompass one of the miracle accounts. The arrangement of the material into a triplicate formulation with the genre of miracle stories culminating in a call to discipleship determines the extent of the pericope.

6. Mark 10:46-52: Healing of Bartimaeus — Miracle Story or Call to Discipleship?

The miracle stories in the New Testament follow the pattern of (1) a difficult problem that needs healing, followed by (2) the performance of the miracle, and (3) a confirmation of the wonder through a demonstration of proof and the amazement of the onlookers.[18] All these elements occur in the narrative

18. See Appendix I, IA3b (pp. 303-4) for a morphology of the genre miracle story.

of Mark 10:46-52. Bartimaeus is not only blind but he must beg for any provisions, and his request for help is met with public scorn from the crowd (10:46-49). Despite these difficulties, Jesus heals him (10:50-52a), and he jumps up and follows Jesus as proof of his healing (10:52b). However, there is no public acclaim and demonstration of awe as is so frequent in miracle stories. Instead, there is a mention of "the way," which as a symbol for the way of discipleship began this section entitled the "Discipleship Catechism" in Mark 8:27. This omission should push the reader to reflect deeper about the genre of this pericope.

In addition, the short healing in 10:52a is preceded by the normal constituent parts of a call to discipleship narrative. Earlier in the Gospel Mark has narrated four standard elements in the calling of Andrew and Peter, James and John, and Levi. Each begins with the initiative of Jesus, who sees a future disciple (1:16, 19; 2:14). Then Jesus calls the person, who in turn leaves something behind and afterward follows Jesus.[19] Following this identical pattern, Jesus stops traveling toward Jerusalem, when he sees Bartimaeus (10:49a). The crowd discerns the call and yells out, "On your feet, he's calling you" (10:49b). Bartimaeus then "throws his cloak aside" (10:50), thus leaving his begging blanket and profession behind. The climax of the passage concludes with the former blind beggar following Jesus along the way (10:52b), his journey of suffering toward the cross. Thus a discipleship story interrupts the healing narrative and takes prominence as the conclusion to a Markan section that begins with another story of a healing of a blind man (8:22-26), which likewise is transformed into a parable of discipleship. Therefore, a sermon or Bible study would notice Mark's alterations to the normal miracle story sequence. The genre of the passage influences and even determines the theme of the pericope.

7. The Genre of the Transfiguration in Matthew (17:1-8)
and Mark (9:2-8)

A similar transformation of genre occurs in the transfiguration narrative of Matthew and Mark. Matthew's structure rehearses the expected genre of a miracle story in which a response of awe follows a divine epiphany. First, the disciples experience a theophanic vision of Jesus transfigured before them as evidenced by his shining face and dazzling white clothes (Matt 17:2). In addi-

---

19. See Appendix I, IA3d (pp. 307-8).

tion, two renowned figures of the Old Testament, Moses and Elijah, whose deaths are not specifically recorded and who come to represent the law and the prophets, appear with him (17:3). To this revelation, the response of Peter must be interpreted positively: "Lord, it is good for us to be here. If you wish, I will put up three shelters — one for you, one for Moses and one for Elijah" (17:4). This mountain location becomes the house of God and a worship shrine for the enraptured disciples. As Joel Marcus explains, "In the pre-Markan narrative, which lacked 9:6, it was regarded as appropriate,"[20] that is, Peter's desire to build the tabernacles seemed honorable.

A second revelation then occurs in Matthew's rendering, a *bath qol* or "voice of God" from the cloud of Shekinah glory: "This is my Son, whom I love; with him I am well pleased. Listen to him!" (17:5). Again the disciples are overcome with fear and fall on their faces in awe-struck worship (17:6-7). But afterward, only Jesus, the beloved Son, remains. Moses and Elijah disappear, since Jesus is superior. Consistent with Matthew's theme throughout his Gospel, Jesus is greater than Moses.[21] The miracles in the narrative emphasize Christology.

Mark, on the other hand, develops a different structure that emphasizes discipleship instead. Mark omits the final response of awe and inserts Peter's negative response (9:5-6) between the two epiphanies (9:2-4, 7). In Matthew the recognition of the glorified Jesus along with Moses and Elijah is deserving of three tabernacles, and the voice from heaven causes the disciples to fall on their faces in worship and awe. But Mark's parenthetic comment located strategically at the very center of the narrative demonstrates that Mark interprets the fear negatively: "He (Peter) did not know what to say, they were so frightened." Mark transposes the expected fear of a divine visitation into a negative response of an inappropriate action. The disciples want to remain in the glory of the heavenly mountain whereas in reality they must follow Jesus to the cross (9:13) and join the spiritual warfare in the valley (9:14-29).[22]

---

20. Joel Marcus, *Mark 8–16*. AB 27A (New Haven: Yale University Press, 2009), p. 638.

21. See Chapter 7, A1, "Apologetic Against the Pharisaic Synagogue in the Gospel of Matthew" (pp. 229-34)

22. The phrase "the disciples do not know how to answer Jesus" (9:6) is repeated at Jesus' passion in Gethsemane (14:40), since the disciples are still unwilling to follow a suffering Messiah. Dennis E. Nineham, *The Gospel of St. Mark* (New York: Seabury, 1963), p. 236, adds that "God's will for Christ and the disciples is that they should return into the world and enter upon the path of suffering."

The disciples' misunderstanding is central to Markan theology and thus located at the center of this pericope as the following chiasm demonstrates:[23]

    a. Jesus alone with the disciples (9:2a)
       b. Transfiguration (9:2b-3)
          c. Appearance of Elijah and Moses with Jesus (9:4)
          c. Peter's suggestion of booths for Jesus, Moses, and Elijah (9:5) because he did not know what to say and was afraid (9:6)
       b. Voice from heaven interpreting the transfiguration (9:7)
    a. Jesus alone with the disciples (9:8)

Ernest Best envisions clearly Mark's transformation of the oral tradition. "In the tradition its purpose was christological — to confirm the confession made by Peter of Jesus' true identity. If man, that is Peter, has confessed Jesus as Messiah, God confesses Jesus as his Son."[24] Then Best continues, "Mark has not neglected the original christological setting of the pericope in the tradition but has added another dimension — discipleship — and this in keeping with his whole train of thought in 8:27–10:45."[25] An epiphany is transformed into a discipleship narrative with Peter's lack of understanding (9:6) central. Similar to his earlier misunderstanding (8:33) of the meaning of Jesus' identity, Peter opens his mouth impetuously again and suggests staying on the glorious mountain in three shelters. Mark is creating a second series of narratives in the first cycle of passion prediction, misunderstanding, and teaching on discipleship. Just as Peter's profession of Jesus as Messiah (8:29) produced a passion prediction (8:31) followed by Peter's misunderstanding (8:33) and a lesson on discipleship (8:34-39), so the epiphany of splendor (9:2-4) along with the voice identifying Jesus as God's son (9:7) results in Peter's misunderstanding (9:5-6) followed by a teaching on discipleship as Jesus descends the mountain (9:9-13). The misunderstanding is placed at the center of the passage to give it special prominence. Therefore the message of Matthew and Mark is strikingly different. The exegete and preacher must pay special attention to the genre of a passage.

---

23. From Marcus, *Mark 8–16*, p. 635.

24. Ernest Best, *Disciples and Discipleship: Studies in the Gospel According to Mark* (Edinburgh: T. & T. Clark, 1986), p. 57.

25. Best, *Disciples and Discipleship*, p. 58. Robert H. Stein, *Mark*. Baker Exegetical Commentary of the New Testament (Grand Rapids: Baker, 2008), p. 418, contends that Mark "serves less to emphasize the foolishness of the disciples than to heighten the glory of Jesus," but he is harmonizing the accounts of Matthew and Mark.

8. No Thanksgiving Section in Paul's Epistle to the Galatians

James Bailey points out that the repetition of established content and a structural blueprint from a particular genre such as epistle reinforces the reader's expectations, but "where the pattern is modified, its use subverts in some way the normal social interaction."[26] He offers the example of love letters that normally are patterned with a structured address ("Dearest Eric") and a consistent conclusion ("All my love, Anne"). If suddenly the introduction and ending are altered to "Dear Eric" and "Yours truly, Anne," the modified form results in a startled and troubled reaction from Eric.

Epistolary analysis of the New Testament displays the normal structure of greeting, thanksgiving and prayer, the body of the letter, a paraenetic section, and the farewell. Thus in the Letter to the Galatians when Paul omits his normal thanksgiving section after the address, the Galatians' ears open wide. Then when he replaces the thanksgiving with "I am astonished that you are so quickly deserting the one who called you" (Gal 1:6) and proceeds in verse 8 to the curse formula, "let him be eternally condemned," the Galatians realize that they are in trouble. Alterations in genre should catch the attention of the reader or hearer. As Bailey points out, "An author's selection of a specific genre, thus, is a choice for some viewpoint and against another."[27] Paul alters the regular structure of his epistles to cleverly reveal his viewpoint of the Galatians.

9. Is 1 Corinthians 13:4-7 a Hymn?

Bible studies on the great love poem of 1 Corinthians 13 are very popular. Now the International Standard Bible has attempted to replicate this poetry by structuring 1 Cor 13:4-7 as a hymn in four stanzas, complete with rhyming lines and lyrical rhythm. Let's suppose that you decide tentatively to follow this outline and prepare a Bible study in four points or with four movements, one for each stanza. Does this capture the movement of the text?

---

26. James L. Bailey, "Genre Analysis," in *Hearing the New Testament: Strategies for Interpretation*, ed. Joel B. Green, 2nd ed. (Grand Rapids: Eerdmans, 2010), p. 143.

27. Bailey, "Genre Analysis," p. 144.

International Standard Version
16 lines

⁴Love is always patient,
Love is always kind,
Love is never envious
Or vaunted up with pride.

Nor is she conceited,
⁵And never is she rude,
Never does she think of self
Or ever get annoyed.

She never is resentful,
⁶Is never glad with sin,
But always glad to side with truth,
Whene'er the truth should win.

⁷She bears up under everything,
Believes the best in all,
There is no limit to her hope,
And never will she fall.

Since you are a careful exegete, you decide to compare the English structure with the Greek clauses. In Logos Bible Software you can investigate the clausal outline of 1 Cor 13:4-7 in the *Lexham Clausal Outlines of the Greek New Testament*. You discover that the text does not consist of 16 lines as the ISV suggests but only 15, since this translation has made συγχαίρει δὲ τῇ ἀληθείᾳ ("it rejoices with the truth") into two lines at the end of 13:6 by adding "whene'er the truth should win." In reality the structure consists of a verb pair followed by seven clauses in a row beginning with the negative οὐ, a second verbal pair, and then four positive statements about love each beginning with πάντα ("everything").

Therefore, whereas the ISV mixes two positive qualities with two negative ones in the first stanza, Paul's first point is the positive verb pair that "love is patient and kind." Then Paul contrasts these two positive characteristics with seven negative statements. Third, 13:6 begins a new subsection transforming a negative quality into a positive aspect of love as evidenced by the word "but" and a repetition of a similar verb (οὐ χαίρει ἐπὶ τῇ ἀδικίᾳ, συγχαίρει δὲ τῇ ἀληθείᾳ): "Love does not delight in evil but rejoices with the truth." Finally, Paul ends his description of love with a fourfold series. "Love always protects, always trusts, always hopes, always perseveres." So the Bible study could have four points, but they would not correspond with the four stanzas of the ISV. Instead, the important verb pairs would precede two series of negative and positive descriptions of love as the following outline demonstrates.

A. First verb pair	⁴Ἡ ἀγάπη μακροθυμεῖ,	⁴Love is patient,
	χρηστεύεται ἡ ἀγάπη,	love is kind,
B. Seven negative verbs	οὐ ζηλοῖ, [ἡ ἀγάπη]	It does not envy,
	οὐ περπερεύεται,	it does not boast,
	οὐ φυσιοῦται,	it is not proud.
	⁵οὐκ ἀσχημονεῖ,	⁵ It is not rude,
	οὐ ζητεῖ τὰ ἑαυτῆς,	it is not self-seeking,
	οὐ παροξύνεται,	it is not easily angered,
	οὐ λογίζεται τὸ κακόν,	it keeps no record of wrongs.
C. Second verb pair	⁶ οὐ χαίρει ἐπὶ τῇ ἀδικίᾳ,	⁶ Love does not delight in evil,
	συγχαίρει δὲ τῇ ἀληθείᾳ·	but rejoices with the truth.
D. Four positive verbs	⁷ πάντα στέγει,	⁷ It always protects,
	πάντα πιστεύει,	always trusts,
	πάντα ἐλπίζει,	always hopes,
	πάντα ὑπομένει.	always perseveres.

If you are limited to a couple of English translations, Logos Bible Software offers a plethora of English versions as well as an opportunity to consult the original languages and analyze the structure. Apparently, 1 Cor 13:4-7 is not a hymn in four stanzas.

10. Discerning a Hymn through the Structure of Colossians 1:15-20

Although the presence of prayers and confessions of faith in the New Testament is readily acknowledged, full-fledged hymns are more difficult to discern. The following characteristics are frequently mentioned to affirm the presence of a hymn:

1. Most obvious, of course, would be the use of technical musical expressions.
2. Grammatical indications such as an opening relative pronoun (ὅς) and

predicative relative clauses point to an original liturgical setting. Each stanza of the hymn below begins with this relative pronoun (Col 1:15, 18b) as do the hymns introduced in Phil 2:6 and 1 Tim 3:16.

3. The occurrence of parallelism strongly suggests the presence of poetry. Ralph Martin contends that "a correspondence between words and phrases which are placed in the sentences in an obviously carefully selected position"[28] indicates the presence of a hymn. The second stanza of the hymn below displays some remarkable parallelism.

4. Literary devices such as repetition, alliteration, *inclusio,* and chiasmus can reveal the presence of stanzas or strophes within a hymn. The first stanza in Col 1:15-20 reveals a chiastic structure, and the underlined words in the hymn below demonstrate the repetitions between the two stanzas.

5. Rhetorical indicators are important. Martin pays special attention if the passage contains "a certain rhythmical lilt ascertainable when the passage is read aloud."[29]

6. With regard to content, an abrupt change of subject matter or isolation from the context can demonstrate the presence of preexistent material such as a hymn. For instance, immediately preceding the hymn at Col 1:14 Paul employs the first person plural, and following the hymn in 1:21-23 the second person plural is used, but the third person singular is present throughout the hymn.

Through the use of these characteristics New Testament scholars have detected the presence of hymns in Col 1:15-20; Phil 2:6-11; Eph 1:3-14; John 1:1-18; and 1 Tim 3:16, as well as the book of Revelation.[30]

---

28. Ralph Martin, *Carmen Christi: Philippians 2:5-11 in Recent Interpretation and in the Setting of Early Christian Worship* (London: Cambridge University Press, 1967), p. 12.

29. Martin, *Carmen Christi*, p. 12.

30. See such works as D. R. Carnegie, "The Hymns in Revelation: Their Origin and Function" (Ph.D. diss., London Bible College, 1978); Stephen E. Fowl, *The Story of Christ in the Ethics of Paul: An Analysis of the Function of the Hymnic Material in the Pauline Corpus.* JSNTSup 36 (Sheffield: Sheffield Academic, 1990); G. P. Luttikhuizen, "The Poetic Character of Revelation 4 and 5," in *Early Christian Poetry*, ed. J. Den Boeft and A. Hilhorst. VCSup 22 (Leiden: Brill, 1993), pp. 15-22; R. P. Martin, "New Testament Hymns: Background and Development," *ExpTim* 94 (1983): 132-36; L. Mowry, "Revelation 4–5 and Early Christian Liturgical Usage," *JBL* 71 (1952): 75-84; John J. O'Rourke, "The Hymns of the Apocalypse," *CBQ* 30 (1968): 399-409; James M. Robinson, "A Formal Analysis of Colossians 1:15-20," *JBL* 76 (1957): 270-87; Jack T. Sanders, *The New Testament Christological Hymns: Their Historical Religious Background.* SNTSMS 15 (Cambridge: Cambridge University Press, 1971); Robert H. Smith,

First Stanza of the Hymn: Christ and the Creation

a   [15]He is the image (ὅς ἐστιν εἰκὼν) of the invisible God,

b   the <u>firstborn</u> (πρωτότοκος) over all creation.

c   [16]<u>For by him</u> <u>all things</u> were created:

d1   <u>things in heaven</u>   <u>and on earth,</u>

d1   visible   and invisible,

d2   whether thrones   or powers

d2   or rulers   or authorities;

c   <u>all things</u> were created <u>by him</u> and <u>for him</u>.

b   [17]He is before all things,

a   and in him all things hold together.

Interlude: Pauline Addition about the Church

     [18]And he is the head of the body, the church;

Second Stanza of the Hymn: Christ and the New Creation

a   <u>He</u> is the beginning (ὅς ἐστιν ἀρχή)

a   and the <u>firstborn</u> (πρωτότοκος) from among the dead,

b   so that in everything he might have the supremacy.

b   [19]<u>For</u> God was pleased to have <u>all</u> his fullness dwell <u>in him</u>,

c   [20]and <u>through him</u> to reconcile <u>to himself</u> <u>all things</u>,

c   by making peace through his blood shed on the cross

d   whether <u>things on earth</u>

d   or <u>things in heaven</u>.

In summary, the hymnic nature of Col 1:15-20 is demonstrated by the relative pronoun ὅς that introduces each stanza (1:15, 18), the repetition of vocabulary at key places in the text, the eight-line stanzas, and the chiastic structure of the first stanza as well as the parallelism in the second verse. The development of content as well, from Christ as the mediator of creation to the instrument of the new creation, unifies this passage and sets it apart from the context in Colossians, where the creation is not Paul's subject matter. Yet Paul stitches the hymn into his teaching by adding a line between the stanzas, calling attention to Christ's headship over the church. So the reconciliation is not only cosmic, involving all of creation, but also applied to Christ's special people, the church.

"'Worthy Is the Lamb' and Other Songs of the Revelation," *CurTM* 25 (1998): 500-506; Mark Wegener, "Phil. 2:6-11 — Paul's (Revised) Hymn to Jesus," *CurTM* 25 (1998): 507-17.

Therefore, this christological hymn embedded in 1:15-20 contains two stanzas: (1) Christ and creation and (2) Christ and the new creation. Christ is the image of this invisible God, the firstborn (πρωτότοκος) of the creation in the first stanza and the beginning and firstborn (πρωτότοκος) from the dead in the second stanza. In the first stanza Christ creates all things (1:16), while in the second he reconciles all things (1:20). In this hymn we discover a picture of how the early church praised Jesus and envisioned him as the Lord of this world and the next.

C. The Identification of Literary Techniques

PROCEDURE

Readers are not always aware that literary devices frequently reveal the proposed structure that the author has in mind. Appendix II offers a lengthy list of literary techniques as well as scriptural examples of each. Here we will offer examples of various literary techniques that are employed in Scripture such as chiasm, *inclusio,* and step-parallelism. Whereas we normally concentrate upon the historical details in the Bible, an examination of these particular literary devices can open our eyes to the writing strategies of the biblical authors.

EXAMPLES

1. The Chiasm in Luke 22:40-46: Jesus in the Garden of Gethsemane

Suppose that you are undergoing an intense time of trials and temptation. You decide to investigate how Jesus handled trials in the Garden of Gethsemane. To facilitate this process in Logos 4, call up *Aland's Synopsis of the Four Gospels* from the library and type in Luke 22:39-46 and choose a Greek or English Bible.[31] In the process of comparing the Synoptic Gospels, you notice that the Luke 22 narrative differs dramatically from Matthew and Mark. You are impressed with the ending (22:46), "pray so that you will not fall into temptation," and when you perform a search of εἰς πειρασμόν ("into

---

31. On the Tools menu in Libronix 3, call up the Bible comparisons and investigate the parallel passages and harmonies, esp. §330 in Aland's *Synopsis of the Four Gospels.*

temptation"), you discover that the same phrase is employed at the beginning of the passage in 22:40. Instantly, you recognize this as an example of *inclusio*. With this envelope technique, the emphasis is upon the two ends of the pericope. Then you remember that a chiasm encompasses an *inclusio* and forms a series of symmetrical parallels in an a-b-c-d-c-b-a or similar format. So you read slowly and observe evidence for a chiasm. You notice that Jesus leaves the disciples in 22:41 but returns in verse 45. The "kneeling down" in prayer is contrasted with the later "standing up." Jesus prays in 22:42 with passionate words, but the intensity of his prayer continues in 22:44, where he actively sweats drops of blood. However, the appearance of an angel in the middle of the passage contains no parallel in the narrative. It is therefore the emphatic center of a chiasm. In times of intense trial, God will comfort and strengthen us in some special manner. That is the assurance of the passage.

This pericope can be outlined in the following manner:

    a. (v. 40) Jesus' command to pray so that you do not enter temptation (εἰς πειρασμόν)

        b. (v. 41a) Jesus distances himself from his disciples who are awake

            c. (v. 41b) Kneeling down

                d. (v. 42) Prayer employing passionate vocabulary

                    e. (v. 43) An angel answering the prayer

                d.′ (v. 44) Continued prayer without mentioning words; sweat entails an intensity of prayer

            c.′ (v. 45a) Standing up

        b.′ (v. 45b) Jesus returns to the disciples, who are now sleeping

    a.′ (v. 46) Jesus' repeated command to pray so you do not enter temptation (εἰς πειρασμόν)

If you examine the critical apparatus of the Nestle-Aland Greek text which comes with the Stuttgart Electronic Study Bible, you discover a textual problem in this passage, since several manuscripts omit Luke 22:43-44. So you explore Metzger's *Textual Commentary*, which is found in the Gold edition of Logos Bible Software, and study the evidence to determine the most plausible reading of the ancient text. Does the chiasm disappear if you accept the shorter reading without Jesus' sweating drops of blood and the appearance of an angel? No! Even if you decide that the shorter version is the better text, the center of the chiasm now becomes the prayer, "Father if you are willing, take this cup from me, yet not my will, but yours be done." With both readings you are helped in the struggle against trials and temptations. Trials call us to prayer. The appropriate prayer is one that bids God's will to be done. And God brings comfort in a special manifestation of his presence. Prayer, an acceptance of God's will, and divine comfort in adversity are God's answers to our struggles with temptation. The discovery of a chiasm enhances our understanding of the text.

2. A Chiasm in Mark 4:26-29: Parable of the Seed Growing Secretly

Suppose that in your preaching you normally follow the lectionary. The passage for this Sunday is Mark 4:26-29. Although this parable is difficult to interpret, you refuse to bypass it since it is your assigned text. Reading through the parable, you experience difficulty determining the main point of the story. Tentatively you decide that the gradual growth of the kingdom of God is the theme, since the process of growth is deliberated: "first the stalk, then the head, then the full kernel in the head." After remembering that its genre is parable, you peruse the principles for interpreting parables in Appendix I, Section IIIC, in this book. The fourth principle states that the surprise normally corresponds to the emphasis of Jesus' parables (pp. 346-47). You recognize correctly that the surprise consists of the fact that the soil produces grain all by itself without any help from the planter. Although the farmer scattered the seed, he completely neglected to water the crops, add fertilizer, or pull out the weeds. You are struck as well by the strange Greek word αὐτομάτη ("automatically"), and after attempting a word search, you discover that it is employed only here and in Acts 12:10, where surprisingly Peter's prison door opens automatically. The rarity of this word supplies supplemental evidence that divine sovereignty is the emphasis of the passage.

Next, you observe the larger structure. The parable begins by stating that the kingdom is similar to something. Certainly the future reign and realm of God is not like a person scattering seed but instead like an exceptional harvest. The beginning and end of the parable parallel each other. Then you notice that the threefold process of the growth of grain corresponds with the threefold regular activity of the farmer placed in pairs: (1) night and day; (2) sleeps and gets up; (3) while the seed sprouts and grows. These matching couplets remind you that a chiasm contains corresponding elements. So you attempt a structural outline and discover the following:

a   This is what the kingdom of God is like.
  b   A man scatters seed on the ground.
    c   [27]Night and day,
    c   whether he sleeps or gets up,
    c   the seed sprouts and grows,
      d   though he does not know how.
      d′   [28]All by itself the soil produces grain,
    c′   first the stalk,
    c′   then the head,
    c′   then the full kernel in the head.
  b′   [29]As soon as the grain is ripe, he puts the sickle to it,
a′   because the harvest has come.

When you consult the principles for interpreting a chiasm as specified in Appendix II of this book (p. 359), you are reminded that the emphasis of a chiasm stands in the middle. Therefore the surprise, the unusual wording, and the structure of a chiasm all line up and confirm that the emphasis of the parable is the fact of God's sovereignty in the growth of the kingdom. The two center lines in the chiasm indicate that human ingenuity will never explain the growth of the kingdom, but instead behind the scenes God is producing the fruit all by himself.

3. 1 Timothy 3:16: Various Structures but One Theme

Sometimes it is extremely difficult to decide between various proposals of structure for a particular text. For example, in the liturgical confession or hymn of 1 Tim 3:16 scholars have recommended three competing structural exemplars. The International Standard Version advocates a two-stanza hymn that first describes Jesus' life and then his reception by the world.

Christ's life	In flesh was he revealed to sight,	incarnation
	Kept righteous by the Spirit's might,	baptism
	Adored by angels singing.	resurrection
Reception	To nations was he manifest,	early preaching
	Believing souls found peace and rest,	ensuing belief
	Our Lord in heaven reigning!	heavenly state

A second possibility emphasizes literary parallelism and divides the material into a three-stanza hymn that establishes a contrast between earth and heaven to advocate that Jesus is Lord of both.

He appeared in the body,	Entrance	earthly world
was vindicated by the Spirit,		heavenly world
was seen by angels,	Presentation	heavenly world
was preached among the nations,		earthly world
was believed on in the world,	Enthronement	earthly world
was taken up in glory.		heavenly world

A three-strophe hymn with an *inclusio* or partial chiasm has been proposed as the correct structure as well.[32] Here the first and last lines coordinate with the divine and human exaltation at the center of the hymn.

a	He appeared in human form,	Incarnation
b	was shown to be right by the Spirit,	Divine exaltation
b	and was seen by angels.	
c	He was preached among the nations,	Human exaltation
c	was believed in throughout the world,	
a	and was taken up to heaven.	Ascension

Each of these structures offers insights into the text, but notice that with regard to content Jesus' ascension stands prominently at the conclusion of each. The heavenly state concluding the first structure parallels Christ's enthronement in the second outline and the ascension in the third. Therefore, certainly this verse was composed as an ascension hymn or confession in the early church. The structures can be interpreted differently, but the theme of the ascension is central to each.

4. The Purpose of the Gospel of John Displayed through Inclusios

Unlike much of the biblical literature the fourth evangelist specifically states the purpose for which he is writing. At the end of the Gospel in 20:31, John

32. See Robert H. Gundry, "The Form, Meaning and Background of the Hymn Quoted in 1 Timothy 3:16," in *Apostolic History and the Gospel*, ed. W. Ward Gasque and Ralph P. Martin (Grand Rapids: Eerdmans, 1970), pp. 203-22.

ut these are written that you may believe that Jesus is the Christ, God, and that by believing you may have life in his name." But w...... content that John inserts into the concept and title "Son of God"?

John employs the literary device of *inclusio* to develop his Christology throughout the Gospel. First of all, John defines "Son of God" through the *inclusio* that binds together his discussion of Jesus' fulfillment of the Jewish feasts in chapters 5–10.[33] While communicating the significance of Jesus' healing on the Sabbath, John 5:18 states, "For this reason the Jews tried all the harder to kill him; not only was he breaking the Sabbath, but he was even calling God his own Father, making himself equal with God." The title "Son of God" meant that Jesus was making himself equal with God, therefore divine. As a bookend to reinforce this truth, 10:33-36 returns to this theme. Jesus asks (10:36), "Why then do you accuse me of blasphemy because I said, 'I am God's Son'?" The Jewish leaders are beside themselves with indignation when Jesus employs this title, since Jesus, "a mere man, claims to be God" (10:33). While John is writing his Gospel, the Christians are being thrown out of the synagogue for worshipping Jesus as God (9:34, 38; 16:2). Certainly this grave loss of comradeship could bring despair and disillusionment, but Jesus proclaims that he as the good shepherd of the sheep is leading them out (10:3).[34] The chief shepherd is leading the way because he is God himself.

The more prominent *inclusio* that John employs ties the entire book together. In 1:1 he proclaims that not only was the Logos with God, but "the Word was God." In the final narrative before the purpose statement, John fortifies this theme. When Jesus personally appears to doubting Thomas after the resurrection, Thomas confidently confesses, "My Lord and my God" (20:28). This is the profession of faith that John wants everyone to adhere to: Jesus is God.

The structure of the prologue itself offers proof of a third *inclusio* that emphasizes Jesus' divinity as the Son of God. Just as 1:1 states that "the Word was God," John 1:18 proclaims that "No one has ever seen God, but God the One Only, who is at the Father's side, has made him known." John provides these bookends to the prologue and the entire Gospel to underline his central theme that Jesus is divine.

A fourth *inclusio* ties together Jesus' climatic testimony to himself in 1:51

---

33. Jesus fulfils the Sabbath in ch. 5, the Passover in ch. 6, the water ceremony of the Feast of Tabernacles in ch. 7, the light ceremony of the Feast of Tabernacles in ch. 8 along with the giving of light to the blind in ch. 9, and finally Hanukkah or the Feast of Dedication in 10:22-42.

34. See A4 above (pp. 4-5).

and the resurrection narrative. Jesus prophesies that the disciples will "see heaven open, and the angels of God ascending and descending on the Son of Man." This, of course, recalls Jacob's (Israel's) heavenly vision at Bethel, which literally means "house of God." This scripture is combined with a reference to Dan 7:13, where the Son of Man is ushered into the very presence of God and all nations worship him. The only incident narrated in the Gospel where angels descend and ascend occurs at the resurrection appearance at John 20:12: "and they saw two angels in white, seated where Jesus' body had been, one at the head and the other at the foot." What OT picture related to the house of God is portrayed in this experience? Just as the angels surround the place where Jesus' body lay, so the cherubim stand on either side of the ark of the covenant, where God dwells invisibly on the mercy seat. Therefore the house of God is Jesus (John 2:21); in fact he is the ark of the covenant on which the very presence of God rests. The literary feature of an *inclusio* helps John to convey his purpose in writing the Gospel.

5. Matthew 18:10-14: The Inclusio in the Parable of the Wandering Sheep

Jesus' Parable of the Wandering Sheep in Matthew is distinctively different from the account in Luke 15:3-7. The grammatical description of the sheep diverges with a lost sheep represented in Luke (τὸ ἀπολωλός) but a wandering one in Matthew (τὸ πλανώμενον), so that a different title should be assigned to each parable. Likewise the audience is unique, with outsiders addressed in Luke (tax collectors, sinners, Pharisees, teachers of the law), whereas the ecclesiastical sermon of Matthew 18 is geared toward disciples. Finally, the structure varies. Specifically, Matthew places an *inclusio* (18:10, 14) around the parable (18:12-13), so that experiences in the heavenly realm surround the earthly activity. As a result, the pastoral care of the angels in heaven and God's divine concern for the little ones become a model for the pastoral care of the corresponding shepherds on earth. Notice the *inclusio* in the structure:

Setting in heaven: 18:10
    A   [10]See that you do not look down on one of <u>these little ones</u>.
    B   For I tell you that their angels in heaven always see the face of my <u>Father in heaven</u>.
Setting on earth: 18:12-13 The parable itself
Setting in heaven: 18:14

      B′   ¹⁴In the same way your <u>Father in heaven</u> is not willing
      A′   that any of <u>these little ones</u> should be lost.

Jesus introduces guardian angels in Matt 18:10 who continually and faithfully bring the concerns and care of the spiritually immature on earth before God in heaven. Likewise, God himself is not willing that any should wander from the fold. This chiastic *inclusio* sets the stage for the behavior of human shepherds on earth. With that same concern, earthly pastoral care-givers will search out that one sheep that has wandered off and gather the lamb back into the nurturing fold. As the context after the parable in Matthew indicates, the theme is church discipline with regard to the immature. The literary devices of repetition and envelope technique reinforce the meaning of the parable and equip the reader to understand its significance.

6. The Purpose of Step-Parallelism: Luke 15:4-10, Lost Sheep and Coin

A step-parallelism differs from a chiasm or an *inclusio* through the repetition of a continuous structure such as a-b-c-d; a-b-c-d. This duplication establishes a recurring pattern so that the sequence becomes a significant contribution to the intended meaning of the author, who wants this pattern repeated in the life of his or her readers. In the parables of the Lost Sheep and Lost Coin below I have underlined the duplication of vocabulary and placed the ten-stage step-parallelism on the left margin. These ten steps can be divided more simply into three basic movements: (1) having to losing; (2) search to find; and (3) gather together and be joyful.

Parable of the Lost Sheep Luke 15:4-7

  A. Having to Losing
      1. man   ⁴<u>Suppose</u> one of you
      2. possessions   <u>has</u> a hundred sheep
      3. losing one   and <u>loses one</u> of them.

  B. Search to Find
      4. question   <u>Does</u> he not leave the ninety-nine in the open country
         about a search   and go after the lost sheep
      5. end of the search <u>until</u> he <u>finds it</u>?
      6. finding   ⁵<u>And when</u> he <u>finds it,</u>
         he joyfully puts it
         on his shoulders   ⁶and goes home.

C. Gather Together and Be Joyful

7. gathering	Then he <u>calls his friends and neighbors together</u>
8. invitation	<u>and says</u>, "<u>Rejoice with me</u>;
9. reason for gathering	<u>I have found my lost</u> sheep."

10. joy in heaven
    over a repentant
    sinner
	[7]<u>I tell you</u> that in the same way there will be more
	<u>rejoicing</u> in heaven <u>over one sinner who repents</u>
	than over ninety-nine righteous persons who
	do not need to repent.

Parable of the Lost Coin Luke 15:8-10

A. Having to Losing

1. a woman	[8]Or <u>suppose</u> a woman
2. possessions	<u>has</u> ten silver coins
3. losing one	and <u>loses one</u>.

B. Search to Find

4. question about a search	<u>Does</u> she not light a lamp, sweep the house and search carefully
5. end of the search	<u>until</u> she <u>finds it</u>?
6. finding	[9]<u>And when</u> she <u>finds it</u>,

C. Gather Together and Be Joyful

7. gathering	she <u>calls her friends and neighbors together</u>
8. invitation	<u>and says</u>, "<u>Rejoice with me</u>;
9. reason for gathering	<u>I have found my lost</u> coin."
10. joy in heaven over a repentant sinner	[10]In the same way, <u>I tell you</u>, there is <u>rejoicing</u> in the presence of the angels of God <u>over one sinner who repents</u>.

Preachers should pay attention to the step-parallelism. This series of three movements can become the outline of their sermon. Frequently homilies based upon this text climax with the finding of the lost sheep or coin. But the final climactic movement involves the community. Jesus wants to establish a pattern among his people so that when one is lost, there is a prolonged intensive search until the lost is found. But then the community meets together and celebrates so that the new convert becomes the most important member of the community. The joy is profound and unparalleled since the shepherd-evangelist rejoices (15:5), the community rejoices (15:6), and the angels in heaven rejoice (15:7). The step-parallelism pattern provides a paradigm for the continuing life of the church.

7. Luke's Technique of Parallel Alternating Narratives: Acts 1:1–6:7

As a sophisticated writer, Luke enjoys the use of literary devices such as parallel structured narratives. In the first section of the book of Acts, which demonstrates the miraculous growth of the church, Luke alternates narratives dealing with the church's inward life together and their outward journey of mission. The first sketch portrays the 120 believers as waiting and praying for power from on high with one mind and heart (Acts 1:1-26). Then the outward mission becomes prominent through the blowing wind of the Spirit and the astonishing speaking in the tongues of all the gathered nations. As a result, Peter's powerful preaching establishes a Christian community of more than three thousand in one Pentecost day (2:1-41). In the next scene, Luke returns to a picture of the spiritual life of the early Jerusalem church and describes the power of their life together in word, fellowship, sacraments, and prayer (2:42-47). Alternating again to the outward journey, Luke depicts how the healing ministry of the church was used by God for growing the mission of the community in the world (3:1–4:22). Then, in what seems like a duplicate to the end of chapter 2, Luke describes the inner dynamics of the church, this time from an economic viewpoint emphasizing the sharing of possessions so that there is not a needy person among them (4:23–5:11). These parallel narratives continue with the outward journey of the community, highlighting the powerful signs and courageous testimony of the disciples (5:12-42), followed by a final depiction of the leadership of the early Jerusalem church in caring for the poor among them (6:1-7).

Luke employs this literary device to demonstrate that the captivating growth of the church proceeds both from the dynamic vitality of the church's relationships and from their bold outreach ventures into the world outside their attractive community. Through the alternating of parallel narratives, Luke is proclaiming a powerful message about the magnetic appeal of Jesus through his newly-formed, Spirit-filled community. The outreach techniques of the early church include both centripetal evangelism by attracting members to its vital inner life and centrifugal evangelism by moving outward towards new converts. Luke's message, which he hopes will be repeated by every generation of Christians, is written into the literary device of alternating parallel narratives.

Study and Discussion Questions

1. We have witnessed how chapter divisions interrupt the thematic flow of the narrative, as in the two controversy dialogues about the Sabbath in Mark 2:23–3:6. Both Luke 13:10-17 and 14:1-6 also portray healings on the Sabbath and should be read together. Notice as well Jesus' habit of linking together a story about a man and a woman both here and in Luke 13:18-21 and 15:1-10. What is the relationship between the type of healing Jesus performs (Luke 13:11, 16; 14:2) and the application to everyday life in 13:15 and 14:5? (You may have to discover what dropsy is before you understand the passage.) What is the theme of both passages?

2. Is a chapter division at Deuteronomy 13 appropriate? What does Deut 12:32 refer to when it says, "See that you do all I command you." Notice as well 13:18, "keeping all his commands that I am giving you today." What is the literary device connecting these two verses called, and why would it be employed here? What is so important about the laws in Deuteronomy 13 that these bookends are placed around it?

3. Mark entitles the book he wrote a "gospel" (Mark 1:1). Similarly the gospel is preached to the first Gentiles in Acts 10:36-43. How is the flow of the written Gospel of Mark similar to the oral preaching of the gospel in Acts 10? How then would "preached history" be an apt description of a gospel? Reflect upon the audience to whom Mark might be re-preaching the message of Jesus, and ponder how relevant this preached history would be.

4. If the genre of gospel can be described as preached history or kerygmatic biography, how does this account for the unique passages in Matthew such as 1:23; 2:15, 18, 23; 4:15-16; 8:17; 12:17-21; 13:35; 27:9-10? If we picture Matthew as a member of a Christian synagogue across the street from a Pharisaic synagogue, what message about Jesus is Matthew attempting to preach to his fellow Jews?

5. A miracle story contains three parts: (1) the extreme difficulty of the disease; (2) the performance of the healing; and (3) the confirmation of the miracle as well as the reaction of awe from the bystanders. When these expected occurrences are altered, the perceptive reader should pay attention (see B6 above; pp. 16-17). In the healing of the epileptic boy, Luke 9:37-43 climaxes the narrative with the statement, "And they were all amazed at the

greatness of God." Now turn to the Gospel of Mark and describe how he concludes this narrative. Remember the discipleship catechism section encompasses Mark 8:21–10:52. Why does Mark omit the reaction of awe from the crowd in the healing of the epileptic and instead talk about prayer (Mark 9:28-29)?

6. We have witnessed an *inclusio* tying together John's Gospel. What are the connections between the birth and burial/resurrection accounts in the Gospel of Matthew? How do the beginning and end of Matthew narrate both a hostile story and a friendly one that are interwoven in a positive-negative-positive-negative-positive pattern? For an insightful diagram diagnosing a parallel structure, consult Raymond Brown, *The Death of the Messiah*. ABRL (New York: Doubleday, 1994), 2:1302. What is at the center of each chiasm? What is equivalent to the name "Immanuel" (Matt 1:23) in 28:16-20? In the Great Commission the gospel is brought to the Gentile nations. How is this foreshadowed in Jesus' birth? Herod lies by insisting that he wants to worship the baby king (2:8). What parallel falsehood occurs in the resurrection narrative? How is the Trinitarian baptismal formula (28:19b) already witnessed in Jesus' baptism in Matt 3:16-17?

7. If you eliminate the heading (Eccl 1:1) and the conclusion (12:9-14) to the book of Ecclesiastes, what is the *inclusio* that surrounds the teaching material? How is this idea reinforced through repetitions throughout the book on the subject of labor, pleasure, and riches?

8. We encounter another Lukan example of alternating parallel narratives in the birth narratives of John the Baptizer and Jesus. For example, in the angel's foretelling of the birth of John, Luke builds a fivefold parallel with the prediction of the birth of Jesus:

John (Luke 1:11-20)	Jesus (Luke 1:28-38)
(a) The angel Gabriel appears	(a) The angel Gabriel appears
(b) Zechariah is startled	(b) Mary is startled
(c) Message of a birth to elderly people	(c) Message of a virgin birth
(d) Questioning response: How am I to know this?	(d) Questioning response: How can this be?
(e) Sign: Zechariah reduced to silence	(e) Sign: Mary's relative conceives in old age

What message would Luke be proclaiming through paralleling both the predictions (1:5-25; 26-38) and the births (1:57-80; 2:1-40) of John and Jesus? What is the significance that the encounter of Mary with Elizabeth is placed at the center of these parallel narratives? (See esp. 1:41.)

9. The Gospels and other Semitic literature are filled with parallelism. But once in a while authors break up parallel structures to add a line that becomes the emphasis of the passage. Study the parallelism between the two sayings of Jesus about garments and wine in Mark 2:21-22 and write out the similar structure. Which line does not fit the parallelism? What then would be the emphasis that Jesus and Mark are intending to underline?

10. The simple literary technique of verbal repetition frequently exposes the emphasis of a particular pericope. In Libronix 3 there is a handy method of constructing a vocabulary list of any passage. If you want to discover the repetitions in 2 Cor 1:3-7, open NA27. In Libronix 3, when you press Control and N after opening NA27, a new document box will appear into which you should type "2 Corinthians 1:3-7." After clicking OK to create a blank Vocabulary List user document, open the Properties dialog. There select Greek, OK, and click on Add where you select NA27 from the drop-down box. Then type "2cor 1 3-7" in the reference box, click OK, and you can then sort the vocabulary by Frequency (Descending). You will notice that, besides the short expected words, you encounter παράκλησις ("encouragement") six times, παρακαλέω ("to encourage") four times, πάθημα ("suffering") four times, and θλῖψις ("tribulation") in two occurrences. Place these concepts together in your own words and you have discovered the theme of the passage. Now repeat this exercise with 2 Cor 5:18-21 and Gal 3:14-29, or in the Hebrew language try 2 Kings 1, paying attention to the word "come down," and 2 Samuel 11, which emphasizes the verb "send." For Logos 4 a similar method of determining the important words in a passage is under development.

CHAPTER 2

The Grammatical Route

Using an Exegetical Microscope

Grammatical exegesis has remained a priority throughout the history of interpretation. In this chapter we pay close attention to the minute details of the text as if peering into a microscope. Traveling down the grammatical route, we begin with an analysis of the text itself and discover examples where determining the correct Greek text is the first step in exegesis. Then we will proceed to word study, the interplay of words in phrases, and an analysis of clauses. Next with regard to sentence structure, we will investigate how word order assists the interpreter in locating the emphasis of the author. Finally, we will compare English versions of the Bible and study the benefits of employing several types of translations.

A. Textual Criticism

PROCEDURE

We possess more than 5,700 Greek manuscripts of segments of the New Testament, yet none of them are exactly alike. How do we determine the correct reading? Textual criticism is the field that examines the documents, categorizes the texts according to age, place of origin, and similarity to other manuscripts, and then offers external and internal criteria for determining the correct text. External evidence considers the age of the manuscripts and their distribution throughout major centers of the ancient world. Eldon Epp exemplifies the thinking of the majority of textual critics in specifying internal criteria for determining the original text.[1]

1. A variant's status as the shorter or shortest reading.
2. A variant's status as the harder or hardest reading.
3. A variant's fitness to account for the origin, development, or presence of all other readings.
4. A variant's conformity to the author's style and vocabulary.
5. A variant's conformity to the author's theology or ideology.
6. A variant's conformity to Koine (rather than Attic) Greek.
7. A variant's conformity to Semitic forms of expression.
8. A variant's lack of conformity to parallel passages.
9. A variant's lack of conformity to OT passages.
10. A variant's lack of conformity to liturgical forms and usages.
11. A variant's lack of conformity to extrinsic doctrinal views.

Although each of our manuscripts read differently, the overwhelming majority of variants are inconsequential, comprised mainly of spelling differences, the presence or absence of the article, changes in word order, and accidental omissions. Daniel Wallace contends that "only about 1% of the textual variants are both meaningful and viable" and that "significant textual variants that alter core doctrines of the NT have not yet been produced."[2] We will present two examples below to offer the reader a taste of how textual criticism is applied to significant texts.

EXAMPLES

1. Jude 22-23: Triplicates in the Epistle of Jude

Some English versions (KJV, NKJV, NEB) of Jude 22-23 describe two groups of addressees, while other translations (RSV, NRSV, NIV, TNIV) distinguish three categories of people. The NKJV, for instance, states, "And on some have compassion, making a distinction; but others save with fear, pulling *them*

---

1. Eldon Jay Epp, "The Eclectic Method in New Testament Textual Criticism: Solution or Symptom?" in *Perspectives on New Testament Textual Criticism: Collected Essays, 1962-2004.* NovTSup 116 (Leiden: Brill, 2005), p. 158; repr. from *HTR* 69 (1976): 243.

2. Daniel B. Wallace, "The Gospel According to Bart: A Review Article of *Misquoting Jesus* by Bart Ehrman," *JETS* 49 (2006): 330, 347.

out of the fire, hating even the garment defiled by the flesh." The TNIV, on the other hand, reads "Be merciful to those who doubt; save others by snatching them from the fire; to others show mercy, mixed with fear — hating even the clothing stained by corrupted flesh." If external evidence is examined, excellent Greek manuscripts contain both readings (two groups in B C* K L P Byzantine manuscripts; three groups in ℵ A). So how do we ascertain which reading is superior?

If we explore Jude's literary style, we discover his preference for threes. Jude employs triadic structures in verses 2, 4, 5-7, 8, and 11.

Jude 2   Triple greeting: "Mercy, peace, and love be yours in abundance."

Jude 4   Three attributive participles as subjects: those whose condemnation was written about long ago; those who pervert the grace of God; those who deny Jesus Christ.

Jude 5-7   Three groups are destroyed: people who came out of Egypt; unholy angels; Sodom and Gomorrah.

Jude 8   Three behaviors of ungodly people: they pollute their own bodies, reject authority, and heap abuse on celestial beings.

Jude 11   Three examples: "the way of Cain . . . Balaam's error . . . Korah's rebellion."

To visualize these threefold structures in the Greek, you can consult the *Lexham Clausal Outlines* of Jude in Logos Bible Software and observe the triad of attributive participles in verse 4, the three main verbs in verse 8, and the three verbs of the ὅτι clause in verse 11. In addition, Metzger's *Textual Commentary* confirms our supposition when it concludes,

> In view of the author's predilection for arranging his material in groups of three (as in verses 2, 4, 8, in the examples of judgment in verses 5-7, and of sin in ver. 11), a majority of the Committee was disposed to prefer as original the triple arrangement of the passage, and to regard the other forms as aberrations that arose partly from scribal inattentiveness, partly from indecision concerning the sense of διακρίνεσθαι in ver. 22 (in ver. 9 it means "to contend" with someone; here, however, it must mean "to doubt"), and partly from concern to provide a main clause after three (or two) relative clauses.[3]

3. Bruce M. Metzger, *A Textual Commentary on the Greek New Testament*, 2nd ed. (Stuttgart: Deutsche Bibelgesellschaft, 1994), p. 659.

Therefore, a threefold exhortation at the end of Jude is the best reading, and the TNIV contains the superior translation. The text must be established before grammatical exegesis can begin.

2. Mark 1:1: Son of God?

Since your Bible study on the Gospel of Mark begins this week, you need to study a portion of Mark 1. The Second Gospel begins with the phrase "the beginning of the gospel." So you perform a word study of the term "gospel" and discover that it occurs in Mark 1:14-15 as well. This term then functions as a frame[4] around the beginning of Mark's Gospel that consists of John's ministry and Jesus' baptism. In the Bible study, students will use either the NIV translation or the TNIV. But when you consult these two versions, you notice that Mark 1:1 is divergent. The NIV reads "The beginning of the gospel about Jesus Christ, the Son of God" while the TNIV states "The beginning of the good news about Jesus the Messiah." Should the title "Son of God" be included in your Bible study of this passage?

To arrive at an answer, you attempt to discover other English versions that omit this title "Son of God." To answer this query, click on "Text Comparison" under the "Tools" heading of Logos 4 and survey the various versions, or alternatively in Libronix 3 choose "Tools," then "Bible Comparison" and "Passage in All Versions." Through this process, you discover that the TNIV is the only major translation to omit this title.[5] For the TNIV to display such peculiarity, strong arguments are needed. You decide to consult the experts and turn to Metzger's *Textual Commentary* in the Gold edition of Libronix. The authors there conclude that "the combination of B D W *al* in support of υἱοῦ θεοῦ is extremely strong." Therefore, the best manuscripts support "Son of God" in the text. Also its absence in some documents can be explained. "The absence of υἱοῦ θεοῦ in ℵ* θ 28ᶜ *al* may be due to an oversight in copying, occasioned by the similarity of the endings of the *nomina sacra*."[6]

---

4. See Markan intercalations and frames in Appendix II, C (pp. 359-60).

5. Less well-known editions have omitted "Son of God" at Mark 1:1: The New World Translation; *The Twentieth Century New Testament* (1904; repr. Chicago: Moody, 1961); *The Complete Gospels: Annotated Scholars Version,* ed. Robert J. Miller (Sonoma: Polebridge, 1992); and the 1946 edition of the RSV New Testament, although "Son of God" was included in the full Bible of 1952.

6. Metzger, *Textual Commentary,* p. 659. The *nomina sacra* are abbreviations of titles that look alike.

The eye of the copyist could have moved easily from the οὖ endings of Ἰησοῦ Χριστοῦ ("Jesus Christ") and accidentally skipped over υἱοῦ θεοῦ ("Son of God").

You wisely decide to perform your own study of the terms "Messiah" and "Son of God" in the Gospel of Mark. When you execute a Bible search of the term "Messiah" in the TNIV, you discover that Χριστός is employed eight times in Mark, with the next occurrence at 8:29. If you click this text, Logos Bible Software opens a window so you can study the context. Here Peter confesses Jesus as Messiah, but then suddenly denies Jesus' additional identity as the suffering Son of Man. Apparently the title "Messiah" does not convey everything that Mark wants the reader to know about Jesus' identity. This is confirmed when you read the narrative about the healing of the blind man (8:22-26) placed immediately before Peter's confession of the Messiah. Just as the blind man needs a second touch before he can see perfectly, so Peter needs a second touch before he embodies a complete Christology and a true discipleship vision. To picture Jesus as the miracle-working Messiah is not enough; in addition, one must confess Jesus as the suffering Son who must go to the cross and lead his followers down a similar path of discipleship. Therefore the title "Son" is crucial to Mark's understanding of Christology.

In your search of the terms "Son of God" or "Son" in Mark, you discover as well that the Roman centurion recites the confession of Jesus as "Son of God" at the crucifixion in 15:39. This christological declaration stands as a climactic conclusion in Mark's Gospel. The title "Son of God" really structures the Gospel so that at Jesus' baptism the voice from heaven is aimed at Jesus, confirming his Sonship (1:11). Then at the transfiguration (right after Peter's confession) the voice from heaven reveals Jesus as the Son of God to the chosen disciples (9:7). The final revelation occurs right after Jesus' death when the centurion, acting like a voice from heaven, proclaims for all to hear (in particular the Gentiles) that Jesus is the Son of God (15:39). Unlike Peter, the centurion makes the complete christological confession that Jesus is Son of God in his suffering at the cross. The important role that the title "Son of God" plays in the Gospel surely indicates that Mark would want to include this phrase at the very beginning of his Gospel in 1:1.

Therefore, both external and internal evidence indicate that the NIV, not the TNIV, should be followed in Mark 1:1. In the process you have discovered the importance of the titles "Messiah" and "Son" in your investigation into a textual problem in Mark's Gospel.

B. Word Study

Grammatical analysis at the ground level is word study. The various lexicons and grammars in Logos Bible Software are invaluable in performing exegetical research. The Greek text as well is already analyzed and grammatically identified so that you do not have to rely upon your memory. Simply placing the curser upon the Greek word supplies the morphological data in the left bottom corner of the screen. The following examples demonstrate how the grammatical data as well as etymologically similar forms enlighten the meaning of particular passages of Scripture.

EXAMPLES

1. 1 Thessalonians 4:17: The Nature of the Rapture

With regard to eschatology, the nature of the rapture is continually debated. Will Jesus return upon the clouds, rapture his saints, and return to heaven for a period of time so that the earth is devoid of Christians? Or will Jesus return, rapture his saints, and then proceed to earth to judge the living and the dead? Everyone agrees that this doctrine is propounded in 1 Thess 4:17, but how are we to understand this meeting with the Lord in the air? Enlighenment occurs when we attempt to establish the meaning of the term ἀπάντησις ("a meeting") by allowing one Scripture to interpret another.

If you perform a search on the lemma form of ἀπάντησιν in 1 Thess 4:17, you discover that this word also occurs in Matt 25:6 and Acts 28:15. In the Parable of the Ten Virgins in Matthew, the wise maidens go out to meet the bridegroom and then accompany him to the wedding banquet in order to celebrate together. Also in Acts, the Christians from Rome travel as far as the Forum of Appius and the Three Taverns to meet Paul and then escort him into the city of Rome. The established pattern consists of the citizens traveling to meet a dignitary and then ushering that person back to their original location. If we apply this information to 1 Thess 4:17, the results of this word study reinforce the interpretation that the saints are raptured and accompany Jesus to earth to begin his eternal reign. Word studies open up the meaning of the text.

2. The Present Tense in 1 John 3:6 and Matthew 7:7

The Greek language is more specific than English and can create distinctions that are not possible in modern languages. For instance, the Greek tenses supply vital information for interpretation. The aorist tense is the default tense that specifies snapshot action. The present and imperfect tenses, on the other hand, describe ongoing motion-picture activity. Therefore, the careful reader should always check the Greek verb information to discover what type of action is conveyed.

For instance, in 1 John 3:6 the NRSV reads "No one who abides in him sins." This translation could create great confusion for inexperienced readers of the Bible, since they might fear that their continued sinning would disqualify them from being a Christian or become convinced that Christians will arrive at a state where they will no longer commit sins. But the Greek employs the present tense, which specifies motion-picture action (πᾶς ὁ ἐν αὐτῷ μένων οὐχ ἁμαρτάνει). Therefore the NIV translation is superior: "No one who lives in him keeps on sinning." Christians who are continually being made holy by Christ do not commit the same sins over and over again throughout their lifetime.

Likewise, those who have struggled with unanswered prayer might be tempted to deny the truth of Matt 7:7, "Ask and it will be given to you; seek and you will find; knock and the door will be opened to you." But again, the Greek employs the present tense in each of the imperatives (αἰτεῖτε . . . ζητεῖτε . . . κρούετε) so that the New Living Translation (NLT) better conveys the meaning, "Keep on asking, and you will receive what you ask for. Keep on seeking, and you will find. Keep on knocking, and the door will be opened to you." The specificity of the Greek tenses enables us to arrive at a correct interpretation and a more biblical view of prayer.

3. 1 Peter 1:7: Agreement in Person, Number, and Gender

The grammatical formulations of person, number, and gender can supply the needed information for a correct understanding of the biblical text. For instance, in 1 Pet 1:7 there is confusion whether one's faith or the tested genuineness of one's faith is of greater worth than gold. The NIV states that "These have come so that your faith — of greater worth than gold, which perishes even though refined by fire — may be proved genuine and may result in praise, glory and honor when Jesus Christ is revealed." On the other hand, the English Standard Version (ESV) reads, "so that the tested genuineness of your faith — more precious than gold . . . may be found to result in praise and glory and honor." Which is correct?

The interpreter must pay attention to the Greek phraseology: τὸ δοκίμιον ὑμῶν τῆς πίστεως πολυτιμότερον χρυσίου. Here the word faith (πίστεως) is feminine, while the testing (δοκίμιον) and the participle "more precious" (πολυτιμότερον) are neuter. Therefore, the ESV has the correct translation; the tested genuineness of our faith is more precious than gold. Peter is demonstrating through imagery the value of faithful persistence in the midst of adverse circumstances. Grammatical exegesis again proves its worth.

4. Luke 22:31-32; John 1:50-51; 3:7-12: Singular and Plural

Frequently English translations do not allow the reader to determine whether an author intends you singular or you plural. For instance, in Luke 22:31-32 the NIV reads, "Simon, Simon, Satan has asked to sift you (plural ὑμᾶς) as wheat. But I have prayed for you (singular σοῦ)." One could easily become confused and think that Satan was only harassing Peter and not the other disciples. Editors can employ footnotes to clarify this distinction, but a more appropriate method involves the use of "all of you," as the ISV: "Simon, Simon, listen! Satan has asked permission to sift all of you like wheat."

Similarly, in John 1:50 Jesus speaks individually to Nathaniel, "You will see greater things than these," but then follows with a prophetic word for all the disciples, "Truly, truly I tell all of you, you will see heaven standing open and the angels of God going up and coming down to the Son of Man." The ISV again catches appropriately the switch to the second person plural.

In addition, the Gospel of John frequently switches between singular and plural to apply Jesus' message to the contemporary hearers at the time when John wrote his Gospel. In John 3:7 Jesus begins by speaking to Nicodemus personally, but in 7b applies the message to John's entire audience: "You (singular) should not be surprised at my saying, 'You (plural) must be born again.'" Similarly, in 3:11 Jesus and Nicodemus begin the conversation, but in the end the debate is really between the Christians and unbelieving Jews: "I tell you (singular) the truth, we (Christians) speak of what we know, and we (Christians) testify to what we (Christians) have seen, but still you people (unbelieving Jews) do not accept our testimony." This same device is employed by John in the conversation between Jesus and the woman at the well in chapter 4. The woman represents all the Samaritans, just as Nicodemus represents all the Jewish leadership. The reference to a group is indicated by the use of the first person plural (4:12, 20-22, 25, 42) instead of the singular. For readers to pick up these nuanced distinctions, they must pay attention to switches in the Greek pronouns.

5. Ephesians 4:12: One Single Comma

Ephesians 4:12 discusses the function of pastor-teachers. Surprisingly, a single comma in the English text creates a completely different philosophy of ministry for the church. In the 1952 edition of the RSV, Eph 4:12 assigned three tasks to the leaders of the church: God gave "pastors and teachers, for the equipment of the saints, for the work of ministry, for building up the body of Christ." However, the 1971 edition removed the comma after "saints" so that pastors and teachers "equip the saints for the work of ministry, for building up the body of Christ." Notice that the comma after the word "saints" is now omitted. Therefore, the pastor-teachers have one task, "to equip the saints," and the people perform two functions, "to do the work of ministry" and "to build up the rest of the church."[7]

This change is justified when one performs a word study of the Greek text. There is an important alteration of prepositions from the single use of πρὸς to the double usage of εἰς:

πρὸς τὸν καταρτισμὸν τῶν ἁγίων	to equip the saints
εἰς ἔργον διακονίας,	for the work of ministry,
εἰς οἰκοδομὴν τοῦ σώματος	for building up the body
τοῦ Χριστοῦ.	of Christ.

The leaders of the church equip the people, and the members do the work of ministry and build up the body of Christ. This shift of prepositions dramatically contrasts with the triad of εἰς phrases in Eph 4:13, which describes three parallel results that are obtained when the leaders and members work together in performing their functions in the church. The results of this team ministry climax in all of us together reaching (1) the unity of the faith and the knowledge of the Son of God; (2) mature adulthood; and (3) the whole

---

7. The recent ISV still includes the comma: "to perfect the saints, to do the work of ministry, and to build up the body of Christ."

measure of the fullness of Christ. Furthermore, the context supports an emphasis upon lay ministry, since in the conclusion at 4:16 the subject of the verb "makes the body grow" is not "the pastors and teachers" but "the whole body." It is the entire body of Christ that makes the body grow. Grammatical data, word studies, and context all support the same conclusion. Leaders equip and the people do the ministry.

The colorful nuances of the Greek noun καταρτισμὸν ("equipping") in Eph 4:12 are difficult to determine since it occurs only here in the Greek Bible. But other searches in Logos Bible Software can uncover similar roots. If one attempts a morphological search in the NIV by choosing Logos Greek Morphology and typing in g:katarti (g for Greek and *katarti* as the root of words connected to "equip"), several interesting references to the Greek verb καταρτίζω are revealed. Such passages as Matt 4:21; 1 Cor 1:10; and Luke 6:40 throw light on the meaning of "equip."

In Jesus' calling of James and John to discipleship, καταρτίζω contains the imagery of repairing nets, implying that "equipping the saints" means repairing people's lives. 1 Corinthians 1:10 employs the additional imagery of reconciling two conflicting parties. Paul states, "I appeal to you, brothers, in the name of our Lord Jesus Christ, that all of you agree with one another so that there may be no divisions among you and that you may be perfectly united (κατηρτισμένοι) in mind and thought." Therefore, "equipping the saints" involves training people to work together cooperatively and peacefully. Finally, Luke 6:40 describes modeling behavior so that the training of the saints implies a process whereby the student resembles the teacher: "A student is not above his teacher, but everyone who is fully trained (κατηρτισμένος) will be like his teacher." In this example, a search of the verb form adds important content to the meaning of the noun form καταρτισμὸν in Eph 4:12. To equip the saints encompasses repairing people's lives, training them in conflict management, and modeling Christlike behavior. Therefore, a thorough exegesis includes a study of the various derivative forms of a Greek root.

6. *Philippians 2:9 and 1:29: Etymologically Similar Forms*

Additional light shines upon a passage when similar words are searched or etymologically related forms are consulted. For instance, ἐχαρίσατο (χαρίζομαι) in Phil 2:9 is usually translated, "gave him the name that is above every name." But this verb is closely related with the noun χάρις, meaning "grace." Therefore, the passage could be translated that God graced Jesus with the name above every name. In Phil 1:29 Paul applies this same term to the believer: "For it has been granted (ἐχαρίσθη) to you on behalf of Christ not only to believe on him, but also to suffer for him." Surprisingly, God's grace is visible not only in the vibrant faith that we manifest but also when we have the opportunity to suffer for Christ. Grace is everywhere!

Similar Greek words include the following:

χάρισμα = "charisma, gift"
χαρά = "joy"
εὐχαριστέω = "to be thankful"
εὐχαριστία = "thanksgiving" or "the Eucharist"
χαρίζομαι = also meaning "to forgive"

The interconnection of these words from the same root provides a possible sermon illustration or an edifying Bible study comment so that people recognize the abundant grace freely bestowed upon us by God. Forgiveness, thanksgiving, joy, our celebration of the Lord's Supper, and the spiritual gifts we possess are all intimately connected with God's grace.

7. οὐ and μή in Luke 6:39; Romans 9:20-21; 1 Corinthians 9:8

The Greek language utilizes two distinct words for the negative, so that the careful researcher can distinguish whether questions expect a positive or negative reply. The terms μή or μήτι expect a negative answer, whereas the words οὐ or οὐχὶ anticipate a positive response. Both are exemplified in Luke 6:39. There Jesus inquires, "Can a blind man lead a blind man? Will they not both fall into a pit?" The Greek specifies that the first question should be answered negatively (μήτι δύναται τυφλὸς τυφλὸν ὁδηγεῖν), whereas the second insists on a positive reply (οὐχὶ ἀμφότεροι εἰς βόθυνον ἐμπεσοῦνται). Word choice determines the expected answer to each question.

Likewise in Rom 9:20-21 the switch in negatives offers an exegetical clue to the expected answer. Will what is molded say to its molder, "Why have you made me thus?" Certainly not, since the Greek negative μή is employed. Has the potter no right over the clay? Of course he does, since the Greek negative οὐκ occurs in this question.

Or finally in 1 Cor 9:8 the intended meaning is clarified through word usage. In discussing the rights of an apostle, Paul authoritatively asks, "Do I say this on human authority?" No, he does not, as indicated by the use of the Greek negative μὴ (Μὴ κατὰ ἄνθρωπον ταῦτα λαλῶ). Then Paul alters the negative in the very next question to positively assure his audience that the law says the same thing (ἢ καὶ ὁ νόμος ταῦτα οὐ λέγει; "doesn't the Law say the same thing?"). Paul carefully employs vocabulary to strengthen his arguments. Grammatical distinctions (some found only in Greek) greatly clarify the intended meaning of the biblical text.

8. "Submit" in Ephesians 5:21-22

Frequently people begin a quotation of Scripture with Eph 5:22, "Wives, submit to your husbands as to the Lord." However, if one refers to the original Greek, no verb is present in the sentence. Literally, the text states, "wives, to one's own husband as to the Lord." Readers without a knowledge of Greek should consult the *Lexham Greek-English Interlinear of the New Testament* or the *English-Greek Reverse Interlinear New Testament* in Logos Bible Software, where the two languages are compared. To discover the verb, one must examine the previous verse. The imperative from 5:21 must be carried over to 5:22 in order to understand the meaning "submit" when it applies to husband-wife relationships. This entails that the passages 5:21 and 5:22 must be read together. To understand the biblical view of the marriage relationship, the reader must begin with 5:21, "Submit to one another out of reverence for Christ." That is the foundation upon which everything following is built.

Therefore, mutual submission is the key. Based upon this underpinning, the wife must place the husband first by submitting to him before her own agenda. Likewise, as 5:25 indicates, the husband must place his wife's needs and concerns before his own by loving his wife as Christ loved the church. The omission of the verb in 5:22 leads to an important insight into the text. Mutual submission is the basis upon which Paul expounds the marriage relationship and applies this principle both to the woman and to the man. Paul addresses the woman before the man in 5:22, but in the concluding verse of the passage (5:33) he reverses the order and exhorts the husband first: "However, each one of you also must love his wife as he loves himself, and the wife must respect her husband." The rights of each person give way to an emphasis upon one's responsibility to put the other person first, just as 5:21 underscores at the beginning.

9. "Joy" and "Rejoice" in Philippians

Paul's Letter to the Philippians could be entitled "A Chorus of Joy." In the beginning thanksgiving Paul reports, "I always pray with joy because of your partnership in the gospel" (1:4-5). Likewise, when he concludes the correspondence, he states "Finally, my brothers, rejoice in the Lord" (3:1) and "Rejoice in the Lord always. I will say it again: rejoice" (4:4). When Paul is feeling great by recalling the sweet fellowship he experienced with the Philippians, he rejoices. He labels the community "his joy and crown" (4:1). Paul testifies that he experiences complete joy when they are one in spirit and purpose (2:2), and he knows that at his arrival "your joy in Christ Jesus will overflow on account of me" (1:26). But Paul can also rejoice in his sufferings, even at the point of death: "For to me, to live is Christ and to die is gain" (1:21). With deep conviction Paul contends, "Even if I am being poured out like a drink offering on the sacrifice and service coming from your faith, I am glad and rejoice with all of you" (2:17). Through a simple word study of the terms "joy" and "rejoice" we have created an edifying Bible study.

Paul speaks about joy some fourteen times in four short chapters. However, sometimes he employs a verb while in other passages he uses a noun. How do we discover all these occurrences? In Logos 4 in the search menu you should click the Morph search, change the range to Philippians in the NIV (or your preferred Bible) and designate "Logos Greek Morphology." Then type in g:xa (where g indicates Greek and xa the first two letters of the Greek words for "joy," "rejoice," etc.), and the various options for "joy" and "rejoice" will appear. You will discover five texts under the noun and nine references under the verb.[8] Now you have a word study process that can locate all the words about joy in Paul's Epistle to the Philippians.

---

8. In Libronix 3 you can use the search icon and then type in "rejoice," choose the NIV, designate the range as "special" and type in "Philippians," and you will find eight references in six verses. Now repeat the procedure with "joy" and you will have six more. But if you know Greek, you can unearth all the occurrences in one process if you place a star behind the root χα* and use the Greek morphological Bible search. To type in Greek you can change the keyboard from English to Greek to Hebrew by hitting the shift and alt keys consecutively. Now you have 17 verses to investigate, since the word "grace," which is similar to the root "joy," is included. If you search *χα* you have 20 verses to inspect, since the similar word "thanksgiving" is added to the search. The advantage of searching in the Greek morphology is that sometimes English translations employ various words for the same Greek term, so that the NIV speaks about being "glad" in 2:28 and employs the noun "joy" in 1:26, where it is not found in the Greek.

C. Analysis of Phrases

PROCEDURE

A phrase is a group of connected words without a verbal element such as a main verb, participle, or infinitive. Especially important for exegetical reasons are the various uses of the genitive case. In the examples below we demonstrate the significance of distinguishing various types of genitive constructions as well as the importance of searching for repeated phrases in the context.

EXAMPLES

1. The Interpretation of Genitive Phrases: 1 Thessalonians 1:3

In 1 Thess 1:3 Paul remembers the church's work of faith (τοῦ ἔργου τῆς πίστεως), their labor of love (τοῦ κόπου τῆς ἀγάπης) and their endurance of hope (τῆς ὑπομονῆς τῆς ἐλπίδος). To capture the full impact of these phrases, I would advise that you attempt a translation without employing the word "of" for the genitive. Various English translations are possible, since the genitives can be categorized as appositive genitives, attributive genitives (genitives of quality), attributed genitives, or genitives of origin.

First we will define these genitive categories and give examples of each. With an appositive genitive, you can use an equal sign to clarify the meaning. When at Pentecost the invitation is extended to the crowd to receive the gift of the Holy Spirit (τὴν δωρεὰν τοῦ ἁγίου πνεύματος, Acts 2:38), an appositive genitive is employed meaning that the gift = the Holy Spirit. Or when Jews received the sign of circumcision (σημεῖον περιτομῆς, Rom 4:11), it was circumcision itself that was the sign. Or when Paul speaks about the guarantee of the Spirit (τὸν ἀρραβῶνα τοῦ πνεύματος, 2 Cor 5:5), he is not promising a guarantee which the Spirit will bestow. No, the guarantee is the Spirit.

Attributive and attributed genitives are relatives of each other: both function as adjectives. With the attributive genitive, the noun in the genitive case functions as an adjective, whereas with the attributed genitive, the noun preceding the genitive functions as the adjective in English. So the expression "the appearance of glory" in Titus 2:13 (ἐπιφάνειαν τῆς δόξης) is properly translated in English "the glorious appearing," an attributive genitive. However, the phrase "the fruit of work" in Phil 1:22 (καρπὸς ἔργου) must mean "fruitful work," so that the preceding word becomes the adjective while the genitive becomes a noun in English as an attributed genitive. These divergent usages even occur within a few verses of each other, so that Eph 4:19 (ἐργασίαν ἀκαθαρσίας) must be translated as an attributive genitive, "an impure work," while Eph 4:17 (ἐν ματαιότητι τοῦ νοὸς) means "a futile mind," thus an attributed genitive.

A fourth category, the genitive of origin or source, can best be rendered in English by "whose origin is" or "produced by." Therefore, the "fruit of the Spirit" (καρπὸς τοῦ πνεύματός) in Gal 5:22 is best categorized as a genitive of origin, indicating that the fruit is produced by the Holy Spirit. You can obtain more information about these distinctive genitives by studying such grammars as Daniel Wallace's *Greek Grammar Beyond the Basics* or Blass-Debrunner-Funk's *A Greek Grammar of the New Testament and Other Christian Literature* (BDF) — all available in Logos Bible Software.[9] In addition, Albert Lukaszewski offers his opinion on the use of each genitive in the Logos resource, *The Lexham Syntactic Greek New Testament: Expansions and Annotations.*[10]

Now let's use this information to interpret the possible translations of 1 Thess 1:3. If the genitive is an appositive genitive, then the work would be faith itself, the labor would equal love, and endurance would be the same as hope. However, this last expression in the series ("endurance which is hope") makes little sense and argues against the use of an appositive genitive for the other expressions. The New Living Translation seems to favor an attributive genitive but inconsistently applies this category to the text. The NLT reads, "we think of your faithful work, your loving deeds, and the enduring hope," so that the first two phrases are attributive, but a strange switch substitutes an attributed genitive in the third expression. Surely Paul would not have switched the use of the genitive in the middle of a sentence without notifying the reader. With more consistency the ISV employs an attributed genitive throughout. It states, "we constantly remember how your faith is active, your love is hard at work, and your hope in our Lord Jesus Christ is enduring." The NIV and TNIV, on the other hand, choose for a genitive of origin: "your work

9. For the genitive, see Daniel B. Wallace, *Greek Grammar Beyond the Basics* (Grand Rapids: Zondervan, 1996), pp. 72-136; and Friedrich Blass, Albert Debrunner, and Robert W. Funk, eds., *A Greek Grammar of the New Testament and Other Christian Literature* (Chicago: University of Chicago Press, 1961), #491-520.

10. Lukaszewski is helpful but not infallible, as evidenced by his categorization of "salt of the earth" in Matt 5:13 as a partitive genitive, whereas "light of the world" in Matt 5:14 is an objective genitive. I take them both as objective genitives.

produced by faith, your labor prompted by love, and your endurance inspired by hope." To decide between these usages of the genitive, the exegete must observe which one best conforms to the context and the style of the author.

A search of the three topics of faith, hope, and love reveals several parallels (1 Thess 5:8; 1 Cor 13:13; Col 1:4-5). Because these three qualities of faith, hope, and love are central to Paul's theology at several points, they would be the expected emphasis of the passage. Because nouns receive more emphasis than adjectives in an English sentence, a translation with attributed genitives seems appropriate at first glance, since it highlights a working faith, a laboring love, and an enduring hope. However, the idiom "work of faith" in 1 Thess 1:3 appears alien to a mature Pauline theology and should catch the eye of the careful exegete, since later in his writings Paul always contrasts faith and works. Searching for a similar expression in Paul's correspondence with the Thessalonians, we discover a helpful parallel in 2 Thess 1:11. There two genitive phrases are placed next to each other so that the text reads literally, "to fulfill every purpose of good and work of faith" (πληρώσῃ πᾶσαν εὐδοκίαν ἀγαθωσύνης καὶ ἔργον πίστεως). Because the first genitive is certainly attributive ("good purpose"), similar Pauline style provides the best evidence for an attributive genitive in the second expression of ἔργον πίστεως ("faithful work") as well. The parallel in 2 Thess 1:11 rules against an attributive genitive in 1 Thess 1:3 as found in the ISV. Thus the translation of the NIV seems preferable since "work produced by faith" makes good sense and Paul's three primary character qualities of faith, hope, and love are given prominence as nouns in the translation. Through the use of the various possibilities of interpreting the genitive and through consulting analogous passages from the same author, we have discovered the preferred translation.

2. Subjective and Objective Genitives: Doctrines of Demons in 1 Timothy 4:1

The distinction between a subjective and objective genitive can be extremely important for exegesis. When the noun before a genitive can be reformulated into a verb, then the phrase can be either a subjective or objective genitive. Therefore the expression in Rom 16:25, "the proclamation of Jesus Christ," can either mean "Jesus' proclamation of the gospel" (subjective genitive) or "the proclamation about Jesus Christ" (objective genitive). How are we to understand the expression "the baptism of Jesus"? If interpreted as a subjective genitive, then Jesus is the subject performing the baptism, a phenomenon denied in John 4:2. However, if the expression "baptism of Jesus" is categorized as an objective genitive, then Jesus' own baptism in the Jordan is implied, which is the more likely scenario.

A third grammatical option suggests the presence of a plenary genitive that encompasses both subjective and objective meanings.[11] For instance, at 2 Cor 5:14, "the love of Christ controls us" (ἡ γὰρ ἀγάπη τοῦ Χριστοῦ συνέχει ἡμᾶς) could refer both to Christ's love for us and our love for Christ. Therefore Wallace translates this verse, "The love that comes from Christ producing our love for Christ . . . constrains us."[12] In resolving such exegetical debates, the context is always the deciding issue. Since the following verse (5:15) highlights both Christ dying for us and our "no longer living for ourselves but for him," a plenary genitive is possible in 2 Cor 5:14.

1 Timothy 4:1 predicts that the last times will be characterized by "doctrines of demons" (διδασκαλίαις δαιμονίων), which can be interpreted as either a subjective or objective genitive. Will there be an abundance of teaching about demons (objective genitive) in the end times, or will demonized or heretical doctrines abound (subjective genitive)? Although each of the above hypotheses are grammatical possibilities, the context favors a subjective genitive, since this phrase is coupled with "deceitful spirits" (πνεύμασιν πλάνοις) and specific heretical doctrines are mentioned in 1 Tim 4:3. Since the context of 1 Timothy 4 centers upon heretical movements in the last times and not demonology, a subjective genitive (demonized doctrines) is the better translation.

3. The Genitive Phrase πίστις Ιησοῦ: "Faith in Jesus" or "Faithfulness of Jesus"

Ever since the Reformation, texts such as Rom 3:22, 26; Gal 2:16; 3:22 have been employed to emphasize justification by faith. Martin Luther lived and was willing to die on the contention that believers are justified, not by keeping the law, but by faith in Jesus Christ. But now authors including Richard Hays and Tom Wright have argued that the genitive expression πίστις Ἰησοῦ

---

11. I assume the wisdom of Moises Silva, *Biblical Words and Their Meaning: An Introduction to Lexical Semantics* (Grand Rapids: Zondervan, 1983), p. 151: "We should assume one meaning unless there are strong exegetical (literary, contextual) grounds to the contrary."

12. Wallace, *Greek Grammar Beyond the Basics*, p. 59.

Χριστοῦ should be translated "the faithfulness of Jesus Christ" instead of "faith in Jesus Christ."[13]

To analyze this exegetical problem, attempt a search of this phrase in Logos Bible Software, and then decide if the expression πίστις Ἰησοῦ Χριστοῦ is an objective genitive ("faith in Jesus Christ") or a subjective genitive (Jesus Christ's faith or faithfulness).[14] Recently the ISV has, for the first time in a standard English translation, rendered this expression as a subjective genitive. Therefore, instead of the traditional understanding of Gal 2:16, "we know that a person is justified not by the works of the law but through faith in Jesus Christ" (NRSV), the ISV reads, "we know that a person is not justified by the works of the law but by the faithfulness of Jesus Christ." Likewise, Rom 3:22 is not translated "This righteousness from God comes through faith in Jesus Christ to all who believe" (NIV), but instead it comes "through the faithfulness of Jesus Christ to all who believe." Thus the works of the law are not contrasted with our faith in Christ but the finished work of Jesus.

Certainly we are justified by Christ's faithful work on the cross as well as by placing our faith in that finished work of Christ; both are true. But what is the emphasis in these Pauline passages? Grammatically, both genitive expressions are equally possible. In the end, you the reader must decide which is the more appropriate. Advocates of the new view of Paul contend that it is redundant in Rom 3:22 to state both that "This righteousness from God comes through faith in Jesus Christ" and then to repeat "to those who believe." However, I prefer to think of this duplication as a Pauline emphasis. Personally, I still favor the traditional interpretation, since I believe Paul employs the term "grace" not "faith" when referring to the finished work of Christ and "the faithfulness of God" (Rom 3:3, 21). He does not employ the phrase "the faithfulness of Christ" when speaking about divine action. Furthermore, the antithesis between "works of the law" and πίστις Χριστοῦ is most naturally understood as Paul's way of posing the alternatives on the human side. Therefore, the phrase διὰ τῆς πίστεως ("through faith") always means human faith in Paul (Rom 3:25, 30, 31; Eph 3:12, 17; Col 2:12). Which-

---

13. See Richard B. Hays, "Πίστις and Pauline Christology: What Is at Stake?" in *The Faith of Jesus Christ: The Narrative Substructure of Galatians 3:1–4:11*, 2nd ed. (Grand Rapids: Eerdmans and Dearborn: Dove, 2002), Appendix 2, pp. 272-97, who disagrees with James D. G. Dunn, "Once More, ΠΙΣΤΙΣ ΧΡΙΣΤΟΥ," in Appendix 1, pp. 249-71. See N. T. Wright, "The Letter to the Romans," *NIB* 10 (1994): 473-74.

14. In Logos Bible Software the resource *Lexham Syntactic Greek New Testament: Expansions and Annotations* by Albert Lukaszewski categorizes genitive phrases, but on these occasions he does not make a choice between objective or subjective genitive.

ever position is true, the difference in translations is determined by an analysis of this genitive phrase. Grammatical exegesis is fundamental.

4. 1 Timothy 3:1: πιστὸς ὁ λόγος, "Faithful Is the Saying"

Phrases can be searched in Logos Bible Software as well as individual words. When we search the phrase πιστὸς ὁ λόγος ("the faithful saying"), we discover that this expression is employed in the Pastoral Epistles on five occasions: 1 Tim 1:15; 3:1; 4:9; 2 Tim 2:11; and Titus 3:8.

Frequently this phrase in 1 Tim 3:1a is viewed as referring to 3:1b, "Whoever aspires to be an overseer desires a noble task." Although this chapter division dominates all English translations, the Nestle-Aland Greek text places this phrase at the end of the last paragraph so that the faithful saying refers to "But women will be saved through childbearing — if they continue in faith, love, and holiness with propriety." To easily view the structural divisions of various Bible versions in Logos Bible Software, click the "Tools" menu, followed by "Passage Analysis" and "Compare Pericopes." There you can decide which Bible versions you would like to compare, and the software will report the beginning and conclusion of each pericope. Regarding 1 Tim 3:1a, which is correct, the English versions or the Greek edition? Put another way, suppose you are preaching a series of sermons on the five faithful sayings in the Pastoral Epistles. Would you apply the faithful saying of 1 Tim 3:1 to the calling of ministers and elders as a noble task?

A search of key words in each faithful saying can enlighten this difficult problem. Turning to the first of these five faithful sayings, you determine that the word "save" is crucial: "Christ Jesus came into the world to save sinners" (1 Tim 1:15). So you attempt a search of σώζω ("save," 1 Tim 1:15; 2:15) as well as σωτήρ ("Savior," 1 Tim 4:10; Titus 3:6), and σωτηρία ("salvation," 2 Tim 2:10, referring to vv. 11b-13) and discover that one of these terms is employed near each reference to a faithful saying.

> 1 Tim 1:15b "Christ Jesus came into the world to <u>save</u> sinners — of whom I am the worst."
> Titus 3:5b-6 "He <u>saved</u> us through the washing of rebirth and renewal by the Holy Spirit, whom he poured out on us generously through Jesus Christ our <u>Savior</u>."
> 1 Tim 4:10 "We have put our hope in the living God, who is the <u>Savior</u> of all men, and especially of those who believe."

The trustworthy saying in 2 Tim 2:11b-13 is described as "salvation in Christ Jesus" by Paul in 2:10: "I endure everything for the sake of the elect, that they too may obtain the <u>salvation</u> that is in Christ Jesus, with eternal glory."

Each of these faithful sayings is therefore about salvation, meaning that the phrase πιστὸς ὁ λόγος in 1 Tim 3:1a more likely refers backward to 1 Tim 2:15.

Sometimes the reference to a faithful saying points backward (1 Tim 3:1; Titus 3:8), while on three occasions the faithful saying comes afterwards (1 Tim 1:15; 4:9; 2 Tim 2:11). Thus, even though you might wish that the faithful saying in 1 Tim 3:1a would refer forward to the call to ministry (3:1b), exegetical evidence supports another conclusion. Since each πιστὸς ὁ λόγος phrase speaks about salvation, the faithful saying in 1 Tim 3:1a is probably that "people will be saved if they continue in faith, love, and holiness," which Paul in turn applies to a context about women in the church by adding the words "women" and "through childbearing." Therefore, the NIV (as well as most versions) is mistaken in its delimitation of paragraphs as demonstrated by our study of a phrase in the Pastoral Epistles.

D. Clausal Analysis

PROCEDURE

A clause is a sentence or a part of a sentence that includes a verb, participle, or infinitive. Frequently one clause can be embedded within another. Logos Bible Software includes several resources that are helpful in identifying and searching clauses. The simplest is the *Lexham Clausal Outlines of the Greek New Testament,* where you will find each clause grammatically analyzed, with the main clause placed closest to the left margin and dependent clauses indented with tabs. The *Lexham Syntactic Greek New Testament* is more detailed, including the identification of phrases, the interconnecting words between clauses, and an explanation of the parts of speech. With the *Open Text Syntactically Analyzed Greek New Testament and Clause Analysis* you can search a variety of clausal constructions and observe arrows that display the interconnection of clauses as well as the number of clauses per chapter. For the Old Testament, you should employ the *Hebrew Bible Anderson-Forbes Analyzed Text,*[15] while

15. In Logos Bible Software the *Lexham Clausal Outlines of the Greek New Testament*

the prominent NT resource is *The Cascadia Syntax Graphs of the New Testament* developed by Andi Wu and Randall Tan for the Asia Bible Society.

In the following examples we will concentrate our attention upon determining the adverbial idea of participles, the identification of conditional sentences, and the differentiation between prohibitions and changes of tenses, since these are the most helpful skills to acquire in analyzing clauses. By adverbial idea we mean the various possibilities for translating adverbial participles, which include (1) temporal (before, while, after); (2) causal (since, because); (3) conditional (if); (4) concessive (although); (5) means (by means of); (6) manner (use the "-ing" ending); (7) purpose (in order that); (8) result (so that, then, as a result).

EXAMPLES

1. Colossians 2:11-12: Baptism Replaces Circumcision

Colossians 2:11 states that "in Him (Christ) you were also circumcised" ('Ev ᾧ καὶ περιετμήθητε). Then verse 12 adds an adverbial participle, "having been buried with him in baptism" (συνταφέντες αὐτῷ ἐν τῷ βαπτισμῷ). What is the relationship between circumcision, the OT sign of entrance into the covenant, and baptism, the NT seal of access to a relationship with God?

Various English versions interpret the relationship differently and therefore punctuate the sentences in distinct ways. The NLT attempts to simplify the translation by including shorter sentences, but in the process separates baptism both from spiritual circumcision and resurrection and seems to imply that there are three main verbs: "You were circumcised. . . . You were buried. . . . You were raised." The ISV, on the other hand, connects the temporal participle with the following main verb so that it reads, "When you were buried with him in baptism, you were also raised with him." But in attempting this tie between baptism and new life, the ISV breaks the parallelism between the two phrases ἐν ᾧ καὶ that begin each sentence: "In him also you were circumcised. . . . In him also you were raised." This sentence pattern

---

were produced by Dean Deppe; the *Lexham Syntactic Greek New Testament* by Albert L. Lukaszewski; the *Open Text.org Syntactically Analyzed Greek New Testament* by Matthew Brook O'Donnell, Stanley E. Porter, Jeffrey T. Reed, and Randall Tan; and the *Hebrew Bible Anderson-Forbes Analyzed Text* by Francis I. Anderson and A. Dean Forbes.

is supported by the Pauline parallel in Rom 6:3-9,[16] so that being crucified with Christ and raised to new life parallels being circumcised and raised with him in Col 2:11-12.

Therefore, the adverbial participle συνταφέντες ("buried") establishes some connection between circumcision and "buried in baptism." Traditionally, the "-ing" ending is employed for adverbial participles (NIV), but I would recommend that you choose an adverbial idea for participles. The *Lexham Clausal Outlines* categorize the various participles for the reader. This resource suggests that συνταφέντες is a temporal adverbial participle, meaning that the best translation reads, "you were circumcised when you were baptized." Certainly, this is not the only correct assessment. The adverbial idea could be categorized as "means" as well, with the resultant translation, "you were circumcised by means of being buried with him in baptism." Both translations demonstrate a connection between circumcision and baptism, so that baptism takes the place of circumcision. The interconnection of clauses offers a theological interpretation of the content of the text. Does the resulting translation argue for infant baptism? See study question 4 at the end of this chapter for further reflection on the importance of grammatical exegesis.

2. Colossians 2:13-15: The Meaning Is in the Structure

If you started with English Bible versions, it would be extremely difficult to uncover the structure of Col 2:13-15. As is evident in the diagram on page 60, the NLT contains seven sentences, the NIV three, and the NAB one. Which is correct?

If you consult a reverse interlinear with morphological identifications or color code the text in Logos Bible Software and search for verbs, you discover only four verbs in this passage, but the verb "to be" ("which was against us" in 2:14) is not a main verb but part of a relative clause beginning with "which" (ὅ). Therefore, the three primary actions are (1) Christ made you alive with him; (2) he took the written code out of the middle; and (3) he made a public spectacle of the principalities and powers. Now it is important to classify the remaining participles and decide to which main verb they are attached. Here we can receive assistance from the *Lexham Clausal Outlines* in Logos Bible Software. The participles appear to create a pattern, with a temporal participle before the main verb in each case and a participle of means

---

16. Rom 6:4 explains, "We were therefore buried with him through baptism into death."

New Living Bible	New International Bible	New American Bible
[13]You were dead	[13]When you were dead	[13]And even when you were dead

because of your sins and
  because your sinful
  nature was not yet
  cut away.
	in your sins
	  and in the uncircumcision
	  of your sinful nature,
	God made you alive
	  with Christ.
		(in) transgressions
		  and the uncircumcision
		  of your flesh,
		he brought you to life
		  along with him,
		  having forgiven us
		  all our transgressions;

Then God made you alive with Christ.		
He forgave all our sins.		
	He forgave us all our sins,	[14]obliterating the bond

[14]He canceled the record	[14]having canceled
	  the written code,
		against us,
		  with its legal claims,

that contained
  the charges against us.
	with its regulations,
	  that was against us
	  and
	  that stood opposed to us;
		which was opposed to us,

		he also removed it
		  from our midst,
		  nailing it to the cross;

He took it
and destroyed it
  by nailing it
    to Christ's cross.
	he took it away,
	
	  nailing it
	    to the cross.	

[15]In this way, God
disarmed
  the evil rulers
  and authorities.
	[15]And having disarmed
	  the powers and authorities,
	he made a public spectacle
	  of them,
	  triumphing over them
	  by the cross.
		[15]despoiling
		  the principalities
		  and the powers,
		he made a public spectacle
		  of them,
		  leading them away
		  in triumph by it.

He shamed them
  publicly by his victory
  over them on the
  cross of Christ.		

(like NCV, TEV)	(For many translations 13b-14a is one sentence)	(ASV, KJV also)

following the main verb. In 2:13 Paul points out that Christ made us alive when we were dead in sins by means of forgiving our trespasses. In 2:14 Christ took the law out of the middle when he canceled the written code by means of nailing it to the cross. In 2:15 Christ made a public example of the devil when he disarmed the powers by means of triumphing over them.

Through this structure we perceive that Christ overcame the three great enemies of sin, the law, and the devil. Each victory is portrayed with a unique image. First, we are described as traveling from death to life when our sins were forgiven. Forgiveness is so dramatic that Paul pictures it like the beginning of a new life.

In the second description, the imagery of "taking something out of the middle" seems cryptic at first until we consult the parallel passage in Eph 2:14. There we discover from a Greek lexicon that the middle wall (μεσότοιχον) "is used figuratively in reference to the partition in the Temple in Jerusalem, which set off the court of the Gentiles from the rest of the Temple area."[17] Christ united Jews and Gentiles by erasing the sign in the Court of the Gentiles that reported that death would ensue if any uncircumcised person advanced any closer to the temple.

Similarly with the third imagery, we must consult a Bible dictionary to discover that the conquering of principalities and powers entails "to make a public show or spectacle as the Romans did when they exposed their captives and the spoils of the conquered enemies to public view in their triumphal processions."[18] Paul imaginatively combines graveyard, temple, and political images to display Christ's finished victorious work over the enemies of sin, the law, and the devil. Electronic tools have simplified and shortened the task of understanding the structure of the text, while the interconnection between the participles and the main verbs has opened our eyes to fresh insights into God's word. Therefore, the New American Bible stands closest to the Greek structure since it divides the passage into three sentences, whereas the NIV ties the written code to the list of sins that stand against us, not the regulations of the Jewish law that separate Jews from fellowship with Gentiles.

---

17. J. P. Louw and E. A. Nida, *Greek-English Lexicon of the New Testament: Based on Semantic Domains,* electronic edition of the 2nd ed. (New York: United Bible Societies, 1989), 1:90.

18. Spiros Zodhiates, *The Complete Word Study Dictionary: New Testament,* electronic ed. (Chattanooga: AMG, 1993), G11165.

3. Philippians 2:6-8: Eliminating the "-ing" Endings from Participles

As an exercise to eliminate the "-ing" endings from participles, attempt a more nuanced translation of Phil 2:6-8 employing the various adverbial ideas such as temporal, causal, conditional, concessive, purpose, result, means, and manner. The ASV follows the traditional mode of using "-ing" endings:

> ⁶who, <u>existing</u> in the form of God, counted not the being on an equality with God a thing to be grasped, ⁷but emptied himself, <u>taking</u> the form of a servant, <u>being</u> made in the likeness of men; ⁸and <u>being</u> found in fashion as a man, he humbled himself, <u>becoming</u> obedient *even* unto death, yea, the death of the cross.

You can easily identify the participles in Phil 2:6-8 by employing the Libronix morphological filter to color code the various parts of speech. For instance, I employ a darkening of colors for Greek tenses: present indicative = yellow highlighter; imperfect = orange; future = red; aorist = green; perfect = blue; pluperfect = gray; and future perfect = brown. Likewise, for nouns I place a double square around the vocative, whereas the nominative = orange underline; the genitive = green underline; the dative = blue underline, and the accusative = brown underline. For the Greek moods I use a black underline for the subjunctive and a double black underline for the optative, whereas the imperatives are encircled with a red box, participles with a green box, and infinitives with a blue box. For our visual generation such a procedure proves vitally important.

After identifying the participles, now replace the "-ing" endings with a particular adverbial idea. What do you think of the following translation? What adverbial ideas have I employed for the various participles?

> <u>Although</u> he was in the form of God, he did not consider seizing equality with God but he emptied himself <u>by means of</u> taking the form of a slave <u>so that as a result</u> he could become the likeness of men. <u>After</u> he appeared as a man, he humbled himself <u>by means of</u> obedience unto death, yes death upon a cross.

Notice how the removal of the "-ing" endings clarifies the connection between clauses and infuses the translation with life. The choice of the adverbial idea is, of course, a conjecture on my part, but each translation fits well into the context, which in the end is the determining factor.

The president of our seminary in a recent chapel talk argued that this *kenosis* passage should begin, "because Christ was in the form of God," not "although he was in the form of God." He argued that it is the very nature of God to empty himself in self-giving service. Because God's character is completely composed of altruistic love, God could arrive at no other possibility than the incarnation as a human person. This alternative adverbial idea for the participle creates a new window into the personhood of the deity.

This procedure of "trying out the various options" can offer new insights into texts that we have read hundreds of times. The plethora of English translations, as well, argues for more specificity and differentiation when translating adverbial participles. Whether you conclude that a causal or concessive idea best fits Christ's emptying of himself, determining the adverbial idea of the participles offers new possibilities of translation that can produce fruitful insights.

*4. Adverbial Participles Made into Main Verbs:
Colossians 2:7 TEV and NLT*

Participles can be employed as main verbs if they are designated as independent rather than adverbial participles and are not connected with any other verb in the context.[19] But some English versions transform participles into main verbs in order to establish short sentences for easy comprehension and in the process conceal the main point of the sentence. For instance, in Col 2:6-7 the TEV creates five consecutive commands, with the last four all involving adverbial participles:

1. [6]Since you have accepted Christ Jesus as Lord, live in union with him.
2. [7]Keep your roots deep in him,
3. build your lives on him,
4. and become stronger in your faith, as you were taught.
5. And be filled with thanksgiving.

Therefore, it appears to the reader that these are all unconnected imperatives, whereas in reality the four imperatives are somehow related to the verb "live in union with him" (literally, "walk").

19. Independent participles substituting for main verbs can be found, for instance, as indicative verbs in Rom 5:11; 12:6; 2 Thess 3:8; 2 Cor 10:15; Luke 6:13, etc. and more frequently as imperatives with seventeen instances in Rom 12:9-19, five examples in Phil 2:2-4, and several examples in the hortatory sections of 1 Peter (1:13-14; 2:12, 18; 3:1, 7-9; 4:8-9).

The NLT, on the other hand, generates a series of three imperatives: (1) "continue to follow him"; (2) "let your roots grow down into him"; and (3) "let your lives be built on him," followed by two result clauses: (1) "then your faith will grow strong"; and (2) "you will overflow with thankfulness."

> [6]And now, just as you accepted Christ Jesus as your Lord, you must continue to follow him. [7]Let your roots grow down into him, and let your lives be built on him. Then your faith will grow strong in the truth you were taught, and you will overflow with thankfulness.

Every translation is an interpretation, and the NLT implies that the completion of rootedness in Christ and the establishment of a solid foundation will result in strong faith and increased thankfulness.

However, in the Greek, Col 2:6 contains the only imperative, while 2:7 follows with four adverbial participles, thus implying that all four participles describe the action of the one main verb. The primary theme is continuing to walk or live in Christ. How is this accomplished? The four participles (with the first two connected with "and") are best translated by the adverbial idea of means, since they appear in parallel sequence and supply the means by which believers continue to live in Christ. Therefore, a clausal outline would look something like the following:

comparative clause	[6]Ὡς οὖν παρελάβετε τὸν Χριστὸν Ἰησοῦν τὸν κύριον, So then, just as you received Christ Jesus as Lord,	
imperative	ἐν αὐτῷ περιπατεῖτε, in him continue to live,	
1st adv ptcs <u>means</u>	[7]ἐρριζωμένοι καὶ ἐποικοδομούμενοι [7]rooted and built up	ἐν αὐτῷ in him,
2nd adv ptc <u>means</u>	καὶ βεβαιούμενοι strengthened	τῇ πίστει in the faith
comparative clause	καθὼς ἐδιδάχθητε, as you were taught,	
3rd adv ptc <u>means</u>	περισσεύοντες and overflowing	ἐν εὐχαριστίᾳ. with thankfulness.

Paul is only giving one command: walk (or live) in Christ. This is contrasted with the negative command in 2:8: "Watch out that no one takes you captive." In between, Paul describes three ways to walk in Christ: (1) by means of being rooted and built up in him; (2) by means of being strengthened in the faith; and (3) by means of thanksgiving.[20] If the first image is one of tree roots deeply settled into the soil to produce a sturdy foundation, then the second picture consists of a tree trunk that is solid and firm,[21] while the third description of "increasing in thanksgiving" may connote the branches and leaves increasing in stature and producing a mature tree. This entire process of growth is the means by which "living in Christ" is described. The participles enhance, expand, and broaden the meaning of the main verb.

This example demonstrates the importance of categorizing adverbial participles and determining if they are (1) temporal; (2) causal; (3) conditional; (4) concessive; (5) manner; (6) means; (7) purpose; or (8) result. To discern the emphasis of the author, the main verbs must be identified and distinguished from the participles that are connected with the main verb in order to accentuate its theme.

5. Discerning the Main Verb in Mark 5:25-27

If you only consult the English text, you would surely imagine that Mark 5:25-27 consists of several sentences rehearsing the story of a hemorrhaging woman.

> [25]And a woman was there who had been subject to bleeding for twelve years. [26]She had suffered a great deal under the care of many doctors and had spent all she had, yet instead of getting better she grew worse. [27]When she heard about Jesus, she came up behind him in the crowd and touched his cloak.

But in reality, the Greek text contains only one main verb.

To discover the central thought of the passage, the non-Greek reader can consult a Greek interlinear or reverse interlinear from Logos and even color code the various parts of speech so that the main verb stands out

---

20. The ISV contains the one command in 2:6 but then appears to make the first two participles causal and the third temporal ("For you have been rooted in him and are being built up and strengthened in the faith, just as you were taught, while you overflow with thanksgiving"). However, this is not the best translation, since the phrases "in him," "in the faith," and "with thanksgiving" appear to be parallel.

21. The Greek word βεβαιόω means "firm in commitment, established, strengthened" according to BDAG, p. 172.

prominently. Or if you have studied Greek, you can consult my *Lexham Clausal Outlines*. There you will discover that seven participles precede the main verb, which as the climax of the passage mentions that the woman touches (ἥψατο) Jesus. This touching is significant, since the story of the bleeding woman (Mark 5:25-34) is combined into a Markan sandwich with the narrative of the dead girl (5:21-24, 35-43) to whom Jesus also reaches out and touches in the healing process. According to OT ceremonial legislation, whenever someone touches a bleeding woman or a corpse, they become unclean (Lev 15:19-33; 22:4; Num 19:11-22). However, instead of Jesus becoming unclean, the victims are healed. Jesus' kingdom actions are fulfilling and thus replace the OT ceremonial laws, so that now Jesus the Messiah cleanses people. Discerning the main verb in the passage contributes to discovering the central theme of the narrative.

6. The Adverbial Idea in Hebrews 6:6 and the Perseverance of the Saints

Hebrews 6:4-6 offers another interesting example where adverbial participles can be translated with a variety of adverbial ideas or uses. The NIV and ISV translations of Heb 6:6 differ, with the NIV employing a causal connotation to the participles ("because") while the ISV translates using a temporal connection ("as long as" or "when").

> NIV: [4]It is impossible for those who have once been enlightened . . . [6]to be brought back to repentance, <u>because</u> to their loss they are crucif<u>ying</u> the Son of God all over again and subject<u>ing</u> him to public disgrace.

> ISV: [4]For it is impossible to keep on restoring to repentance time and again people who have once been enlightened . . . <u>as long as</u> they continue to crucify to themselves the Son of God and to expose him to public ridicule.

What difference does this decision make? Calvinists and Arminians have been debating for centuries the doctrine of "once saved, always saved." A conclusion about the adverbial idea in Heb 6:6 could determine your theological view on the perseverance of the saints. Will those who have fallen away never be able to be restored <u>because</u> they continue to crucify the Son of God by their unbelief and lifestyle, or will they not be restored <u>as long as</u> they continue their behavior. This last translation assumes that God could change their hearts and preserve their faith in the end, whereas the translation "because" merely indicates why they cannot be restored to grace. So a decision on the adverbial idea could affect the treasured beliefs that we embrace, demonstrating again the importance of grammatical constructions in the interpretation of the Bible.

7. *Conditional Sentences: Acts 5:38-39 and Matthew 4:3, 9*

Greek conditional clauses are ripe with exegetical fruit. So a review of the various types of conditional sentences is crucial in order to glean exegetical insights from biblical examples. A good place to start is the creation of a collection of several Greek grammars in Logos Bible Software. First, choose under "Tools" the category "Collections" and then type in "Greek grammar." From the resulting list select such resources as the *Greek New Testament Insert* by Chapman and Shogren, *Elements of New Testament Greek* by Nunn, *Syntax of the Moods and Tenses in New Testament Greek* by Burton, and BDF, Wallace's *Greek Grammar Beyond the Basics,* or A. T. Robertson's *A Grammar of the Greek New Testament in the Light of Historical Research,* which are supplemental resources in Libronix.[22] Then perform a basic search of first or second class conditions to review the grammatical distinctions between the various conditional sentences. You will discover that first class logical conditions assume that the speaker intends the protasis (the "if" clause) as true while a second class contrary-to-fact condition assumes that the author considers the statement false.

With this background you can turn to sentences in the Greek where an alteration of a class of conditional sentences occurs in the immediate context. For instance, in English translations like the NIV, the protases in Acts 5:38-39 are translated the same: "For if their purpose or activity is of human origin, it will fail. But if it is from God, you will not be able to stop these men." However, in the Greek Acts 5:38 is a third class condition with ἐάν and the subjunctive, while Acts 5:39 is a first class condition employing the indicative mood with εἰ and frequently translated by "since." Acts 5:38 functions

---

22. Benjamin Chapman and Gary S. Shogren, *Greek New Testament Insert* (Quakertown, PA: Stylus Publishing, 1994); H. P. V. Nunn, *The Elements of New Testament Greek* (Cambridge: Cambridge University Press, 1923); Ernest DeWitt Burton, *Syntax of the Moods and Tenses in New Testament Greek,* 3rd ed. (Edinburgh: T. & T. Clark, 1898); A. T. Robertson, *A Grammar of the Greek New Testament in the Light of Historical Research,* 2nd ed. (New York: Hodder & Stoughton, 1915).

as an anticipatory condition with the subjunctive, implying something hypothetical. But in Gamaliel's speech given by Luke in Acts 5:39, the switch to a first class condition can best be translated, "but since it (the apostles' activity) is from God, you will not be able to stop these men." It is assumed by Luke that the apostles are speaking from God himself. Grammatical distinctions clarify the meaning of the text.

Likewise, a switch of conditions occurs in the temptations of Jesus by the devil. Matthew 4:3 states, "If you are the Son of God, tell these stones to become bread," while 4:9 reads, "All this I will give you, if you will bow down and worship me." However, in the Greek 4:3 is a first class condition, while 4:9 is an anticipatory third class conditional sentence. Therefore, 4:3 could be translated, "since you are the Son of God," with the devil assuming that this statement is true. However, "if you will bow down and worship me" is not assumed to be true but is a hypothetical statement that must be answered through some future action. Of course, we know from the story that Jesus does not surrender to the devil's wishes. But these examples demonstrate that the Greek text should be consulted when studying conditional sentences. There are 339 examples of logical first class conditions and 51 examples of contrary-to-fact conditional sentences that you can explore in the New Testament.

8. 1 Peter 3:14 and 1 Peter 4:14: Comparing Conditional Sentences

A conditional sentence with the optative mood is rare in the New Testament. You could perform a morphological search in Logos Bible Software to detect all the optatives in the New Testament or narrow the focus down to optatives with a conditional using the Greek word εἰ ("if"). This can be accomplished by performing a morphological search in the NIV (or any Bible with a reverse interlinear in Libronix) and placing a @ sign in the box and then choosing "Verb" and "Optative" under "Mood."

Let's say you are studying 1 Peter to discover more about the theme of persecution. You pause and stop reading at 1 Pet 3:14, "But even if you should suffer for what is right, you are blessed." When you consult the Nestle-Aland text in Libronix, you discover that the optative mood is employed (εἰ πάσχοιτε). Peter is speaking about persecution that *might happen* someday in the future. So you perform a Bible search of "if and blessed" in a literal version such as the NASB and discover that a similar expression is used in 1 Pet 4:14: "If you are insulted because of the name of Christ, you are blessed." But this time, instead of an optative protasis the indicative is employed.

1 Pet 3:14 ἀλλ᾽ εἰ καὶ <u>πάσχοιτε</u> διὰ δικαιοσύνην, μακάριοι
1 Pet 4:14 εἰ <u>ὀνειδίζεσθε</u> ἐν ὀνόματι Χριστοῦ, μακάριοι

Peter alters the grammatical construction from a fourth class condition to a first class condition, from the hypothetical optative to the true-to-reality indicative. Something appears to have changed in the circumstances of Peter and/or his readers to account for this significant alteration of grammar. A logical conclusion asserts that persecution has begun and Peter now wants to address this new situation by employing a new type of conditional sentence. To support this hypothesis, many scholars point to the theme of eschatology in 4:7 ("The end of all things is near"), which frequently concludes a letter. In addition, notice the doxology at 1 Pet 4:11b after a series of paraenetic imperatives as well as the new address in 4:12, "dear friends."[23] After concluding his initial letter, Peter appears to have heard from his readers about a wave of persecution heading their direction and picked up his pen again to instruct them about "the painful trial that they were suffering" (1 Pet 4:12). Now he employs the indicative mood to bless his readers (4:13). The change in conditional sentences offers valuable exegetical information about the conditions that motivated Peter's writing of this epistle.

9. Prohibitions: John 20:17 and Ephesians 5:18

Just as there are various grammatical techniques to create conditional sentences in Greek, so the careful reader must distinguish two types of prohibitions. One category of negative commands utilizes the aorist subjunctive with μή, while the more exegetically significant usage employs the imperative in the present tense. Here continuity is presumed so that present tense prohibitions are frequently translated "stop doing what you are doing" (depending upon the context, of course).

An interesting example is found in John 20:17, which the ASV translates, "Touch me not; for I am not yet ascended unto the Father." Most readers are mystified by this statement and ask, "Why would Jesus not permit Mary to touch him? Could human contact affect his divine condition or divine contact transform Mary's countenance?" Notice that the grammatical data in

---

23. E.g., eschatology is a concluding theme in 1 Thessalonians 4–5, 1 Corinthians 15, 2 Peter 3, and Didache 16; doxologies conclude many letters; and final paraenesis occurs in Hebrews 13 and 1 Tim 6:17-20.

Logos Bible Software report that Jesus' statement is a prohibition coupled to a present imperative (μή μου ἅπτου). Therefore, the NASB more accurately translates this expression, "Stop clinging to Me." The present tense implies continuing action, "stop continuing to hold me." The disciples should not attempt to hold on to Jesus and keep him physically present since the eternal and omnipresent presence of Jesus through the Spirit depended upon his ascension. It is for our benefit that Christ left this earth. Mary had to stop wishing that Jesus would continue his earthly presence with them. Thus, a correct appraisal of the grammatical data offers a needed exegetical insight and a corresponding appropriate translation.

Likewise, the prohibition in Eph 5:18 employs the present tense rather than the aorist subjunctive: μὴ μεθύσκεσθε οἴνῳ, ἀλλὰ πληροῦσθε ἐν πνεύματι. Therefore, the exegete can translate this sentence, "Stop being drunk with wine and continually (present tense) be filled with the Spirit."[24] The Greek grammar proves that a one-time filling with the Holy Spirit is not enough.

10. The Third Person Imperative Following a Second Person Imperative

One grammatical device to apply a command emphatically to each individual is to follow a second person plural command with a third person singular imperative. Carroll Osburn explains, "In this emphatic imperatival usage, the speaker attaches such tremendous importance to the command that he makes it clear with the third person imperative that not a single member of the group is exempt."[25] In the Hebrew OT, 2 Kgs 10:19 is a good example, since the general command of Jehu to the prophets of Baal to enter his presence is followed up with an individual emphasis, "See that no one is missing." Likewise, Zech 7:10 first employs a second person plural imperative: "Do not oppress the widow or the fatherless, the alien or the poor." But the next sentence alters the command to the third person singular: "In your

---

24. With regard to the translation "stop," the interpreter should be warned that only the context determines if the present prohibition means "stop," since as James L. Boyer, "A Classification of Imperatives: A Statistical Study," *Grace Theological Journal* 8 (1987): 43 claims, a previous action is denied in the context on 32 occasions of a total of 174 occurrences in the New Testament.

25. Carroll D. Osburn, "Interpreting Greek Syntax," *Biblical Interpretation: Principles and Practice,* ed. F. Furman Kearley, Edward P. Myers, and Timothy D. Hadley (Grand Rapids: Baker, 1986), p. 242.

hearts do not think evil of each other."[26] This personalization of the text can be particularly effective to drive home the application.

In the NT,[27] Jesus begins the Parable of the Sower with a general exhortation, "Listen" (Ἀκούετε, Mark 4:3), but concludes with an individual application employing a third person singular imperative, "He who has ears to hear, let him hear" (ἀκουέτω, 4:9). Through this formula Jesus highlights the individual response that is necessary. Similarly, at Pentecost in Acts 2:38 Peter issues a general call to repentance (μετανοήσατε), which is immediately followed by an emphatic personal exhortation, "and be baptized, every one of you, in the name of Jesus Christ for the forgiveness of your sins." The alteration of the type of imperative makes sure that the response of each individual person is given due attention.

E. Examining Word Order

PROCEDURE

The emphasis in a sentence can frequently be determined through unusual word order. However, this is not visible in English translations, since the Greek word order diverges in a manner that does not sound appealing to the English trained ear. Therefore, the Greek text or a Greek-English interlinear should be consulted. Although the interlinear can sound very wooden, the emphasis can frequently be diagnosed.

EXAMPLES

1. 2 Corinthians 2:4; 1 Peter 4:10; and John 10:9:
Words Placed Outside a Clause

Sometimes a word is placed outside a clause for emphasis. We will offer an example from a ἵνα (purpose, result) clause, a comparative clause, and a conditional clause. After reading the NIV of 2 Cor 2:4 ("I wrote you . . . with

---

26. Osburn, "Interpreting Greek Syntax," p. 242, lists Exod 16:29; Josh 6:10; and 1 Macc 10:63 in addition to these OT examples.

27. Raymond Elliott, "Functions of the Third Person Imperative Verb Forms in the Greek New Testament," *Notes on Translation* 69 (1978): 30-31, offers a list to which Osburn, "Interpreting Greek Syntext," p. 242, n. 34, adds Matt 5:31; 8:13; 1 Cor 7:17; 1 Tim 4:12; and 2 Pet 3:8.

many tears, not to grieve you but to let you know the depth of my love for you"), it is very difficult to determine whether Paul is emphasizing one particular concept. But if you create a Layout in Logos Bible Software (called a Workspace in Libronix 3) with the Greek and English translations vertically tiled, then you notice that the word "love" is placed before the ἵνα clause in which it belongs (ἀλλὰ τὴν ἀγάπην ἵνα γνῶτε). Paul's love for the Corinthians is accentuated in the Greek text, not his tears.

For the sake of emphasis, Greek words are regularly placed outside other dependent clauses such as comparative clauses as well. The ISV translates 1 Pet 4:10, "As good managers of God's grace in its various forms, serve one another with the gift each of you has received." Here in English the term "each" is buried in the middle of the sentence, whereas in the Greek it is strategically placed first and outside the καθώς clause in which it belongs (ἕκαστος καθὼς ἔλαβεν χάρισμα). The NIV at least places the word "each" first in the sentence in an effort to afford it the needed emphasis: "Each one should use whatever gift he has received to serve others." This call to individual responsibility in the use of one's gifts is highlighted when the word order is given its due attention.

With regard to conditional clauses, one might be tempted to highlight "whoever" when reading John 10:9 ("I am the gate; whoever enters through me will be saved"). But the accent is not upon the human person but upon Christ since the phrase "through me" is placed outside the "if" clause (δι' ἐμοῦ ἐάν τις εἰσέλθῃ σωθήσεται). The text literally says, "through me, if anyone comes, he will be saved." The divine action of Jesus is accentuated, as is appropriate in God's word. Attention to word order supplies the reader with exegetical nuggets that are unattainable if the Greek text is not investigated in some form.

2. *Matthew 12:27: The Positioning of Interrogatives*

In Greek as well as English, question words normally occur at the beginning of a sentence. Therefore, when words are positioned before the interrogative pronoun, the author is calling attention to this prioritized concept.

By reading the NIV of Matt 12:27 it is extremely difficult to detect the accent of the sentence: "And if I drive out demons by Beelzebub, by whom do your people drive them out?" But in the Greek, the phrase "your children" or "your people" is positioned outside the question: οἱ υἱοὶ ὑμῶν ἐν τίνι ἐκβάλλουσιν. So the emphasis is upon "your sons" or "your followers." This totally changes the impact of the saying. Instead of the Pharisees causing a division between Jesus and the crowds over the role of the devil in Jesus' exorcisms, Jesus' answer polarizes the Pharisees from their own followers.

3. Matthew 1:20; Hebrews 10:12; and Hebrews 13:8: Isolated Elements

Sometimes a verb, participle, infinitive, or pronoun intervenes in a noun phrase separating two parts of the sentence that normally belong together. As a result, the emphasis usually lies with the isolated element. For instance, in Matt 1:20 the noun phrase "Holy Spirit" is separated by the verb "to be" (ἐκ πνεύματός ἐστιν ἁγίου). Therefore, the emphasis is upon the fact that the child born to Mary out of wedlock is holy. This accent in the Greek structure could be captured by an English translation that belabors the fact that the Spirit is the Holy Spirit; an appropriate translation might read, "the child in Mary's womb is holy, out of the Holy Spirit," or "the child in Mary's womb is from the Spirit who is holy." This particular emphasis is supported as well by the context, where women are included in Jesus' genealogy (Matt 1:3, 5, 6) who did not at first sight seem holy, characters like Tamar, Rahab, and Bathsheba.

To make sense of Heb 10:12, the words "one sacrifice" must be held together when translated into English, "But when this priest had offered for all time <u>one sacrifice</u> for sins." However, in the Greek these two words are separated by a prepositional phrase and a participle (οὗτος δὲ <u>μίαν</u> ὑπὲρ ἁμαρτιῶν προσενέγκας <u>θυσίαν</u>). This "moving up" of the word μίαν ("one") in the sentence places the emphasis upon the single sacrifice of Christ. The context should reinforce this emphasis, which indeed it does with the contrast between "day after day" and "again and again" (Heb 10:11) versus the "one sacrifice" that generates perfection (10:14).

Reading an English translation of Heb 13:8, it is difficult to ascertain whether any element in the sentence is accented: "Jesus Christ is the same yesterday and today and forever." Students unfamiliar with Greek can consult an interlinear Bible from Libronix to detect a significant deviation in word order. In between the phrase "yesterday, today, and forever" the author places the pronoun "the same" (Ἰησοῦς Χριστὸς ἐχθὲς καὶ σήμερον <u>ὁ αὐτὸς</u> καὶ εἰς τοὺς αἰῶνας). The consistent character of Jesus Christ is the emphasis. In our rapidly changing culture, where trends, fads, and fashions shift with incredible speed, Jesus Christ remains the same as the anchor of our lives. The Greek word order reveals the emphasis in the sentence.

4. Romans 11:13-14 and Matthew 14:33:
Genitive Modifiers before the Noun

In Greek, the genitival modifier normally follows the noun. According to
Stanley Porter, this is true 96 percent of the time for Paul and 99 percent for
Luke.[28] Alterations of established word order again underscore the emphasis
of the author. In Romans 9–11, where Paul discusses the relationship of God
to the Jewish people, he refers to himself as the apostle of the Gentiles
(ἐθνῶν ἀπόστολος, 11:13). The emphasis in the Greek is not on "apostle" but
upon "the Gentiles," which adds significantly to Paul's theme in these chapters. Again the context witnesses to this emphasis when it states Paul's purpose: to "arouse my own people to envy and save some of them" (11:14). Context and word order cooperate together to reveal to the reader what the
author is highlighting.

In Matt 14:33, at the conclusion of Jesus' miraculous walking upon the
sea, the disciples proclaim the significant christological confession, "Truly
you are the Son of God." The Greek, however, reads literally, "truly, of God,
the Son, you are" (ἀληθῶς θεοῦ υἱὸς εἶ). Thus the change of word order in
the Greek, with "God" placed before "Son," even more dramatically calls attention to Jesus' close relationship with the Father, since the genitival modifier is placed before the noun.

5. John 1:18 and Revelation 21:22: First Position in the Sentence

The first position in the sentence is normally reserved for the most important element.[29] The NIV of John 1:18 rearranges two Greek sentences into
one English statement, "No one has ever seen God, but God the One and
Only, who is at the Father's side, has made him known." Through the use of
commas, this translation captures the emphasis upon "God the One and
Only," which in the Greek is placed at the beginning as subject of the second
sentence. However, the English is unable to highlight "God" in the first sentence, which is likewise the initial grammatical element (Θεὸν οὐδεὶς
ἑώρακεν πώποτε· μονογενὴς θεὸς ὁ ὢν εἰς τὸν κόλπον τοῦ πατρὸς ἐκεῖνος
ἐξηγήσατο). The emphasis throughout is upon Jesus as God. This peculiar

---

28. Stanley E. Porter, *Idioms of the Greek New Testament*, 2nd ed. (Sheffield: Sheffield
Academic, 1995), pp. 290-92.
29. See BDF, §472.2.

word order is reinforced by a literary analysis of John 1:1-18, where an *inclusio* connects John 1:1 and 1:18 with a stress upon the divinity of Christ in each verse.[30]

A second example occurs in Rev 21:22. Throughout the book John initiates a sentence with the familiar apocalyptic phraseology, "I saw." However, at the very end in 21:22, the noun "temple" is spotlighted in first position, although English translations again position the verb first. The NIV reads, "I did not see a temple in the city, because the Lord God Almighty and the Lamb are its temple." But a literal translation asserts, "a temple I did not see in it" (καὶ ναὸν οὐκ εἶδον ἐν αὐτῇ). The absence of a temple in the new earth is the focus, not the perception of the seer. Effective exegesis can only occur if the Greek word order is consulted.

F. English Translations

PROCEDURE

For a full-orbed understanding of the Bible the serious student should consult several English versions based upon different translation policies (word for word, dynamic equivalence, and free translations). The best tool for such an analysis is the "Parallel Bible Versions" resource in Libronix 3 found under "Bible Comparison" in the "Tools" menu, which is entitled "Text Comparison" in Logos 4. In addition, for a line-by-line comparison of the four Gospels you can consult the section numbers from Kurt Aland's *Synopsis of the Four Gospels*.[31] After studying several versions, it is frequently helpful to form your own translation of particularly important sections of the text in order to internalize its meaning.

A beneficial literal English version is the NASB, which attempts to translate Greek words with the identical English equivalents. The NIV and NLT, on the other hand, favor dynamic equivalence, whereas the TEV is a more free translation but still not a paraphrase like *The Message* by Eugene Peterson or Kenneth Taylor's *The Living Bible*, which adopt contemporary metaphors. Since each type of Bible version is valuable for certain occasions, I suggest creating a Layout in Logos Bible Software where all three types are

---

30. See Chapter 1, C4 above, "The Purpose of the Gospel of John Displayed through *Inclusios*" (pp. 29-31).

31. I suggest the Greek-English edition (Stuttgart: German Bible Society, 1972).

placed side by side on the screen for easy observation. For instance, with re-gard to Jesus' first beatitude in Matt 5:3, the NASB offers a word-for-word translation, 'Blessed are the poor in spirit." The NLT employs a dynamic equivalent, replacing "in spirit" with "realize their need for him." *The Message* transforms the imagery into a contemporary expression, "You're blessed when you're at the end of your rope." Each of these renderings can be helpful for the exegete and communicator in different situations.

EXAMPLES

1. Romans 8:28: Two Different Possible Translations[32]

Sometimes Bible verses memorized as a child take on a fresh understanding when read in contemporary versions. The traditional wording of Rom 8:28 according to the KJV states that "we know that all things work together for good to them that love God, to them who are the called according to *his* pur-pose." However, this reading is being challenged by an innovative option that interprets "God" as the subject and "all things" as the direct object.[33] The ISV reads, "We know that he works all things together for the good of those who love God who are called according to his purpose." English versions are almost evenly split on which translation is correct:

> We know that all things work together for good to those who love God. (KJV, ASV, NRSV, ESV, NKJV, NAB)

> We know that he works all things together for good to those who love God. (NASB, RSV, NIV, TNIV, TEV, ISV, NJB, NLT)

32. Really three translations are possible. The Spirit from the previous verses could be the subject as the NEB translates, "and in everything, as we know, he (meaning the Holy Spirit from verses 26-27) cooperates for good with those who love God." However, the change of subjects from Spirit to God has occurred earlier in 8:27: "And he who searches our hearts (i.e., God) knows the mind of the Spirit." See Carroll D. Osburn, "The Interpretation of Romans 8:28," *WTJ* 44 (1982): 108. For further discussion, compare the arguments in favor of this interpretation in Matthew Black, "The Interpretation of Romans viii 28," *Neotestamentica et Patristica: Eine Freundesgabe, Herrn Professor Dr. Oscar Cullmann*, ed. W. C. van Unnik. NovTSup 6 (Leiden: Brill, 1962), pp. 166-72, with the arguments against this reading by C. E. B. Cranfield, "Romans 8.28," *SJT* 19 (1966): 204-15.

33. More correctly it is labeled an adverbial accusative describing how God does this working together, since the verb συνεργεῖ is an intransitive verb.

Both possibilities are supported by the Greek text, depending upon whether πάντα ("all things") is the subject or the direct object with the ending of συνεργεῖ as the subject. Although the traditional reading is the most memorized and well known, the new translation is favored by the fact that the direct object precedes the verb in Rom 8:29-30 as well. The four occurrences of οὓς ("those") in the immediate context are certainly the direct objects to the verbs "foreknew," "predestined," "called," and "justified." In addition, the traditional rendering can produce a faulty theology that naively projects that all things turn out good for the Christian. Frequently the life of a Christian is filled with more intense struggles, conflicts, and demands of giving. Therefore, we should probably begin to memorize this text by asserting, "God is working in all things for good."[34] But whatever version you favor, this example demonstrates that multiple translations should be consulted to assure a full understanding of the text.

2. Ezra 4:14 and Acts 1:4: Literal Translations

Various English equivalents of the original Hebrew or Greek wording dictate divergent translations. Consider, for instance, the reading of Ezra 4:14 in two very popular English versions, the NIV and NRSV. The NIV reads, "Now since we are under obligation to the palace and it is not proper for us to see the king dishonored, we are sending this message to inform the king." Therefore, you might be surprised when you turn to the NRSV and find "Now because we share the salt of the palace and it is not fitting for us to witness the king's dishonor, therefore we send and inform the king." What does "being under obligation to the palace" have to do with "eating salt with each other"? When you examine the *Biblia Hebraica Stuttgartensia* (or a Hebrew interlinear), you discover that the NRSV follows a word-for-word translation (דִּי־מְלַח הֵיכְלָא מְלַחְנָא) in the tradition of the ASV, RSV, and ESV (the NAB and NJB also read "salt" here). On the other hand, the NIV chooses a dynamic equivalent, since "eating salt" no longer has a cultural meaning in Western society.

An understanding of the cultural milieu contributes an additional dimension to this text. If we investigate the ancient Near Eastern background to eating salt, we discover a cultural ceremony involving the ratifying of agreements. When the participants ate salt in the palace (NRSV), they were

---

34. Textually, this reading is supported by the important manuscripts of 𝔓[45], A, and B.

confirming their loyalty to the king so that they were under an obligation of service (NIV). Such a ceremony was entitled a salt covenant. Eating bread with salt ratified an agreement for troth, fidelity, fellowship, and faithfulness between parties.[35] After agreeing to such a covenant, the smallest injury inflicted on someone's possessions or person was considered a crime, so that the guilty party was despised as a wretch deserving reproof and detestation from everyone. In fact, the Arabic terms for "salt" and "treaty" are identical, and the Persian word for a "traitor" is *namak haram,* "untrue to salt" or "faithless to salt."[36] Once an Arab has received in his tent even his worst enemy and has eaten salt with him, he is bound to protect his guest as long as he remains. The famous story of Ali Baba and the Forty Thieves contains an intriguing example where the captain of the robber band who had visited Ali Baba in order to murder him was unwilling to partake of any food that contained salt. However, the faithful slave girl, Morgiana, became suspicious of this carefulness and decided to check out the identity of this person who would not eat salt, only to discover that it was her master's mortal enemy.[37]

This social covenant also took on cultic significance in the religious life of the Near East and is described in the Bible as the salt covenant (Lev 2:13; Num 18:19; 2 Chr 13:5; cf. *Jubilees* 6:3-4; 21:11; Acts 1:4). Israel placed salt upon their sacrifices to confirm their covenant with God, whereby he would protect them and they would offer their unconditional allegiance. The reference in Acts 1:4 is particularly interesting, since it apparently involves a salt covenant between the apostles and Jesus before he ascended into heaven. The NIV reads, "On one occasion, while he was eating with them, he gave them this command." What was Jesus eating with his disciples? The Greek employs the term συναλιζόμενος from ἁλίζω, meaning "to salt." The authoritative BDAG lexicon lists as one of the possible translations "to eat salt with" and refers to a salt covenant in the explanation.[38] Jesus was apparently cut-

---

35. See Harry Fleddermann, "The Discipleship Discourse (Mark 9:33-50)," *CBQ* 43 (1981): 73.

36. See Dean B. Deppe, "The Imagery of Salt in the Sayings of Jesus: An Exegetical Study of Mark 9:49-50; Luke 14:34-35 and Matthew 5:13?" (Th.M. diss., Calvin Theological Seminary, 1978), p. 8.

37. For other examples, cf. Henry Clay Trumbull, *The Covenant of Salt as Based on the Significance and Symbolism of Salt in Primitive Thought* (New York: Scribner's, 1899), pp. 25-32.

38. See also Charles Cutler Torrey, *The Composition and Date of Acts* (Cambridge: Harvard University Press, 1916), p. 23.

ting a salt covenant with his disciples. Jesus promised to send the powerful Holy Spirit (1:4b), and his followers covenanted to bring the gospel to the whole world (1:8). Therefore, an examination of several translations including, of course, the original languages results in new critically important information about a Near Eastern ritual.

3. Psalm 45:6/Hebrews 1:8-9; Isaiah 7:14/Matthew 1:23: *The Old in the New*

Every Bible version contains its own philosophy of translation that is essential for the English reader to understand. Let's examine different principles of translation when Old Testament quotes appear in the New Testament. On the menu in Libronix 3, if you go to "Tools; Bible Comparison; Parallel Passages and Harmonies; Source; Old Testament Quotes in the New Testament (HCSB)," you will locate a program that compares the OT passage with a NT quote. If you choose the book of Hebrews, the software will generate all the OT passages quoted in this significant book. Alternatively, with Logos 4 you can examine the parallel examples in the resource *Old Testament Quotes in the New Testament* by H. David Philipps.[39]

When you select the NIV as your standard reference, you discover that under Heb 1:8-9 the OT and NT texts are exactly alike: "Your throne, O God, will last forever," etc. However, if you consult the RSV, Ps 45:6 reads, "Your divine throne endures forever and ever. Your royal scepter is a scepter of equity," while the NT quote in Hebrews states, "Thy throne, O God, is forever and ever, the righteous scepter is the scepter of thy kingdom." They differ quite dramatically, so that Psalm 45 seems to refer to the king's throne and scepter whereas the NT text specifically designates the throne and scepter as the Son's. Here the reader uncovers a different translation policy. The RSV attempts to understand the Scripture within the context of the original readers, so that Psalm 45 refers to the Davidic king while Hebrews 1 designates the divine Christ. The NIV, on the other hand, purposely demonstrates the fulfillment of the OT in the NT, so that both are translated identically. Both perspectives are important for a full meaning of the text, since the text was meaningful during Israel's monarchy but received an additional fulfillment through the coming of Jesus Christ in the New Testament. This different

---

39. For NT allusions of the Old Testament, examine in Logos Bible Software the resource *Old Testament Quotations and Allusions in the New Testament* by David A. Jones.

translation policy indicates the importance of reading the Bible in more than one version. Both the continuity between the testaments like the NIV and the progressive movement of salvation from one covenant to the next like the RSV need to be emphasized.

For a second example, generate the OT quotations in the Gospel of Matthew. You will notice in the very first reference comparing Isa 7:14 and Matt 1:23 that the texts are identical again in the NIV. However, the RSV reads "a young woman shall conceive" in Isaiah but "a virgin shall conceive" in Matthew. Again, the RSV translators attempt to reproduce a text that is understandable in the original situation where the prophecy was spoken. They conclude that the prophecy concerned the events of Hezekiah's war with the Assyrians (Isaiah 36–37) and did not refer originally to a virgin birth.[40] Only the second fulfillment in the New Testament involved a unique virgin birth. The NIV, on the other hand, attempts a christological interpretation of both passages. Presuppositions play a role in translation practices, and the mature reader should investigate the translation policy of each of the English versions.

4. 2 Samuel 11:4 and Joel 2:18-19: Hebrew Tenses

The determination of the English tense from the Hebrew original is particularly difficult because of the fluidity of the language. Although the Hebrew perfect normally is translated by a simple past tense, the NIV sometimes renders the Hebrew perfect or participle with a past perfect English equivalent. For instance, in 2 Sam 11:4, when David commits adultery with Bathsheba, the NIV reads, "Then David sent messengers to get her. She came to him, and he slept with her. (She <u>had purified</u> herself from her uncleanness.)" Here the NIV implies that Bathsheba was no longer ritually unclean by employing the past perfect tense, "she had purified herself." But the NRSV demonstrates another translation option by rendering the text, "Now she was purifying herself after her period." Both English translations are possible, but the context favors the NRSV. Here the author is documenting David's sin. Apparently his evil is not only moral but also religious and cultic. This literary aside is ironic. While she is purifying herself according to

---

40. However, a miraculous birth could be in the mind of Isaiah as well. Even if every male died in the war with the Assyrians, God would cause a virgin to give birth and continue the history of Israel.

the law, David is making himself impure both morally and ritually. It is a double dastardly deed.[41]

Another significant translation variant occurs in Joel 2:18-19a. The NIV (along with the KJV, NKJV, NASB, NLT) employs the future tense, so that these verses become a impending prophecy: "Then the Lord will be jealous for his land and take pity on his people. The Lord will reply to them. . . ." However, the TNIV has changed the NIV to a past tense (along with the ASV, RSV, NRSV, TEV, ESV, NET): "Then the Lord was jealous for his land and took pity on his people. The Lord replied to them. . . ." Why has this alteration occurred in the updating of a similar translation? In the Hebrew language the sequential imperfect can be translated in a variety of ways. Therefore, exegetes must attempt to determine whether the context involves a future promise or a present example of the Lord dealing with his people through the prophet. Joel 2:12-13 pictures an event occurring now: "Even now," declares the Lord, "return to me with all your heart, with fasting and weeping and mourning. Rend your heart and not your garments. Return to the Lord your God, for he is gracious and compassionate." As the narrative continues, the Lord proves that he is indeed gracious and compassionate when in verse 18 he "took pity on his people." Therefore, the context indicates proof of a genuine repentance, with the result that the Lord took pity and answered them.[42] The context governs the tenses of the verbs, proving that a future prophecy is unlikely. Again it is important to investigate the various translations to verify that different possibilities exist for interpreting the text.

5. The Benefits of a Dynamic Equivalent Translation for New Christians

For many Christians who have not grown up in the church, cryptic biblical imagery, obscure metaphors, and complicated theological jargon cause confusion and consternation. Therefore, besides word-for-word translations, it is important to consult a dynamic equivalent translation such as the New Living Bible that explains ancient imagery and complex theological terms. For

---

41. For another example of the past perfect, see below Chapter 7, C4, "The Tenses in Genesis 2:8 and 2:19" (pp. 256-58).

42. See Walter C. Kaiser, Jr., *Preaching and Teaching from the Old Testament: A Guide for the Church* (Grand Rapids: Baker Academic, 2002), p. 163.

instance, the authors avoid using terms such as "justification," "sanctification," and "regeneration" as carryovers from Latin translations, and in their place provide renderings such as "we are made right with God," "we are made holy," and "we are born anew." In addition, a typical modern reader might be confused by the literal text of Mark 9:49, "everyone will be salted with fire," so the NLT renders this verse, "everyone will be tested with fire." Likewise, instead of "bind on earth" and "loose on earth" in Matt 18:18 the NLT explains, "I tell you the truth, whatever you forbid on earth will be forbidden in heaven, and whatever you permit on earth will be permitted in heaven."

Conservative Christians might have trouble that the NLT adds the following underlined words not directly extracted from the original text. However, the resulting clarity is hard to dispute. Luke 10:11 explains the purpose of an ancient Jewish practice, "We wipe even the dust of your town from our feet to show that we have abandoned you to your fate." The meaning of "hate" is clarified in Luke 14:26: "If you want to be my disciple, you must hate everyone else by comparison."

In a dynamic equivalent translation additional words not exactly found in the original clarify the meaning for the contemporary reader. Antiquated phraseology is explained to the reader using the latest scholarly research. "Played the pipe and sang the dirge" (TNIV) in Luke 7:32 becomes "played wedding songs and funeral songs." The aphorism "With the measure you use, it will be measured to you" (Mark 4:24) is changed to "The closer you listen, the more understanding you will be given." Each of these translations faithfully captures the original meaning but employs wording that communicates to contemporary people. Therefore, various translations should be consulted, not only to offer a variety of possible readings but to clarify for the contemporary reader the meaning of difficult metaphors and outdated practices.

6. *Examples from* The Message *by Eugene Peterson*

Paraphrase versions of the Bible have been extremely popular in the church, especially Kenneth Taylor's *The Living Bible* in the 1970s and Eugene Peterson's *The Message* today.[43] How do we evaluate these contemporary free

---

43. Kenneth N. Taylor, *The Living Bible, Paraphrased* (Wheaton: Tyndale House, 1971); Eugene H. Peterson, *The Message: The Bible in Contemporary Language* (Colorado Springs: Navpress, 1993).

translations, each the work of only one person? Certainly they can be beneficial when studying passages of the Bible that have lost their impact due to familiarity. In the advertisements for this Bible paraphrase, the pop singer Amy Grant exclaims, "Since being given a copy of *The Message,* I haven't wanted to put it down. I'm always reading on to find out what happens next, and it constantly takes me by surprise." Likewise, Bono, the lead singer of the rock group U2, witnesses to the value of Peterson's work: "It has been a great strength to me. He's a poet and a scholar, and he's brought the text back to the tone in which the books were written."[44]

Free translations frequently paint word pictures of the text that are both memorable and relevant. The triumphant passage Romans 8 may lose its luster through continued repetition, so Peterson's creative imagery frequently produces new insights for the contemporary reader. Instead of the traditional language in Rom 8:1, "there is now no condemnation," Peterson composes a picture: we "no longer have to live under a continuous, low-lying black cloud." Likewise, in 8:3 the penetrating image, "God went for the jugular when he sent his own Son," is grippingly unforgettable. Instead of just asserting that the law was powerless, *The Message* again sketches a portrait: "The law always ended up being used as a Band-Aid on sin instead of a deep healing of it." Another free translation, J. B. Phillips's paraphrase of the New Testament, depicts as well a helpful etching of "the creation waiting in eager expectation" (Rom 8:19) when he describes all nature "standing on tip-toe," anticipating the revelation of the glorious transformation of the children of God.[45]

However, the reader must be careful not to assume that every thought of the author in a paraphrase traces back to the biblical text. For instance, the imagery Peterson employs to describe the Spirit of life in Rom 8:2 ("The Spirit of life in Christ, like a strong wind, has magnificently cleared the air") is not a translation of the Greek text but an additional thought of the author. Furthermore, by altering the biblical imagery with contemporary word pictures, paraphrases sometimes convey a different message from the one originally intended by the author. For instance, Peterson loses the comical imagery of having a tree stuck in your eye (Matt 7:3) when he transforms "Why do you look at the speck of sawdust in your brother's eye and pay no attention to the plank in your own eye?" into "It's easy to see a

---

44. For these quotes, see the back cover of the 2002 edition of *The Message.*

45. J. B. Phillips, *The New Testament in Modern English: Student Edition* (New York: Macmillan, 1958).

smudge on your neighbor's face and be oblivious to the ugly sneer on your own." Instead of systematically describing the armor of a soldier in Eph 6:14-17 through a series of pictures, Peterson simply states, "Truth, righteousness, peace, faith, and salvation are more than words." Furthermore, he overlooks the repetition of the word "stand," so that the flow of the book of Ephesians from sit (Eph 1:20; 2:6) to walk (4:1, 17; 5:2, 8, 15) to stand (6:11, 13, 14) is no longer obvious. Although he employs the expressions "standing up to everything the devil throws" and "you'll still be on your feet," the victory of a soldier in the Lord's army is not clearly captured. Therefore, a paraphrase should never be used by itself, but always alongside a standard translation of the Bible.

STUDY AND DISCUSSION QUESTIONS

1. With regard to textual criticism, list some reasons why a particular text is chosen over others. Go to Goggle Scholar and type in "Rules of Textual Criticism" and read several of the articles for enlightenment.

2. In the NIV translation of Matt 27:17, Pilate asks the crowd during Jesus' trial, "Which one do you want me to release to you: Barabbas, or Jesus who is called Christ?" The TNIV translation, however, reads "Which one do you want me to release to you: Jesus Barabbas, or Jesus who is called the Messiah?" The difference traces back to the divergence of early Greek manuscripts. But how does the reading "Jesus Barabbas" make sense historically? What could be the reason why Barabbas's first name was erased from many manuscripts?

3. Word study is important at Gen 12:3. Should the Hebrew word "blessed" (וְנִבְרְכוּ) be translated passively like the NIV, "all peoples on earth will be blessed through you"? Or is the more appropriate meaning the reflexive like the RSV, "and by you all the families of the earth shall bless themselves"? If the verse is read passively, then Abraham and his offspring are viewed as a channel of blessing. If the Scripture is translated reflexively, then they are viewed as a paradigm of blessing. To come to your own position, investigate Hebrew grammars for clarification, e.g., *An Introduction to Biblical Hebrew Syntax* by Bruce K. Waltke and M. O'Connor, esp. p. 395, which supports the passive. Why does Robert B. Chisholm, *From Exegesis to Exposition*, pp. 111-12, argue for the reflexive translation?

4. What does the connection between circumcision and baptism discovered in the discussion of Col 2:11-12 above say about infant baptism? Does circumcision on the eighth day support the baptism of children? Or is the physical infant of OT circumcision now replaced by the spiritual baby of NT baptism? I will leave that question to your reflection upon the importance of this adverbial participle. Interestingly, the NLT begins Col 2:12 with these words: "When you came to Christ, you were 'circumcised.'" Does the expression "came to Christ" have any parallel in the Greek, or is it an interpretation? Check an interlinear or reverse interlinear in Logos Bible Software to evaluate this English translation. Theological interpretations must have grammatical backing.

5. Genitive phrases can be translated quite differently by various Bible versions.

   a. Ephesians 2:20 (ἐποικοδομηθέντες ἐπὶ τῷ θεμελίῳ τῶν ἀποστόλων καὶ προφητῶν) is translated by the TEV, "built upon the foundation laid by the apostles and prophets," but by *The Message*, "He used the apostles and prophets for the foundation." What is the difference, and which type of genitive is employed by the two versions?

   b. 2 Corinthians 4:4 reads τὸν φωτισμὸν τοῦ εὐαγγελίου τῆς δόξης τοῦ Χριστοῦ, which the KJV translates, "the light of the glorious gospel of Christ," but the TEV states, "the light that comes from the Good News about the glorious Christ." What category of genitive does the TEV employ for τοῦ εὐαγγελίου ("the gospel")? What category of genitive goes the TEV employ for τοῦ Χριστοῦ? From the context, do you think the translation should be "glorious Christ" or "glorious gospel"?

   c. In Rom 1:5 the genitive "obedience of faith" (εἰς ὑπακοὴν πίστεως) is translated by C. E. B. Cranfield, "obedience that consists of faith,"[46] while the NIV reads "obedience that comes from faith." What is the difference, and what type of genitive is chosen by the various versions?

   d. Ephesians 4:9 states that Christ "descended into the lower parts of the earth" (κατέβη εἰς τὰ κατώτερα [μέρη] τῆς γῆς). If Jesus' descent into hell or hades is meant, what type of genitive is employed? If the incarnation of Christ is in mind, what genitive category would be employed? Which do you think is correct?

6. After studying John 13:17 and Gal 1:8-9, determine the importance for meaning in the change between the various types of conditional sentences. In Acts 18:14-15 what kind of distinction is the proconsul, Gallio, making when he employs two conditional sentences in his evaluation of the accusation directed by the Jews against the Christians? What significance for meaning can be drawn from the fact that John 8:19 and 18:36 are second class contrary-to-fact conditions?

7. Frequently the disruption of word order reveals the author's emphasis in a sentence. Check the following ἵνα clauses (2 Cor 12:7; Gal 2:10; Col 4:16; Acts 19:4; and Rev 18:4) to determine the emphasis in these Scriptures through certain vocabulary being removed from the purpose clauses.

   46. C. E. B. Cranfield, *On Romans: and Other New Testament Essays* (Edinburgh; T. & T. Clark, 1998), p. 66.

8. Words are placed outside of temporal and conditional clauses for emphasis. Determine what is given prominence in the temporal clauses located in John 7:27; 11:29, 32, 33; 16:21 and the conditional clauses in Matt 15:14; John 12:32; 1 Cor 6:4; 7:13; 15:2.

9. Examine the following verses by creating a Layout in Logos 4 (called a Workspace in Libronix 3) where you can compare the Greek text with English translations and determine which element in the sentence was removed from a question or indirect question and placed first for emphasis (Mark 14:68; Acts 5:35; 11:17; Rom 9:19; 11:2; 14:4, 10; 1 Cor 6:1; 14:16; and 1 Pet 4:18).

10. Determine how the word order in the following texts provides insights into the author's emphasis: Matt 15:14; 25:24; Mark 4:11; 8:17; 11:13; Acts 25:25; Rom 12:4; 1 Cor 7:7; Heb 6:16; 7:11; 10:32; Jas 1:2; and 1 Pet 2:12; 4:2; 5:3.

11. Hebrew tenses have been variously translated in Ps 67:6. The NIV reads, "Then the land <u>will</u> yield its harvest, and God, our God, <u>will</u> bless us," while the NRSV states, "The earth <u>has</u> yielded its increase; God, our God, <u>has</u> blessed us." If you check the Hebrew or an interlinear, you will discover that the first verb is a QTL Perfect (נָתְנָה), but the second verb is a YQTL imperfect (יְבָרְכֵנוּ). So what do you think of the ESV's translation, "The earth has yielded its increase; God, our God, shall bless us"? What two ways is the Hebrew imperfect translated? What does that imply as you evaluate the following translation of the NASB-95, "The earth has yielded its produce; God, our God, blesses us"?

12. In addition to the continuing nature of the Greek present and imperfect tenses (the progressive or durative sense), they can also be translated in an iterative and conative sense. The iterative entails the repeated nature of an action rather than its continuous nature. How does this explain the verbs in Luke 2:41; Acts 2:45; and 1 Cor 11:26? The best translation for the conative is "to try" or "to attempt." Construct a conative translation of Matt 3:14; Mark 15:23; Acts 26:28; and 1 Cor 9:8. Which English versions recognize this sense? How about Gal 1:13: does it have both a conative and durative verb?

13. Sometimes the present tense is used when a past tense is expected, the so-called historical present. The purpose is to establish vividness so that it feels like a past event is happening right now. Notice in the temptations of Jesus that the English translations of Matt 4:5, 8 read "the devil took him," whereas

the Greek employs the present tense. What does this say about the devil's temptations? Similarly, the present tense can be used when the future is expected in order to magnify the certainty of the coming event. Whereas the book of Revelation normally employs the future tense (notice Rev 22:3-6), the futuristic present is employed in 22:7, 12, 20. What does this say about Christ's second coming?

14. In Greek the strongest possible negative statement is constructed through the use of οὐ μή with the subjunctive and entitled the emphatic future negation. How does this shine additional light upon the statements in Mark 13:2; 14:31; Matt 24:35; and John 4:14; 6:35?

15. Unattainable wishes in Greek are expressed in the imperfect indicative. How does this help explain Paul's meaning in Rom 9:3 and Gal 4:20? Attainable wishes, on the other hand, are constructed by employing the optative mood. How does this shine light upon Mark 11:14 and Acts 8:20?

16. The hipʿil in Hebrew expresses a causative sense. How is this important in the translation of Ps 13:1? Is God intentionally hiding his face, that is, purposely withdrawing the consciousness of his presence from the author? Also examine Ps 8:7 (8:6 English); 18:28; and 68:9-10 (68:10-11 English) and explain the significance of the hipʿil.

17. What is the controversy surrounding the King James Version of the Bible? Consult the web page http://www.leaderu.com/orgs/probe/docs/kjvdebat .html. Why is there so much heat in the debate over the NIV versus the TNIV? Check the internet at http://www.tniv.com and http://www.no-tniv .com (http://www.cbmw.org).

18. Luke 17:37 (ὅπου τὸ σῶμα, ἐκεῖ καὶ οἱ ἀετοὶ ἐπισυναχθήσονται) is sometimes translated "Where the body *is*, there the eagles will be gathered together," or by other versions, "Where the corpse is, there the vultures will gather." Examine all your English versions in Logos Bible Software and determine which translations favor which reading. How did Matthew understand the text in 24:28? Since Jesus and John the Baptizer sometimes use doubletalk cleverly to mean two things at once (Mark 9:49a; Luke 3:16b), is it possible that both are intended? How would this affect Jesus' audience?

CHAPTER 3

The Structural Analysis Route

Employing a Skeleton Snapshot

In Chapter 1, we analyzed the genre and literary features of a biblical passage by using our infrared exegetical camera to view what many readers cannot see behind the text. Then in Chapter 2 we took our microscope to investigate the grammatical details. Now we want to view the skeleton of a text, to visualize the entire structure and examine how the grammatical details fit together into the final product. First of all we will scrutinize the structures of entire books in the New Testament, then look at paragraphs, and finally employ clausal outlines to enlighten the internal structure of various biblical paragraphs.

A. The Structure of Various Biblical Books

1. The Ending of the Gospel of Mark and Its Discipleship Structure

The ending of the Gospel of Mark is a notorious knotty problem. Up until the twentieth century in Germany and about 1950 in the English-speaking world, the dominant position maintained that Mark 16:9-20 was the original ending. However, since the work of Julius Wellhausen in Germany and R. H. Lightfoot in England,[1] the prevailing opinion in the second half of the twentieth century claimed that Mark intended his Gospel to end at 16:8. Now in

---

1. For Wellhausen, see Morna D. Hooker, *The Gospel According to St. Mark,* Black's New Testament Commentaries (London: Black, 1991), p. 391. R. H. Lightfoot, *The Gospel Message of St. Mark* (London: Oxford University Press, 1950), pp. 80-97.

the beginning of the twenty-first century, evangelical scholars have pushed for the position that the end of Mark was lost.[2] How can a discussion of the skeleton structure of Mark benefit this controversy?

Frequently I repeat a standard quip in my classes, "the meaning is in the structure." For Mark's Gospel the reader must notice the repeated cycles where the disciples begin positively but struggle at the end because of the rejection of the message of Jesus. Through each cycle of the Jesus tradition, Mark is attempting to develop a deeper and more solid commitment by confronting the Christian community with the struggles they will face at the time of his writing. The first cycle embarks with the disciples dramatically choosing to follow Jesus by leaving their professions (1:16-18) and families (1:19-20) but concludes with the disciples and Mark's readers witnessing the rejection of Jesus' message by the Jewish leaders (3:6). In the second cycle Jesus appoints the Twelve to be "with him" as the new Israel, endows them with his own authority, and trains them as apostles (3:13-19), but they must face rejection from their own townsfolk as Jesus did at Nazareth (6:1-6a). In the third cycle, the disciples take the lead in the gospel mission (6:7-30) while Jesus supervises their ministry, but now they struggle with their own faith. Even though the disciples are warned that they could become outsiders (4:13), in the end they are overcome with blindness, misunderstanding, forgetfulness, and obduracy (8:17-21).

This initial call, training, and sending forth in mission of the disciples leads to a section where Jesus' devotees are tested in their ability to persevere in a discipleship of the cross. Again this section commences positively, with Peter proclaiming that Jesus is the Messiah (8:29). But in Mark 8:34 Jesus issues a new call, "If anyone would come after me, he must deny himself and take up his cross and follow me." Whereas the disciples are taught everything they need to know to follow a crucified Messiah (8:27–10:52), in the end they betray (14:43-45), deny (14:66-72), and abandon Jesus (14:50-52). Thus rejection is manifested not only in spiritual blindness and misunderstanding but in the disciples' very actions. In the final cycle, the women replace the Twelve and, like their counterparts, commence their discipleship by leaving all behind (15:40-41). They follow Jesus all the way from Galilee and according to Mark are the only loyalists present at the cross. Yet the final scene pictures them closed-mouthed and fearful at the prospect of following a crucified Messiah (16:8). Rejection has infiltrated Jesus' entire spiritual family.

2. See the commentaries of Robert H. Gundry, Craig A. Evans, Ben Witherington III, R. T. France, and Robert H. Stein.

From this rehearsal of the skeleton structure of Mark's Gospel, it is clear that the expected content of Mark 16:8 would center on rejection. Therefore, the fear and flight in 16:8 should not be interpreted positively as a hurried return to the apostles based upon the overwhelming awe of the experience. Nor is additional narrative needed, since a conclusion of rejection is the normal ending of each section.[3] The women flee in fear just as the disciples did in the garden of Gethsemane (14:50). The women's negative response must be interpreted as a struggle with a discipleship of the cross. From an analysis of the structure we can conclude that Mark's Gospel ended at 16:8, even though at first these words seem strange and anticlimactic to the initial reader.

2. The Cleansing of the Temple and the Structure of John's Gospel

Since the cleansing of the temple is narrated in the last week of Jesus' passion in the Synoptic Gospels (Mark 11:15-19) but as Jesus' first prophetic act in Jerusalem in the Fourth Gospel (John 2:13-22), several scholars conclude that there must have been two cleansings of the temple.[4] However, when we survey the first half of John's Gospel, the careful reader discerns that the material is organized, not according to chronological history, but through similar content.

As Raymond E. Brown points out,[5] the Fourth Gospel can be divided into the section "From Cana to Cana" in chapters 2–4 and the fulfillment of the Jewish feasts in chapters 5–10. Just as the subject matter of the various feasts organizes the third part of the Book of Signs, so John 2–4 is concerned with the fulfillment of Jewish institutions and with the salvation of all the people groups of Palestine. Based upon the plethora of symbolic overtones in John's Gospel, it is likely that the writer is using the town of Cana to allude to the conquest of the land of Canaan so that Jesus in his ministry is giving

3. However, Robert H. Stein, *Mark*. Baker Exegetical Commentary of the New Testament (Grand Rapids: Baker, 2008), p. 287, agrees with the first three cycles but then contends that the ending of Mark in 16:8 is positive in nature.

4. For support of two cleansings, see William Hendriksen, *Exposition of the Gospel According to John* (Grand Rapids: Baker, 1953), p. 120. For arguments on both sides, see Leon Morris, *The Gospel According to John*, rev. ed. NICNT (Grand Rapids: Eerdmans, 1995), pp. 167-69.

5. Raymond E. Brown, *The Gospel According to John*. AB 29 (Garden City: Doubleday, 1966), pp. cxl-cxli.

the Promised Land back to the New Israel. When the true Israelites believe in Jesus as exemplified through Nathaniel (1:47-49), then the eschatological age has arrived, so that Jesus' sign at the wedding feast in Cana represents the new age of abundance (Amos 9:13b). The best wine is saved for now (John 2:10). Likewise, the second sign at Cana demonstrates the continual harvest expected in the new age (John 4:35-38), as prophesied in Amos 9:13a.

What events will happen in the new age? First of all, the Messiah will establish a new temple. Therefore, John places the cleansing of the temple at the beginning of Jesus' ministry, since the most important institution in Judaism must be fulfilled by Jesus. John reveals that the temple Jesus had spoken of was his body (2:21), so that the new temple has arrived. Now every group of people must come to worship Jesus as the new temple. First, the Jewish leaders through the person of Nicodemus are replaced by those who are born again by water and the Spirit (3:1-12). Then, all the followers of John the Baptizer must turn to Jesus, since as John concedes, "He must become greater; I must become less" (3:30). John 4 then describes the turning of the Samaritans to Jesus, so that through the woman at the well they all believe that Jesus is the "Savior of the world" (4:42). Finally, salvation comes to the royal official's family, who represent the Gentiles who believe with their entire household (4:53) as the Gentile believers in the book of Acts (Acts 11:14; 16:15, 33; 18:8). So the new age witnesses the coming of the true Israelites, the entire Baptist movement, the Samaritans, and the Gentiles to faith in the Messiah, Jesus.

From this synopsis of the flow of material it becomes evident that John is organizing his Gospel to preach a message and not just to recite historical happenings. Therefore, we need not conclude that Jesus cleansed the temple twice. The Synoptic writers use the temple cleansing to display the reason why Jesus was crucified (Mark 11:18), whereas for John the raising of Lazarus from the dead becomes the initiating event of Jesus' passion (John 11:47-57). The events themselves are historical, but the interpretation of the events is theological. The writers structure the Gospels differently to express the full meaning of the events. Within the structure lies the meaning.

3. Conflict in the Early Church and the Structure of the Acts of the Apostles

C. H. Turner proposed a structure to the Acts of the Apostles where each section concluded with a summary statement about the growth of the church.[6] Furthermore, each section begins with a miraculous work of the Holy Spirit, demonstrating the real source of all spiritual and numerical growth. Therefore, the first section beginning with the physical presence of the Holy Spirit in wind and fire at Pentecost resulting in 3000 Jewish converts concludes with the summary, "So the word of God spread. The number of disciples in Jerusalem increased rapidly, and a large number of priests became obedient to the faith" (6:7). Interestingly, Luke consistently narrates a difficult controversy that the church confronted before each summary of God's providential growth. Here the problem of the internal dissension between the Aramaic- and Greek-speaking believers over the treatment of widows (6:1-6) is placed immediately before this summary statement to proclaim that the Holy Spirit's power overcomes any human disagreement.

In the next section, the reader encounters a special revelation of the Holy Spirit to the Greek-speaking Stephen (6:8; 7:55-56), the arrival of the Holy Spirit in Samaria only after the apostles come from Jerusalem, and the miraculous lifting and placing of Philip in the wilderness to speak to the Ethiopian eunuch who is reading Isaiah 53. This progression demonstrates that the gospel is also intended for Greek-speaking Jews, the half-breed Samaritans, and the God-fearers who have joined Israel as Gentiles. The section concludes, "Then the church throughout Judea, Galilee and Samaria enjoyed a time of peace and was strengthened. Living in the fear of the Lord and encouraged by the Holy Spirit, it increased in numbers" (9:31). God even caused growth in the midst of persecution and turned the person breathing out murderous threats into the apostle to the Gentiles (9:1-30).

In the third section of Acts, the conversion of the Gentiles at the home of the centurion Cornelius becomes prominent. The Holy Spirit falls upon the Gentiles even before they are baptized (10:44-48), so that the section concludes, "the word of God continued to increase and spread" (12:24). Here the opposition of a tyrant ruler and the loss of one of the twelve apostles cannot stop God's work (12:1-23).

In the fourth section, the gospel spreads beyond Palestine to all of Asia Minor when the Holy Spirit sets apart Paul and Barnabas for God's special missionary endeavors (13:2-3). This section narrates Paul's first and second missionary journeys until they reach the edge of Europe. As a result, "the

6. C. H. Turner, "Chronology of the NT," in *A Dictionary of the Bible,* ed. James Hastings (New York: Scribner, 1902-1904), 1:421. See the International Bible Society's edition of the Bible in 2007 as *The Books of the Bible,* where this structure is incorporated into a text without chapters and verses.

churches were strengthened in the faith and grew daily in numbers" (16:5). This growth summary is offered immediately following a division in the apostolic team that could have completely halted the spread of the gospel (15:37-41). But now, instead of only one missionary team, the Holy Spirit can utilize the efforts of two, Paul and Silas as well as Barnabas and Mark.

In the fifth section, the gospel transcends the boundary between Asia and Europe. In Acts 16:6-7 we witness the Holy Spirit forbidding Paul to enter the provinces of Asia and Bithynia. So he journeys for a while without a mission until a vision from the Holy Spirit calls Paul to travel over to Europe. As 19:20 concludes, "In this way the word of the Lord spread widely and grew in power." Every obstacle to the gospel was overcome, including the power of Satan, persecution, and battles with the occult (19:13-19).

The final section begins with Paul's decision in the Spirit to return first to Jerusalem and then advance to the heart of the empire at Rome. This initiates Paul's passion, where he faces all the false accusations of the Jewish leaders and prison at the hand of the Romans similar to Jesus. But the final chorus of joyous exaltation (28:28) is that "God's salvation has been sent to the Gentiles and they will listen!" The unbelief of the Jewish leaders cannot halt the movement of God's Spirit. The gospel has been preached in the capital city of Rome before the emperor, and the story can cease. Here again in the book of Acts we encounter how the author employs the structure of the book to proclaim a powerful message. The meaning is in the structure.

4. The Purpose of the Parallel Flow of Material in Luke-Acts:
Lukan Symmetry

The Gospel of Luke and the Acts of the Apostles must be studied together. The hyphenated title Luke-Acts, which Henry Cadbury coined in 1927, offers a perspective upon these books that cannot be ignored.[7] As Robert Smith points out,

> That hyphenated label may seem inelegant or even barbarous, yet it is
> useful in the extreme; for it handily summarizes a hard-won position that

7. Henry J. Cadbury, *The Making of Luke-Acts* (New York: Macmillan, 1927). For the opposing view that "the hyphenated Luke-Acts ought to be retired," see Mikeal C. Parsons and Richard I. Pervo, *Rethinking the Unity of Luke and Acts* (Minneapolis: Fortress, 1993, and Patricia Walters, *The Assumed Authorial Unity of Luke and Acts: A Reassessment of the Evidence.* SNTSMS 145 (Cambridge: Cambridge University Press, 2009).

is (or should be) a presupposition for all investigations of the Third Gospel and the Book of Acts: the entire work from Luke 1.1 to Acts 28.31 is a unified whole . . . and neither should be studied in isolation from the other.[8]

What was Luke's purpose in structuring these two books in a similar manner? First I will chart the parallel development of the content and then examine its significance. Hopefully, you as the reader will not be intimidated or lulled to sleep by the long lists that follow, but the abundance of parallels between Luke and Acts is overwhelming.

The symmetry of Luke-Acts is witnessed, first of all, in the following general characteristics:[9]

1. Each book has three sections: a ministry at home (Galilee or Jerusalem), an extensive travel narrative occupying 37 percent of Luke (Luke 9:51–19:44) and 38 percent of Acts (12:25–21:16), and a passion narrative constituting about 23 percent of Luke's first book (Jesus' arrival in Jerusalem through his ascension) and 24 percent of Acts (Paul's arrest from Acts 21:27 through 28:31).[10]

2. The geography is reversed, so that Jesus' trip from Galilee, his travel narrative through Samaria and Judea, and his ministry in Jerusalem, which each begin with a rejection narrative (4:14-30; 9:51-55; 19:41-48), correspond to the outward successful movement of the church from Jerusalem to Judea and Samaria and finally the ends of the earth (Acts 1:8). Therefore, any resurrection appearances in Galilee are omitted by Luke.

3. Both books are addressed to the same person, Theophilus, cover about thirty years of history, and are written in a sequel format, so that Luke ends and Acts begins with the ascension (Luke 24:50-51; Acts 1:9-11), the empowering from on high (Luke 24:49; Acts 2), the preaching of repentance and forgiveness of sins (Luke 24:47; Acts 2:38), and a reference to witnesses (24:48; Acts 1:8, 22; 2:32).

4. Through an *inclusio,* Luke-Acts begins and ends in the capital of the Roman empire and with the Roman emperor himself (Luke 2:1; Acts 28:16, 19).

8. Robert Smith, "Theology of Acts," *CTM* 42 (1971): 527.

9. See Charles H. Talbert, *Literary Patterns, Theological Themes, and the Genre of Luke-Acts.* SNTSMS 20 (Missoula: Scholars, 1975).

10. David E. Aune, *The New Testament in Its Literary Environment.* LEC 8 (Philadelphia: Westminster, 1987), p. 119.

5. The temple motif provides a stylized symmetrical structure, so that
   (a) the Gospel begins and ends in the temple (Luke 1:9; 24:53); (b) the
   birth narrative commences and concludes in the temple (1:9; 2:41-49);
   (c) Jesus' ministry is inaugurated and terminated in the temple (4:9;
   21:37); and (d) the book of Acts opens with the church worshipping
   in the temple (2:46), while Paul's arrival at the temple instigates his trial
   in Jerusalem (21:26-31), just as Jesus' cleansing of the temple led to his
   arrest.

6. The gospel extended to the Gentiles begins and ends Luke-Acts, with
   Simeon in the birth narrative speaking of the baby Jesus as "the light for
   revelation to the Gentiles" (Luke 2:32) and Acts 28:28 concluding that
   the Gentiles will listen.

Second, beyond these general characteristics, the sequence of the narratives in Luke-Acts is remarkably symmetrical, as demonstrated by the close
to twenty parallels between Luke and Acts.

1. The birth of Jesus (Luke 1–2) parallels the birth of the church (Acts 1–2)
   where (a) both occur through the work of the Spirit (Luke 1:15, 35, 41, 67;
   Acts 1:2, 5, 8, 16); (b) the revelations in each instance are undergirded
   with prayer (Luke 1:10; Acts 1:14); (c) angels announce Jesus' coming
   (Luke 2:9-12) and his second coming (Acts 1:10).

2. Forty days elapse before Jesus' ministry (Luke 4:1-2, 14), and forty days
   of resurrection appearances precede Jesus' ascension into heaven (Acts
   1:3) and the disciples' ministry.

3. The disciples are listed (Luke 6:14-16; Acts 1:13) with Peter given precedent (named first and given primary leadership in Acts 1:15), so that the
   Twelve now become the 120 (12 × 10).

4. After prayer the Spirit descends in physical form, both at Jesus' baptism
   (Luke 3:21-22) and at Pentecost (Acts 1:14, 24; 2:1-4). A voice from heaven
   in Luke is paralleled by heavenly tongues in Acts 2:4.

5. Both Jesus' ministry on earth and his ministry through the church open
   with a sermon that emphasizes the fulfillment of prophecy and highlights the rejection of Jesus (Luke 4:16-30; Acts 2:14-40).

6. The first demand of the kingdom and the first demand of apostolic
   preaching is repentance (Luke 3:3; Acts 2:38).

7. Conflicts with religious leaders begin at the outset (Luke 5:29–6:11; Acts
   4:1–8:3).

8. Deceivers in the community appear early in the narrative (Luke 6:16;

Acts 5:1-11), so that both Judas as well as Ananias and Sapphira tragically lose their lives.

9. Jesus embarks on his ministry by manifesting the healing power of God's rule (Luke 4:31-37); now Peter and the apostles do the same in the name of Jesus (Acts 3:6). Compare Acts 9:32-35 with Luke 5:24-26 and Acts 9:40 with Luke 8:54.

10. The mission of the seventy to extend Jesus' ministry (Luke 10) is paralleled by the mission of the seven to extend the apostles' ministry (Acts 6–8).

11. Stephen has a transfiguration experience where his face shines (Acts 6:15) seeing Jesus at God's right hand (7:55), just as during the ministry of Jesus an epiphany of Moses and Elijah occurs with Jesus transfigured (Luke 9:28-36).

12. Jesus' rejection in Samaria (Luke 9:51-53) as the apostles travel toward Jerusalem is paralleled in Acts by the positive reception of the Samaritans as the apostles travel from Jerusalem (Acts 8:4-25).

13. Peter's confession of faith stands as the turning point of the Gospel (chapter 9), and Paul's conversion is the turning point of Acts (chapter 9), so that Peter's profession controls the following material by leading to the travel narrative and the destination of Jerusalem, just as Paul's conversion (9:15-16) reveals that he will carry Jesus' name before Gentiles (the travel narrative of Acts 13:1–20:38) and suffer much for Jesus' name (the passion narrative of Acts 21–28).

14. A centurion, well-spoken of by the Jews, sends messengers both to Jesus and to Peter to ask them to bring the message of salvation to their house (Luke 7:1-10; Acts 10).

15. Herod Antipas's intention to kill Jesus (Luke 13:31) is paralleled by the threat on Peter's life by Herod Agrippa I (Acts 12:1-19).

16. At the middle of each book, Luke narrates a story about Jewish exorcists who attempt to drive out evil spirits (Luke 9:49-50; Acts 19:11-19).

17. Three instances of rejection begin each section of Jesus' travel narrative (9:51-55; 13:22-35; 17:11-17) and correspond to three crucial rejections by the Jewish leaders on Paul's missionary journeys (13:46, Pisidian Antioch; 18:6, Corinth; 19:9, Ephesus).

18. Paul delivers a farewell speech in Acts 20, revealing that he will not see the believers again, just as Jesus offers a discourse foretelling the future before his death (Luke 21).

19. Jesus' prediction about a future persecution in Luke 21:12-13 ("They will lay hands on you and persecute you. They will deliver you to synagogues

and prisons, and you will be brought before kings and governors, and all on account of my name. This will result in your being witnesses to them") is fulfilled by Paul in his suffering.

Finally, a third list of remarkable narrative similarities involves the events of Paul's passion (Acts 21–28), which are written by Luke in such a manner to imitate the suffering of Jesus.

1. Both Jesus and Paul travel to Jerusalem under divine necessity (Luke 13:33; Acts 20:22), knowing that suffering and even death await them, although their closest friends misunderstand them but are unable to persuade them otherwise (Luke 9:45; 18:34; Acts 21:4, 12-14).

2. In each case, three passion predictions are narrated in their trips to Jerusalem (Luke 9:22, 44; 18:32; Acts 20:22-23 at Ephesus; 21:4 at Tyre; 21:11 by Agabus at Caesarea), revealing that they will be delivered into the hands of the Gentiles (Luke 18:32; Acts 21:11).

3. Jesus surrenders to God's will in the garden of Gethsemane (Luke 22:42, "Not my will but yours be done"), just as in Acts 20:36-37 Paul kneels down and prays with his friends before his arrest in Jerusalem and at 21:14b asserts, "The Lord's will be done."

4. Both initially receive a good reception in Jerusalem (Luke 19:37; Acts 21:17-20a), but their entering the temple leads to their arrest (Luke 19:45-48; Acts 21:30-33).

5. Forty men plot with the chief priests and elders to trap Paul (23:13-15), just as chief priests and elders conspire with Judas to capture Jesus (Luke 22:4).

6. Jesus is accused of declaring he will destroy the temple, and Paul is accused of defiling the holy place (21:26-30); similarly,the charges against Paul before Felix (Acts 24:5-6) resemble the accusations against Jesus before Pilate (Luke 23:1-2).

7. Both Jesus and Paul are associated with Zealots; Jesus is selected to be crucified instead of Barabbas (Luke 23:18-19) and killed between two revolutionaries (Luke 23:32), while Paul is confused with an Egyptian who recently stirred up a revolt and led four thousand assassins into the wilderness (Acts 21:38).

8. In the Roman trial, each defendant is accused by the high priest and the leaders of the Jewish people (Luke 23:2, 5, 10; Acts 25:2, 7, 11, 15-17; 26:2) who demand the death penalty (Luke 23:18, 21, 23; Acts 25:24).

9. The Gentile rulers proclaim three times that Paul has done nothing

worthy of death (before Felix 23:29; Festus 25:25; and Agrippa 26:31), just as Pilate attempts to release Jesus on three occasions (Luke 23:16, 20, 22).

10. In each book there is a Herod who opposes the Christian movement in the middle (Luke 13:31-33; Acts 12) and end of the story (Luke 23:15, Herod Antipas; Acts 26:32, Herod Agrippa II). In both trials before Herod, the accused is returned to the governor without being found guilty.

11. Both Jesus and Paul endure four trials, with Jesus placed before the Sanhedrin, Pilate, Herod, and Pilate again (Luke 22:66; 23:1, 8, 13) and Paul tried before the Sanhedrin, Felix, Festus, and Herod Agrippa (Acts 23, 24, 25, 26).

12. Jesus' death and resurrection is mirrored in Paul's sea journey to Rome, where Paul is saved from the storm (27:43-44) with all his shipmates (27:24), just as Jesus is raised from the dead and saves everyone through it.

13. The supper on the ship (taking, blessing, breaking bread, 27:35) parallels either the Last Supper before Jesus' upcoming death or the appearances of the risen Jesus where he eats bread (Luke 24:30, 41-43), so that the narrative of Jesus' death and resurrection is being recalled.

14. An angel appears to strengthen Paul in the narrative of the storm at sea (Acts 27:23), just as Luke depicts an angel that strengthens Jesus in the garden of Gethsemane (Luke 22:43).

15. Paul is pictured by Luke as taking charge of the ship, even though he is not the captain or the centurion (27:21, 31-32, 34, 42-43); likewise, Jesus takes charge on the cross, even though he is being crucified (Luke 23:28, 34, 43, 46).

16. Jesus' prediction that "not a hair of your head will perish" is fulfilled through Paul's sea ordeal (Luke 21:18; Acts 27:34), so that the saying is employed in both books in a context of witnessing before the authorities.

17. According to Richard Rackham, "The rest and peace of the three winter months at Malta, when the apostle was entirely cut off from the outside world and his old life, is like the rest of the three days in the grave (Luke 23:50-56; Acts 28:1-10)."[11]

18. The ministries of Jesus and Paul conclude on the note of the fulfillment of Scripture (Luke 24:32, 44-45; Acts 28:23, 26-28).

19. Luke finishes the Gospel with Jesus' command to go to all nations (24:47), and Acts ends with a comment about the Gentiles that "they will listen" (28:29).

---

11. Richard B. Rackham, *The Acts of the Apostles: An Exposition* (1912; repr. Grand Rapids: Baker, 1978), pp. 477-78. I include this, even though it is the weakest of the parallels.

The reading of these three extensive lists at one sitting can be quite over-whelming. Luke must have some important purpose for these symmetrical constructions. The prologue of each book supplies the answer. Acts 1:1 ex-plains that in the Gospel Luke "wrote about all that Jesus began to do and to teach," implying that the second volume is about what Jesus *continued* to do and to teach. Therefore, the designation "Acts of the Apostles" is really a faulty title; more appropriate is the heading, "The Continuing Acts of Jesus." Jesus was not just active when he walked this earth, but now he is acting from heaven through his body, the church. Jesus' ministry both in its glory and its suffering is being carried on through the church. What an astonishingly high view of church history is demonstrated in the book of Acts! Through these extensive parallels Luke is attempting to instill within the church a sense of her majestic calling. Through the Holy Spirit the teaching and deeds of Jesus continue. This message Luke incorporates into the very structure of his book.

5. Structures in the Book of Revelation

First-time readers of the book of Revelation frequently respond with sheer terror. The number 666 elicits doomsday predictions. The scary grotesque beasts with seven heads and the tail of a dragon that sweeps a third of the stars out of the sky cause a mixture of angst and confusion. But if the reader inves-tigates the purpose of apocalyptic literature, this fear should change to com-fort. In a time of chaos and confusion, the apocalyptic seer writes for the en-couragement and edification of the church. History is not out of control; God is sovereign and working out his purposeful plan. Therefore, the prophet demonstrates through an orderly calendar of events how God has control over time and eternity. The book of Revelation is neatly divided into groups of seven, so that perfect order is restored upon history: seven churches (chs. 2–3), seven seals (6:1–8:5), trumpets (8:6–11:19), and bowls (chs. 15–16), seven mystic figures (chs. 12–14), and seven great enemies defeated (chs. 17–20). In addition, seven beatitudes are sprinkled throughout the book to offer bless-ing continually to God's people (1:3; 14:13; 16:15; 19:9; 20:6; 22:7; 22:14). Some authors[12] even contend that seven scenes of heavenly worship are clearly visi-ble (4:2-11 + 5:8-14; 7:9-17; 11:15-18; 13:1-15; 14:1-5; 15:2-4; 19:1-8).

The rotation of material in the book of Revelation also generates com-

---

12. Stanley P. Saunders, "Revelation and Resistance: Narrative and Worship in John's Apocalypse," in *Narrative Reading, Narrative Preaching,* ed. Joel Green and Michael Pasquarello III (Grand Rapids: Baker Academic, 2003), p. 139.

fort. Heavenly scenes dominated by praise and worship regularly precede earthly scenes of increasing agony and destruction. For instance, the rich heavenly worship of chapters 4–5 prepares the reader for the devastation of a quarter of the earth in 6:8, a third of the earth in 8:7-8, climaxing in total annihilation in 16:3-4. The reader is supposed to envision the terror on earth through a heavenly eternal perspective of divine sovereignty. The following rotation of material structures the entire Apocalypse.

1a. Ch. 1	A vision of Christ reigning in heaven.	
1b. Chs. 2–3	Letters to seven earthly churches.	
2a. Chs. 4–5	Adoration of God and Christ exalted in heaven.	
2b. Ch. 6	The seven seals opened; the last times on earth. (6:8: a quarter of the earth is destroyed.)	
3a. 7:1–8:5	The sealing of the saints, the great multitude before the throne, and silence in heaven.	
3b. 8:6–11:14	The seven last trumpets upon the earth. (8:7-8: a third of earth is destroyed.)	
4a. 11:15–12:12	The war in heaven is completed and God's temple in heaven is opened (11:19), which parallels the open door in heaven seen in 4:1.	
4b. 12:13–13:18	The dragon and beasts devour and pollute the earth.	
5a. Chs. 14–15	The song of the 144,000 and the heavenly prophecy that Babylon is fallen.	
5b. Chs. 16–18	The seven bowls on earth (16:1-20: God's wrath is poured out on all things.)	
6a. 19:1-18	The threefold hallelujah in heaven and the revelation of the rider on the white horse.	
6b. 19:19–20:10	The dragon and the beasts on earth attempt a final attack but are soundly defeated.	
7. 20:11–22:21	Heaven and earth are united in Christ.	

From such evidence, Elisabeth Schüssler Fiorenza challenges the notion that injustice and oppression are at the center of the universe for the Apocalyptist. Instead, "Revelation's central theological query is, To whom does the earth belong? Who is the ruler of this world? The book's central theological symbol is therefore the *throne*."[13] Likewise, Allan Boesak entitles his volume on Revelation *Comfort and Protest* to demonstrate that the Christian is not endangered or powerless because of the events described in this last book of the Bible.[14] When we review the overall purpose of a book, the individual details sometimes take on new meaning. A thoughtful understanding of the purpose of apocalyptic literature creates a completely different impression of the book of Revelation. The purpose is revealed in the structure.

6. One Hundred Fifty Psalms but Five Books

Children in Sunday school learn that the Hebrew Psalter consists of 150 psalms. Frequently, the first and last psalms are even memorized. However, rarely are they taught that these psalms comprise five volumes. What is the significance of this structure?

The five books of psalms comprise the collections 1–41, where the divine name Yahweh is prominent; 42–72, where the title Elohim is employed; 73–89, which includes an anthology assigned to Asaph (73–83) and the Sons of Korah (84–85, 87–88); 90–106, centering upon The Lord Reigns collection (93–100); and finally 107–150, which comprise the so-called Egyptian Hallel (111–118), the Songs of Ascent (120–134), the final Davidic king collection (138–145), and the Praise the Lord psalms (146–150). In the Greek LXX, each of the first four books ends identically: Γένοιτο γένοιτο ("Let it be, let it be"). In Hebrew, the conclusions of books one and four proclaim a repeat chorus, "Praise be to the LORD, the God of Israel, from everlasting to everlasting," with Book One concluding "Amen and Amen" (41:13), while Book Four wraps up, "Let all the people say, 'Amen!' Praise the LORD" (106:48). Books Two and Three likewise finish with a double "Amen." The additional line terminating the second collection, "This concludes the prayers of David son of Jesse," must be left over from a previous edition of psalms, since a group of Davidic psalms are located at the end of the Psalter as well (86, 101, 103, 109, 110, 122, 124, 131, 133, 138–145).

---

13. Elisabeth Schüssler Fiorenza, *Revelation: Vision of a Just World* (Minneapolis: Fortress, 1991), p. 120.

14. Allan A. Boesak, *Comfort and Protest: Reflections on the Apocalypse of John of Patmos* (Philadelphia: Westminster, 1987).

Regarding the first book, the Davidic psalms begin with Psalm 3, so that the first two psalms are introductory. Significantly, Psalm 1 as a wisdom psalm turns a hymnbook that is directed at God into a divine revelation of the law of God that is aimed at the human community.[15] Psalm 2 then introduces the royal psalms when God installs his king as Son of God on Mount Zion (2:6-7). Psalm 150 supplies an appropriate finale to the book with its tenfold "praise him," framed by the more extensive exaltation, "Praise the Lord."

But what significance did a collection of five books have for Israel? Here we must remember that the books of Moses were entitled the Pentateuch. The authoritative law of God that shaped the life and customs of ancient Israel comprised five volumes. To establish the authority of other genres of literature, the material was likewise divided into five sections. When the psalms were placed into five books, they became not just human devotion and worship of God but the infallible revelation of God to his people.[16]

This identical procedure developed with other genres of literature. With regard to apocalyptic literature, the book of *Enoch* developed into five volumes. Similarly, wisdom literature as exemplified in Ecclesiastes was assigned five distinct parts,[17] and the exemplar of rabbinic literature, *Pirke Aboth,* comprised five Pereqs, since the sixth chapter is not original.[18] In addition, when later authors attempted to continue writing the history of Israel, they resorted to five narrative volumes, as represented in Jason of Cyrene's Maccabean history (2 Macc 2:23). So when Matthew penned a Gospel, he also divided the Jesus tradition into five sermons (Matthew 5–7, 10, 13, 18, 24–25)[19] to designate this material as authoritative teaching for Israel. In

---

15. See Brevard S. Childs, *Introduction to Old Testament Theology as Scripture* (Philadelphia: Fortress, 1979), pp. 513-14; Gerald T. Sheppard, "Canonization: Hearing the Voice of the Same God Through Historically Dissimilar Traditions," *Int* 36 (1982): 23; Claus Westermann, "The Formation of the Psalter," *Praise and Lament in the Psalms* (Atlanta: John Knox, 1981), p. 253.

16. See James Luther Mays, *The Lord Reigns: A Theological Handbook to the Psalms* (Louisville: Westminster John Knox, 1994), p. 122; and Carl J. Bosma, "Discerning the Voices in the Psalms: A Discussion of Two Problems in Psalmic Interpretation, Part 2," *CTJ* 44 (2009): 159.

17. See John C. Hawkins, *Horae Synopticae: Contributions to the Study of the Synoptic Problem,* 2nd ed. (Oxford: Clarendon, 1909), pp. 163-64.

18. R. H. Charles, *The Apocrypha and Psuedepigrapha of the Old Tetament in English* (Oxford: Clarendon, 1913), 2:710.

19. See Benjamin W. Bacon. "The 'Five Books' of Moses against the Jews," *Exp* 15 (1918): 56-66 and *Studies in Matthew* (London: Constable, 1930), chs. 12-16.

the second century, Papias continued this trend with his five volumes on the sayings of Jesus (συγγράμματα), which Eusebius called βιβλία (*Hist. eccl.* 3:39). Finally, Irenaeus assigned the same authoritative rubric to his genre of apologetic when he partitioned his *Against Heresies* into five books around 180 C.E.

With this as background, we must conclude that the division of the book of Psalms into five volumes is of utmost importance. The structure produced a new meaning for the material.

7. The Flow of Psalms 120–122 in the Psalms of Ascent

Is there any orderly arrangement to the collections of psalms within the five books of the Hebrew Psalter? This is very difficult to discern for most collections, but the first three Songs of Ascent (Psalms 120–122) form a journey narrative where the pilgrims finally arrive at the temple in Jerusalem. Then the remaining Psalms of Ascent contain a plethora of allusions to liturgical expressions employed by the priests and worshipping community. In addition to the introductory liturgical formula "let Israel say" (Pss 124:1; 129:1), these include the following:

> Psalm 124:8 "Our help is in the name of the Lord, the Maker of heaven and earth."
> Psalms 125:5b; 128:6b "Peace be on Israel."
> Psalm 128:1 "Blessed are all who fear the LORD, who walk in his ways."
> Psalm 128:5 "May the LORD bless you from Zion all the days of your life."
> Psalm 131:3 "Israel, put your hope in the Lord both now and forevermore."
> Psalm 132:9 "May your priests be clothed with righteousness; may your saints sing for joy."
> Psalm 134:3 "May the Lord, the Maker of heaven and earth, bless you from Zion."

This structure of the Psalms of Ascents must have been particularly meaningful to the nascent pilgrim headed to Jerusalem for the first time.[20]

In Psalm 120, the song writer is in distress because he dwells in Meshech

---

20. See Leslie C. Allen, *Psalms 101–150,* rev. ed. WBC 21 (Dallas: Word, 2002), p. 194, for a background in a pilgrim feast as well as other suggestions.

and lives among the tents of Kedar (120:5).[21] As Leslie C. Allen explains, "The particular relevance for the psalm's eventual incorporation into a manual of processional songs for pilgrims seems to lie in a reinterpretation of v 5. It became a vehicle for the homesickness of devout expatriate Jews. Their place of residence in various parts of the Diaspora was no home away from home."[22] Psalm 121 follows with a journey through the mountains where the path is so treacherous that one's foot can easily slip resulting in a dangerous fall (121:3). However, the Lord is pictured as the traveling protector who watches over Israel night and day (121:4). Finally, in 122:1-2 the community rejoices, because now "our feet are standing in your gates, O Jerusalem." In the temple the people "praise the name of the Lord" (122:4) and "pray for the peace of Jerusalem" (122:6-8). The peace and security experienced in Jerusalem (122:7) stand dramatically opposed to life away from the temple where the devotee lives among those who hate peace (120:6). Therefore, a series of psalms that were recited at a pilgrim feast are even structured by a pilgrim journey. The structure provides a meaningful arrangement of relevant content for a yearly event in the history of Israel. Structure supples meaning to God's people.

B. Grammatical and Literary Structure

PROCEDURE

Now we turn from macrostructures that organize an entire book or collection to examples of grammatical and literary structures in individual passages. After an analysis of the words, phrases, and clauses in Chapter 2, it is important to read the text as paragraphs. The interpreter must think in terms of paragraphs.[23] A sense unit of the author becomes a paragraph in the text, which becomes an organizing thought of the reader. In paragraph or discourse analysis, the exegete pays attention to the relationship between clauses and sentences. These include the following relationships: sequence,

21. The parallelism of Meshech and Kedar does not presuppose geographical proximity, since Meshech was located in the far north (northeast of Cilicia and east of Cappadocia) while Kedar is associated with the Syro-Arabian desert.

22. Allen, *Psalms 101–150*, p. 199.

23. See Gordon D. Fee and Douglas Stuart, *How to Read the Bible for All Its Worth: A Guide to Understanding the Bible*, 2nd ed. (Grand Rapids: Zondervan, 1993), pp. 54-55.

progression, summary, contrast, particularizing, generalizing, promise, illustration, question/answer, assertion/action, cause/result, and so forth.[24]

Biblical writers construct their paragraphs in a unique manner. For example, James 1 begins each small paraenetic paragraph with an exhortation (1:2, 5, 9, 13, 16, 19, 22) and finishes with his own fitting conclusion or explanation (1:4, 7-8, 11b, 14-15, 25). Between this material James employs previously known teaching material (1:3, 6a), religious aphorisms (1:13b, 20), illustrations from nature (1:6b) and everyday experience (1:23-24), OT language (1:10b-11a), and allusions to sayings of Jesus (1:5b).[25] Paul in Romans, on the other hand, develops extensive arguments and the use of diatribe. A helpful tool for the study of discourse analysis within the Greek and English New Testament are the two volumes by Steven Runge which are an add-on in Logos Bible Software, *The Lexham Discourse Greek New Testament,* and *The Lexham High Definition New Testament ESV Edition.*[26]

In addition to analyzing the flow of the paragraph, it is crucial to evaluate what holds the paragraph together. Here the exegete pays special attention to repetitions, series of arguments, catchwords, questions and answers, and conclusions that are drawn from a series of examples. To identify the conclusion, markers like "therefore" or "finally" are normally employed (or in the Greek, οὖν, διό, ὥστε, ἄρα). A Bible Search in Logos Bible Software will bring up all the occurrences of the word "therefore" in an English Bible. In order to ascertain which Hebrew and Greek words are employed, you can right click on any of the references to "therefore" and choose "Bible Word Study," which will produce diagrams charting the words in the original languages with color coding indicating the more common words employed. If you click on any of the Hebrew or Greek words, Logos Bible Software will compose a complete list of examples.

24. See George H. Guthrie, "Discourse Analysis," in *Interpreting the New Testament: Essays on Methods and Issues,* ed. David Alan Black and David S. Dockery (Nashville: Broadman & Holman, 2001), p. 267.

25. See Dean B. Deppe, *The Sayings of Jesus in the Epistle of James* (Chelsea, MI: Bookcrafters, 1989), p. 60.

26. Steven Runge, *The Lexham Discourse Greek New Testament* (Bellingham: Logos Research Systems, 2008); Steven Runge, *The Lexham High Definition New Testament ESV Edition* (Bellingham: Logos Research Systems, 2008). For an explanation of all the linguistic devices which Runge has annotated, see *The Lexham Discourse Greek New Testament: Glossary* and *The Lexham High Definition New Testament: Introduction,* additional resources in Logos Bible Software. For a more detailed study, see Runge's *A Discourse Grammar of the Greek New Testament: A Practical Introduction for Teaching and Exegesis,* a 2010 product of Logos Bible Software.

In the following section we will demonstrate how repetitions, exegetical arguments, and rhetorical devices tie together biblical paragraphs.

EXAMPLES

1. 1 Peter 1:3-12: Future, Present, and Past Salvation

Repetitions frequently create a structural flow to a paragraph. 1 Peter rotates between kerygmatic and hortatory sections.[27] The first kerygmatic section consists of 1 Pet 1:3-12, where the theme of salvation binds the paragraph together. The term σωτηρία occurs in 1:5, 9, 10, but with a different emphasis in each. Peter begins rejoicing in the future salvation (1:3-5) that will be revealed in the last times (ἀποκαλυφθῆναι, 1:5), then celebrates the present salvation (1:6-9) that is revealed in Jesus Christ (ἀποκαλύψει, 1:7), and concludes by delighting in the past salvation that the OT prophets proclaimed as a previous revelation (ἀπεκαλύφθη, 1:12). Repetition ties this section together.

In the first section, notice that God has given us new birth into (εἰς) a threefold future reality: (1) a living hope (1:3); (2) a heavenly-kept inheritance (1:4); and (3) a ready-to-be-revealed salvation (1:5). In the middle section, observe the double use of ἄρτι ("now," 1:6, 8), so that the readers are rejoicing now even though they are presently experiencing various trials as well. In the final section, Peter clarifies that the prophets already testified to this twofold experience of trials and joy since they "predicted the sufferings of Christ and the glories that would follow" (1:11). Therefore, this repetition of terms both divides the paragraph into three sections but also binds it together with the theme of salvation.

2. Luke 3:21-22; 4:18-19; Acts 9:15-17; Luke 1–2: Lukan Call Narratives

The repetition of distinctive elements in various calls to mission bind together a group of passages in Lukan literature. We will discover that a Lukan call narrative consists of four elements: (1) the entrance of a divine epiphany; (2) empowerment with the Spirit; (3) endowment with self-consciousness; and (4) an explanation of mission.

27. See below Chapter 4, A1, "Kerygmatic and Hortatory Sections in the Epistles" (pp. 132-33).

Jesus' baptism functions as his call to ministry. Before this time, Jesus is a disciple of John the Baptizer in the wilderness, but afterwards he moves to Galilee and begins his ministry of healing and teaching. An inspection of the baptism of Jesus narrative in Luke 3:21-22 reveals a grammatical structure of three impersonal infinitives following the main verb Ἐγένετο ("It happened"). After Jesus is baptized (aorist participle βαπτισθέντος) but while he is praying (present participle προσευχομένου), three events occur:

1. heaven is opened (ἀνεῳχθῆναι τὸν οὐρανὸν);
2. the Holy Spirit descends (καταβῆναι τὸ πνεῦμα τὸ ἅγιον); and
3. a voice from heaven confirms to Jesus his messianic identity (φωνὴν ἐξ οὐρανοῦ γενέσθαι) and explains his mission agenda.

Whereas Mark evidences a simple structure of three sentences (Mark 1:9-11) relating what Jesus did, what Jesus saw, and what Jesus heard, Luke constructs this infinitive triplicate to divulge the three elements integral to the call of Jesus.[28] God is initiating the new age of the kingdom; the heavens are opened. Second, God is pouring out his divine power; the Holy Spirit descends. Third, a particular person is endowed with a special identity or self-consciousness. In this case, a voice from heaven confirms to Jesus his identity as God's beloved Son.

If you employ the Passage Guide in Logos Bible Software for Luke 3:21-22, the Mackie Literary Genre Coding categorizes this passage as an Identity Narrative. A call narrative always alters someone's identity. This divine gift of self-consciousness includes an explanation of mission that frequently becomes a fourth element in a call narrative. The voice from heaven, "This is my beloved Son in whom I am well pleased," combines Ps 2:7 (a messianic psalm) and Isa 42:1 (the first of four Suffering Servant songs). As a result, Jesus' mission involves the calling to be a suffering servant Messiah. The messianic task will not primarily involve political rule or economic provision or miraculous works as the devil shortly will tempt Jesus to perform (Luke 4:1-13), but instead suffering and death. This repetition of elements in a call narrative structures the Lukan paragraph and can offer an outline for the modern preacher or Bible study leader as well.

This analysis of Luke 3:21-22 enables the reader to discern these standard elements in other call narratives in Lukan literature. Jesus' first sermon in

---

28. For an evaluation of the individual emphases of the Gospel writers, see below Chapter 4, B1, "The Baptism of Jesus Narrative in All Four Gospels" (pp. 141-44).

Luke 4:18-19, which recalls and fulfills Isaiah 61, contains all four of these elements as well. Now Jesus is revealing his calling to the public. The entrance of a new dimension of the kingdom has begun, since the Year of Jubilee has arrived (4:19); the Spirit of the Lord is upon Jesus in power (4:18a); Jesus recognizes his identity as the anointed one (4:18b); and his mission is to preach good news to the poor and to set free the blind and oppressed (4:18c) in order to inaugurate the year of the Lord's favor. These four elements structure Jesus' first public sermon.

Luke's hero, Paul, likewise experiences a call narrative that imitates the elements in the call of Jesus.[29] In Paul's conversion and call to ministry in Acts 9:15-17, the Damascus road encounter initiates a new revelation of the kingdom where the heavens are opened (9:3-6), followed by an empowerment by the Spirit (9:17), an endowment with self-consciousness (9:15a), and an explanation of Paul's mission (9:15b-16). The time of the Gentiles has now arrived, and God calls the apostle to the Gentiles. The Holy Spirit falls upon Paul in a powerful manner whereby his blind eyes are miraculously opened and his confusion removed. Through Ananias, Paul's new identity and the content of his mission are revealed: "This man is my chosen instrument to carry my name before the Gentiles and their kings and before the people of Israel. I will show him how much he must suffer for my name." Paul's call to ministry structures the remaining chapters of the book of Acts. The central section of Acts describes Paul proclaiming the name of Jesus to the Gentiles through his missionary journeys. The last third of Acts then portrays Paul's suffering through his various trials. These four elements of a Lukan call narrative provide the flow for Paul's conversion and even affect the larger structure of the book of Acts.

Finally, the birth narratives in Luke also exhibit these same structural characteristics. The following four outlines demonstrate how Luke structures the call of John the Baptizer through revelations to his father, Zechariah, and how Jesus' mission and message are revealed to Mary, his mother, as well as the devout temple-dweller, Simeon.

A. The Angel's Epiphany to Zechariah about John the Baptizer (Luke 1:11-17)

   1. Entrance of a divine epiphany: the appearance of the angel of the Lord in the temple to Zechariah (Luke 1:11).

---

29. See above in A4, "The Purpose of the Parallel Flow of Material in Luke-Acts: Lukan Symmetry" (pp. 94-100), how Luke structures the Gospel and the Acts of the Apostles similarly.

2. Empowerment with the Spirit: "And he will be filled with the Holy Spirit even before he is born" (Luke 1:15b).

3. Endowment with self-consciousness: "He will be great in the sight of the Lord. He is never to take wine or other fermented drink" (Luke 1:15a) means that he will be a Nazarite (Num 6:4-5).

4. Explanation of mission: "And he will go on before the Lord, in the spirit and power of Elijah, to turn the hearts of the parents to their children and the disobedient to the wisdom of the righteous — to make ready a people prepared for the Lord" (Luke 1:17).

B. The Epiphany of Zechariah about John the Baptizer (Luke 1:67, 76)

1. Entrance of a divine epiphany: the prophecy of Zechariah (Luke 1:67).

2. Empowerment with the Spirit: "Zechariah was filled with the Holy Spirit and prophesied" (Luke 1:67).

3. Endowment with self-consciousness: "And you, my child, will be called a prophet of the Most High" (Luke 1:76a).

4. Explanation of mission: "for you will go on before the Lord to prepare the way for him" (Luke 1:76b).

C. The Epiphany to Mary about Jesus (Luke 1:26-38)

1. Entrance of a divine epiphany: the appearance of the angel Gabriel (Luke 1:26).

2. Empowerment with the Spirit: "The Holy Spirit will come upon you, and the power of the Most High will overshadow you" (Luke 1:35).

3. Endowment with self-consciousness: "He will be great and will be called the Son of the Most High" (Luke 1:32).

4. Explanation of mission: "The Lord God will give him the throne of his father David, and he will reign over the house of Jacob forever" (Luke 1:32-33).

D. The Confirming Praise of Simeon regarding Jesus (Luke 2:25-35)

1. Entrance of a divine epiphany: the divine message of the holy ones, Simeon and Anna, in the temple (the prophecies in Luke 2:34-35, 36, 38).

2. Empowerment with the Spirit: "The Holy Spirit was upon him" (Luke 2:25).
   "It had been revealed to him by the Holy Spirit" (Luke 2:26).
   "Moved by the Spirit, he went into the temple courts" (Luke 2:27).

3. Endowment with self-consciousness: "a light for revelation to the Gentiles and the glory of your people Israel" (Luke 2:32).

4. Explanation of mission: "This child is destined to cause the falling and rising of many in Israel and to be a sign that will be spoken against" (Luke 2:34).

The repetition of four elements in a Lukan call narrative enables the reader to discern a pattern in the narratives that can be used to structure Bible studies and sermons on the books of Luke-Acts.

3. Romans 5:1-11: Paul's Glorying and Qal Wahomer arguments

The paragraphs in Romans 1–8 are structured by exegetical arguments. The rabbis at the time of Jesus such as Hillel distinguished seven exegetical principles called *Middoth*.[30] These include (1) *Qal Wahomer* (a fortiori argument from light to heavy, expressing "how much more"); (2) analogy *(Gezerah Shawah)*; (3) a standard conclusion based on one passage *(Binyan 'ab mikathub 'ehad)*; (4) a standard conclusion based on two passages *(Binyan 'ab mishene kethubim)*; (5) general and particular *(Kelal upherat, upherat ukelal)*; (6) analogy with another passage *(Kayoze' bo bemaqom 'aher)*; and (7) proof from the context *(Dabar halamed me'inyano)*.[31] A concentration of fortiori arguments dominates Romans 5 so that the conclusions in this chapter evidence a greater logical flow than the already accepted facts previously given in Romans.

The dominant structural element in Rom 5:1-11 is the repetition of the

---

30. Tosephta, *Sanh.* 7:11 records seven that Hillel commended to the elders at Petherah.

31. See Richard N. Longenecker, *Biblical Exegesis in the Apostolic Period* (Grand Rapids: Eerdmans, 1975), pp. 33-38, for a compact explanation.

verb καυχάομαι ("to boast"). First Paul takes pride in and boasts about the future hope of the glory of God in 5:2 (<u>καυχώμεθα</u> ἐπ' ἐλπίδι τῆς δόξης τοῦ θεοῦ). Then he glories in tribulations in 5:3a (οὐ μόνον δέ, ἀλλὰ καὶ <u>καυχώμεθα</u> ἐν ταῖς θλίψεσιν). Paul supports such boasting, not only because of the benefits to our character (5:3b-5), but also because of how much greater our life in Christ will be in the eternal future. Here Paul climaxes the paragraph with *Qal Wahomer* arguments (5:9-10). If we think being declared righteous now is great, how much better (πολλῷ οὖν μᾶλλον, 5:9) will be the experience of complete salvation in the future! If while we were enemies of God, Christ still died for us, how much more (πολλῷ μᾶλλον, 5:10) abundant life will we experience now that we have become God's friends! The exegetical device of *Qal Wahomer* solidifies Paul's arguments.

Then in 5:11 we encounter the third use of Paul's boasting formula (καυχώμενοι), this time concerning the present riches that we have in Christ. Now we have received reconciliation! Again this glorying is undergirded by *Qal Wahomer* arguments in 5:15-21. How much greater (πολλῷ μᾶλλον, 5:15) are the gift and grace of God than our trespasses! If death reigned through Adam, how much more (πολλῷ μᾶλλον, 5:17) will righteousness reign through Christ! These a fortiori arguments lead to an unmistakable conclusion as evidenced by two successive "therefore" words (Ἄρα οὖν) at the beginning of 5:18: "Consequently, just as the result of one trespass was condemnation for all men, so also the result of one act of righteousness was justification that brings life for all men." This conclusion is placed in the comparison/contrast format as evidence by the ὥσπερ γὰρ . . . οὕτως καὶ ("for just as . . . so also") sequence in triplicate (5:18, 19, 21). Just as the result of one trespass was condemnation, so also the result of one act of righteousness is justification. Just as through the disobedience of the one man many were made sinners, so also through the obedience of one man many are made righteous. Just as sin reigned in death, so also grace reigns for eternity through Jesus Christ our Lord. The repetition of exegetical arguments structures the pericope.

From this elucidation of discourse analysis in Romans 5, one can see the importance of searching the phrase πολλῷ μᾶλλον ("how much more") in discerning the presence of a fortiori arguments. In the reading of paragraphs, certain pat phrases frequently reveal the presence of conclusions, comparisons, progressive sequences, and illustrations. Finally, the importance of discerning repetitions cannot be underestimated. Thus, in Romans 5 we have witnessed how Paul's boasting first about future glories, then about the results of tribulation, and finally about the present riches experienced in Jesus Christ binds this paragraph together.

4. Greco-Roman Rhetorical Training and New Testament Structures

Some New Testament theologians contend that biblical writers like Paul organized their material according to the oratory skills that they learned in their Greco-Roman rhetorical training.[32] Rhetorical analysis organizes speeches and documents into four to six major sections.[33] Like an effective introduction, the *Exordium* establishes rapport between the speaker and the audience, creates interest in the upcoming content, and frequently foreshadows the impending subject matter. The *Narratio* then states the proposition to be argued with appropriate background information and rationale. The *Partitio* was added later as a separate unit to enumerate the opponent's arguments. The *Probatio* is central to the speech, since it presents the important arguments backed up by quotations from supportive authorities and effective examples. Some of the rhetorical handbooks attach here a section entitled the *Refutatio* to counter each argument earlier elicited by the opponents. Finally, the *Peroratio* summarizes the major points and educes a final appeal to the audience's reasoning abilities or to arouse their supportive emotions.

Benoît Standaert discerns this rhetorical structure in the Gospel of Mark:[34]

A. Mark 1:1-13 *Exordium* (*prooemium;* introduction)
B. Mark 1:14–6:13 *Narratio* (*prosthesis*)
C. Mark 6:14–10:52 *Probatio* (*pistis* or *confirmation*)
D. Mark 11:1–15:47 *Refutatio*
E. Mark 16:1-8 *Peroratio* (*epilogos* or *conclusion*)

However, the Gospel of Mark is dominated by a Jewish background, not Greco-Roman rhetoric. Furthermore, the miracle section of Mark 4:35–8:21 is broken up by Standaert, and the discipleship catechism (Mark 8:22–10:52) no longer

32. See Thomas H. Olbricht, "An Aristotelian Rhetorical Analysis of 1 Thessalonians," in *Greeks, Romans, and Christians: Essays in Honor of Abraham J. Malherbe,* ed. David L. Balch, Everett Ferguson, and Wayne A. Meeks (Minneapolis: Fortress, 1990), p. 221; Richard N. Longenecker, *Galatians.* WBC 41 (Dallas: Word, 1990), pp. 112-13.

33. See Appendix 1, ID2 (pp. 324-27), for a morphology of this material. For a compact description of these sections, see Jeffrey A. D. Weima, "What Does Aristotle Have to Do with Paul?" *CTJ* 32 (1997): 460-61.

34. Benoît Standaert, *L'Evangile selon Marc: Composition et genre littéraire* (Zevenkerken-Brugge: Stichting Studentenpers Nijmegen, 1978), pp. 27-29, 51.

stands central to the structure.[35] Finally, as Adela Yarbro Collins maintains, "The main problem with this approach is that 6:14–10:52 is still narration, even if it has more strongly didactic character than the preceding material."[36]

Similarly, the letters of Paul demand epistolary analysis rather than a background in these rules for oral discourse. Paul, in fact, acknowledges that he is unskilled in speaking (2 Cor 11:6), since many witnessed his unprofessional public presentations (10:10). As Bruce Winter concludes, Paul "renounced the use of oratory in preaching as inappropriate, for it was designed to draw attention to the messenger and his rhetorical abilities, and not the content of his message."[37] Therefore, for most of the writers of the New Testament a background in oratory training cannot be assumed.

The only New Testament writer that betrays undeniable influence from the classic rhetoricians is Luke. As a trained physician he undoubtedly received an excellent Hellenistic education. Ben Witherington discovers rhetorical arguments in the speeches of the book of Acts. Specifically, Paul's sermon in the Hellenistic synagogue at Pisidian Antioch (Acts 13:14-41) contains persuasive speech including, according to Witherington, (1) an *exordium* (13:16), (2) a *narratio* (13:17-25), (3) a *propositio* (13:26), (4) a *probatio* (13:27-37) using proofs from the senses (13:30-31), the law, and other recognized written authorities (13:27, 29, 33-35) as well as evidence where there is general agreement (13:32-33, 37) and things admitted by all parties (13:28, 29, 36), and finally (5) a *peroratio* or final exhortation (13:38-41).[38] However, these conclusions can be disputed, since Paul's speech is a Jewish sermon that rehearses the history of salvation and centers upon the kerygma of Jesus' death and resurrection like the other sermons in Acts (2:14-40; 3:12-26; 7:2-53; 10:34-43).

More convincing are the speeches at 17:16-31 to the Areopagus in Athens and Paul's apology before King Agrippa in chapter 26. Witherington discovers the following division of material:

1. *Exordium* (17:22-23a; 26:2-3);
2. *Narratio* (26:4-21 with a *propositio* at 26:22-23 and 17:23b);[39]

---

35. For additional criticisms of Standaert, see Ernest Best, *Mark: The Gospel as Story* (Edinburgh: T. & T. Clark, 1983), pp. 103-4.

36. *Mark.* Hermeneia (Minneapolis: Fortress, 2007), p. 90.

37. Bruce Winter, "Is Paul among the Sophists?" *RTR* 53 (1994): 35, quoted in Weima, *CTJ* 32 (1997): 466.

38. Ben Witherington III, *The Acts of the Apostles: A Socio-Rhetorical Commentary* (Grand Rapids: Eerdmans and Carlisle: Paternoster, 1998), p. 407.

39. The absence of a *narratio* in Acts 17 is explained by Witherington, *Acts,* p. 518, as a re-

4. *Probatio* (17:24-29; 26:25-26 includes a *refutatio* and a digression with added information); and

5. *Peroratio* (17:30-31; 26:27-29).[40]

Therefore, it is possible that rhetorical arguments structure some of the speeches in Acts, but the influence of Greco-Roman rhetorical education is very limited in the New Testament literature.

C. Clausal Outlines

PROCEDURE

Greek clausal outlines are invaluable in the diagnosis of the structure of paragraphs within a biblical book. Frequently, English translations transform participles into main verbs and confuse the syntactical relationships within a pericope. Clausal outlines clarify matters of coordination and subordination. To discover how to construct a Greek clausal outline, read the introduction to the *Lexham Clausal Outlines of the New Testament* in Logos Bible Software.

EXAMPLES

1. Ephesians 3:14-19: Three ἵνα Clauses

While performing a clausal analysis of Paul's prayer in Eph 3:14-21, the attentive reader discovers a repetition of three ἵνα (purpose) clauses. If these stand as a progression, then this passage illustrates three purposes for prayer. First, Paul bows his knees in order that God may strengthen the reader with power within (3:16). Second, he prays for power to comprehend the riches of God's love (3:18). Finally, Paul intercedes that the Ephesian Christians may be filled with all the fullness of God (3:19). The *Lexham Clausal Outlines* clarify the structure, which consists of one main verb followed by three pur-

---

duplication of vv. 18-19, "namely, the charges that Paul was a dilettante, guilty of sound-byting Greek philosophy, and that he was guilty of offering new teaching, proclaiming foreign deities, and his statement of the facts about his speaking about Jesus and the resurrection."

40. Witherington, *Acts*, pp. 518, 737-38.

pose clauses. Two infinitives follow each of the first two ἵνα clauses to explicate their meaning, but the last ἵνα clause stands climactically alone.

main verb	¹⁴Τούτου χάριν For this reason	κάμπτω I kneel	τὰ γόνατά μου πρὸς τὸν πατέρα, before the Father,
rel clause		¹⁵ἐξ οὗ πᾶσα πατριὰ ἐν οὐρανοῖς καὶ ἐπὶ γῆς ὀνομάζεται, from whom his whole family in heaven and earth derives its name	
1st purpose	¹⁶ἵνα δῷ (I pray)	ὑμῖν κατὰ τὸ πλοῦτος τῆς δόξης αὐτοῦ that out of his glorious riches	
1st comple inf	δυνάμει κραταιωθῆναι he may strengthen you with power	διὰ τοῦ πνεύματος αὐτοῦ through his Spirit εἰς τὸν ἔσω ἄνθρωπον, in your inner being,	
2nd comple inf	¹⁷κατοικῆσαι τὸν Χριστὸν so that Christ may dwell	διὰ τῆς πίστεως through faith ἐν ταῖς καρδίαις ὑμῶν, in your hearts.	
adv ptcs result/means (and I pray)	ἐν ἀγάπη that you in love	ἐρριζωμένοι καὶ τεθεμελιωμένοι, being rooted and established	
2nd purpose	¹⁸ἵνα ἐξισχύσητε may have power		
1st comple inf	καταλαβέσθαι to grasp	σὺν πᾶσιν τοῖς ἁγίοις with all the saints	
indir quest/dir obj	τί τὸ πλάτος how wide	καὶ μῆκος καὶ ὕψος καὶ βάθος, and long and wide and deep	
2nd comple inf	¹⁹γνῶναι τε and to know		
direct object	τὴν ὑπερβάλλουσαν τῆς γνώσεως ἀγάπην τοῦ Χριστοῦ, this love of Christ that surpasses knowledge		
3rd purpose	ἵνα πληρωθῆτε that you may be filled	εἰς πᾶν τὸ πλήρωμα τοῦ θεοῦ. to the measure of all the fullness of God.	

Discerning the structure of the pericope enables the communicator to construct a meaningful and well-organized Bible study or sermon.

Interestingly, Paul has already offered a prayer for the Ephesians in 1:15-23, at its normal location in a letter after the thanksgiving of 1:3-14. Why would Paul offer a second prayer? To answer this question we have to examine the structure of the first prayer. There as well Paul's prayer contains only one main verb: Paul never ceases (οὐ παύομαι) in his offering of thanksgiving and petition (1:16). But this time Paul adds only one ἵνα clause; he prays that God may give the Ephesians a spirit of wisdom and revelation (1:17).[41] Then, by means of having their hearts enlightened (1:18a), three results will occur. They will possess an intimate knowledge of the hope of God's calling, the riches of God's glorious inheritance among the saints, and the unlimited greatness of God's power among those who believe (1:18-19). Here the emphasis stands firmly on God's action and the results of prayer, not upon human need and the Ephesians' petitions expressed to God to meet this need. Therefore, Paul must move to his knees again in chapter 3. There the three ἵνα clauses call attention to the needs of the Ephesian Christians, climaxing in the all-comprehensive petition that they be filled with all the fullness of God. Clarifying the structure through a clausal outline enables the reader to understand the flow of the epistle.

2. Ephesians 5:18-21: The Results of Being Continually Filled with the Spirit

In order to create short compact sentences, English translations frequently change Greek participles into main verbs. This process, however, creates a series of seemingly unconnected sentences where the main thought is difficult to discern. For instance, in Eph 5:18-21 the NIV creates a succession of commands with only 5:20 translated like a participle with an "-ing" ending.

> [18]Do not get drunk on wine, which leads to debauchery.
> Instead, be filled with the Spirit.
> [19]Speak to one another with psalms, hymns and spiritual songs.
> Sing and make music in your heart to the Lord,
>   [20]always giving thanks to God the Father for everything,
>   in the name of our Lord Jesus Christ.
> [21]Submit to one another out of reverence for Christ.

However, in the Greek 5:19-21 in its entirety is composed of adverbial participles that must be connected to some verb in the context. The closest main

---

41. Here the ἵνα clause is not a purpose clause but a subfinal or substantival ἵνα, which changes the structure of the passage. See below under C5, "Two Clausal Outlines of Colossians 1:9-11a."

verb is "be filled with the Spirit" in 5:18, so there must be some relationship between "being filled with the Spirit" and the participles "speaking to one another," "singing and making music," "always giving thanks," and "submitting to one another." The most likely adverbial idea connecting the context is that of result. As a result of being continually filled with the Spirit,[42] Christians express their joy with songs of praise and thanksgiving as well as displaying a submissive spirit.

To catch this idea of "result," the ISV translates these verses with the word "then" and the future tense.

> [19]Then you will recite to one another psalms, hymns, and spiritual
>   songs.
> You will sing and make music to the Lord with your hearts.
> [20]You will always give thanks to God the Father for everything
>   in the name of our Lord Jesus Christ.
> [21]And you will submit yourselves to one another out of reverence for
>   Christ.

The diagnosis of these clauses clarifies a clear structure in the passage. The continual filling of the Holy Spirit will result in four experiential manifestations: (1) the upbuilding of one another with songs of praise; (2) uplifting anthems and music; (3) thankful speech in every circumstance; and (4) mutual submission. A clausal outline unveils structural connections not visible in some English translations.

3. Hebrews 12:1-2: Discovering the Main Verb

If the reader attempts to create a clausal outline of a passage from the English text, a variety of possibilities frequently result. Contemporary translation policies aim at shorter sentences, so that dependent participles are treated as main verbs. For instance, in Heb 12:1-2 the NIV contains three main imperatives, the ESV two commands, and the ISV only one imperative. Which is correct? How many main points is the passage emphasizing? Observe the English clausal outlines below:

---

42. See above, Chapter 2, D9, "Prohibitions: John 20:17 and Ephesians 5:18" (pp. 69-70), for the significance of the present tense.

New International Version

¹Therefore, since we are surrounded by such a great cloud of witnesses,
1st imper   let us throw off everything that hinders and the sin that so easily entangles,
2nd imper   and let us run with perseverance the race marked out for us.

New International Version

3rd imper   ²Let us fix our eyes on Jesus, the author and perfecter of our faith,
                        who for the joy set before him endured the cross,
                                        scorning its shame,
                        and sat down at the right hand of the throne of God.

English Standard Version

¹Therefore, since we are surrounded by so great a cloud of witnesses,
1st imper   let us also lay aside every weight, and sin which clings so closely,
2nd imper   and let us run with endurance the race that is set before us,
                        ²looking to Jesus, the founder and perfecter of our faith,
                        who for the joy that was set before him endured the cross,
                                        despising the shame,
                        and is seated at the right hand of the throne of God.

International Standard Version

1st ptc   ¹Therefore, having so vast a cloud of witnesses surrounding us,
2nd ptc   and throwing off everything that hinders us
                        and especially the sin that so easily entangles us,
main imper   let us keep running with endurance the race set before us,
3rd ptc   ²looking off to Jesus, the pioneer and perfecter of the faith
                        who, in view of the joy set before him endured the cross,
                                        despising its shame,
                        and has sat down at the right hand of the throne of God.

The three parallel imperatives in the NIV imply that the author is making three main points: (1) let us throw off; (2) let us run; and (3) let us fix our eyes. The ESV, on the other hand, places less emphasis upon "fixing our eyes" and emphasizes (1) let us lay aside; and (2) let us run. Finally, the ISV translates the text with only one imperative (let us keep running) and three participles (having, throwing off, looking).

This conundrum of translations can only be solved by turning to the Greek Nestle-Aland text. If you construct a visual filter in Logos Bible Software and color code verbs and participles, you discover that only one main verb stands out in Heb 12:1-2a, "let us keep running." Perseverance in running the Christian race is then the prominent point that the passage is emphasizing. Subordinate to the main verb are three participles: (1) a causal ἔχοντες (because we have a cloud of witnesses); (2) a temporal ἀποθέμενοι (after putting off); and (3) a participle of means ἀφορῶντες (by means of looking to Jesus).

The following Greek clausal analysis places the main verb at the left margin with the participles indented one tab and placed underneath each other. This allows for an easy recognition of the flow of the passage.

| adv ptc causal | ¹Τοιγαροῦν καὶ ἡμεῖς τοσοῦτον ἔχοντες |
| | Consequently also we such having |

| adj ptc/dir obj | περικείμενον ἡμῖν νέφος μαρτύρων, |
| | setting around us cloud of witnesses |

| adv ptc temp | ὄγκον ἀποθέμενοι πάντα καὶ τὴν εὐπερίστατον ἁμαρτίαν, |
| | weight putting off every and the ensnaring sin |

| hort subjun | δι᾽ ὑπομονῆς τρέχωμεν |
| | through endurance let us run |

| adj ptc/dir obj | τὸν προκείμενον ἡμῖν ἀγῶνα |
| | the lying before us race |

| adv ptc means | ²ἀφορῶντες εἰς τὸν τῆς πίστεως ἀρχηγὸν καὶ τελειωτὴν |
| | looking unto the of faith beginner and finisher |

| appositive | Ἰησοῦν, |
| | Jesus |

| rel clause | ὃς ἀντὶ τῆς προκειμένης αὐτῷ χαρᾶς |
| | who in place of the lying before him joy |

| 1st verb rel clause | ὑπέμεινεν σταυρὸν |
| | endured cross |

| adv ptc means | αἰσχύνης καταφρονήσας |
| | shame despising |

| 2nd verb rel clause | ἐν δεξιᾷ τε τοῦ θρόνου τοῦ θεοῦ κεκάθικεν. |
| | at the right hand and of the throne of God sat down |

This clausal outline can easily turn into an outline for a Bible study or homily where the main verb of the structural outline becomes the prominent point of the message. In summary, Heb 12:1-2 has one main verb (τρέχωμεν, "let us run"), a hortatory subjunctive. There are three adverbial participles, one causal, one temporal, and one means. Therefore, the author is concentrating on one point: let us run with perseverance. Three subpoints undergird this theme: the reason that we can run with perseverance is the cloud of witnesses (ἔχοντες); the precedent for running is the laying aside (ἀποθέμενοι) of everything that hinders, and the means for running is fixing our attention upon Jesus (ἀφορῶντες). David Alan Black suggests the following sermon outline, using the triad of participles as the three points expounding the main theme of perseverance:[43]

Theme: Running the Race of the Christian Life with Perseverance
A. Our Encouragement (having so great a cloud of witnesses);
B. Our Entanglements (laying aside every encumbrance);
C. Our Example (fixing our eyes on Jesus).

When we think of faith, we usually picture the heroes of faith in Hebrews 11 who courageously acted upon the unseen realities of the spiritual world and received a reward. Discourse analysis can be employed effectively to gain insights into Hebrews 11. George Guthrie demonstrates that

> Hebrews 11 has a very high level of cohesiveness due to formal, semantic, and pragmatic relationships. Formally, the author often presents his material in a pattern: the word *pistei* ("by faith"), followed by the name of the exemplar of faith, followed by the action or event by which faith was expressed, and then the positive outcome. Semantically the words are meaningful because of a historical backdrop that is understood — the names "fit together" because they form a tapestry of figures from the Old Testament era. . . . Pragmatically, the examples serve a unified purpose — to challenge the hearers to live by faith.[44]

But the Greek term πίστις has two connotations: faith and faithfulness. Surrounding the call to miraculous faith in Hebrews 11 the reader encounters two passages that underscore faithfulness. Both 10:32-39 and 12:1-3 employ the noun (ὑπομονή, 10:36; 12:1) and verb form (ὑπομένω, 10:32; 12:2-3) of endurance or perseverance. Therefore, this *inclusio* of persevering faithfulness encircles a chapter emphasizing miraculous faith. The definition of faith that the author of Hebrews wants to emphasize here is persevering faith. Only one imperative is emphasized in 12:1-2; one theme should dominate our sermon or Bible study: we run the race with perseverance. Faith demands endurance.

---

43. David Alan Black, *Using New Testament Greek in Ministry: A Practical Guide for Students and Pastors* (Grand Rapids: Baker, 1993), p. 79.
44. Guthrie, "Discourse Analysis," pp. 258-59.

4. Jude 20-21: How Many Commands?

Since it is extremely difficult to determine the main verb from an English translation, I will offer one more example demonstrating the necessity of consulting a Greek Bible for a structural outline. In Jude 20-21, the NRSV employs four commands, the NLT three commands, the New Century Version (NCV) two imperatives, and the TNIV one imperative. Which is correct? Compare the following translations to visualize the confusion.

A. NRSV: 4 commands
   [20] But you, beloved, <u>build</u> yourselves up on your most holy faith;
   <u>pray</u> in the Holy Spirit;
   [21] <u>keep</u> yourselves in the love of God;
   <u>look forward</u> to the mercy of our Lord Jesus Christ that leads to eternal life.

B. NLT: 3 commands (see also NIV)
   [20] But you, dear friends, must <u>build each other up</u> in your most holy faith, <u>pray</u> in the power of the Holy Spirit,
   [21] and <u>await</u> the mercy of our Lord Jesus Christ, who will bring you eternal life. In this way, you will keep yourselves safe in God's love.

C. NCV: 2 commands
   [20] But dear friends, <u>use</u> your most holy faith to build yourselves up, praying in the Holy Spirit.
   [21] <u>Keep</u> yourselves in God's love
   as you wait for the Lord Jesus Christ with his mercy to give you life forever.

D. TNIV: 1 command (see also NET)
   [20] But you, dear friends, by building yourselves up in your most holy faith and praying in the Holy Spirit,
   [21] <u>keep</u> yourselves in God's love
   as you wait for the mercy of our Lord Jesus Christ to bring you to eternal life.

The Epistle of Jude is an apologetic letter against heresy. How must Christians contend for the faith? The various English translations of Jude

20-21 confuse the emphasis for the reader. In reality, only the TNIV directly imitates the Greek. There is only one imperative, τηρήσατε, "keep yourselves in the love of God." As the readers fight heresy, they are exhorted to complete this task in love. In Jude 1 the readers are described as <u>loved</u> (ἠγαπημένοις) by God the Father and <u>kept</u> (τετηρημένοις) by Jesus Christ. Now in Jude 21 they must similarly <u>keep</u> themselves in the <u>love</u> of God (ἑαυτοὺς ἐν ἀγάπῃ θεοῦ τηρήσατε) as they struggle with untruth. This is the central message of the passage, but you must either read Greek or employ an interlinear to clearly visualize this emphasis.

Interestingly, Jude employs three participles in this verse along with the one focal imperative. This diagnosis matches the style of Jude, who repeatedly employs grammatical triplicates to make his point.[45] This literary preference offers additional proof that the one imperative (keep yourselves in the love of God) is the main point with three subsidiary participles undergirding this command. We can keep ourselves in the love of God by means of building ourselves up in faith and by praying in the Holy Spirit as we wait for the mercy of Jesus. Discerning the relationship between clauses produces a structure that enlightens the meaning.

5. *Two Clausal Outlines of Colossians 1:9-11a*

Sometimes choosing between two clausal outlines can be difficult. In Paul's prayer in Col 1:9-11, is he stating various purposes why he is entreating God or is the content of his request prominent? In my clausal outline in Logos Bible Software entitled the *Lexham Clausal Outlines of the Greek New Testament*, I preferred a structure of five purpose statements explaining why Paul is praying, one with a ἵνα clause, the second employing an infinitive of purpose, and the last three as adverbial participles. Then the purposes for Paul's unending supplication would be:

1. in order that the Colossians might be filled with the knowledge of God's will;
2. in order that they walk worthy of the Lord;
3. in order that they bear fruit in every good work;
4. in order that they increase in the knowledge of God; and
5. in order that they be strengthened with all power.

45. See above, Chapter 2, A1, on Jude 22-23 (pp. 39-41).

However, the repetition of "knowledge" in numbers 1 and 4 above makes it unlikely that Paul is constructing a fivefold list of purpose clauses through different grammatical constructions. Unlike what we have seen in Paul's prayer in Eph 3:14-19 where three parallel ἵνα clauses are employed,[46] here the variant grammatical clauses signal a different usage. A less common function of a ἵνα clause is the substantival or subfinal usage that functions like a direct object answering the question "what" rather than "why."[47] Then Paul's prayer would consist of the request that the Colossians know God's will (the ἵνα clause) for the purpose that they walk worthy of the Lord (the infinitive clause), which will take place by means of the Colossians bearing fruit in every good work, increasing in the knowledge of God, and being strengthened with all power (the three adverbial participles). Therefore Paul's central prayer is for the Colossians to be filled with the knowledge of God's will rather than a fivefold list of purposes for praying. This becomes the prominent theme around which a sermon or Bible study would be constructed.

Here are the two possible analyses of the Greek clausal outline, with the correct grammatical choices underlined:

subject	[9]Διὰ τοῦτο καὶ ἡμεῖς, Through this also we	
rel clause	ἀφ᾽ ἧς ἡμέρας ἠκούσαμεν, from which day we heard	
main verb	οὐ παυόμεθα ὑπὲρ ὑμῶν we do not cease on behalf of you	
supple ptc	προσευχόμενοι καὶ αἰτούμενοι, praying and asking	
purpose or <u>substantival</u>	ἵνα πληρωθῆτε τὴν ἐπίγνωσιν τοῦ θελήματος αὐτοῦ in order that you might be filled the knowledge of the will of him	
prep phrase	ἐν πάσῃ σοφίᾳ καὶ συνέσει πνευματικῇ in all wisdom and understanding spiritual	
inf purpose	[10]περιπατῆσαι ἀξίως τοῦ κυρίου εἰς πᾶσαν ἀρεσκείαν, to walk worthy of the Lord in all favor	
1st adv ptc purpose or <u>means</u>	ἐν παντὶ ἔργῳ ἀγαθῷ καρποφοροῦντες in every work good bearing fruit	

---

46. See above, C1 (pp. 115-17).

47. See Daniel B. Wallace, *Greek Grammar Beyond the Basics* (Grand Rapids: Zondervan, 1996), pp. 474-76.

2nd adv ptc	καὶ αὐξανόμενοι	τῇ ἐπιγνώσει τοῦ θεοῦ,
purpose or <u>means</u>	and increasing	in the knowledge of God
3rd adv ptc	¹¹ἐν πάσῃ δυνάμει	δυναμούμενοι.
purpose or <u>means</u>	with all power	being empowered.

To substantiate the correct structure we turn to the parallel prayer in Paul's letter to the Ephesians, which was probably written at the same time during Paul's imprisonment in Rome. Here we encounter the only other place where Paul employs the Greek word παύω, "to cease doing something." Again my initial proposal consisted in a structure of three purpose clauses employing a ἵνα clause, an adverbial participle, and an articular infinitive with εἰς. However, the adverbial participle is placed by Paul in the accusative case and must modify the subject of the following infinitive (accusative of respect), namely ὑμᾶς. Therefore, Paul has not constructed three parallel purpose clauses, but his central request is that God will give the Ephesians a spirit of wisdom and revelation (the ἵνα clause) so that as a result they might know (the infinitive result or purpose clause) the three things that are listed in the indirect questions of verses 18b-19a by means of having the eyes of their hearts enlightened (the adverbial participle). Thus in Eph 1:16-19a we encounter a substantival ἵνα clause as the main request, a result or purpose clause employing an infinitive, and an adverbial participle of means exactly as in Col 1:9-11.

main verb	¹⁶οὐ παύομαι I do not cease		
supple ptc	εὐχαριστῶν giving thanks	ὑπὲρ ὑμῶν on behalf of you	
supple ptc	μνείαν ποιούμενος remembrance making	ἐπὶ τῶν προσευχῶν μου, upon the prayers of me	
substantival or purpose	¹⁷ἵνα that	ὁ θεὸς τοῦ κυρίου ἡμῶν the God of the Lord of us	Ἰησοῦ Χριστοῦ, Jesus Christ
appositive		ὁ πατὴρ τῆς δόξης, the Father of glory	
verb ἵνα	δώη might give	ὑμῖν πνεῦμα σοφίας καὶ ἀποκαλύψεως to you the spirit of wisdom and revelation	
prep phrase		ἐν ἐπιγνώσει αὐτοῦ, in the knowledge of him	

adv ptc <u>means</u> or purpose	¹⁸πεφωτισμένους τοὺς ὀφθαλμοὺς τῆς καρδίας [ὑμῶν] having been enlightened the eyes of the heart of you
art inf purpose	εἰς τὸ εἰδέναι ὑμᾶς in order to know you
1st indir question	τίς ἐστιν ἡ ἐλπὶς τῆς κλήσεως αὐτοῦ, what is the hope of the call of him
2nd indir question	τίς ὁ πλοῦτος τῆς δόξης τῆς κληρονομίας αὐτοῦ ἐν τοῖς ἁγίοις, what (is) the riches of the glory of his inheritance in the saints
3rd indir question	¹⁹καὶ τί τὸ ὑπερβάλλον μέγεθος τῆς δυνάμεως αὐτοῦ and what (is) the exceeding greatness of the power of him

This analysis confirms which clausal outline is correct and directs the reader to the central request, in each case listed through a ἵνα clause. The content of the prayer is similar in both Colossians and Ephesians: to possess the wisdom and knowledge of God. From these examples the attentive reader can clearly see the exegetical and homiletical payoff in discovering the appropriate clausal outline for a biblical passage.

STUDY AND DISCUSSION QUESTIONS

1. Study Psalm 100. Notice that there are seven imperatives and that the middle command receives additional content (דְּעוּ). What is the relationship between the imperatives right before and after this middle statement? What important content does the Psalmist place right at the center of the poem?

2. Identify the threefold chorus (1:6, 12, 14) in the hymnlike passage Eph 1:3-14. Is this a Trinitarian hymn?[48] If so, what are the activities of the Father, Son, and Holy Spirit? In the Greek, Eph 1:3-14 is one sentence. How many sentences do English translations employ? What is the main verb that Paul is emphasizing?

3. The Letter to the Ephesians can be simply structured by the three verbs: sit, walk, stand. Paul instructs this church first to be seated in the heavenly places in Christ and realize their identity (1:20; 2:6), then to walk or live this identity out in everyday life (4:1, 17; 5:2, 8, 15), and finally to stand (6:11, 13, 14) and not surrender any of their gains in the Christian life. What is important about this process for the Christian? Where else does Paul emphasize "standing" at the end of a letter? Perform a Bible Search of the NIV with the word "stand" to discover this information. Psalm 1:1, instead, uses the order "walk, stand, sit." How does that process lead us right into the middle of evil?

4. The central theme of John's first letter is found in 1:5: "This is the message we have heard from him and declare to you: God is light; in him there is no darkness at all." Then John offers various tests for walking in the light in 1 John 2:3–5:12.[49]

    (1) Test of keeping the commandments (2:3-5a).
    (2) Test of walking as Jesus walked (2:5b-8).
    (3) Test of love (2:9-17).
    (4) Test of staying with the church (2:18–3:10).
    (5) Test of loving one another (repeated) (3:11-18).
    (6) Assurance that we are passing the tests (3:19-24).
    (7) Test of discerning the spirit of the antichrist (4:1-6).
    (8) Test of love (repeated for a third time) (4:7-21).

48. Compare this outline with the findings of discourse analysis by Johannes P. Louw, "A Discourse Reading of Ephesians 1.3-14," in *Discourse Analysis and the New Testament: Approaches and Results,* ed. Stanley E. Porter and Jeffrey T. Reed. JSNTSup 170 (Sheffield: Sheffield Academic, 1999), pp. 308-15.

49. For the structure of 1 John 1:6–2:2, see above Chapter 1, A2 (pp. 2-3).

    (9) Summary of tests (5:1-5).

   (10) The final proof of truth is the testimony of God (not our passing the tests) (5:6-12).

What is "walking in the light"? Why is the test of love mentioned on more than one occasion? Reflect upon how you are doing in these tests. If we pass the tests, what five certainties can we experience in 1 John 5:13-20? Notice the verb "we know" (οἴδαμεν).

5. The body of the book of Jude in between the letter opening and the doxology appears to be structured by an a-b-b-a chiasm.[50]

    A 3   The general appeal: believers must contend for the faith.

    B 4   The general reason for the appeal: the danger of false teachers.

    B′ 5-19 The specific reason for the appeal: the judgment of the false teachers.

    A′ 20-23 The specific appeal: exhortations revealing how to contend for the faith.

How does the second A section complete the first A section? How does the second B section solve the dangers illustrated in the first B section? Frequently Christians suppose that contending for the faith means critically denouncing opponents. What positive exhortations does Jude conclude with instead?[51]

6. The book of Hebrews is commonly structured as five homilies before a final chapter of general exhortations. To exalt the majesty and preeminence of Christ, the author proclaims

    a. Christ's superiority to angels (1:1–2:18).

    b. Christ, superior to Moses and Joshua (3:1–4:13).

    c. Christ, superior to the Aaronic priesthood (4:14–7:28).

    d. Christ, the mediator of a better covenant (8:1–10:31).

    e. The superiority of true faith and faithfulness (10:32–12:29).

---

50. For negative evaluations of extended chiasms that supposedly cover entire biblical books, see Appendix II, B (pp. 354-60). However, Jude is short enough for a chiasm to be remembered and thus effective.

51. For preaching ideas, see Richard J. Bauckham, *2 Peter and Jude.* WBC 50 (Waco: Word, 1983), p. 32; and Andrew J. Bandstra, "Onward Christian Soldiers — Praying in Love with Mercy: Preaching on the Epistle of Jude," *CTJ* 32 (1997): 136-39.

If these are sermons, what texts does the author reflect upon in 1:5-14; 3:7-11; 5:1-10; 8:1-13; and 10:37-38? How do these sermons describe the relationship between the Old and New Testaments? What exhortations are given to believers in each sermon? See Heb 2:1-4; 3:12–4:13; 4:14-16 and 5:11–6:12; 10:19-31; and 12:1-29.

7. The NIV at Mark 5:25-27 possesses six main verbs. However, the Greek only emphasizes one main verb. Check an interlinear or the Lexham Clausal Outline in Logos Bible Software and identify the main verb. This same verb is also repeated in 5:28, 30, 31 and so must be central to the meaning of the text. In the Markan sandwich, Jesus also grabs the hand of a dead girl (5:41). What happens according to the Old Testament when a person makes contact with a bleeding woman or a corpse (Lev 15:19-33; Num 19:11-22)? How does Jesus fulfill these passages? How would this relate to Mark's statement that the new wine must be placed into new wineskins (Mark 2:22)?

8. Determining the outline of a passage can aid in the structure of a Bible study or sermon. Adverbial clauses are extremely helpful for sermonic purposes, since they can serve as subpoints in a sermon or Bible study. Read Isa 9:1-6 and Isa 55:6-13 and locate the three *kī* (כִּי) clauses found as the first word in Isa 9:3, 4, and 5 and 55:8, 10, and 12. Use this information to construct an outline of the passages for a Christmas sermon on Isaiah 9 and a call to conversion sermon from Isaiah 55 for those who need to know God's abundant pardon.

9. The book of Genesis can be structured by what is called in Hebrew the *Toledoth* or in English "generations." Notice Gen 2:4: "These are the generations of the heavens and the earth." In Logos Bible Software, search the word "generations" or "Toledoth" in the Hebrew text to discover where this phrase is employed at strategic places in Genesis. What does this say about how God works with his people?

10. Notice in the prophecies against the nations in Amos 1–2 how the seer condemns the countries to the north (1:3-5), the west (1:6-10), the east (1:11–2:3), and the south (2:4-5). What are these countries? What nation does the prophet conclude with in 2:6-16? Certainly they must have thought that they were the righteous ones as God circled them with the fire of his anger. How are we sometimes not able to look at our own sinfulness? What sins do you think are prevalent among the people of God? Notice that Amos concludes his book with renewal in 9:11-15. What does this renewal look like, and how can we apply it to our day?

11. Pay close attention to the three cycles of judgment followed by predictions of future salvation in the Prophecy of Micah (#1: 1:2–2:11; 2:12-13; #2: chs. 3 and 4–5; #3: 6:1–7:7; 7:8-20). What are the elements in God's salvation? Now pay attention to the four punishment and restoration cycles in Isaiah 1–12 (#1: 1:2-31; 2:1-5; #2: 2:6–4:1; 4:2-6; #3: 5:1–8:20; 8:21–9:7; #4: 9:8–10:34; 11:1-16 with a liturgical ending in ch. 12). How is God's salvation described here? Does this pattern demonstrate how God works with his people?

12. For evaluating the benefits of discourse analysis, study what insights George Guthrie gained in understanding Heb 6:17 and Joel Green with regard to Luke 3:1-20 through the use of this method of investigation.[52] How does Andries Snyman apply discourse analysis to Paul's Letter to Philemon?[53] How do Jeffrey Reed, Guthrie, and Moisés Silva apply discourse analysis to Paul's Letter to the Philippians in unique ways?[54] Can discourse analysis provide an outline for 1 John? Compare the findings of Robert Longacre and Birger Olsson.[55] For those interested in discourse analysis of the Old Testament, other works can be consulted.[56]

---

52. Guthrie, "Discourse Analysis," pp. 262-67; and Joel B. Green, "Discourse Analysis and New Testament Interpretation," in *Hearing the New Testament: Strategies for Interpretation* (Grand Rapids: Eerdmans, 1995), pp. 218-39.

53. Andries H. Snyman, "Discourse Analysis: A Semantic Discourse Analysis of the Letter to Philemon," in *Text and Interpretation: New Approaches in the Criticism of the New Testament*, ed. P. J. Hartin and J. H. Petzer. NTTS 15 (Leiden: Brill, 1991), pp. 83-99.

54. Jeffrey T. Reed, *A Discourse Analysis of Philippians: Method and Rhetoric in the Debate over Literary Integrity.* JSNTSup 136 (Sheffield: Sheffield Academic, 1997), ch. 4; George H. Guthrie, "Cohesion Shifts and Stiches in Philippians," in *Discourse Analysis and Other Topics in Biblical Greek,* ed. Stanley E. Porter and D. A. Carson. JSNTSup 113 (Sheffield: Sheffield Academic, 1995), pp. 36-59; and Moisés Silva, "Discourse Analysis and Philippians," in Porter and Carson, *Discourse Analysis and Other Topics,* pp. 102-6.

55. Robert Longacre, "Towards an Exegesis of 1 John Based on the Discourse Analysis of the Greek Text," in *Linguistics and New Testament Interpretation: Essays on Discourse Analysis,* ed. David Alan Black (Nashville: Broadman, 1992), pp. 271-86; and Birger Olsson, "First John: Discourse Analyses and Interpretations," in Porter and Reed, *Discourse Analysis and the New Testament,* pp. 369-91.

56. Cynthia L. Miller, "Discourse Functions of Quotative Frames in Biblical Hebrew Narrative," in *Discourse Analysis of Biblical Literature,* ed. Walter R. Bodine. SBL Semeia Studies (Atlanta: Scholars, 1995), pp. 155-82; Ernst R. Wendland, *The Discourse Analysis of Hebrew Prophetic Literature: Determining the Larger Textual Units of Hosea and Joel* (Lewiston: Mellen, 1995); and Wendland, ed., *Discourse Perspectives on Hebrew Poetry in the Scriptures* (New York: United Bible Societies, 1994).

CHAPTER 4

The Literary Context Route

Using a Wide-Angled Lens

A wide-angled lens stretches the picture in order to provide a broadened scenario of what is happening at the time you take a photo. Similarly, an analysis of the context before and after a particular biblical passage delivers a broadened awareness of the significance of the pericope you are studying. In this chapter we will first examine a series of examples where the context plays an important role in understanding the significance of a biblical text. Then in the second section we will study how authors take an identical event but place the proceedings in different contexts to offer a distinct perspective. Here we will employ redaction criticism to compare the four Gospels and how they handle particular episodes in the life of Jesus.

A. The Context Surrounding the Pericope

PROCEDURE

Context is everything! Exegesis must always analyze a text within contexts: literary, historical, and ideological. In this chapter we will analyze examples where the literary context is of utmost importance. Chapter 5 then considers the historical background as the context for interpretation, while Chapter 6 investigates the role which the history of interpretation plays in broadening the context for the exegete. Finally, Chapter 7 discusses the ideological and theological context from which writers write and interpreters interpret. The author's placement of material and events before and after a particular episode supplies a wide-angled lens to view correctly the significance of a particular scene. Without context, we interpret in a vacuum.

EXAMPLES

1. Kerygmatic and Hortatory Sections in the Epistles

The various contexts of the biblical letters require divergent reading techniques. If you analyze Paul's Epistle to the Romans, you notice that Romans 12 (especially vv. 9-21) is composed of one ethical and relational command after another, whereas Romans 1–8 contains a very tightly organized series of doctrinal themes. You have unveiled a different literary context. To substantiate the disparate mood of Romans 12, you can employ the "Morph River" in Logos Bible Software to discover where the biblical writers employ the majority of imperatives. Under the "Tools" menu and the "Passage Analysis" bar, you will discover the "Morph River" icon at the bottom of the screen. Adjust the data so that you are calculating "Verbs by Mood." Then if you type in Romans 1–11 in the box above, the statistical analysis informs you that 62.7 percent of the verbal forms are indicative, while only 1.8 percent consist of imperatives. If you modify the domain to Romans 12, then the identical 17.5 percent are indicative as well as imperative with the addition of 27 percent imperatival participles. Therefore, commands constitute an amazing 44.5 percent of Romans 12. Likewise, Ephesians 1–3 is comprised of 38.2 percent indicatives and only .8 percent imperatives, whereas Ephesians 4–6 incorporates 19.8 percent imperatives and 11.2 percent participles employed as imperatives. We have discovered that the first part of Romans and Ephesians comprises mostly indicative verbs, whereas a high concentration of imperatives occupies the second part of each epistle. Theologians describe this phenomenon as the imperative based upon the indicative. Doctrine always precedes practice. What we do should be based upon who we are. Our Christian identity found in Romans 1–8 and Ephesians 1–3 determines the way we live and act (Romans 12–15; Ephesians 4–6). We have to become who we already are in Christ.

Now if you construct a "Morph River" of the imperatives in the book of 1 Peter, a distinct pattern is revealed. Instead of the commands at the conclusion of the book, the indicative and imperative rotate throughout the epistle so that a kerygmatic section precedes a hortatory section four times throughout the letter.

First kerygmatic section (1:3-12): Our Full Salvation.

First hortatory section (1:13–2:3): Growing Up into Salvation.

Second kerygmatic section (2:4-10): Christ and the Church; Living Stone and Living Stones.

Second hortatory section (2:11–3:12): A Christian Social Code.

Third kerygmatic section (3:13-22): Christian Suffering Based on Christ's Victory.

Third hortatory section (4:1-11): Christian Duty.

Fourth kerygmatic section (4:12-19): Persecution as Participating in Christ's Suffering.

Fourth hortatory section (5:1-14): Faithful Service from Leaders and Church Members.

The interpretation of the kerygmatic sections will differ from the hortatory portions because of context.

Now you can employ the "Morph River" tool again or add a visual filter to the text to color coat the imperatives in the Letter of James. Notice that they are sprinkled throughout the letter. In fact, the 108 verses of James contain some 54 imperatives, so that the more appropriate title is The Paraenesis of James. James assumes that his audience has already internalized the kerygma of the gospel, which is only discernable at 1:18 ("He chose to give us birth through the word of truth, that we might be a kind of firstfruits of all he created"). The overwhelming majority of James's work concentrates on the imperatives of the Christian life. Therefore, within letters of instruction the reader must establish if the context is one of doctrine or exhortation.

2. ἡγέομαι ("Count") in the Letter to the Philippians

Both the context before and after a particular passage contribute significantly to its interpretation. Suppose you are writing a sermon on Phil 2:3, "in humility count (ἡγούμενοι) others better than yourselves." You could limit your research to the immediate context of 2:1-4, but then you would miss some exciting discoveries on how Paul employs the term ἡγέομαι ("to lead, suppose, count") throughout the letter.

While searching the lemma, you detect that the root is also employed in Phil 2:6 and 3:7-8 (2:25 as well). Whereas 2:3 is an exhortation to members of the church, 2:6 establishes the christological foundation: Jesus "did not consider (ἡγήσατο) equality with God something to be grasped, but made himself nothing, taking the very nature of a servant." The command to count others better than oneself does not stand alone as a human achievement, but is based upon the example of self-sacrifice evident in Jesus himself. Philippians 3:7-8, on the other hand, is a personal testimony by Paul. Just as Jesus, the Son of God, emptied himself, likewise Paul, a human follower, did not grasp for status but counted (ἡγέομαι) any personal righteousness as dung and refuse. These two passages, then, become the grounding for the exhortation to count others better than one's self in 2:3. We have the powerful examples of Jesus and Paul to equip us in this endeavor. The fuller context offers both a christological depth to the sermon and a personal illustration in the life of Paul.

Word study leads the interpreter to contexts still to come, but grammatical connections force the sensitive reader to consider carefully the past verses. The term ἡγούμενοι ("counting") in 2:3 is an independent participle functioning as an imperative in a series of seven commands. The structure is complicated with two imperatives in 2:2 (πληρώσατέ, "make full") and 2:5 (φρονεῖτε, "think") surrounding an imperatival ἵνα clause ("think the same things") and four independent participles (ἔχοντες, φρονοῦντες, ἡγούμενοι, σκοποῦντες in 2b-4) employed as imperatives.[1] These seven commands are then based upon the four conditional clauses of 2:1: "If you have any encouragement from being united with Christ, if any comfort from his love, if any fellowship with the Spirit, if any tenderness and compassion." If these four spiritual realities are true, then the reader can perform these seven commands. The four "if clauses" establish a platform of union with Christ, the bond of his durable love, the fellowship of the Holy Spirit, and the compassion of Christ's character. Based upon this solid foundation, we are able to "count others better than ourselves." The preceding and following contexts of 2:3 supply the soil, the nourishment, and the supporting structure to hold up the tender seedling of 2:3, "but in humility consider others better than yourselves."

3. Psalm 8: Surrounded by Laments

We do not usually think of context when we study the psalms; instead, we treat each psalm individually. But the psalms were collected together and arranged in a certain order, as evidenced by the fact that Book I of the psalms

---

1. See my *Lexham Clausal Outlines of the New Testament* in Logos Bible Software.

consists entirely of Yahweh songs while the divine name Elohim is constantly employed in Book II. The Davidic psalms begin with Psalm 3, and surprisingly the first series of poems are dominated by laments. However, one psalm stands out as strikingly different — Psalm 8. We hear five cries of lament before Psalm 8 and five expressions of grief following Psalm 8.[2] Listen to the repeated chorus at the beginning of these lament psalms:

Psalm 3:1 O LORD, how many are my foes!
Psalm 4:1 Give me relief from my distress.
Psalm 5:1 O LORD, consider my sighing.
Psalm 6:1 O LORD, do not rebuke me in your anger.
Psalm 7:1 Save and deliver me from all who pursue me.
Psalm 9:13 O LORD, see how my enemies persecute me!
Psalm 10:1 Why, O LORD, do you stand far off?
Psalm 11:2-3 For look, the wicked bend their bows. . . . When the foundations are being destroyed, what can the righteous do?
Psalm 12:1 Help, LORD, for the godly are no more.
Psalm 13:1 How long, O LORD?

These desperate cries to God include exclamations of anguish, prayers for relief, pleas for deliverance, questions of bewilderment, and climax in the wail, "How long?"

Notice, however, that Psalm 9 does not begin its lament until the song is half finished. Normally, personal laments begin with a dirge and climax with deliverance and praise, but Psalm 9 strangely reverses this order. Instead, this poem commences with praise and thanksgiving (1-2), a celebration of victory (3-6), an acknowledgement of the reign of God (7-8), a profession of trust (9-10), and a call to praise (11-12). Why this unique ordering of material? Notice as well that the last verse of Psalm 7 is filled with praise: "I will give thanks to the LORD because of his righteousness and will sing praise to the name of the LORD Most High" (7:17). Here we encounter a frame around Psalm 8 that serves to introduce this unique proclamation of the majestic name of God. This frame is reinforced by an *inclusio* surrounding the psalm itself with the repeated chorus, "O LORD, our Lord, how majestic is your name in all the earth!" (8:1, 9). In this vast sea of lament, one psalm protrudes above like a

---

2. See John H. Stek, *The NIV Study Bible Revised* (Grand Rapids: Zondervan, 2002), p. 794. According to Stek, each of the five psalms before and after Psalm 8 have 64 poetic lines.

lighthouse directing the reader home, namely Psalm 8. To prepare for this epiphany the psalmist introduces this change of tone with Ps 7:17 and reverses the normal order of a lament to continue the praise with 9:1-2: "I will praise you, O Lord, with all my heart; I will tell of all your wonders. I will be glad and rejoice in you; I will sing praise to your name, O Most High."

This progression of psalms broadcasts a message about human existence. Life is filled with outward tragedy and defeat as well as inward mourning, bewilderment, and gnawing questions. But in the midst of this distress Psalm 8 stands as a beacon announcing the glory of the Lord. The picture of human beings outside Psalm 8 is depressing. Psalms 9 and 10 conclude by underlining the mortality of human beings: "let the nations know they are but men" (9:20) and the description "man, who is of the earth" (10:18). On the other hand, directly at the center of Psalm 8 is the stunning confession, "Yet you have made them (i.e., human beings) a little lower than God, and crowned them with glory and honor" (NRSV). In the midst of lament and despair Psalm 8 offers a divine perspective on life. All of the verbs of Psalm 8 except for verse 3 promote God as the subject of the sentence. We are called to place our hope and attention upon the majestic name of God, the glory of God and his providence in creation, and in particular upon the true portrait of human beings as exalted image bearers of God himself.

Apparently the context of the psalms can provide important clues to the meaning of the individual pieces of poetry.[3]

4. Psalm 119:176: Confession of Sin or Profession of Loyalty?

The concluding verse of the longest psalm in the Bible states, "I have strayed like a lost sheep. Seek your servant" (Ps 119:176a). At first glance, the psalmist appears to offer a confession of sin and a plea for renewal. Especially if the reader is familiar with Jesus' parables about the Lost Sheep, the Lost Coin, and the Lost Son in Luke 15, the self-evident conclusion seems that the author is placing himself in a negative light as someone wandering from God's commandments. But context is everything! Throughout Psalm 119 the speaker utters confessions of innocence. In 119:11 he proclaims, "I have hidden your word in my heart that I might not sin against you," and in 119:16, "I

---

3. Several writers contend that Psalm 19 is the pivot point in the concentric arrangement of Pss 15-24. See Carl J. Bosma, "Discerning the Voices in the Psalms: A Discussion of Two Problems in Psalmic Interpretation, Part 2," *CTJ* 44 (2009): 159.

delight in your decrees; I will not neglect your word." These professions of loyalty run throughout each acrostic stanza of the psalm. But the persuasive proof lies in the immediate context. The very last phrase of the psalm confesses, "I have not forgotten your commands" (119:176b).

Therefore, the context reveals that the attentive reader must fill the expression "lost sheep" with an alternative meaning. The psalmist has not fallen from God's pathway of righteousness; instead, this expression refers to the outward situation of the psalmist. Enemies have created such a perilous situation for the author that he is like an abandoned sheep without the tender care of the shepherd. He is vulnerable and about to be devoured by the enemy. In the midst of a difficult situation, the psalmist is protesting his innocence and calling attention to his devotion to Yahweh and his love for God's precepts. The interpretation of particular imagery like "a lost sheep" is always controlled by the context.

5. Mark 11:22-23: Casting a Mountain into the Sea

At first sight, Mark 11:22-23 appears to speak about an abundance of faith that is capable to move any obstacle, even a mighty mountain. "Have faith in God," Jesus answered. "I tell you the truth, if anyone says to this mountain, 'Go, throw yourself into the sea,' and does not doubt in his heart but believes that what he says will happen, it will be done for him." Confirmation for this hypothesis seems to come from the close parallel in Matt 17:20 (cf. Matt 21:21 for the context parallel to Mark 11:22-23), "I tell you the truth, if you have faith as small as a mustard seed, you can say to this mountain, 'Move from here to there' and it will move. Nothing will be impossible for you." This passage is placed right between the healing of the demonized boy and the promise of a miracle catch of a fish with the temple tax in its mouth. Certainly Matthew is emphasizing the need for miraculous faith.

However, only the Markan context contains the literary device of an intercalation, commonly entitled a Markan Sandwich. Mark attaches the sayings about faith, prayer, and forgiveness (Mark 11:22-25) to the cursing of the withered fig tree, which serves as a sandwich (11:12-14, 20-21) around the temple action (11:15-19). Just as the fig tree (symbolizing Israelite leadership)[4] is cursed and withers away at its root, so will the temple, the promi-

---

4. The withering fig tree is used in judgment statements against Israel (Isa 28:4; Hos 2:12; 9:10; Joel 1:7; Mic 7:1) and Judah (Jer 5:17; 8:13; 24:1-10; 29:17; Hab 3:17).

nent institution of Judaism, be destroyed. The statement about the mountain cast into the sea immediately follows, so that this knoll must be the temple mount according to Mark. If you have faith, the temple mountain will be destroyed along with the sacrificial system. Instead, worship of God through the practices of faith, prayer, and forgiveness will take its place. Just as the love command replaces sacrifices in 12:33, so the practices of faith, prayer, and forgiveness take the place of the temple ceremonies here. If the exegete pays attention to context, there is a greater theological depth here than just the call for miraculous faith.

6. Omitting the Context in Matthew 18:18 and 1 Corinthians 13:8-12

When Bible readers do not highlight the context, faulty interpretations frequently result. As Michael Gorman explains, "A text without a context is a pretext — an excuse for finding one's presuppositions confirmed by the text."[5] In some ecclesiastical circles Matt 18:18 is employed as a text about appropriating the riches of Christ as well as the blessings of this world: "I tell you the truth, whatever you bind on earth will be bound in heaven, and whatever you loose on earth will be loosed in heaven." Claim this verse and earthly as well as heavenly wealth will be loosed and fall into your lap. But the context is not about binding evil spirits or loosing the riches of this world so that I can enjoy them. This logion of Jesus fits into the fourth sermon of Jesus in Matthew, which centers upon relations within the church that include the topics of church discipline (18:15-17) and the forgiveness of offenses (18:21-35). These themes surround our pericope and therefore require that this passage is directed at leaders of the church with regard to the discipline and admonition of the flock. Sin and forgiveness has a corporate dimension that involves the entire community. Individual Christians cannot name a blessing and then claim it by binding the evil spirits. That interpretation fails to match the context.

Those who believe that the gifts of the Spirit such as speaking in tongues have passed away and are no longer available to the church frequently point to 1 Cor 13:8, 10 as a proof text: "if *there are gifts of* prophecy, they will be done away; if *there are* tongues, they will cease; if *there is* knowledge, it will be done away . . . when the perfect comes, the partial will be done away" (NASB). The advent of "the perfect" is then envisioned as the arrival of the

---

5. Michael J. Gorman, *Elements of Biblical Exegesis: A Basic Guide for Students and Ministers* (Peabody: Hendrickson, 2001), p. 69.

canon of Scripture, so that the gifts of the Spirit are no longer needed or available now that we possess the New Testament.[6] However, the context steers the faithful exegete in a different direction. When will the perfect arrive? 1 Corinthians 13:12 states, "For now we see in a mirror dimly, but then face to face; now I know in part, but then I will know fully just as I also have been fully known." The perfect will materialize when we see face to face, when we understand fully. Therefore, the perfection spoken about must be the eschaton, the new heavens and the new earth. The context explains that the gifts of the Spirit will no longer be needed and thus will pass away when we see Christ face to face at his second coming.[7] But in this present age, we should seek all of Christ's gifts for edification and ministry (1 Cor 14:1).

7. The Contexts of Paul's Conversion Experiences in the Book of Acts

Luke narrates Paul's conversion experience three times in the book of Acts (9:1-19; 22:3-21; 26:4-18), and readers would naturally expect these stories to be identical. But surprisingly, each possesses several unique characteristics. In all three narratives the voice from heaven states, "Saul, Saul, why do you persecute me?" (9:4; 22:7; 26:14), but Acts 26 then adds, "It is hard for you to kick against the goads." On the other hand, only in Acts 9 is Paul's reception of the Holy Spirit narrated. Ananias captures a prominent position in the first two accounts of Paul's conversion experience (9:10-18; 22:12-16) but completely disappears in Acts 26, along with Paul's baptism and healing from blindness. Instead, the emphasis falls upon Paul's opening of the eyes of others (26:18), along with his calling to turn people "from darkness to light, and from the power of Satan to God, so that they may receive forgiveness of sins and a place among those who are sanctified by faith." Finally, in the second speech the sending of Paul to the Gentiles concludes the account (22:21: "Go! I will send you far away to the Gentiles"), whereas in 26:17 Paul's deliverance from the Gentiles is mentioned ("I will rescue you from your own people and from the Gentiles").

What accounts for these discrepancies? Again the answer is context. Acts

---

6. Benjamin B. Warfield, *Counterfeit Miracles* (1918; repr. London: Banner of Truth Trust, 1972), p. 6, reasoned that the function of the charismata was tied up with the apostolic witness and connected with divine revelation so that they necessarily passed away with the apostolic age.

7. See Gene L. Green, "'As for Prophecies, They Will Come to an End': 2 Peter, Paul, and Plutarch on 'The Obsolescence of Oracles,'" *JSNT* 82 (2001): 120.

9 consists of a narrative that relates Paul's conversion in a historical fashion, whereas Acts 22 is an apologetic against the Jews and Acts 26 is Paul's defense before a Roman court and the person of Herod Agrippa II, a Jewish king who possessed a Hellenistic intellectual upbringing in the court of the emperor Claudius. With a different audience in each case, Paul extracts divergent details from his conversion and employs distinctive Greek expressions. Since in Acts 8 and 10 Luke emphasizes the work of the Holy Spirit in the inclusion of Samaritans, God-fearing converts to Judaism, and Gentiles into the kingdom of God,[8] in Acts 9 he would naturally emphasize the work of the Holy Spirit when the heart of the apostle to the Gentiles is transformed. Furthermore, the Holy Spirit was a gift exclusively for Christians, so it would not be an appropriate subject when speaking to Jews or Herod Agrippa. Since in Acts 22 Paul was accused of bringing Gentiles into the temple, he would logically mention that he was brought up according to the strictest manner of all zealous Jews (22:3). Coming from this conservative tradition, his ministry to the Gentiles required a divine revelation, with God speaking to him in the temple, "Depart; for I will send you far away to the Gentiles" (22:21).

The polemical nature of Paul's speech is especially visible in Acts 22 and 26. In 22:12 Ananias is described as possessing a good reputation among the Jews, since Paul is offering his defense within Jewish company. The Jews are pictured as "brethren" (22:5), and Paul's persecution of Christians is cited as an example of Paul's zealousness for God (22:3). However, when Paul speaks to the educated literary audience of Herod Agrippa in chapter 26, he employs distinctive rhetoric and stylistic excellence, including classical expressions and complicated Greek sentences.[9] He specifically recites a Greek proverb, "It is hard for you to kick against the goads" (26:14), which has not been found in Hebrew or Aramaic sources.[10] Certainly Paul's comment is aimed at Herod Agrippa himself, who is almost persuaded to be a Christian (26:27-28) but is still kicking against the goads. Before a Roman court Paul emphasizes his close connection with Judaism, since the Romans would not recog-

---

8. See above Chapter 3, A3, "Conflict in the Early Church and the Structure of the Acts of the Apostles" (pp. 92-94).

9. For the rhetorical style, see Ben Witherington III, *The Acts of the Apostles: A Socio-Rhetorical Commentary* (Grand Rapids: Eerdmans, 1998), p. 737; for the stylistic excellence, see F. F. Bruce, *The Book of the Acts,* rev. ed. NICNT (Grand Rapids: Eerdmans, 1988), p. 461; and Ernst Haenchen, *The Acts of the Apostles* (Philadelphia: Westminster, 1971), p. 691.

10. Euripides, *Bacchae* 794-95; Aeschylus, *Agamemnon* 1642; Terence, *Phormio* 1.2.27. Compare *Pss. Sol.* 16:4 and Philo, *De Decalogo* 87. See Gerhard Lohfink, *The Conversion of St. Paul: Narrative and History in Acts* (Chicago: Franciscan Herald, 1976), p. 78.

nize any new religion as legitimate. Paul's expressions include "our religion" (26:5), "our fathers" (26:6), and our twelve tribes (26:7), meaning both Jews and Christians, and the voice from heaven calling Paul to be a Christian is specifically stating as a voice in the Hebrew dialect (26:14). The context of apologetic is the cause for these transformations. Therefore, when interpreting speeches in the biblical record, the audience in each particular context must always be given due attention.

B. Redactionary Activity

PROCEDURE

So far in this chapter we have elicited examples illustrating the importance of context in interpreting particular passages. Now we will demonstrate how the aims of individual authors affect the interpretation of identical stories. This is especially apparent in the four Gospels, where the evangelists situate an event in the life of Jesus into a specific literary context to highlight their own individual themes. Redaction criticism investigates the author's selection and placement of material to determine the theological and kerymatic purposes of each author. We will use the baptism narrative, Peter's confession of Jesus as well as his denials, the triumphal entry, and the tearing of the temple curtain to demonstrate how the context of the evangelist as well as the original setting in the life of Jesus affect the interpretation of a historical event. The final example will consider how the author of Chronicles redacted the traditions from the books of Samuel and Kings through strategic omissions and his special treatment of the material based upon the context within which he wrote.

EXAMPLES

1. The Baptism of Jesus Narrative in All Four Gospels

Earlier we examined the baptism narrative of Jesus in Luke when following the structural analysis route of exegesis.[11] Now we will evaluate how the various Gospel writers employ this passage for their own purposes. In Libronix

---

11. See above Chapter 3, B2, "Luke 3:21-22; 4:18-19; Acts 9:15-17; Luke 1–2: Lukan Call Narratives" (pp. 107-11).

you can bring up pericope 18 in Aland's *Synopsis of the Four Gospels* to visualize all the Gospels at once on your screen.

In Mark the voice from heaven is meant for Jesus, "You are my Son, whom I love; with you I am well pleased" (Mark 1:11). This saying combines Ps 2:7 with Isa 42:1, so that Jesus fulfills the royal psalms as well as the Suffering Servant songs of Isaiah. Mark then portrays this identity of Jesus throughout his book, first in the Galilean ministry, where Jesus is both miracle-working Messiah (Mark 1:16–8:21) and suffering Son of Man (8:22–10:52), and then in the Jerusalem ministry, where Jesus is the prophecy-fulfilling triumphant Messiah and great debater (chs. 11–13) as well as the king of the Jews in his passion and death (chs. 14–15). Only in Mark are the heavens torn (σχιζομένους, 1:10) at Jesus' baptism just as the temple curtain is torn from top to bottom at Jesus' death (ἐσχίσθη Mark 15:38). Jesus' identity as suffering servant Messiah commences with his baptism and is completed at the cross. The purpose of Mark's Gospel is to demonstrate that it was necessary for the promised Messiah to suffer and die and that Christians must likewise take up their cross and follow Jesus in a life of sacrificial discipleship. Mark is the Gospel of the cross. Jesus' peculiar identity is already revealed to him at his baptism. These christological and discipleship purposes control the descriptions of Jesus' baptism.

Matthew, on the other hand, attaches a new section to the context (Matt 3:14-15) where John the Baptizer objects to baptizing Jesus. Consequently, the voice from heaven speaks not to Jesus, but to the Jewish crowd, "This is my Son" (3:17). Why? What is the connection? With regard to the historical context behind Matthew's Gospel, the reader should picture a Christian synagogue on one corner and a Pharisaic synagogue on the other, with the Gospel message offering an apologetic against the accusations of the unbelieving Jews.[12] The leaders of the Pharisees claimed that if Jesus was baptized, he must have committed sin. Furthermore, the one who baptizes is always greater than the one baptized, so John must be superior to Jesus. Through the insertion of Matt 3:14-15 from the Jesus tradition, Matthew faces these challenges head on and points out that John had to be convinced to baptize Jesus, since Jesus wanted to fulfill all righteousness as the perfect Israelite. Matthew defends the church against the accusations of the Jewish synagogue, so that his Gospel could be entitled the apologetic Gospel addressed to unconverted Jews. A sermon or Bible study on Jesus' baptism in Matthew would concentrate on this polemical element and the divine proof from

---

12. See below Chapter 7, A1, "Apologetic Against the Pharisaic Synagogue in the Gospel of Matthew" (pp. 229-34).

heaven that Jesus was the promised one of the Old Testament. In interpreting a Gospel, the context of Jesus as well as the context of the evangelist must be given due attention.[13]

Luke's baptism narrative also reveals some of his redactionary purposes. Luke reports the imprisonment of John before the baptism of Jesus (Luke 3:19-20), so that the era of John appears completed before Jesus' ministry begins. Luke is the theologian of *Heilsgeschichte* who narrates the Gospel as a history of salvation comprising the OT time period of John the Baptizer, the ministry of Jesus, and the history of the church in the book of Acts. Significantly, Jesus is praying while he is baptized as well as during the revelation of the voice from heaven (a present participle). This begins a pattern where Luke introduces the theme of prayer at the strategic turning points in salvation history so that God guides these historical events in response to prayer. The people are praying outside the temple when the revelation concerning the birth of John the Baptist occurs (1:10). Only Luke mentions Jesus praying at his baptism (3:21); before choosing the twelve apostles (6:12); prior to Peter's confession, the turning point of the Gospel (9:18); at the transfiguration, when Jesus' true heavenly identity is revealed (9:28); before teaching the model prayer, "Our Father" (11:1); at the Last Supper to strengthen Peter's faith (22:32); before Jesus' arrest in Gethsemane (22:41-44); and on the cross, where Jesus prays for his enemies (23:34) and recites the Jewish bedtime prayer found in Ps 31:5 (Luke 23:46). History-changing events always happen in a context of prayer.

Charles Talbert[14] calls attention to another unique line in the Lukan baptism narrative, "the Holy Spirit descended on him in bodily form" (Luke 3:22). Talbert contends that the Gospel of Luke contains a polemic against the Docetic heresy that Christ only appeared to be human. These deceptive teachers considered bodily existence as evil and consequently claimed that the divine Christ descended upon Jesus at his baptism but departed before his death. Therefore, Luke called special attention to the physical nature of Jesus' baptism over against these early Gnostics. In the Gospel of Luke Jesus is begotten by God at his virgin birth, not his baptism as the Docetists taught. Furthermore, Luke follows the baptism with Jesus' genealogy as a

---

13. Therefore, Gordon Fee entitles the Gospels "two level" documents and contends that we must think horizontally and vertically. See Gordon D. Fee and Douglas Stuart, *How to Read the Bible for All Its Worth: A Guide to Understanding the Bible*, 2nd ed. (Grand Rapids: Zondervan, 1993), pp. 121-26.

14. Charles H. Talbert, *Luke and the Gnostics: An Examination of Lucan Purpose* (Nashville: Abingdon, 1966), pp. 13-14, 111-13.

human being whose ancestry traces back to the first man, Adam. Additional references to the humanness of Christ follow his death, so that only in Luke's burial account do witnesses physically see the body of Jesus laid in the tomb (Luke 23:55 modifies Mark 15:47). In the resurrection appearances Luke proves that Jesus is not a spirit through the display of his hands and feet (Luke 24:39) and the consumption of broiled fish (24:43). Luke especially emphasizes the ascension, which is a physical ascent of Jesus visible to the natural eye (24:50-51; Acts 1:9-11). Finally, in Acts 20:28-30 Paul warns specifically about a heresy which will infiltrate the Christian community following his departure. In Talbert's view, this is a reference to the Docetic heresy that was becoming popular at the time of Luke. Whatever your view on this issue, the importance of Lukan redaction is difficult to deny.

Finally, in the Johannine baptism account, surprisingly Jesus' baptism is not even narrated. Instead, John the Baptist emphasizes the promise of the baptism of the Holy Spirit that will take place through Jesus (John 1:33). The prominent theme for the evangelist is the witness of the characters to the special titles deserving of Jesus. The voice from heaven is not for Jesus, nor the crowd, but for John the Baptist. John 1:32 reports, "Then John gave this testimony: 'I saw the Spirit come down from heaven as a dove and remain on him.'" The evangelist divides his first chapter into four days bound together by the theme of testimony. On the first day (1:19-28) John the Baptizer draws attention away from himself so that on the next day (1:29-34) John can proclaim his testimony of Jesus as the lamb of God (1:29, 36), the superior one who existed before him (1:30), the one upon whom the Spirit remains (1:32), and the chosen one of God (1:34). The content of these testimonies deepens as the chapter precedes, so that on the third day (1:35-42) John's disciples migrate to Jesus, with Andrew proclaiming Jesus as the Messiah (1:41). Finally, on the fourth day (1:43-51) Philip testifies that Jesus is the one Moses wrote about in the law (1:45), and Nathanael christens him the Son of God, the king of Israel (1:49). Jesus himself culminates the chapter by calling himself the heavenly Son of Man (1:51). This parade of witnesses invites the readers to join the band and offer their own testimony to the significance of Jesus. Thus a sermon or Bible study would appropriately concentrate on the titles the Baptizer assigns to Jesus and culminate in an appropriate testimony to Jesus in today's culture. Jesus' baptism itself is not the point of the narrative.

Treating each of the Gospel writers as a theologian in his own right instead of harmonizing the four Gospels into one account enriches the significance of the historical events. Each Gospel has its own context. Therefore, each Gospel has its own message.

2. Peter's Confession "You are the Christ" in the Synoptic Gospels

The Gospel writers frequently display differing but complementary theological motives in the transmission of the Jesus tradition. Peter's confession of faith for Matthew (Matt 16:13-20) is the high point of the Gospel. Climactically, Peter as the leader of the disciples and the subsequent church asserts the crucial affirmation that Jesus is the Messiah of Israel. Only in Matthew does Peter append to the Markan formulation that Jesus is "the Son of the living God" (16:16b). Only in Matthew does Jesus congratulate Peter for his divine insight: "Blessed are you, Simon son of Jonah, for this was not revealed to you by man, but by my Father in heaven." Only in Matthew does the profession become the occasion on which Simon receives the name Peter, so that Jesus declares, "On this rock I will build my church." Upon Peter's confession the church will prevail over the gates of Hades and withstand all opposition. Jesus gives the church the keys of the kingdom in this revelation at Caesarea Philippi. Many scholars consider this event as a turning point in the Gospel, as evidenced by the formula "from this time on Jesus began" in 16:21 and 4:17, which divides the Gospel into a threefold structure: (1) the person of Jesus the Messiah (1:1–4:16); (2) the proclamation of Jesus the Messiah (4:17–16:20); and (3) the suffering, death, and resurrection of Jesus the Messiah (16:21–28:20).[15] Everything is positive and miraculous.

In the Gospel of Mark, however, we discover a distinctive interpretation of Peter's confession. In Mark, as David Ourisman points out, there is "No praise, no recognition of divine inspiration, no conferral of a new name, no granting of leadership within the church, not even a hint that Peter answered the question correctly."[16] Since in the following verses Peter is forcefully rebuked and identified with Satan himself (8:33), his confession demands supplementation. In fact, since Peter's response is labeled demonic, his confession must parallel the christological utterances of the demons (1:24-25; 3:11-12) that Jesus also silences (8:30), since they similarly omit any allusion to the passion of the Messiah. Merely to entitle Jesus "the Christ" is an insufficient declaration for Mark. The introduction of the suffering Son of Man

15. The most popular outline of the Gospel today is a biographical structure by Jack Dean Kingsbury, *Matthew: Structure, Christology, Kingdom* (Minneapolis: Fortress, 1975). For a competing outline (which I still prefer) based upon the five discourses of Matthew, see Benjamin W. Bacon, "The 'Five Books' of Moses against the Jews," *Exp* 15 (1918): 56-66; and *Studies in Matthew* (London: Constable, 1930), chs. 12-16.

16. David J. Ourisman, *From Gospel to Sermon: Preaching Synoptic Texts* (St. Louis: Chalice, 2000), p. 4.

by Jesus in 8:31 provides the needed christological formulation. Mark cleverly links Peter's confession (8:29) to the double touch healing of the blind man (8:22-26). Just as the blind man required a second touch before he could see perfectly, so Peter needs a second touch. After the first touch of Jesus the blind man can see, just as Peter's confession of Jesus as Messiah is a positive confession of insight into Jesus' identity. However, the blind man cannot see clearly, just as Peter's confession does not allow Peter to envision Jesus clearly. Therefore, the title "Messiah" for Mark is correct but insufficient.[17] Mark's theology affects how he describes the context of Peter's confession of faith.

The profession in Luke 9:18-22 again paints Peter in a positive light as Luke regularly does throughout his Gospel. For instance, in 22:32 Jesus prays personally for Peter so that he will faithfully restore the other disciples in their faith commitment. Likewise, Peter's personal experience at the tomb with Jesus in Luke 24:12 and 24:34 is contrasted with the disbelief of the other disciples (24:11), whereas in Mark 16:7 Peter's restoration is still in the future. Furthermore, by omitting Mark 8:33 where Jesus identifies Peter with Satan, Luke removes Mark's pattern of a discipleship misunderstanding after Jesus' passion prediction (see also Mark 9:31-34 and 10:33-37). Through this process Luke eliminates Peter's misunderstanding of the suffering nature of Jesus' messiahship. In addition, both Matthew and Luke omit the double touch healing of the blind man because their purposes run in a different direction from Mark's. In Luke the disciples are the foundation of the church and therefore portrayed positively.[18] In Mark the disciples, the women, and Jesus' family are portrayed negatively to offer a lesson to a church struggling with a discipleship of the cross.

If we accept the presupposition that the Gospels are preached history, then we can understand the emphases of each Gospel. Against the Pharisaic synagogue Matthew is proclaiming that Jesus is the Messiah and that the community standing upon this profession will prevail over the gates of hades and therefore last forever. Mark is addressing a persecuted church where some have renounced their allegiance to Jesus (13:12-13), so that he is employing the disciples as a foil to call the community to follow Jesus in his victory as Messiah but also in his passion as the suffering servant Son of

---

17. See Dean B. Deppe, "Markan Christology and the Omission of υἱοῦ θεοῦ in Mark 1:1," *Filologia Neotestamentaria* 21 (2008): 50-54; and Jack Dean Kingsbury, *The Christology of Mark's Gospel* (Philadelphia: Fortress, 1983), p. 101.

18. For the ties between Luke and Acts in the portrayal of Peter, see Ourisman, *From Gospel to Sermon*, pp. 76-77. For a further portrayal of a positive Peter in Luke, see pp. 66-67.

Man. Since Nero's persecution is completed when Luke writes, he chooses to highlight the victory of Christianity and so portrays the disciples as heroes. To receive the full meaning of the text, we have to employ redaction criticism and discern both Jesus' message and the respeaking of this history to the situation of the early church by the evangelist preachers. Four separate Gospels are Christ's gift to the church.

3. Luke 19:28-44: A Triumphal Entry?

Palm Sunday is normally remembered as one of the most exciting and exuberant worship services of the church year. The children wave their palm branches in exaltation, even the rocks cannot keep silent (Luke 19:40), and the people shout, "Blessed is the king who comes in the name of the Lord" (19:38). If we expect such a scenario from each Gospel story, we must overlook completely the conclusion of the account in Luke where Jesus weeps, laments, and is weighed down to the point of depression over the future events occurring in Jerusalem (19:41-44).

Each Gospel writer must be read individually to comprehend the total picture of an event in Jesus' life. The Lukan Jesus cannot celebrate and rejoice like the multitude around him. As soon as Jesus rides over the Mount of Olives and his eyes make contact with the buildings of Jerusalem, he weeps uncontrollably (19:41). His tears then turn to words of lament, "If you, even you, had only known on this day what would bring you peace — but now it is hidden from your eyes" (19:42). As 19:38 had already asserted, there is only "Peace in heaven and glory in the highest!" On earth, Jesus' grief continues, and overcome with the unfaithfulness of God's people (19:44b), he prophesies the terrible destruction awaiting Jerusalem and her children (19:43-44a).

Why would Luke emphasize Jesus' pain and rejection when everyone else is thinking joy and blessing? To answer this question, the interpreter must also walk down the exegetical road that concentrates on structure. Luke has divided his Gospel into three sections: Jesus' ministry in Galilee, his circuitous trip to the holy city, and his Jerusalem campaign. Unique to Luke, each of these divisions begins with a rejection. Instead of narrating Jesus' sermon and rejection at Nazareth in the middle of the Galilean ministry like Mark 6:1-6, Luke inaugurates Jesus' ministry with an event where the townspeople of Galilee attempt to murder Jesus, but as in his resurrection, he miraculously escapes out of their hands (Luke 4:14-30). Similarly, as the trip to Jerusalem commences, Jesus is not welcomed but rejected in Samaria, so that the disciples insist on calling down judgment fire from heaven. In fact, each of the three sections of the travel narrative begins with rejection as exemplified by the negative responses of the Samaritans (9:51-55), the Jewish towns and villages as well as Herod (13:22-35), and the nine Jewish lepers who fail to return thanksgiving to Jesus (17:11-18).

Climactically, Jesus enters the capital of Jerusalem, but the recurring rejection of the gospel message causes Jesus to weep and lament. Since this theme of Jesus' rejection is so prominent a Lukan emphasis, it also deserves a pulpit on Palm Sunday. Sometimes like Jesus we are called to perceive the unique significance of events and feel the emotions which others miss. Jesus' inner spiritual makeup moved from joy (19:37-40) to grief (19:41-44) to anger (19:45-46), all on a single day. Jesus' flow of emotion and alteration of consciousness was not controlled by the circumstances of the day but by the leading of the Spirit. Similarly, even though Mark and Matthew do not narrate some of the events that Luke envisions, without the Lukan perspective we would miss an important element of Palm Sunday. Redaction criticism then offers a tool to grasp the total picture of God's revelation.

4. Should We Harmonize Peter's Denials in the Four Gospels?

Faulty interpretations occur when we attempt to harmonize the Gospels without reading the stories separately as complete gospels by themselves with their own individual purpose and setting. In the book *The Battle for the Bible,* Harold Lindsell attempts to prove the inerrancy of Scripture and remove discrepancies by harmonizing the four Gospels.[19] He is troubled by the unique descriptions of Peter's denials in the fourfold witness. By reading the narratives describing Peter's denials in a very literal manner, he determines that there are six different accounts of Peter denying the Lord. Lindsell's "ingenious solution" assumes that Peter denied the Lord three times before the first cock crew and three more times before the signal of the second rooster. He contends this would literally fulfill Mark 14:72, "Before the rooster crows twice you will disown me three times." More importantly, this would remove all the discrepancies from the disparate accounts and prove the Bible reliable according to Lindsell.

The only problem with this proposal is that none of the four Gospels re-

19. Harold Lindsell, *The Battle for the Bible* (Grand Rapids: Zondervan, 1976), pp. 174-76.

cite Peter denying the Lord six times. Matthew, Mark, Luke, and John all dictate that Peter denied Jesus on three occasions. By attempting to harmonize the Gospels, we destroy the original witness of each individual Gospel. In contrast to this approach that transforms minor narrative differences into distinct historical accounts, redaction criticism can be employed to discern the purposes, writing habits, and vocabulary of each individual Gospel writer. Only after redaction criticism is a theological harmonization of the Gospels both credible and useful in the establishment of a biblical theology.

5. The Tearing of the Temple Curtain in the Synoptic Gospels

All three Synoptic Gospels place the tearing of the temple curtain in the crucifixion narrative. However, in comparing Mark and Luke closely (cf. Aland's *Synopsis,* §347), the careful reader notices that the curtain is torn after Jesus' death in Mark and Matthew, while it occurs before his crucifixion in Luke. Furthermore, in Mark 15:38 the curtain is torn in two from top to bottom (εἰς δύο ἀπ' ἄνωθεν ἕως κάτω) while in Luke 23:45 a hole is ripped in the middle (μέσον). What is the significance of this redaction in Luke (if we assume Markan priority)?

Certainly for Mark the destruction of the temple stands as a theme binding the events of Jesus' Jerusalem ministry together. Jesus shuts down temple worship temporarily in his prophetic action against the temple in Mark 11:12-19. Then in 12:11 Mark quotes Ps 118:22 ("The stone which the builders rejected has become the head of the corner") so that a new temple is anticipated with Jesus as the cornerstone. After winning arguments with every group of Jewish leadership in the temple courts (Mark 11:27–12:40), Jesus dramatically predicts the destruction of every brick of this house (ch. 13). At Jesus' trial the Jewish leaders accuse Jesus with the indictment that he will destroy the temple made with hands and build one not made with hands (14:58). Finally, on the cross the passersby mock Jesus, exclaiming, "You who are going to destroy the temple and build it in three days, come down from the cross and save yourself!" Therefore, when the veil of the temple is torn at Jesus' death, it must signify for Mark the destruction of the physical temple complex and its replacement by the person of Jesus through his resurrection after three days.

If you perform a "Bible Word Study" under the "Guides" icon in Logos Bible Software on the English word "temple," you discover that Mark employs the term ἱερόν to refer to the entire physical temple complex in 11:15-16; 12:35; 13:1-3; 14:49. In the Passion Narrative, however, when Jesus wants to refer to his death and resurrection as the destruction and rebuilding of the temple, Mark switches the vocabulary to ναός, meaning "sanctuary" in 14:58; 15:29, 38. Thus Jesus predicts the future destruction of the temple complex as well as the building of a new sanctuary in his resurrection.

Matthew attaches some important theological data to the tearing of the veil (Matt 27:51-53). Only in Matthew does an eschatological earthquake occur at the crucifixion, resulting in people raised from the dead along with the veil of the temple ripping in two. Matthew's context entails that the tearing of the veil must be understood as an eschatological sign; the new age has begun. The life-giving events of the new age, not the destruction of the old temple, become front and center.

Luke transfers the tearing of the temple veil to a time prior to Jesus' death. Before Jesus' parting words, "Father, into your hands I commit my spirit" (Luke 23:46), Luke narrates "And the curtain of the temple was torn in two" (23:45). Immediately before Jesus' death, a hole appears in the middle of the temple curtain. The implication of the narrative is that in his death Jesus passes through this hole into the heavenly sanctuary to perform his priestly work and permanently open access to God to both Jew and Gentile (as signified by the centurion's confession). Therefore, in Luke the tearing of the temple veil is not a sign of the temple's destruction. Luke's theology is identical with that of the book of Hebrews. Hebrews 10:19-20 explains, "we have confidence to enter the Most Holy Place by the blood of Jesus, by a new and living way opened for us through the curtain, that is, his body." Therefore, the hole in the curtain symbolizes the opening of a new way into the very presence of God through Jesus' death.

Although this view of Luke's death narrative is rejected by Raymond Brown,[20] the timing of the tearing as well as the close ties with Hebrews demonstrate that Jesus' priestly role in the temple will endure forever, whereas in Mark the expectation of a messianic destruction of the temple is front and center. By temple Mark means the physical complex, but Luke identifies the temple with the presence of God and therefore maintains a positive view of the temple throughout his Gospel. These theological perspectives on the temple by the Synoptic authors demonstrate the importance of redaction criticism and reading each narrative within its context in the Gospel.

---

20. Raymond E. Brown, *The Death of the Messiah: A Commentary on the Passion Narratives in the Four Gospels*. ABRL (New York: Doubleday, 1994), 2:1102-9, argues that Luke ties together the tearing with the darkness, so that it receives a negative force warning that a continuous rejection of Jesus will bring the destruction of the holy place.

6. Kings and Chronicles: Positive Evaluations
Trump Negative Appraisals

In the Old Testament we encounter a situation of redaction similar to the Gospels when we compare the books of Samuel and Kings with 1 and 2 Chronicles.[21] In his evaluation of Deuteronomistic history that includes the books of Samuel and Kings, Martin Noth contends that the author's presentation of the material is completely negative. The books end with the loss of the northern kingdom and the exile of the southern tribes. The writer "traced the thread of apostasy and decline through Israel's history in order to demonstrate to his exilic contemporaries that Yahweh's judgment in the destruction of Israel and Judah was totally justified."[22] The criticism of the monarchy is especially harsh in the books of Samuel and Kings. Beginning with Saul's rise to power, the theme of evil dominates, since this centralized authority rejects the unity of the tribes based upon God's rule through charismatic figures. Therefore the monarchy was primarily responsible for the falls of Israel and Judah.

The Chronicler, on the other hand, presents a positive view of the monarchy. This is especially apparent in the omission of material from Samuel and Kings. Chronicles narrates the continuous rule by the kings of Judah but ignores the chronological sequence of the northern monarchs. The only exceptions to this policy occur when the northern kings refuse to worship Yahweh in appropriate ways as in the reigns of Jeroboam (2 Chr 10:19; 13:8-9) and Ahab (18:5-7) or when they cause Judah to sin as with King Baasha (2 Chr 16:1-2, 7), King Ahaziah (20:35), and various general references to Israel's rulers (21:13; 28:2). In fact, the Chronicler does not even narrate the fall of Samaria as in 2 Kings 17. For the Chronicler, all Israel exists through the history of the Davidic monarchy.

The positive approach of Chronicles is especially transparent in the idealized descriptions of the reigns of David, Solomon, and Hezekiah. Again the omissions stand out. As Ralph Klein explains, "The Chronicler omits David's controversial struggles with Saul, his adultery with Bathsheba, the murder of Uriah, and the revolt of Absalom. Nothing is said of the weakness

---

21. For a comparison of the texts, see John C. Endres, William R. Millar, and John Barclay Burns, eds., *Chronicles and Its Synoptic Parallels in Samuel, Kings, and Related Biblical Texts* (Collegeville: Liturgical, 1998).

22. Steven L. McKenzie, *The Chronicler's Use of Deuteronomistic History.* HSM 33 (Atlanta: Scholars, 1984), p. 2, summarizes Noth's view and rehearses critical appraisals of it as he compares this literature with the Chronicler's history.

of his final days, the vain efforts of Abishag to warm him, or his vengeful advice to Solomon in 1 Kings 1-2."[23] On the other hand, Abijah's sermon in 2 Chronicles 13 as well as other significant passages (1 Chr 12:39-40; 17:13-14; 22:9-10; 28:6-7) stress the eternal character of the Davidic rule.

The Chronicler contributes a radically revised portrait of Solomon as well. As Klein states,

> Solomon's rise to power did not come through the conniving of Nathan and Bathsheba, who took advantage of David's weakness during his final illness, nor is there any mention of the attempt by Solomon's brother Adonijah, supported by the king's sons and all his royal officials, to usurp the throne. Rather, David, presumably in full command of his powers, designates Solomon as king in fulfillment of the oracle of Nathan (17:15; 22:9-10), and he cites a divine oracle designating Solomon as the king chosen by Yahweh (28:6-7, 10). . . . Solomon's idolatry and apostasy, induced by his many foreign wives, is omitted completely (1 Kgs 10:28b–11:40). Even his journey to sacrifice at the "high place" at Gibeon (1 Kgs 3:2-6) is cast in a different light since according to the Chronicler the tent of meeting/the tabernacle was located there (2 Chr. 1:3-6).[24]

In particular the devotion and commitment of David and Solomon to the temple receives arousing applause from the Chronicler. From 2 Chr 2:1 through 8:16 the building and dedication of the temple is central to Solomon's reign. In addition, David is renowned for his preparations for the building of the temple and his establishment of several classes of temple ministers. Faithfulness in maintaining proper worship becomes the criterion by which kings are judged.

This enthusiasm for the temple is finally renewed by Hezekiah, who functions like David and Solomon and unites all Israel together again to serve Yahweh. As Mark Throntveit maintains, "Through his repair of the temple, reinstitution of worship, and invitation to the North to join in the Passover, Hezekiah restores the ideal situation of David and Solomon that had been lost."[25] The book of Kings devotes the bulk of its account of Heze-

23. Ralph W. Klein, *1 Chronicles*. Hermeneia (Minneapolis: Fortress, 2006), p. 44.
24. Klein, *1 Chronicles*, p. 44.
25. Mark A. Throntveit, "The Relationship of Hezekiah to David and Solomon in the Books of Chronicles," in *Chronicler as Theologian: Essays in Honor of Ralph W. Klein*, ed. M. Patrick Graham, Steven L. McKenzie, and Gary N. Knoppers. JSOTSup 371 (London: T. & T. Clark, 2003), p. 121.

kiah (2 Kgs 18:9–20:19) to political matters such as Sennacherib's invasion, Hezekiah's illness, and Hezekiah's support of Babylon against Assyria. On the other hand, Hezekiah's temple reforms are footnoted in a single verse (2 Kgs 18:4). In stark contrast, as Throntveit points out, "the Chronicler apportions three chapters to the reform (2 Chron. 29–31) and treats the more political concerns that exercised his predecessors in an abbreviated and theologically motivated fashion (2 Chron. 32)."[26] Therefore, Hezekiah restores the spirit of David and Solomon. As Baruch Halpern highlights, "Hezekiah is the last king of whom it is said that Yahweh was with him, saved him, rescued him, gave him any sort of rest, brought foreigners to pay tribute to him, and so forth."[27] Therefore, Israel is reunited at the end of the monarchy according to Chronicles.

In addition, the identical wording of 2 Chr 36:22-23 and Ezra 1:1-3a indicates that the Chronicler is attempting to portray Ezra and Nehemiah as a sequel to his writing. The captivity in Babylon leads to a marvelous restoration of the temple, the rebuilding of the wall around Jerusalem, and the establishment of the law as central to Israel in the following volumes of Ezra and Nehemiah. The Babylonian captivity is not the end, as is the case in the account in the book of Kings.

Therefore, the Chronicler's positive account triumphs over any negative residue left over from the historical descriptions in 1 and 2 Kings. History has moved on, and the context has changed. This author wants to portray the beginning and end of the monarchy as exemplary for Israel at all times and all places. As Walter Brueggemann explains, "This is the David that is necessary for the authorization of a faithful religious community."[28] Therefore, the Chronicler redacts the memoirs of Israel. A subsequent time in history and a new context demand an alternative interpretation of times past, as evidenced in the unique contribution of each account.

---

26. Throntveit, "Relationship of Hezekiah to David and Solomon," p. 106.

27. Baruch Halpern, "Sacred History and Ideology: Chronicles' Thematic Structure — Indications of an Earlier Source," in *The Creation of Sacred Literature: Composition and Redaction of the Biblical Text,* ed. Richard Elliott Friedman (Berkeley: University of California Press, 1981), p. 49. Also burial and accession formulae undergo observable change following the reign of Hezekiah. In the accession formulae the name of the queen mother disappears after Hezekiah, as does the stipulation of internment in the city of David in the burial notices.

28. Walter Brueggemann, "'Vine and Fig Tree': A Case Study in Imagination and Criticism," in *A Social Reading of the Old Testament: Prophetic Approaches to Israel's Communal Life,* ed. Patrick D. Miller (Minneapolis: Fortress, 1994), p. 105.

STUDY AND DISCUSSION QUESTIONS

1. Context sometimes accounts for the use of different terminology in the Synoptic Gospels. For instance, the Lord's Prayer in Luke 11:4 reads, "Forgive us our sins, for we also forgive everyone who sins against us," employing the common Greek word ἁμαρτία. The Matthew account, however, states, "Forgive us our debts, as we also have forgiven our debtors" (6:12), using the financial and economic term ὀφείλημα. How do the four passages (Matt 6:19-21, 22-23, 24, 25-34) following this section on secret piety (6:1-18) relate to our economic life? What is meant by treasures in heaven (6:20)? What is an evil eye (6:23)? (Check Prov 23:6; 28:22 and Matt 20:15, especially in the KJV.) What is another word for "mammon" in Matt 6:24? How does this context in Matthew demonstrate why he employs the term "debts"?

2. The referent "these" in John 21:15, "Do you love me more than these?" (ἀγαπᾷς με πλέον τούτων), can have various meanings. "These" could refer to the boat and the fish, so that Jesus is asking whether Peter loves him more than fishing. Or "these" could refer to the other disciples, resulting in the question, "Do you love me more than you love these human companions?" A third possibility is "Do you love me more than these disciples love me?" Since the resurrection narratives of John 20 are supplemented by a call narrative to be an evangelist-pastor (a fisherman-shepherd) in John 21, which translation does the context favor and why?

3. A change of context can be verified by an alteration of audience and location. Therefore, it is striking that in the Markan telling of the parable of the Sower (4:1-9) Jesus addresses the parable to a crowd from the pulpit of a boat and then gathers his disciples together separately, where he offers a separate interpretation of the parable solely for them (4:10). Notice as well that the parable is spoken to those who need ears to hear (4:3, 9), but the interpretation is aimed at those who have heard already (4:15b, 16b, 18b, 20b). Finally, observe that the three seeds that produce no fruit are contrasted with three seeds that produce thirty, sixty, and a hundredfold in the parable (notice the neuter singular), whereas the interpretation describes four types of soil (notice the masculine plural). Should the parable itself be entitled the parable of the Seed and the clarification to the disciples be called the parable of the Soils? Is Mark 4:14-20 appropriately entitled an interpretation of the parable, or is it in reality a respeaking of the parable to clarify an additional understanding for those who are already disciples? Would you call the parable in

4:3-9 a kingdom parable, whereas 4:14-20 is a discipleship parable? In these separate contexts, how does the meaning of the parable change?

4. Who recites the chorus, "Blessed is he who comes in the name of the Lord"? Your immediate answer is probably the crowd at the triumphal entry of Jesus on Palm Sunday. But look a little closer at the contexts where Jesus predicts this cry. In Luke 13:35 Jesus predicts, "I tell you, you will not see me again until you say, 'Blessed is he who comes in the name of the Lord.'" When is this prediction fulfilled in Luke? But what about the parallel prediction in Matt 23:39? If the Palm Sunday cry occurs at Matt 21:9, when will 23:39 find its fulfillment? Will you be one of the people responding with this chorus? Finally, what psalm is this verse quoting, and what type of psalm is it? Where else in Matthew 21–23 is this psalm alluded to? How would Matthew be employing this psalm to defend Christianity against the Pharisaical accusation that if Jesus is the Messiah, God has rejected his people since the majority of Jews have not followed him?

5. What is the "leaven of the Pharisees"? Mark in his characteristic enigmatic manner does not precisely specify what he means by "Watch out for the yeast of the Pharisees and that of Herod" (Mark 8:15). How do Luke (12:1) and Matthew (16:12) in their independent ways clarify the meaning? How is the particular wording of Matt 16:12 related to the five sermons in Matthew, and especially Matthew 23? How is the clarification in Luke 12:1 related to the context of 11:37-54 as well as the following context of 12:2? How is demanding a sign (Mark 8:11) connected with Herod? See Mark 6:16 and Luke 23:8. Finally, if the leaven for Mark is demanding miracles, how does this fit with his emphasis upon the suffering and passion of Jesus and the cross that the disciples must carry?

6. In Mark 11:23 Jesus proclaims, "I tell you the truth, if anyone says to this mountain, 'Go, throw yourself into the sea,' and does not doubt in his heart but believes that what he says will happen, it will be done for him." It is disputed whether this mountain is symbolic of something that is impossible for humans (Matt 17:20; 21:21), whether a reference to the eschatological splitting of the Mount of Olives in Zech 14:4-5 is intended, or whether Mark is speaking about the temple mount. Which conclusion does the context favor? Where is the destruction of the temple emphasized in Jesus' Jerusalem ministry? Instead of temple sacrifices, what offerings of piety are included in Mark 11:22-25 and 12:33?

7. Kurt Aland's *Synopsis of the Four Gospels* is my favorite book, since it enables the reader to discover the particular emphasis of an author through a line-by-line comparison. For instance, the passion stories of Mark and Matthew are exceptionally close in wording, except that Matthew adds three incidents into the narrative: Judas returns the thirty pieces of silver and regrets his decision (Matt 27:3-10); Pilate washes his hands of Jesus' death after hearing about his wife's dream (27:19, 24); and the responsibility for the crucifixion of the Messiah is laid directly upon the Jewish leadership and people (27:25). How do these additions clarify the audience to whom the Gospel of Matthew is addressed, and how does Matthew call for repentance from the people of his day? See Matt 23:37 and the response of the Jewish leadership to John the Baptizer (21:28-32), Jesus (21:33-46), and Jesus' apostles (22:1-7). What accusation is the Pharisaic synagogue making against the Christian synagogue as evidenced by the unique material that Matthew includes in his Gospel? See Matt 28:13-15; 1:18-19 with the women in the genealogy; 2:1, 23; and 3:13-15. What accusations are made against Christianity today, and how would you defend the Christian faith?

8. Let's assume that you have read in a biblical theology that prayer is an important theme in the Gospel of Luke. Use the method of redaction criticism to discover where Luke adds the fact that Jesus is praying to the narrative he employed from Mark. Search the Greek word προσεύχομαι and compare the uses in Mark and Luke. At what strategic points is Jesus praying in Luke (moments in salvation history whereby God guides the course of events accompanied by human prayer)? What have been the important events in your life where you have witnessed the power of prayer?

9. Whereas the entire Gospel of Mark highlights a discipleship of the cross to enable the Christians to face suffering, Luke has chosen by God's Spirit to emphasize the victory of Christianity. Luke describes the three types of Greco-Roman religion including the mythical religion of the gods and goddesses of the pantheon, the ceremonial religion of the protective idols, and the philosophical religion of the academics. How does Luke demonstrate the superiority of Christianity to each of these in the book of Acts? See 14:11-18; 19:17-41; and 17:16-34. Magic was the everyday religion of the common people in the Greco-Roman empire. How does Luke narrate the triumph of Christianity over magic? See Acts 8:18-24; 13:8-12; 16:16-18; 19:13-20; 28:4-6. How does the Jesus movement triumph over the movement of John the Baptizer? See Acts 19:1-7. How do we experience victory as Christians today?

10. Isaiah 2:1-5 and Mic 4:1-5 are surprisingly similar. Compile a Layout in Logos Bible Software where these passages are placed side by side. Make a list of the similarities and describe the future expectations that are highlighted. Now notice that Isa 2:1 lacks a parallel with Micah 4 and that Isa 2:5 is completely different from Mic 4:4-5. How was this message of hope important to Isaiah in a time where Judah felt abandoned, as illustrated in the context at Isa 2:6? Based upon the context in Mic 3:12, how would this message of hope speak to the situation Micah was prophesying about? What are some present-day situations where these passages could be applied to supply hope and comfort?

CHAPTER 5

The Cultural and Historical Background Route

Using a Telescopic Lens

A telescopic lens attempts to bring the faraway close. The events of the Bible occurred over two thousand years ago in ancient Near Eastern cultures. To understand the Bible, we have to recover the meaning of these events within the original cultural purview. The investigation of this cultural and historical background can proceed in a number of ways, including an analysis of maps, archaeological data, and Jewish and Greco-Roman history. In the first section we will offer a series of examples where reference works on biblical background bring new meaning to the text. Since it is frequently crucial to study the OT background to NT texts or extracanonical works that shine light upon the biblical record, the second section of this chapter will investigate intertextuality. Finally, when interpreting a passage from a particular book of the Bible, it is essential to study the background material, including provenance, authorship, date of writing, and a description of the recipients and their environment.[1] We will conclude with a third section investigating these issues.

A. Historical and Cultural Elements

PROCEDURE

The use of electronic resources greatly reduces the time requirements needed for fruitful research. In Logos Bible Software the researcher can cre-

---

1. Jeannine K. Brown, *Scripture as Communication: Introducing Biblical Hermeneutics* (Grand Rapids: Baker Academic, 2007), pp. 191-92, distinguishes various types of contexts.

ate collections of resources and search the entire inventory. The Scholars Library package includes the following volumes that are helpful in discovering the historical and cultural background of biblical texts:

- Avraham Negev and Shimon Gibson, eds., *The Archaeological Encyclopedia of the Holy Land.* Rev. ed. New York: Continuum, 2001.
- Harold P. Scanlin, *The Dead Sea Scrolls and Modern Translations of the Old Testament.* Wheaton: Tyndale House, 1993.
- Thomas V. Brisco, *Holman Bible Atlas: A Complete Guide to the Expansive Geography of Biblical History.* Nashville: Broadman and Holman, 1998.
- Hanan Isachar, *Images of the Holy Land.* Oak Harbor: Logos Research Systems, 1997.
- Alfred Edersheim, *The Life and Times of Jesus the Messiah.* 1896; Bellingham, WA: Logos Research Systems, 2003.
- A. B. du Toit, *The New Testament Milieu.* Halfway House: Orion, 1998.
- D. Thaine Norris, *Logos Deluxe Map Set.* Oak Harbor, WA: Logos Research Systems, 1997.
- James M. Freeman and Harold J. Chadwick, *The New Manners and Customs of the Bible.* Rev. ed. North Brunswick, NJ: Bridge-Logos, 1998.
- William Mitchell Ramsay, *St. Paul the Traveller and the Roman Citizen.* 1896; Oak Harbor, WA: Logos Research System, 1995.
- Alfred Edersheim, *Sketches of Jewish Social Life in the Days of Christ.* 1876; Bellingham, WA: Logos Research Systems, 2003.
- Alfred Edersheim, *The Temple: Its Ministry and Services as They Were at the Time of Jesus Christ.* 1874; Bellingham, WA: Logos Research Systems, 2003.
- Bruce Malina, Stephan Joubert, and Jan van der Watt, *A Time Travel to the World of Jesus.* Halfway House: Orion, 1997.

Included in this packet as well are Bible dictionaries, such as the *Eerdmans Bible Dictionary, Harper's Bible Dictionary, Holman Illustrated Bible Dictionary,* and *The New Bible Dictionary.* Another invaluable resource that fits the Libronix library and can be bought as a bundle includes the various InterVarsity Press dictionaries, including the *IVP Bible Background Commentary, Dictionary of New Testament Background, Dictionary of Jesus and the Gospels,* and the *Dictionary of Biblical Imagery.*

Now we will examine a series of texts where the cultural and historical background, archaeology,[2] and geography contribute important insights to the understanding of biblical revelation.

1. Luke 10:25-37: The Parable of the Good Samaritan

Suppose you were leading an adult Bible study on the parable of the Good Samaritan in Luke 10:25-37. You could examine the grammar, literary genre of parable, structure, and context of this passage but still miss vital background material. Invaluable information about the terrain between Jerusalem and Jericho, the Jewish view of "neighbor," the importance of hospitality and caring for the needy, and the image of Samaritans in first-century Palestine can be gleaned from dictionaries and encyclopedias. We will demonstrate how a study of the conflicts between Jews and Samaritans enriches an understanding of this Gospel narrative.

In Near Eastern storytelling, the recitation of three occurrences of an event signified its completion.[3] In the parable of the Good Samaritan, the high priest appears first as the spiritual leader at the apex of the religious institutions. Sadly, however, he neglects the needy person at the side of the road. Then the Levite arrives, who as a subordinate religious professional might have more time for an emergency situation, but he again abandons his duty of compassion. Those listening intently to the drama of the parable would expect the third participant to become the hero of the story. Anti-institutional sentiment was prevalent in the first century as in ours, and certainly the audience anticipated the spiritual champion to be a lay leader, who besides working a forty-hour-a-week job also dedicated another forty hours to religious duties. In the first century this person would be the Pharisee. To the crowd's amazement, Jesus presents a Samaritan as the hero. Thus, a background in Semitic storytelling enhances the meaning of the narrative.

A history of the conflicts between Jews and Samaritans also provides essential background material to understand the intense reactions and racial

2. An important recent volume offering insights into the Gospels from archaeology is James H. Charlesworth, ed., *Jesus and Archaeology* (Grand Rapids: Eerdmans, 2006).

3. As examples, think of the three temptations of Jesus in the wilderness, the three seed parables in Mark 4, Jesus' three passion predictions, the mistreatment of the three servants in the parable of the Wicked Tenants, Jesus' three prayers in the garden of Gethsemane, and the three denials of Peter.

prejudice between these two groups. The Samaritans were considered outsiders who had been imported into Israelite territory at the fall of the northern kingdom (2 Kgs 17:24-41). Thus they reminded the Jews of one of the low
points in their national history. In addition, because the five imported nations set up shrines to their own idols (2 Kgs 17:29-34), they were seen as impure and syncretistic with only a thin veneer of Yahwism covering their
deep-seated heathenism.[4] According to the incorrect understanding of
4 Baruch 8:11, the people who established Samaria with their foreign wives
were precisely those who rejected Jeremiah's call to repentance. They were
spiritually insolent and culturally rebellious. Then these mixed breed mon-
grels erected an alternative temple on Mount Gerizim in 332 B.C.E., which so
irritated the Maccabean Jews that John Hyrcanus destroyed it in 128 B.C.E.

During the life of Jesus the conflict intensified again. While the Passover
was being celebrated in Jerusalem (Coponius was procurator in 6-9 C.E.),
the Samaritans strewed human bones in the temple porches and sanctuary
during the night, desecrating the holiness of the temple (Josephus, *Ant.*
18:29-30). As a result, Samaritans were excluded from the Passover for the
first time,[5] and the Sanhedrin declared that Samaritans should be publicly
cursed in the synagogues with a daily prayer requesting that they might not
be partakers of eternal life.[6] This statement takes on special significance for
the parable of the Good Samaritan, since the lawyer begins the conversation
with this question, "What must I do to inherit eternal life?" To inherit eternal
life the lawyer must relate to the person for whom he is praying not to be a
partaker of eternal life. What an irony! The commandment to love one's
neighbor according to Jesus' perspective included the Samaritan, whereas for
the normal Jew only love for one's fellow countryman was entailed. Thus a
journey through a Bible dictionary unveils significant cultural background
material important to interpreting the NT.

The examination of extrabiblical literature can also be profitable. The
Samaritans were despised and not considered Jewish inhabitants, even
though they had lived in Palestine for centuries. Sirach 50:25-26 reports,
"There are two nations that my soul detests, the third is not a nation at all;
the inhabitants of Mount Seir, and the Philistines, and the stupid people liv-

---

4. See T. H. Gaster, "Samaritans," *The Interpreter's Dictionary of the Bible* (Nashville:
Abingdon, 1962), 4:191.

5. James A. Montgomery, *The Samaritans: The Earliest Jewish Sect: Their History, Theology, and Literature* (1907; repr. New York: Ktav, 1968), pp. 84-85.

6. See Walter Wink, "The Parable of the Compassionate Samaritan: A Communal Exegesis Approach," *RevExp* 76 (1079): 210.

ing at Shechem." Indeed, those stupid Samaritans were regarded as being on a level with the Gentiles in all things ritual and cultic. In the Mishnah, *Shevi'it* 8:10 states, "He that eats the bread of the Samaritans is like to one that eats the flesh of swine." These unclean foreigners were forbidden to offer sin offerings in the temple as well (*Sheqalim* 1:5). In fact, in a ruling adopted by the Jewish council in 65-66 C.E., Samaritan women were deemed as "menstruants from the cradle," meaning they lived in a constant state of impurity (*Niddah* 4:1; *b. Shabbat* 16b; *y. Shabbat* 3c). Finally, if a Samaritan became a witness to a bill of divorce, that in itself made the document invalid (*Gittin* 1:5). These background details enhance the surprise in the teaching of Jesus that a Samaritan replaces the priest, Levite, and Pharisee as the hero of the parable.

This extrabiblical information about Samaritans is confirmed in the details of the NT narratives. In John 4:22 Samaritans are regarded as idolaters who worship what they do not know. One of the worst insults that hostile Jews could cast upon Jesus was to call him a Samaritan, but the accusation in John 8:48 is given stronger force yet with demon possession and Samaritan nationality closely identified. "Samaria was considered to be a demon-possessed land,"[7] and Jesus condemns himself by closely associating himself with a Samaritan woman.

But in spite of these negative descriptions, Jesus continually highlights a new positive image of the Samaritans. In John 4 Jesus drinks from the same cup as a Samarian woman, but through this unholy encounter the entire Samaritan community accepts the gospel message. Jesus meets this woman at a well, which recalls the stories of marriage proposals initiated by contact with women at the town's well (Gen 24:10-61; 29:1-12; Exod 2:16-21). Jesus, like Isaac, Jacob, and Moses, finds a wife, but this time it is the Samaritan nation. Such a story would incense Jewish sensibilities, which demanded alienation from such impure people. Later in Luke's Gospel, a Samaritan foreigner (17:18) who distances himself from Jesus because he is an unclean leper (17:12) returns thanks to God for his miracle cleansing and replaces the other, presumably Jewish, lepers as the model of spiritual devotion (17:19). Finally, it is ironic that Jesus' parable took the title "The Good Samaritan," which is a true oxymoron for any Jew in Second Temple Judaism. These examples place the biblical accounts in an unforgettable historical context.

---

7. Klaus Haacker, "Samaritan," in *The New International Dictionary of New Testament Theology*, ed. Colin Brown (Grand Rapids: Zondervan, 1978), 3:463.

2. Mark 6:11: Shaking Off the Dust from One's Feet

Bible students should remember that multiple interpretations of a biblical phenomenon frequently exist. Therefore, several Bible dictionaries or commentaries must be searched. For instance, what does it mean in Mark 6:11 that the disciples were "to shake the dust off your feet as a testimony against them" when their mission was not accepted? The quickest approach is to employ electronic resources and to perform a "Basic Search" in Logos Bible Software of all your computerized dictionaries to explore the background to this concept. Begin by employing the formula Bible = "Mark 6:11." One of the hits in *Harper's Bible Dictionary* explains that, just as washing feet is an act of hospitality in the ancient Near East, so to shake the dust from the disciples' feet is to condemn and reject inhospitality.[8] Therefore, the disciples were not offered the hospitality that true servants of God deserved.

So far we have connected the ritual of "shaking the dust off one's feet" with the importance of hospitality in Jewish culture. In addition, the *Dictionary of Biblical Imagery* (an add-on to Logos Bible Software) states,

> Additional meanings of the imagery of being under the feet include disdain, defilement and judgment. . . . Seating the poor at one's footstool is likewise an act of disdain (Jas 2:3?), as is shaking off the dust of one's feet (Mk 6:11). Pearls are defiled under the feet of swine (Mt 7:6); foreigners defile the land of Israel (Micah 5:5-6), the city of Jerusalem (Lk 21:24) and especially the temple (Is 63:18; Dan 8:13; Rev 11:2) by trampling it underfoot (cf. the removal of shoes on holy ground in Ex 3:5 and 1 Sam 5:5). Treading the winepress is an image of divine judgment (Jer 25:30; Lam 1:15; Joel 3:13; Rev 19:15).[9]

More than mere human inhospitality, this action therefore signifies divine judgment. Human disdain of God's servants has aroused God's righteous anger.

An additional search of *The Exegetical Dictionary of the New Testament* located in the Gold edition of Libronix unveils further significant imagery.

> The disciples, who could not remain in one house, shake off the city's dust that clings to their feet as they leave the city in the way that a Jew shakes

---

8. John Paul Heil, "Foot," *Harper's Bible Dictionary* (San Francisco: Harper and Row, 1985), p. 318.

9. Leland Ryken, James C. Wilhoit, Tremper Longman III, eds., *Dictionary of Biblical Imagery* (Downers Grove: InterVarsity, 1998), p. 906.

off the dust of a Gentile country when he returns to his own country from a journey; thus any form of fellowship is abrogated (cf. *m. Ṭohar.* 4:5; *b. Giṭ.* 8a [*Bar.*]; *b. Ber.* 19b; Acts 18:6).[10]

Normally, Jews shake off the dust when they leave pagan territory; now the disciples are treating their fellow Jews as pagans when they do not accept the gospel message of Jesus. A Jewish gesture of scorn is ironically employed against Jews themselves.

Similarly, when the unbelieving Jews incite God-fearing women in Pisidian Antioch to persecute Paul and Barnabas, the apostles shake the dust from their feet (Acts 13:51) and move on to Iconium.[11] Again they employ a gesture of divine disdain against their own people. Believing faith, not culture or nationality, becomes the criterion of fellowship and acceptability. This gesture contains more significance than at first meets the eye. Investigations into the cultural background unearth treasures that might stay buried without the employment of Bible dictionaries.

3. Judas's Death in Matthew 27:3-10 and Acts 1:18-19

These two texts together produce a conundrum of seemingly unsolvable contradictions regarding Judas's death. Did Judas commit suicide through hanging as Matt 27:5 maintains, or did his body burst open in a fall with his bowels deteriorating as Acts 1:18 suggests? One solution is to harmonize the accounts as Apollinarius did in the fourth century and reported that "Judas did not die by hanging but lived on, having been cut down before he choked to death." Instead of a quick harmonization, we will employ a telescopic exegetical lens to explore whether descriptions of death in the cultural background enlighten these accounts of the death of Judas.

Papias's description of Judas's death in the early second century is even more gruesome and dramatic than Luke's explanation, but special attention

10. Horst R. Balz and Gerhard Schneider, *Exegetical Dictionary of the New Testament* (Grand Rapids: Eerdmans, 1993), 3:471, under χοῦς, dust.

11. In Acts 18:6 Paul shakes out his clothes, which has a precedent in Neh 5:13 as a prophetic sign against the disobedient. In addition, Paul is now innocent of any failure in not fulfilling his calling to preach the gospel. As G. K. Beale and D. A. Carson, *Commentary on the New Testament Use of the Old Testament* (Grand Rapids: Baker Academic, 2007), p. 595, maintain, "The motif of the messenger being free from guilt if the hearers do not accept the message is found in Ezek. 33:1-9; their blood is on their own heads."

must be paid to the fact that a terrible death through bloating because of worms in the bowels signified "ungodliness in this world."

> Judas was a terrible, walking example of ungodliness in this world, his flesh so bloated that he was not able to pass through a place where a wagon passes easily, not even his bloated head by itself. For his eyelids, they say, were so swollen that he could not see the light at all, and his eyes could not be seen, even by a doctor using an optical instrument, so far had they sunk below the outer surface. His genitals appeared more loathsome and larger than anyone else's, and when he relieved himself there passed through it pus and worms from every part of his body, much to his shame. After much agony and punishment, they say, he finally died in his own place, and because of the stench the area is deserted and uninhabitable even now; in fact, to this day no one can pass that place unless they hold their nose, so great was the discharge from his body and so far did it spread over the ground.[12]

As Papias states in the first sentence, he is demonstrating how evil a person Judas was by describing the loathsomeness of his death.

In ancient Near Eastern culture death through bowel disease manifested the negative character of a person's life. For instance, wicked King Jehoram's death is narrated in this fashion: "After all this, the LORD afflicted Jehoram with an incurable disease of the bowels. In the course of time, at the end of the second year, his bowels came out because of the disease, and he died in great pain. His people made no funeral fire in his honor, as they had for his predecessors" (2 Chr 21:18-19). No greater loathsome description of death could portray a king's horrid life.

With regard to the demise of the dastardly villain Antiochus Epiphanes, Josephus (*Ant.* 12:357) reports that in a fit of anxiety Antiochus fell into distemper and died; no worms are reported. But 2 Macc 9:5, 9-10 analyzes the situation differently:

> [5]But the all-seeing Lord, the God of Israel, struck him with an incurable and invisible blow. As soon as he stopped speaking he was seized with a pain in his bowels, for which there was no relief, and with sharp internal tortures. . . . [9]And so the ungodly man's body swarmed with worms, and

---

12. Taken from Papias's fourth book of the *Expositions of the Sayings of the Lord,* quoted in Michael W. Holmes, *The Apostolic Fathers: Greek Texts and English Translations* (Grand Rapids: Baker, 1999), pp. 583, 585.

while he was still living in anguish and pain, his flesh rotted away, and because of the stench the whole army felt revulsion at his decay. [10]Because of his intolerable stench no one was able to carry the man who a little while before had thought that he could touch the stars of heaven.

This less scientific and more contemporary description of Antiochus Epiphanes reveals the revulsion that he created among the Jewish people.

The death of the hated King Herod the Great is described similarly by Josephus (*J.W.* 1:656):

After this, the distemper seized upon his whole body, and greatly disordered all its parts with various symptoms; for there was a gentle fever upon him, and an intolerable itching over all the surface of his body, and continual pains in his colon, and dropsical tumors about his feet and an inflammation of the abdomen, — and a putrefaction of his privy member, that produced worms.[13]

As a fourth example, Luke pictures worms in the death of Herod Agrippa I, who martyred James the apostle: "Immediately, because Herod did not give praise to God, an angel of the Lord struck him down, and he was eaten by worms and died" (Acts 12:23).[14]

In Greco-Roman death accounts of evil persons, the same imagery is employed over and over again, so that we must conclude that such descriptions were meant metaphorically to reveal the reprehensible character of a person. For instance, although Appian pictures Sulla's wonderful retirement, where he became weary of war and power and fell in love with rural life and finally died of a fever (*Bellum Civile* 1:104-5), Plutarch attacks Sulla's character and evil deeds through a description of a loathsome death (*Sulla* 36:3).

For a long time, he was not aware that he had ulcers in the intestines. This resulted in the whole flesh being corrupted and turning into worms. Many people were employed day and night in removing these worms, but they increased far more quickly than they could be removed. Indeed, they came swarming out in such numbers that all his clothing, baths, hand-basins, and food became infected with the corruption and flux. He tried to clean and scour himself by having frequent baths throughout the day;

13. William Whiston, trans., *The Works of Josephus: Complete and Unabridged* (Peabody: Hendrickson, 1987).

14. Josephus's description (*Ant.* 19:350) contains no mention of worms but only "a pain in his belly."

but it was of no use; the flesh changed into worms too quickly, and no washing away could keep pace with their numbers.[15]

Therefore, Luke is not describing the way that Judas died historically, but is offering a theological interpretation of his death. The death of Judas soon after his evil betrayal is historical, but the different interpretations of that death by Matthew and Luke are theological.

Each author offers his own theological interpretation of the events. Matthew employs Zech 11:12-13 and Jer 19:1-13; 32:6-9 to demonstrate how Judas's actions were predicted in Scripture, while Luke quotes Pss 69:25 and 109:8 to emphasize the replacement of Judas by a deserving representative of God. Matthew highlights Judas' remorse (Matt 27:4) so that he confesses his sins and returns the money acknowledging, "I have sinned for I have betrayed innocent blood." Through this event Matthew draws attention away from Judas and Pilate, who washes his hands in a gesture of innocence (27:24) and places the guilt for Jesus' death completely upon the Jewish leaders, who declare, "Let his blood be on us and on our children!" (27:25). Similarly, the interpretations of Judas's death as hanging in Matthew[16] and death through worms consuming the intestines in Luke are intended to offer a theological interpretation of the life of Judas. A study of the cultural background enlightens our understanding of the biblical text.

4. Acts 16:16: A Python Spirit

Demonic exorcisms and the casting out of evil spirits, which at the height of historical-critical exegesis were assigned to an antiscientific age and demythologized, have in our time again become issues of serious research and discussion. In Acts 16 Paul casts out a demon from a woman, and as a result she completely loses her ability to predict the future and her owner's livelihood

15. For descriptions of suicide to polemicize evil people, see the suicide by Razis in 2 Macc 14:37-46 and the suicide of Cato in Appian, *Civil Wars* 2.14.99. The above accounts can be found in Thomas Africa, "Worms and the Death of Kings," *Classical Antiquity* 1 (1982): 1-17.

16. Death by hanging oneself also carried an interpretation of the character of one's life as with (1) the chief baker who plotted against Pharaoh fulfilling Joseph's dream (Gen 40:22; (2) the hanging of the five kings headed by the king of Jerusalem after they attacked those who had made peace with Israel (Josh 10:26); (3) Ahithophel, the advisor to Absalom against David (2 Sam 17:23); (4) the schemer Absalom himself, who was hung by his attractive hair (2 Sam 18:9); and (5) Haman, who worked to destroy the Jewish people in Persia (Esth 7:9-10).

turns bankrupt as well. Grammatical exegesis ties these two events together. The Greek reveals a pun in the text where the same form of the verb (ἐξῆλθεν, Acts 16:18b, 19a) is employed for the spirit leaving and the hope of earning money departing. Second, unusual Greek vocabulary forces the exegete to consult Bible dictionaries to determine the cultural background to this event. Whereas the NIV of Acts 16:16 reports that "she had a spirit by which she predicted the future," the Greek specifically claims that she had a python spirit (πνεῦμα πύθωνα). What is a "python spirit"?

Through performing a "Basic Search" of our electronic dictionaries (Bible = "Acts 16:16"), we discover that the *New Bible Dictionary* quotes Plutarch as Greco-Roman background and informs us that the worship of Apollo was embodied at Delphi in a snake, the Python.[17] Plutarch, who had been a priest at Delphi, speaks of such soothsayers as ventriloquists who uttered words beyond their own control. In addition the *Anchor Bible Dictionary* explains, "According to Greek myth, the *pythōn* was the serpent or dragon that inspired and guarded the oracle at Delphi; the creature was slain by the god Apollo. The word *pythōn* came to mean a divining spirit, and ventriloquists were called *Pythōnes*."[18] The girl's "revelation" is that Paul and Silas are "servants of the Most High God." Since the ethnic background of Philippi is not Jewish (for instance, there are no OT quotes in the Letter to the Philippians), hearers would not think of Yahweh but Apollo as the "Most High God." The gospel of Christ was being undermined and Apollo, the god behind the python spirit, was receiving the credit. The historical background offers an additional insight into the conflicts that were occurring at Philippi.

So far we have examined the cultural background. We could continue our exegesis of this passage by studying Lukan theology since as the *Anchor Bible Dictionary* again explains, "The story of the slave girl manifests considerable Lukan theology."[19] Certainly one of Luke's purposes in writing the book of Acts is to rehearse the victory of Christianity. Christianity triumphs over Judaism, so that Paul's gospel to the Gentiles receives the last word (Acts 26:29; 28:25-28). Christianity triumphs over the Baptist sect, so that its followers turn to Christianity and are baptized with the Holy Spirit that John the Baptizer predicted (19:1-7). Christianity triumphs over heresy and division (5:1-11; 6:1-6; 15:1-41), so that major church growth occurs in spite of

17. D. H. Wheaton, "Python," *New Bible Dictionary*, ed. D. R. W. Wood and I. H. Marshall, 3rd ed. (Downers Grove: InterVarsity, 1996), p. 992, cites Plutarch (*De defectu oraculorum* 9:414E).

18. Robert F. O'Toole, "Slave Girl at Philippi," *ABD*, 6:58.

19. O'Toole, "Slave Girl at Philippi," p. 58.

these events (5:14; 6:7; 16:5). Christianity triumphs over persecution, threats, and heretical as well as political charges, so that the movement's most zealous opponent (Saul) becomes its most ardent proponent (Paul). The specific persecution of Paul at Philippi centered upon greed and economic loss (see 19:24-29), not political rebellion against Rome, but the jail doors flying open dramatically demonstrates divine vindication of all charges. In addition, Christianity triumphs over the power of pagan religions. Here at Philippi as at Lystra (14:11-18), the victory over the gods of the pantheon is emphasized, while at Ephesus (19:23-41) Christianity triumphs over ceremonial religion and at Athens (17:16) over philosophical religion.

Finally, Luke emphasizes that Christianity triumphs over magic. In reality, magic was the prominent religion of the Greco-Roman world. In the book of Acts, Luke ridicules Simon the magician's attempt to buy apostolic power (8:18-24). Similarly, at the beginning of Paul's first missionary journey Elymas the sorcerer is blinded by Paul and completely loses his influence (13:6-12). Later, demons physically overwhelm counterfeit Jewish exorcists, and as a result sorcery books worth fifty thousand drachmas are burned (19:13-20). In contrast, Paul is not harmed by a vicious snake bite (28:4-6), so that the natives of Malta alter their view of him from a murderer to a god. Magic's ignorant superstitions become the catalyst for the spread of the gospel. Similarly, here at Philippi a woman with the power of fortune-telling loses her abilities when Paul rebukes her in the name of Jesus (16:16-18). Both cultural background and literary background are vistas for the reader to explore.

5. Revelation 3:14-22: The Geography of Laodicea

Geographical details also contribute exegetical insights when the cultural background is examined. John wrote a letter to the church at Laodicea in Rev 3:14-22 that cannot properly be interpreted without allusions to the geography behind the scenes. The reference to the church as lukewarm (3:16) points to the geographical location of Laodicea between the hot springs at Hierapolis (six miles north), which fall over a three hundred foot high cliff, and the cold waters of Colossae about ten miles distant. Laodicea is lukewarm in between these two cities. Furthermore, the expression "pride in riches" (3:17) recalls the fact that Laodicea was the wealthiest city in Phrygia and a prominent banking center. In addition, the phrase "I do not need a thing" (3:17) has been connected with Laodicea's unaided recovery from an

earthquake during Nero's reign.[20] Likewise, buying white clothes to wear
(3:18) originates from the fact that Laodicea was famous for raising black
sheep. Finally, the mentioning of salve to anoint their eyes (3:18) derives
from the medical school in Laodicea, which was famous for producing a
healing ointment to improve eyesight. These descriptive geographical and
historical details contain rich exegetical applications.

Regarding the use of specific resources, volumes on Bible background as
well as Bible dictionaries offer illustrations about Laodicea from Greco-
Roman writers, including the reports of Pseudo-Aristotle (*Mirab. Auscult.*
58) and Galen (*De sanitate tuenda* 6:12).[21] In Logos Bible Software you can
employ the "Passage Guide" tool and read the insights that commentaries
have to offer. For instance, in the *New International Greek Testament Commentary* by Greg Beale (from the Gold edition), you will discover a lengthy
section on OT background. Similarly, the *Word Biblical Commentary* by David Aune (also in Libronix format) includes helpful material under the
heading "Historical-Geographical Setting."[22]

6. Matthew 7:24-27; Luke 6:47-49: The Parable of the Two Builders

The exploration of geography also enlightens the parable of the Two
Builders. If you examine this parable in Aland's *Synopsis* §75 or §83, you notice that Matthew places the emphasis upon the crisis with a fourfold repetition of the catastrophe in Matt 7:25 and 7:27: "The rain came down; the
streams rose, and the winds blew; and beat against that house." Meanwhile,
Luke only repeats the one line that "the torrent struck that house." On the
other hand, Luke 6:47-49 emphasizes the building of a sturdy foundation
through the threefold repetition of the verb (dug, went deeper, and laid a
foundation) which is more obvious in Greek (ἔσκαψεν καὶ ἐβάθυνεν καὶ
ἔθηκεν) and whose importance demands a more literal English version.
Young's Literal Translation (YLT) in Libronix, for instance, reads, "he is like
to a man building a house, who did dig, and deepen, and laid a foundation

20. William M. Ramsay, *Letters to the Seven Churches and Their Place in the Plan of the
Apocalypse* (London: Hodder and Stoughton, 1904), p. 428.

21. See Colin J. Hemer, *The Letters to the Seven Churches of Asia in Their Local Setting.*
BRS (Grand Rapids: Eerdmans and Livonia: Dove, 2001), pp. 96-97; and F. F. Bruce,
"Laodicea," *ABD*, 4:230.

22. G. K. Beale, *The Book of Revelation.* NIGTC (Grand Rapids: Eerdmans, 1999), pp.
297-301; David E. Aune, *Revelation 1–5:14.* WBC 52A (Dallas: Word, 2002), pp. 249-50.

upon the rock" (Luke 6:48). These divergent geographical descriptions lead the careful exegete toward some interesting conclusions about the meaning of each parable.

Matthew's version is a crisis parable that calls for an immediate response to join the kingdom cause of Jesus through obedience to the instruction that he has just given in the Sermon on the Mount. In the midst of the eschatological crisis of Jesus' proclamation of the kingdom of God, the hearer must make an immediate decision. In Matthew's Palestinian geography, the flash floods abruptly pour down the mountainside in the desert so that a well-built house must be constructed upon the rock outside the sandy wadi.

On the other hand, Luke composes his Gospel for an urban Hellenistic community like Antioch and so pictures a singular river that yearly floods its banks and carries away the buildings without foundations.[23] In Hellenistic geography, one must dig down to build a foundation, whereas the bedrock lies on the surface in Palestine. Luke is therefore calling for a deepening of discipleship so that the digging, going deeper, and laying a foundation upon rock (6:48) corresponds to Jesus' earlier call to "come to me and hear my words and put them into practice" (6:47). This dual description of a three-fold action creates an intimate correspondence between a storm and discipleship. Therefore, in Luke the parable becomes a discipleship parable rather than a crisis similitude. The reader must be aware of the different building techniques in Palestine and the Diaspora to fully comprehend these similar parables. We are given a glimpse here of Luke's urban audience and the middle-class Greek speakers whom he wishes to address. Again the commentaries, dictionaries, and reference works in Logos Bible Software contribute to a more thorough understanding of the text.

B. The Old Testament as Background

With regard to specific quotes and recognized allusions to the OT, Libronix contains two helpful tools. The first resource limits itself to quotations, *Old Testament Quotations in the New Testament (HCSB)*, while the other in-

---

23. See Arland J. Hultgren, *The Parables of Jesus: A Commentary* (Grand Rapids: Eerdmans, 2000), p. 135; Michael J. Knowles, "'Everyone Who Hears These Words of Mine': Parables on Discipleship," in *The Challenge of Jesus' Parables,* ed. Richard N. Longenecker. McMaster New Testament Studies (Grand Rapids: Eerdmans, 2000), p. 288; Klyne Snodgrass, *Stories with Intent: A Comprehensive Guide to the Parables of Jesus* (Grand Rapids: Eerdmans, 2008), pp. 330-31.

cludes allusions, *Old Testament Quotations and Allusions in the New Testament* (David A. Jones) located under Tools; Bible Comparison; Parallel Passages and Harmonies; Source; Old Testament Quotes in the New Testament (Jones) in Libonix 3. In Logos 4 you can examine the resource *Old Testament Quotes in the New Testament* by H. David Philipps.

1. Numbers 6 and Psalm 67: The Aaronic Blessing Extended

Intertextuality is the study of how an earlier biblical text affects the repetition of similar concepts and vocabulary later in the history of redemption. For example, the Aaronic benediction found in Numbers 6 is strikingly similar to the introduction of Psalm 67.

> Numbers 6:24-26
> [24]The LORD bless you and keep you;
> [25]the LORD make his face shine upon you and be gracious to you;
> [26]the LORD turn his face toward you and give you peace.

> Psalm 67:1-2
> May God be gracious to us and bless us
> and make his face shine upon us
> [2]that your ways may be known on earth, your salvation among all
>   nations.

One grammatical difference is the switch from the pronoun "you" to "us," so that now the speaker is included among the recipients of blessing. But the major addition in Psalm 67:2 involves an extension of the blessing from the people of Israel to the entire world of nations.

The benediction upon God's people now becomes a missionary blessing to all people. As Marvin Tate explains, "The speaker is not identified, but it is plausible to think of a priest leading a congregation in a prayer for blessing which will bring forth praise and reverence for Yahweh from the peoples of the world."[24] National barriers are lifted and the plan of salvation extended to the entire world. Therefore, the psalmist calls all nations to testify to God by singing his praise. The refrain in verses 3 and 5 repeatedly emphasizes this extension of blessing, "May the peoples praise you, O God; may all the peoples praise you." This missionary task of the people of God finally gets

---

24. Marvin E. Tate, *Psalms 51–100*. WBC 20 (Dallas: Word, 2002), p. 155.

concretized in the Great Commission of Jesus to "Go and make disciples of all nations" (Matt 28:19). Intertextuality thus demonstrates the extension of the covenant as the blessing of Abraham and the Aaronic blessing resound in the vocabulary of later texts of Scripture.

2. Luke 1:78: The Rising Sun

A line of the Song of Zechariah in Luke 1:78 is difficult to interpret: "the rising sun (ἀνατολὴ ἐξ ὕψους) will come to us from heaven to shine on those living in darkness." What is this "rising sun"? For the preacher who during Advent must return yearly to Matthew 1–2 and the first two chapters of Luke, a lucid understanding of each verse of these Christmas songs is critical to sufficient sermon material. A search of the OT background is frequently beneficial. In Logos Bible Software you can search through the Septuagint (LXX) on the lemma ἀνατολή. Unfortunately, in this case there are close to two hundred occurrences of this term. Which references are the most important? This is where past research experts who have written commentaries and dictionary articles prove invaluable. To gain access to this information, you can perform a basic search in Logos 4 in your established collection of Bible dictionaries by typing Luke 1:78 in the box.[25] In the *Dictionary of Jesus and the Gospels* (an add-on to Libronix), you will uncover this explanation:

> Moreover, the *anatolē*, or "dayspring," of verse 78, a difficult word which contains within its range of meaning reference both to the sprouting up of a plant and the rising of a star, seems to refer to the "sprout" or "root" of David (Jer 23:5; cf. Zech 3:8; 6:12). The images are combined in Revelation 22:16 in which the exalted Christ declares, "I am the root and offspring of David, the bright morning star." The hymn seems an answer to those hopes later formalized in the fifteenth benediction of the great synagogue prayer, the eighteen benedictions *(šəmōneh 'eśrēh)*, "Let the shoot of David speedily spring up and raise his horn in Your Salvation. . . . May you be blessed, O Lord, who lets the horn of salvation flourish."[26]

---

25. You can perform a basic search in Libronix 3 of Bible dictionaries using the formula: Bible = "Luke 1:78."

26. S. C. Farris, "Zechariah's Song," in *Dictionary of Jesus and the Gospels*, ed. Joel B. Green and Scot McKnight (Downers Grove: InterVarsity, 1992), p. 895.

Here we are given three OT passages to consult. Jeremiah 23:5 as well as Zech 3:8 and 6:12 all refer to the coming of my servant, the Branch (ἀνατολή). The rising one is the messianic branch but also the star of Num 24:17, which predicts that "a star will rise (ἀνατελεῖ) out of Jacob." This conclusion is reinforced by the use of ἀνατολή to refer to the star of Bethlehem in the Matthean birth narrative at Matt 2:1, 2, 9. Therefore, Luke 1:78 should be translated "rising star" rather than "sun," as Raymond Brown notes in his book *The Birth of the Messiah*.[27] The OT background found in passages about the branch and the star enlighten the darkness of a cryptic Greek term in the birth narrative of Jesus.

3. The Scriptural Background to Jesus' Parables

To receive the full impact of Jesus' parables, the reader must be familiar with the OT. In the parable of the Mustard Seed (Luke 13:18-19; Matt 13:31-32) the kingdom of God is inaugurated as the smallest seed in the Near Eastern world but launches into a tree where all the nations of the earth can find shade. Jesus employs Ezek 31:1-9 as a foil to tell a new but familiar sounding story with surprising twists. In the passage in Ezekiel, the world-dominating power of Assyria is compared to a colossal cedar of Lebanon that "towered on high, its top above the thick foliage" (Ezek 31:3) with overshadowing branches like the garden of God in paradise (31:8). All the birds of the air nest in its boughs, meaning that Assyria has authority over the entire world (see also Dan 4:12).

But now, Jesus recites a parable about a mustard seed, the tiniest seed known in Palestine, instead of a story concerning a gigantic cedar. In addition, we learn from the Mishnah, Judaism's most prominent book after the OT, that the mustard seed was banned from gardens in Jerusalem because it was a despicable invasive weed.[28] As David Buttrick explains, the parable "seems to be a deliberate burlesque of the mighty cedar of Lebanon, a symbol

---

27. Raymond E. Brown, *The Birth of the Messiah* (Garden City: Doubleday, 1979), p. 374.

28. *Kil'ayim* 3:2 states that "No kind of seeds do they sow in a garden bed, but all kinds of vegetables do they sow in a garden bed. Mustard and smooth chick-peas (alternate translation: small chick-peas) [are considered] kind[s] of seeds." Snodgrass, *Stories with Intent*, p. 220, contends that erroneous assumptions have been drawn from this passage, which only applies to small gardens and not larger gardens. Whichever is true, the contrast with Ezekiel 31 is still dramatic.

of national power and triumph. Instead of a mighty cedar, Jesus pictures a weed, indeed, a weed regarded as a public nuisance."[29] Most "respectable" first-century people regarded Christianity as a nuisance, a tiny marginal religious movement composed of commoners. But Jesus has great plans for this insignificant band: "Do not be afraid, little flock, for your Father has been pleased to give you the kingdom" (Luke 12:32). The tiniest seed will produce a sprawling tree where all the nations of the earth will find comfortable shade. Jesus will establish his kingdom through a tiny flock of marginalized, unrespectable disciples. What a contrast with the similar parable in Ezekiel 31!

Coupled with the parable of the Mustard Seed stands the parable of the Leaven (Luke 13:20-21; Matt 13:33). Here again Jesus employs a negative symbol, this time associated with sinful corruption as is evident from 1 Cor 5:7, "Get rid of the old yeast that you may be a new batch without yeast — as you really are." In the OT only unleavened bread could be placed on the altar and employed at Israel's feasts. The smoke of anything leavened was a putrid odor to a holy God (Lev 2:11). In the NT Jesus warns against the leaven of the Pharisees, which is hypocrisy (Luke 12:1). Paul identifies leaven with malice and evil while unleavened represents sincerity and truth (1 Cor 5:8). In addition Paul warns those who follow anyone who teaches justification by works and not by faith alone that "a little yeast works through the whole batch of dough" (Gal 5:9). However, in Jesus' parable the kingdom of God is compared to leaven. In fact, a marginalized woman using the reviled Jewish symbol of leaven can bake enough bread to fill up a modern day semi-truck and feed between 100 and 150 people. Similarly, a despised group of fishermen and peasants will mightily permeate the dead lump of religious Judaism with their preaching about the kingdom of God.

But the full meaning of the text is not grasped until the designation "three seahs of flour" is aligned with Gen 18:6. There Sarah, the wife of Abraham, employs this exact amount of flour to produce a feast to welcome God himself into their tent. This OT allusion entails that God himself has arrived in the ministry of Jesus. Therefore, when the NIV transposes three seahs or measures of fine flour into "a large amount of flour," the English reader is prohibited from making a connection with the OT narrative behind it. Jesus is building his parable based upon God's visit to Abraham and Sarah. Intertextuality supplies the reader with crucial additional meaning.

In another Gospel pericope (Matt 18:21-22), Jesus' comment to Peter in

---

29. David Buttrick, *Speaking Parables: A Homiletic Guide* (Louisville: Westminster John Knox, 2000), p. 53.

extending the forgiveness of God from seven times to an unheard-of seventy-seven times recalls the curse of Lamech in Gen 4:24: "If Cain is avenged seven times, then Lamech seventy-seven times." In the ministry of Jesus divine forgiveness, not the damnation of a curse, is extended to the nth degree. Therefore, in the parable that follows (Matt 18:23-27), the master forgives the servant ten thousand talents, an amount equal to sixty million denarii, where one denarius was the average daily wage in Palestine. Put another way, ten thousand talents would be 204 metric tons of precious metal. At this rate it would take the servant more than 164,000 years to reimburse the king. Through hilarious exaggeration Jesus reverses the curse of Cain and Lamech with immeasurable abundant grace.

Again, in the parable of the Sower the productive ground of the kingdom produces one hundredfold (Mark 4:8, 20). This remark summons up the OT passage where Isaac, after sojourning in the land of Canaan for many years, finally plants crops and reaps one hundredfold (Gen 26:12). The retaking of the promised land is at hand in the ministry of Jesus. The gift of the land to Israel is fulfilled in the coming of the Messiah, Jesus of Nazareth.

Finally, in reciting the parable of the Lost Sheep Jesus is fulfilling what God himself does in Ezek 34:11-12: "For this is what the Sovereign LORD says: I myself will search for my sheep and look after them. As a shepherd looks after his scattered flock when he is with them, so will I look after my sheep." Jesus' example of pursuing the lost sheep of Israel (Matt 15:24) becomes a call to the disciples to seek the lost sheep on the mountainside (Matt 18:12, based upon Ezek 34:6), even if they have to leave the ninety-nine behind. These examples clearly demonstrate how crucial an exploration of the OT background is in our exegesis of the NT books. If we miss the trajectory backward to previous literature, we will overlook the intention of the author.

4. Fishers of People (Mark 1:17): OT Backdrop or Geographical Background?

Sometimes the importance of the OT background needs to be weighed over against the contemporary cultural milieu.[30] The metaphor of fishing was em-

---

30. For instance, in the parable of the Lost Sheep just discussed, should shepherds be viewed against the contemporary despised marginalized herders of Jesus' time or against an OT background, where the shepherds like David were the rulers of Israel? In that parable we concluded that an OT background was more probable, since Jesus constantly employs OT material in his parables.

ployed by the OT prophets to display God's wrath and judgment in plucking Israel out of the water of their homeland. Amos 4:2 warns, "The Sovereign LORD has sworn by his holiness: 'The time will surely come when you will be taken away with hooks, the last of you with fishhooks'" (see Ezek 17:20). One of the closest expressions to "fishers of men" is Jer 16:16, which gives notice, "But now I will send for many fishermen, declares the LORD, and they will catch them. After that I will send for many hunters, and they will hunt them down on every mountain and hill and from the crevices of the rocks." From these texts one would assume a negative meaning to the phrase "fishers of people," so that the disciples would be calling forth judgment on Israel. In that case Peter would be the rock (Mark 3:16) who crushes God's people with words of repentance, and James and John, the sons of thunder (3:17), would call down fire and destruction as they desired to do in Luke 9:54.[31]

The clearest alternative to a background in the OT use of fishing is to posit the Sea of Galilee and the vocation of the disciples as the backdrop for Jesus instilling new meaning into the symbol of fishing. Instead of the undertone of violently snatching fish from their natural environment, Jesus would be employing a missionary connotation of gathering all nations into the net of the kingdom of God (see Matt 13:47). This would fit with a positive use of fish in this saying as well as the employment of bread in the feeding of the five thousand and four thousand, especially if the twelve baskets left over symbolized the feeding of Israel whereas the seven containers (Mark 8:19-21) stood for the Gentile nations of Canaan (see Acts 13:19). The extracanonical book Joseph and Aseneth 21:21 functions as a helpful parallel: "by his beauty he caught me, and by his wisdom he grasped me like a fish on a hook, and by his spirit, as by bait of life, he ensnared me, and by his power he confirmed me, and brought me to the God of the ages and to the chief of the house of the Most High, and gave me to eat bread of life, and to drink a cup of wisdom, and I became his bride for ever and ever."[32] Then the understanding of "fishers of people" would be primarily positive as a call to missionary work.

Joel Marcus contends that the faithful exegete does not have to choose among the various interpretations. Then "fishers of people" would be "a multivalent image that includes their future missionary preaching, their future teaching, and their future exorcisms . . . all of which are understood as a

---

31. For a connotation of judgment, see Charles W. F. Smith, "Fishers of Men: Footnotes on a Gospel Metaphor," *HTR* 52 (1959): 187-203; and Wilhelm H. Wuellner, *The Meaning of "Fishers of Men"* (Philadelphia: Westminster, 1967).

32. James H. Charlesworth, *The Old Testament Pseudepigrapha* (Garden City: Doubleday, 1985), 2:237-38.

participation in God's eschatological war against demonic forces."[33] How-ever, since the context of the metaphor is the calling of disciples along the Sea of Galilee and not a milieu similar to the OT prophets, it seems better to posit a missionary meaning. As R. T. France notes, "In the context of 'good news' this [i.e., the negative interpretation] can hardly be Jesus' meaning, nor does it correspond to the task the disciples will be given later in the gos-pel."[34] Although an OT background must always be explored, sometimes the context leads us in a different direction.

C. Basic Background Information for Biblical Books

PROCEDURE

So far we have examined how the cultural background and the OT enlighten the text. Now we will turn to the basic background information pertaining to a biblical book, including the provenance, date of composition, authorship, recipients, and purpose of the work. We will offer two instances where an in-vestigation of the introductory background material is vital to an interpreta-tion of the Pauline Epistles, followed by two examples from the Gospels.

EXAMPLES

1. Slavery and Paul's Epistle to Philemon

When contemporary readers imagine the slavery described in the Epistle to Philemon, we immediately identify it with racial prejudice, bigotry, and a life-long oppressive environment where the slave is conscripted against his or her will. In line with our experience, we picture all slavery as an intolerable situa-tion incompatible with the Christian faith. Are we reading our conceptions of slavery back upon the NT? These questions demonstrate the importance of re-searching background material to the biblical books through Bible dictionar-ies and articles in theological periodicals.

The *International Standard Bible Encyclopedia* (an add-on in Logos Bible Software) perceptively rehearses the differences between ancient enslavement

---

33. Joel Marcus, *Mark 1–8*. AB 27 (Garden City: Doubleday, 2000), p. 185.

34. R. T. France, *The Gospel of Mark*. NIGTC (Grand Rapids: Eerdmans, 2002), p. 96.

and the types of slavery we are familiar with. In stark contrast to New World slavery prevalent in the seventeenth through nineteenth centuries, Greco-Roman slavery was not a permanent condition but rather only a temporary phase of life. Very few persons are known to have reached old age in slavery; instead, pertinent inscriptions indicate that roughly 50 percent were set free by the age of thirty. Manumissions were entirely normal and expected. More than one thousand release contracts were inscribed on the sacred wall in Delphi. In fact, "At the beginning of the century owners were manumitting their slaves with a frequency that provoked Augustus Caesar to introduce laws restricting the numbers and ages of those who could be lawfully manumitted."[35]

A second difference concerns the initiation process. Rather than forced slavery, Greco-Roman enslavement was for the most part a voluntary process. As Bartchy explains,

> Large numbers of people sold themselves into slavery for various reasons, above all to enter a life that was easier and more secure than existence as a poor, freeborn person, to obtain special jobs, and to climb socially. It is quite likely that the Erastus mentioned in Rom. 16:23 as the 'city treasurer' *oikonómos tēs póleōs)* of Corinth had to sell himself to the city (as a form of 'bonding insurance') in order to secure this responsible position. . . . Many non-Romans sold themselves to Roman citizens with the justified expectation, carefully regulated by Roman law, of becoming Roman citizens themselves when manumitted. The money that one received from such a self-sale into slavery usually became the beginning of the personal funds *(peculium)* that would later be used to enter freedom under more favorable circumstances, e.g., with former debts extinguished.[36]

Slavery was therefore for many a beneficial process that they voluntarily entered.

Third, ancient slavery had no connection to race or the stigma of a particular excluded social class. "In outward appearance it was usually impossible to distinguish among slaves, freedmen, and free persons. Neither the slave's clothing nor his or her race revealed a legal or social status. Patterns of religious life, friends, or work did not separate slaves from freed persons or freeborn workers."[37] In fact, slaves held respected positions in society, includ-

---

35. Scott S. Bartchy, "Slavery," *International Standard Bible Encyclopedia*, ed. Geoffrey W. Bromiley (Grand Rapids: Eerdmans, 1979), 4:545.

36. Bartchy, "Slavery," p. 543.

37. Bartchy, "Slavery," p. 544.

ing tutors of persons of all ages, physicians, nurses, executives with decision-making powers, and managers of households, ships, and estates. Capable slaves were given an excellent education at their owner's expense, including famous philosophers (Epictetus), teachers (Verrius Flaccus), grammarians (Palaemon), and administrators (Felix).[38] Craig deVos adds, "In the collectivist, authoritarian and patriarchal cultures of the Greco-Roman world of the first century we would not expect much difference in these two types of relationships. The act of manumission did not significantly change the circumstances of most slaves, or how they were perceived or treated."[39] These types of descriptions break all of our stereotypes about slavery.

Scriptural teaching on slavery must be understood in this context. Owning and using men and women as slaves were taken entirely for granted by all ancient teachers. Therefore, Paul had no grandiose plans of demanding the total demolition of this entire system of serfdom. But what exactly was Paul's purpose in writing this letter to Philemon? The traditional understanding states that "Onesimus was a slave of Philemon in Colossae (cf. Col. 4:9) who had not only run away from his master (Phlm. 15-16) but had also absconded with some of Philemon's money or possessions (vv. 18-19)."[40] Then Paul is either asking that Onesimus's debt be applied to his account (vv. 18-19) and that Philemon allow Paul to use his services as a forgiven slave,[41] or Paul is requesting not to delay Onesimus's manumission because of any misdeeds.[42] If Paul was asking for Onesimus's freedom, he is speaking of a normal everyday occurrence.

Recently this traditional interpretation has been accused of unjustly defending the master rather than the slave and therefore displaying a vested interest in the establishment leading to social prejudice. The upcoming mainline view[43] now states, "Far from running away from his master, Onesimus is

38. Bartchy, "Slavery," p. 544.
39. Craig S. deVos, "Once a Slave, Always a Slave? Slavery, Manumission and Relational Patterns in Paul's Letter to Philemon," *JSNT* 82 (2001): 100.
40. Murray J. Harris, *Colossians & Philemon*. Exegetical Guide to the Greek New Testament (Grand Rapids: Eerdmans, 1991), p. 241.
41. DeVos, "Once a Slave, Always a Slave?" p. 105, states, "Therefore, Paul's intention in his letter to Philemon was not to persuade Philemon to manumit Onesimus, but to bring about a fundamental change in their relationship, such that the master would treat his slave no longer as a slave, but as a brother or honoured guest."
42. Bartchy, "Slavery," p. 545. See deVos, "Once a Slave, Always a Slave?" p. 90, notes 3 and 4, for those in favor and against the view that Paul was asking Philemon for manumission.
43. See D. A. Carson and Douglas J. Moo, *An Introduction to the New Testament*, 2nd ed. (Grand Rapids: Zondervan, 2005), p. 591.

in fact deliberately running to a friend of the master in hope that, through the friend's intervention, he might be happily restored to his master."[44] However, to imagine Onesimus traveling some 1200 miles from Colossae to Rome to seek help from a friend of his master seems far-fetched. Furthermore, Paul continually calls attention to Philemon's faith and love for fellow Christians (vv. 5, 7), and the conditional clause in verse 18, "if he has wronged you at all or owes you anything," seems to imply that the slave is in the wrong rather than the master.[45] Whatever the purpose of the letter, we perceive a positive attitude from Christians toward the slave Onesimus. The NT cannot be accused of racial prejudice.

Besides searching out the cultural background and purpose of the letter, epistolary analysis should lead us to the identical positive attitude toward the slave Onesimus. Paul's "brief masterpiece of sensitive persuasion"[46] begins with a letter opening where Paul identifies himself with Onesimus's condition as a slave. Paul's self-designation as a prisoner (δέσμιος) rather than his normal title "apostle" places him in the same situation as Onesimus and is not simply due to his current imprisonment, since he does not employ this title in Philippians, Colossians, or Ephesians. In the joy formula (v. 7) of the thanksgiving section, Paul remarks that Philemon has refreshed the hearts of the saints (τὰ σπλάγχνα τῶν ἁγίων ἀναπέπαυται διὰ σοῦ), but then employs this fact in verse 20 to request that Philemon now refresh Paul's heart (ἀνάπαυσόν μου τὰ σπλάγχνα) by allowing Onesimus, Paul's very heart (v. 12), to be his apprentice in the gospel proclamation. In the body of the letter Paul employs an appeal formula (vv. 9-10) where he claims that Onesimus has become his son, a family member. Likewise, he calls Philemon "brother" (vv. 7, 20), so that by inference Philemon is also the brother of Onesimus (v. 16), his slave. Therefore, a completely new family relationship is envisioned. In the closing hortatory section of the letter, Paul creates a pun on Onesimus's name to demonstrate his usefulness. The expression, "that I may have some benefit (ὀναίμην) from you in the Lord" (v. 20), recalls Onesimus's name, just as in verse 11 Paul has described Onesimus as useful both to Philemon and Paul. Thus a slave is endowed with positive connotations throughout each standard part of the letter.

Paul suggests that Philemon is performing the correct action by return-

---

44. Brian Rapske, "The Prisoner Paul in the Eyes of Onesimus," *NTS* 37 (1991): 195-96.

45. See Jeffrey A. D. Weima, "Collected Readings & Class Notes: The Pauline Letters & Their Message for the Church," Calvin Theological Seminary Class Syllabus, p. 248.

46. Bartchy, "Slavery," p. 545.

ing Onesimus to Paul's service. The normal action required of runaway slaves was to return them to their master by not providing a place of refuge (Symmachus, *Letters* 9, 140), but Paul reverses this standard procedure and requests that Onesimus would be returned to him. In fact, Philemon the master must picture himself as a slave as well since Paul could order him to do this (v. 8) since he owes Paul his very self (v. 19). The positions of master and slave no longer have significance in the Christian community.

The above material demonstrates that a study of the background material to a biblical book frequently breaks our modern stereotypes, introduces us to new possible interpretations not yet envisioned, and employs literary devices that were common to the readers of that day but unfamiliar to a contemporary audience.

2. Work Ethic and 2 Thessalonians

In 1 Thess 5:14 Paul instructs the church to admonish the idle (ἀτάκτους). This behavior stands over against the example of the apostolic team who "did not live in idleness among them" (ἠτακτήσαμεν, 2 Thess. 3:7). Then in 2 Thess 3:6 Paul warns to "keep away from every brother who is idle (ἀτάκτως; see 3:11) and does not live according to the teaching you received from us." This statement in turn reminds the reader of 1 Thess 4:11, where Paul likewise commands, "Make it your ambition to lead a quiet life, to mind your own business and to work with your hands, just as we told you." How can a study of the background to this epistle help us understand what is occurring in Thessalonica?

The Greek term ἄτακτοι possesses two possible meanings, either of which is appropriate in the Thessalonian situation. As Jeffrey Weima explains, "One is derived from its use in military contexts to depict soldiers who would not keep step or follow commands — that is, those who were 'obstinate' or 'rebellious.' The other stems from its use in the papyri of the Hellenistic period to describe students or workers who failed to do their work — that is, those who were 'idle' or 'lazy.'"[47] Paul is therefore alarmed about the rebelliously idle. These people were unwilling to work (2 Thess 3:10) already at Paul's original visit (1 Thess 4:11; 2 Thess 3:10), relying on oth-

---

47. Jeffrey A. D. Weima, "'How You Must Walk to Please God': Holiness and Discipleship in 1 Thessalonians," in *Patterns of Discipleship in the New Testament*, ed. Richard N. Longenecker. McMaster New Testament Studies (Grand Rapids: Eerdmans, 1996), p. 113.

ers for their sustenance (1 Thess 4:12), and becoming a financial burden (2 Thess 3:8) to the Thessalonian congregation (3:11). Who are these disorderly meddlers, and why are they acting in this manner?

Because Paul never specifically articulates the root cause of the ἄτακτοι problem, commentators differ regarding the background of 2 Thess 3:6-15. Should an eschatological backdrop be posited, or do sociological factors take precedence?[48] Simply stated, the eschatological view imagines a group of idlers who believe that, since the end of the world is near, work is a waste of time. Christ is returning immediately, so why put one's time and effort into building an earthly future that will soon pass away? An alternative version concentrates on realized eschatology and contends that the Thessalonians thought that the day of the Lord had already come spiritually and therefore they were experiencing the eternal Sabbath rest, which did not require work.[49] Evidence in favor of an eschatological proposal is the repeated reference to Christ's return in the Thessalonian correspondence (1 Thess 4:13–5:11, 23; 2 Thess 2:1-17). Weima points out that "the problem of idleness, which is raised twice in 1 Thessalonians (4:11-12; 5:14), frames the extended discussion of matters concerning Christ's return."[50] Therefore, eschatology and idleness must be connected.

Although this eschatological explanation stands as the traditional view, the preponderance of modern scholars denies any connections between eschatological expectations and the ἄτακτοι problem. They point to Paul's silence in not explicitly connecting eschatology to the problem of the rebellious idlers. In fact, Paul's discussion appears to be entirely ethical without theological overtones. Furthermore, the expectation of an immediate return of Christ in other biblical passages created a stricter ethic and not laziness. In 1 Cor 7:5, 24-26 those who expect an immediate return of Christ are willing to forgo sexual relations and remain celibate in order to participate in kingdom work. In Gal 4:15 the community is eager to tear out their eyeballs to offer Paul improved eyesight to perform his apostolic calling. Eschatological nearness produces commitment and self-sacrifice, not laziness.

48. For a summary of the history of interpretation see Benjamin Ribbens, "The Eschatological Origin of the 'Ataktoi' in Thessalonica" (Th.M. diss., Calvin Theological Seminary, 2009), pp. 1-10.

49. See Greg K. Beale, *1-2 Thessalonians*. IVP New Testament Commentary 13 (Downers Grove: InterVarsity, 2003), pp. 247-64.

50. Weima, "How You Must Walk to Please God," p. 113. He adds on page 114 that eschatological excitement has led to idleness in a variety of religious groups over the centuries. See also Ribbens, "Eschatological Origin of the 'Ataktoi,'" pp. 129-30.

Instead, this rebellious laziness appears to be present even before Paul arrived on the scene, before the conversion of the Thessalonians. Following this line of thinking, many researchers prefer sociological reasons for the Thessalonians' disdain for work.[51] They had adopted the Greek repulsion for manual labor rather than Paul's model lifestyle of working with one's hands while preaching the gospel (1 Thess 4:11; Acts 18:3; 20:34-35). This attitude became inflated when they were converted to Christianity, because now they were free children of God and did not expect to work like slaves. David Aune thinks that they possessed an elevated sense of self-importance born out of their new spiritual condition.[52] They formed relationships with Christian patrons who would support them with money, food, and representation. This resulted in Paul's accusation that they were exploiting the generosity of their new Christian patrons. Bruce Winter even thinks that Paul's counsel was to dissolve all patron-client relationships.[53]

In contrast to these views, other scholars point out that patronage did not necessarily produce laziness. Part of the client's daily routine was accompanying one's patron to the public square in order to applaud their speeches and support their public policies so that their economic and political interests would be promoted. Thus Weima points out that patronage "involved sufficient activity that clients would not likely be accused of idleness."[54] In addition, why would rich Christians continually support those who were simply being lazy and greedy?[55] Significant questions even exist regarding the prevalence of patronage in Roman Thessalonica.[56] The Greco-Roman writings that degrade manual labor represent the views of the affluent and cultured, which does not seem to represent Thessalonian demographics.[57] Furthermore, if Paul opposed patronage, one would expect references in

---

51. Abraham J. Malherbe, *The Letters to the Thessalonians*. AB 32B (New York: Doubleday, 2000), pp. 256-60, 454-57, contends that this group conformed their lives to Epicurean social values. For a summary of sociological explanations, see Ribbens, "Eschatological Origin of the 'Ataktoi,'" pp. 61-76.

52. David C. Aune, "Trouble in Thessalonica: An Exegetical Study of I Thess 4.9-12; 5.12-14; and II Thess. 3.6-15 in Light of First-Century Social Conditions" (Th.M. thesis, Regent College, 1989), p. 92.

53. Bruce W. Winter, "From Secular Clients to Christian Benefactors," in *Seek the Welfare of the City: Christians as Benefactors and Citizens* (Grand Rapids: Eerdmans, 1994), pp. 48-50.

54. Weima, "How You Must Walk to Please God," p. 115.

55. Ribbens, "Eschatological Origin of the 'Ataktoi,'" p. 72, asks this question.

56. See Ribbens, "Eschatological Origin of the 'Ataktoi,'" pp. 67-68.

57. Ribbens, "Eschatological Origin of the "Ataktoi,'" pp. 61-63.

other letters as well. Finally, Paul does thoroughly integrate eschatological and ethics in 1 and 2 Thessalonians.[58]

In describing the Thessalonian situation, Charles Wanamaker asserts that "A careful reading suggests that Paul had three principal concerns regarding the church: he believed that the church was undergoing oppression (2 Thess 1:4-6); he was worried that his converts were deviating from a correct understanding of the day of the Lord (2:1-12); and he was troubled by a report that some members of the community were indolent and exercising a disruptive influence on the community (3:6-15)."[59] Together these three purposes reveal both difficult socio-economic relationships and a distorted theology. Troublesome social-economic conditions seem crucial in forming a context in which this problem of rebellious idleness could arise. In all likelihood, these new believers were affected by their culture and thus were easily repulsed by manual labor. But because religious justification of unseemly behavior is a common phenomenon, this group in Thessalonica used the nearness of Christ's coming as an excuse for laziness and so became rebellious to Paul's apostolic teaching. Therefore, an investigation of the background to the book of 2 Thessalonians should give due regard to both eschatology and the social conditions infecting the church.[60]

3. Sayings from the Cross in the Four Gospels

When I was a pastor/preacher in a local church, we would plan an afternoon ecumenical service each year commemorating the seven last words of Christ on Good Friday. Numerous participants imagined that all seven sayings were contained in each Gospel. They would harmonize all the Gospels together so that Jesus' cry of forsakenness need not be taken too seriously, since in a few moments he would call God his father again ("Father, forgive

58. See the series of examples in Ribbens, "Eschatological Origin of the 'Ataktoi,'" pp. 84-86.

59. Charles A. Wanamaker, *The Epistles to the Thessalonians: A Commentary on the Greek Text.* NIGTC (Grand Rapids: Eerdmans, 1990), p. 58.

60. Several scholars consider both factors. See Ernest Best, *A Commentary on the First and Second Epistles to the Thessalonians.* HNTC (New York: Harper and Row, 1972), pp. 175-76, for an eschatological background and p. 334 for a sociological description; I. Howard Marshall, *1 and 2 Thessalonians.* NCB (Grand Rapids: Eerdmans, 1983), pp. 219, 223, 253 for sociological analysis and p. 131 for the eschatological situation; Heinz Schürmann, *The First Epistle to the Thessalonians* (London: Burnes and Oates, 1969), pp. 157-58.

them") and recite triumphantly, "It is finished." However, the sayings of Jesus on the cross must be interpreted against the background of each individual Gospel.

To uncover where each saying of Jesus is narrated in your English Bibles, you can employ a Gospel harmony that uses the red-lettering feature in Logos Bible Software like *A Harmony of the Synoptic Gospels* by Burton and Goodspeed.[61] By examining the crucifixion passage, you discover that the first Gospel, Mark, only transmits one saying, "My God, my God, why have you forsaken me?" (Mark 15:34; Matt 27:46). Apparently Mark wants his community to dwell upon the forsakenness of Jesus. At the center of the book Jesus predicts his suffering on three successive occasions (8:31; 9:31; 10:33), and at the climax Jesus dies a despised death on the cross alone and alienated from his disciples. Since the persecuted church of Mark's time will undergo such a severe sense of forsakenness, he wishes to remind them of the faithful endurance of Jesus in the midst of seeming abandonment. Therefore, Mark omits the resurrection appearances (16:9-20 is a later addition) to center the community's attention on the cross, so that they hear the call to voluntary suffering. The situation of the community to which Mark is writing determines which sayings from the cross he incorporates into the narrative.

In addition to assimilating almost the entirety of Mark's Passion Narrative, Matthew inserts three noteworthy pericopes into his Gospel. With remorse, Judas reimburses the Jewish leaders the thirty pieces of silver (Matt 27:1-10) so that he no longer bears the primary guilt for Jesus' death. Pilate as well repeatedly attempts to free Jesus and finally washes his hands of the matter protesting his innocence (27:24). Matthew then adds that the Jewish populace take primary responsibility for the death of Jesus, reciting almost an oath formula, "Let his blood be on us and on our children!" (27:25). The Gospel of Matthew is an apologetic against the Jewish synagogue, pointing out their need for repentance and the forgiveness offered through Jesus' death. To carry out this agenda, Matthew inserts these three passages into Mark's treatment of Jesus' death. Again, the author's situation affects which material from the Jesus-tradition is included in the narrative.

Luke recites three additional crucifixion sayings of Jesus, each portraying a dimension of Luke's purpose in preparing the Gospel record. Luke's crucifixion account can be divided into three sections, each constructed around one utterance of Jesus. In Luke 23:26-34, the author introduces the

---

61. You can easily employ the red-lettering feature in Libronix 3 as well (Tools; Options; Bible Tools; General) and call to the screen Aland's *Synopsis of the Four Gospels* §347.

personnel at the cross, including Simon of Cyrene, the mourning women, the fellow criminals, and the soldiers who crucify Jesus. At this point Jesus declares, "Father, forgive them, for they do not know what they are doing." Here we encounter the Lukan theme of the magnitude of God's forgiveness as savior. The picture of Jesus as the selfless Christ thinking only of others like the soldiers and the thief becomes a model for the followers of Jesus, so that the saying is repeated when Stephen, the first Christian martyr, likewise forgives his enemies (Acts 7:60).

The second paragraph in Luke's crucifixion narrative focuses upon the mockery of Jesus (Luke 23:35-43). In the midst of extreme ridicule from the rulers, people, soldiers, and a fellow criminal, Jesus responds to the repentant murderer with compassion, "Today you will be with me in paradise." This action reinforces the Lukan theme of Jesus' warmhearted contact with the marginalized and leftovers of society. Christ's last companion on earth and first comrade in heaven becomes a lowly prisoner.

Finally, Jesus' death itself is portrayed in Luke 23:44-49, centering upon his loud cry of confidence and victory, "Father, into your hands I commit my spirit." Luke-Acts celebrates the victory of Christ and Christianity over any and all obstacles.[62] Rather than rehearsing Jesus' suffering and forsakenness, Luke omits *"Eloi, Eloi, lama sabachthani"* (Mark 15:34) and replaces it with a positive prayer of assurance. The double Lukan motif of prayer and victory raises its head also here in the crucifixion narrative. Therefore, Luke's unique motifs in the crucifixion narrative correspond perfectly with his major emphases elsewhere.

Finally, the Gospel of John also contains three cross sayings of Jesus, but again all novel utterances. To be lifted up on the cross is the first stage of exaltation in Johannine theology (John 12:32). Therefore, the sayings from the cross demonstrate Jesus' exaltation, so that he is fulfilling Scripture and initiating the mission of the community that will follow him. Christ is sovereignly in control of everything that happens. Jesus gives his mother to the care of the beloved disciple (19:26-27), so that the Christian community composed of the apostles, women, and Jesus' family (Acts 1:14) is inaugurated. When he says "I am thirsty" (John 19:28), Jesus is not exasperated but is purposefully fulfilling Scripture. Furthermore, the thirst he is experiencing is not physical exhaustion but a thirst to drink the cup of God's will (18:11; 4:34; 12:27). Finally, the expression "it is finished" is not a regret that his life is over or a sigh of relief that his suffering is concluded, but a trium-

---

62. See above the ending of section A4, "Acts 16:16: A Python Spirit" (pp. 167-69).

phant exclamation point upon the crucifixion narrative signifying that the work of redemption is finished. In his victory Jesus is the chief prophet who fulfills the Scriptures, the high priest who concludes the sacrificial system, and the eternal king who conquers sin, death, and hell. The purpose of the Gospel "that you may believe that Jesus is the Christ, the Son of God, and that by believing you may have life in his name" (20:31) is evident in the exalted portrayal of Jesus in his death. When the overall purposes and themes of each Gospel are rehearsed, the individual details of the crucifixion narrative take on fuller significance as the reader glimpses the big picture.

4. Mark 9:49-50: The Uses of Salt and Markan Background

More than 97 percent of Mark's material is paralleled in Matthew and 88 percent in Luke, so that only thirty-one verses of Mark are not found in one of these Gospels.[63] Therefore, the content of this unique material must be important to the purposes of Mark, but not the other Gospel writers. Mark includes three sayings about salt in Mark 9:49-50, a salt prophecy, salt parable, and salt exhortation, with only the salt parable paralleled in the Q material of Matt 5:13 and Luke 14:34-35. The importance of these salt sayings is evidenced by their placement as the climax of Jesus' final sermon in Galilee at Capernaum (Mark 9:35-50).

Salt prophecy: Mark 9:49	"Everyone will be salted with fire."
Salt parable: Mark 9:50a	"Salt is good, but if it loses its saltiness, how can you make it salty again?"
Salt exhortation: Mark 9:50b	"Have salt in yourselves, and be at peace with each other."

How can an investigation of the background material to the Gospel of Mark equip the reader to determine the purpose of these various references to salt in the Second Gospel?

The Gospel of Mark presents a crucified Messiah who is requesting the discipleship community to join him in taking up the cross and being willing

---

63. Bruno de Solages, *A Greek Synopsis of the Gospels: A New Way of Solving the Synoptic Problem* (Leiden: Brill, 1959), p. 1052.

to sacrifice themselves in martyrdom (8:34) rather than deny the Christian faith and betray their brothers and sisters to death (13:9, 12-13). These salt sayings speak relevantly to this crisis that the Markan community is experiencing. First of all, Jesus predicts that the fire of persecution will encompass the community. "They will be salted with fire" alludes to the salt that was placed upon sacrifices for burnt offerings (Ezek 43:24; Ezra 6:9-10), grain offerings (Lev 2:13; *T. Levi* 9:14), and incense offerings (Exod 30:35; Lev 24:7 LXX). This is confirmed by the addition of Mark 9:49b in the Byzantine text tradition, "and every sacrifice shall be salted with salt" (KJV). Certainly the expression "salted with fire" was difficult to understand, and the early community probably placed this commentary in the margin to enlighten Mark 9:49a. Jesus' prophecy predicted that the discipleship community would become like a sacrifice placed into the fire.

The salt parable is then a warning against not continuing in one's commitment to a discipleship of the cross. It is possible for the community to lose its saltiness. Salt was employed as a preservative to prevent decay. If the community does not possess this preservative, they will be good for nothing. It will take the salt of the gospel to be able to persevere when the community is placed upon the sacrificial altar.

Finally, Jesus closes with an exhortation to maintain peaceful relations with each other. This use of salt alludes to the salt covenant, which promised loyalty to one another (Lev 2:13; Num 18:19; 2 Chr 13:5; *Jub.* 6:3-4; 21:11; Acts 1:4).[64] Instead of brother betraying brother and children causing their parents to be put to death (Mark 13:12), the community is exhorted to maintain a covenant of peace. These three sayings are tied together, so that the exhortation to cut a salt covenant and the call to be salted as a preservative equip the community to face the coming situation of required sacrifice. Therefore, these unique verses in Mark 9:49-50 must be interpreted within the overall purpose of the Gospel of Mark. Indeed, the salt sayings offer a porthole into the message of Jesus for the Markan community.

Throughout this chapter we have employed a telescopic lens as an exegetical tool to recover the historical background, the OT allusions, and the introductory material of specific books of the Bible. In the process the text has come alive with meaning.

---

64. See Dean B. Deppe, "The Imagery of Salt in the Sayings of Jesus: An Exegetical Study of Mark 9:49-50; Luke 14:34-35 and Matthew 5:13" (Th.M. diss., Calvin Theological Seminary, 1978). We have discussed the salt of the covenant above in Chapter 2, F2, "Ezra 4:14 and Acts 1:4: Literal Translations" (pp. 77-79).

STUDY AND DISCUSSION QUESTIONS

1. The background for a NT passage frequently traces back to the OT. The parable of the Wicked Tenants (Mark 12:1-12 par.) begins with the Song of the Vineyard from Isa 5:1-7. Read both passages and discuss why Jesus would recall this passage from the prophet. Is Jesus singing his lovesong over the vineyard one last time and if there is no response Isaiah 5 will occur? Or will another outcome happen? See Mark 12:9.

2. The meaning of the term "Son of Man" is notoriously difficult to determine. How is the Son of Man described in Ps 8:4? (See also Ezek 2:1; 3:1; 4:1; 5:1; 6:1; etc.). Contrast this depiction with the portrayal of the Son of Man in Dan 7:13-14. Why would Jesus want to hide his true identity in the mysterious phrase "Son of Man"?

3. While quoting Isa 40:3, Luke 3:4 states, "Prepare the way for the Lord, make straight paths for him." For whom are the paths made straight in the Isaiah context? How does Luke alter this? What theological statement is Luke confessing? Luke 8:39a also changes Mark 5:19 to read "God" instead of "Lord." What significance does this bring to Luke's statement in 8:39b?

4. At the transfiguration, the voice from heaven declares, "This is my Son, whom I love. Listen to him" (Mark 9:7). The OT background for the last sentence is in all likelihood Deut 18:15: "The LORD your God will raise up for you a prophet like me from among your own brothers. You must listen to him." What significance does this give for the presence of Moses at the transfiguration? What are the disciples supposed to listen to: Jesus' words of exaltation in Mark 9:1, or the words about a suffering Son of Man in 9:12-13, or both? What is wrong with Peter's desire to build three tabernacles on the mountain? What kind of Christ should the disciples be ready to follow when they listen to both Mark 8:29 and 8:33-34?

5. 1 John 2:2 teaches that Jesus Christ, the righteous one, is the ἱλασμός for our sins. What is the cultural background to this term? The KJV, ASV, and ESV translate the verse, "He is the propitiation," while the RSV reads, "He is the expiation." Perform a search of "expiation" in a Bible Dictionary like Harper's Bible Dictionary found in Logos Bible Software. What is the difference in meaning between these two terms? Why are many conservative translations wary of losing the translation "propitiation"? Is the Good News

translation (TEV) attempting to avoid the issue by simply explaining that Jesus is "the means by which our sins are forgiven"? The NIV, NRSV, ISV, and NET translate the verse, "He is the atoning sacrifice." Are they attempting to capture both interpretations?

6. Revelation 21:1 boldly proclaims that in the new heaven and new earth there will be no sea. To determine the significance of this statement, the Near Eastern background must be explored. How is the sea portrayed in the stories about Noah and Jonah? Read Ps 104:5-9. What was the importance of the boundary that God set? What then is the significance of Jesus calming the sea in Matt 8:23-27 and walking over the sea like dry ground in Matt 14:22-33?

7. One of the principles set forth in Scripture is that the spiritual battle against the forces of evil must be won before victory will ensue against human forces. In the ten plagues against Pharaoh, what then is the significance that the first plague consists of the river turning to blood? How was the Nile River pictured by the Egyptians? In Canaanite mythology Baal was the god of fertility who was in charge of the Jordan River, providing nourishment for the land of Palestine. What was the significance that when the ark of the covenant touched the Jordan River it began to dry up (Josh 3:13-17)? What was the spiritual victory that Jesus won for his people and the consequent application to human beings?

8. In Acts 28:11 Paul arrives in Rome with the twin gods Castor and Pollux as the figureheads on his ship. Consult a Bible Dictionary in Logos Bible Software and investigate what message this would give to the Roman officials. Second, how would the conclusion that Paul and Jesus were revolutionaries (Luke 23:2, 19; Acts 21:38) inhibit the proclamation of the gospel? How does this explain the change from Mark 15:39 to Luke 23:47? Notice the three times in Luke 23:4, 14, 22 where Pilate proclaims that Jesus is not guilty. What message was Luke attempting to display to the Roman Empire?

9. Sometimes the words of Jesus are the background for understanding the meaning of a passage. Revelation 6 describes the opening of the seven seals. The descriptions parallel Jesus' prediction of the destruction of Jerusalem and the end of the world (Matt 24:3). Compare the first seal with Luke 21:8; the second seal with 21:9-10; the third with 21:11b; the fourth with 21:11c; the fifth with 21:12; and the sixth seal with 21:25. If Revelation 6 has as its background the eschatological discourse of Jesus that predicted the destruction

of the temple, where in the book of Revelation does John narrate the fall of Jerusalem in symbolic terms? Where does he envision the end of the world?

10. Extrabiblical literature occasionally offers cultural understandings that are helpful in interpreting the Bible. For instance, various expectations of the coming Messiah are described in the Dead Sea Scrolls. The Aramaic Apocalypse 4Q246 states, "He will be called son of God, and they will call him son of the Most High. . . . His kingdom will be an eternal kingdom, and all his paths in truth and uprightness." The Messianic Apocalypse 4Q521 explains, "for the heavens and the earth will listen to his Messiah . . . and upon the poor he will place his spirit . . . freeing prisoners, giving sight to the blind, straightening out the twisted . . . and the Lord will perform marvellous acts such as have not existed, just as he said for he will heal the badly wounded and will make the dead live, he will proclaim good news to the meek, give lavishly to the needy, lead the exiled and enrich the hungry."[65] Where are these descriptions of the Messiah paralleled in the Gospel narratives?

11. The discovery of the Dead Sea Scrolls has altered the translations of our Bible. All Bible versions before the discovery of the Scrolls (like the KJV) include one couplet in Ps 145:13, "Thy kingdom *is* an everlasting kingdom, and thy dominion *endureth* throughout all generations." However, more recent translations like the NIV add "The LORD is faithful to all his promises and loving toward all he has made." This is an acrostic psalm. What does that designation mean, and how does this structure help us solve the mystery of the additional line in Psalm 145? Check out the Hebrew text or an interlinear and discover which letter of the alphabet was missing in this psalm.

12. The radicalness of Jesus' view of women can be determined only when Jewish literature from near his lifetime is compared with the Gospels. Philo, a Jewish leader in Egypt in the first century, stated that "It is suitable for (married) women to stay indoors and to live in retirement . . . never even approaching the door" (*De specialibus legibus* 3:169). In the educational process two separate rooms existed in the synagogue, the Sabbath room for worship and the men's room for education (Josephus, *Ant.* 16:164). Rabbi Eliezer (90 C.E.) even declared that "If a man gives his daughter a knowledge of the law,

---

65. Florentino García Martínez, *The Dead Sea Scrolls Translated: The Qumran Texts in English*, 2nd ed. (Grand Rapids: Eerdmans, 1996), pp. 138, 394.

it is as though he taught her lechery" (*Soṭah* 3:4). In Luke 10:38-42, Mary sits at the Lord's feet and Jesus asserts that "Mary has chosen what is better, and it will not be taken away from her." What is implied about Jesus' relationship to women in this passage and how does Jesus' view differ from the quotations of his contemporaries?

13. The picture of God as a gracious being is frequently surprising in Jesus' parables, especially when similar rabbinic parables are compared. For instance, contrast Jesus' parable of the Laborers in the Vineyard (Matt 20:1-16) with the parable of the Exceptional Laborer recited in the Jewish Targum, *Sifra on Lev.* 26:9. What themes are developed differently?

> They parable a parable. Unto what is the matter like? It is like a king who hired many laborers. And along with them was one laborer that had worked for him many days. All the laborers went to receive their pay for the day, and this one special laborer went also. He said to this one special laborer: "I will have regard for you. The others, who have worked for me only a little, to them I will give small pay. You, however, will receive a large recompense."
>
> Even so both the Israelites and the peoples of the world sought their pay from God. And God said to the Israelites: My children, I will have regard for you. The peoples of the world have accomplished very little for Me, and I will give them but a small reward. You, however, will receive a large recompense. Therefore, it says, "And I will have regard for you."[66]

---

66. Harvey K. McArthur and Robert M. Johnston, *They Also Taught in Parables: Rabbinic Parables from the First Centuries of the Christian Era* (Grand Rapids: Zondervan, 1990), p. 58.

CHAPTER 6

The History of Interpretation Route

Using a Motion Picture Exegetical Camera

A. The Major Commentators

PROCEDURE

When seminary students ask me what commentaries to use in their exegetical preparation, I always say, "Study the text yourself first and only then open the commentaries to see what you missed." In order to evaluate one's conclusions and add to the thoroughness of one's personal exegesis, you can consult a plethora of excellent commentaries. Sometimes we choose the most recent commentaries, presuming that they are the best. But comprehensive exegesis employs commentaries from various perspectives, from different time periods in church history, and volumes that are grammatical, literary, as well as theologically oriented. The first section of this chapter concentrates on recent commentaries that offer new solutions to old problems. The conclusion of the chapter will investigate how a stroll through commentaries from other periods of church history enlightens the text.

EXAMPLES

1. Micah 4:4 and 1 Kings 4:25: Sitting Under One's Vine and Fig Tree

After a personal exploration of a biblical text, wisdom advocates the additional step of examining a commentary to open your eyes to insights you may have overlooked. The prophet in Mic 4:4 envisions a future vista where "Everyone will sit under their own vine and under their own fig tree, and no one will make them afraid, for the LORD Almighty has spoken." This imagery of sitting underneath one's own vine and fig tree conveyed a message of shalom, well-being, harmony, rest, and prosperity. This identical description is used to portray the reign of Solomon in 1 Kgs 4:25:[1] "During Solomon's lifetime Judah and Israel, from Dan to Beersheba, lived in safety, each man under his own vine and fig tree." The most natural interpretation is to link these two descriptions together and envisage the reign of Solomon as an example *par excellence* of prosperity, happiness, comfort, security, and salvation in Israel. In this picture all individuals possess their own property where they can relax from the drudgery and exhaustion of work under the shade and comfort of a fruit tree. They can partake of the luxuries of grapes and figs and not worry that some enemy will remove this standard of living. Placing these two texts side by side offers both a future scenario of shalom and a realized eschatology already experienced here and now in our daily lives in the world. God's salvation is both already and not yet.

However, recent commentators like Walter Brueggemann suggest that these two texts are intended as contrasts rather than as comparisons. This conclusion shines an entirely new light upon a seemingly familiar scripture. According to Brueggemann, the narrator is speaking in ironic ways to show that Solomon's political experiment did not work. 1 Kings 4 sets the statement of Micah 4 in an "utterly incongruous context of Solomonic arms and oppression."[2] The prophet Micah was speaking positively about an ideal future that included the promise that "Nation will not take up sword against nation, nor will they train for war anymore" (Mic 4:3). However, in 1 Kgs 4:26 "Solomon had four thousand stalls for chariot horses, and twelve thousand horses." Oppression reigned because the territories "brought tribute and were Solomon's subjects all his life" (4:21). A central empire like Solomon's inevitably contains inequalities, so that many "also brought to the proper place their quotas of barley and straw for the chariot horses and the other horses" (4:28). Therefore, Brueggemann maintains that "Solomon is remembered as a patron of a self-serving theodic settlement that permitted

---

1. In Hebrew the text is numbered as 1 Kgs 5:5 and in the LXX it is placed after 2:46.

2. Walter Brueggemann, "'Vine and Fig Tree': A Case Study in Imagination and Criticism," in *A Social Reading of the Old Testament: Prophetic Approaches to Israel's Communal Life* (Minneapolis: Fortress, 1994), p. 102.

power, wealth, and wisdom in disproportionate measure. . . . For Solomon
was a patron for the justification of a self-serving system that benefitted the
patron and those who enjoyed his patronage."[3]

In this scenario Solomon's empire was exactly what the prophet Samuel
had warned against when Israel demanded a king (1 Sam 8:11-15).

> [11]He said, "This is what the king who will reign over you will do: He will
> take your sons and make them serve with his chariots and horses, and
> they will run in front of his chariots. [12]Some he will assign to be com-
> manders of thousands and commanders of fifties, and others to plow his
> ground and reap his harvest, and still others to make weapons of war and
> equipment for his chariots. [13]He will take your daughters to be perfumers
> and cooks and bakers. [14]He will take the best of your fields and vineyards
> and olive groves, and give them to his attendants. [15]He will take a tenth of
> your grain and of your vintage and give it to his officials and attendants.

Therefore the descriptions in 1 Kgs 4:25 are completely ironic and violate
God's intention to stand alone as the leader of Israel (1 Sam 8:6-7). As
Brueggemann contends,

> The use of the "vine and fig tree" metaphor in Mic. 4:1-4 shows a poet in
> Israel practicing bold imagination, evoking an alternative community yet
> anticipated. And on the basis of that, the narrative of 1 Kings 4:20-28
> (Hebr. 4:20–5:8) is an example of ironic criticism, designed to show that
> the present royal order, absolute and comprehensive in its claims, cannot
> keep its promises.[4]

Micah's dream of disarmament is totally reversed in 1 Kings 4. Furthermore,
the description in 4:20 that "The people of Judah and Israel were as numerous as the sand on the seashore; they ate, they drank and they were happy"
cannot be meant literally, since "When some live so extravagantly, others
must have paid."[5] The "peace and prosperity" system of Solomon (4:24) is
surely a system of exploitation, as is evident in 1 Kings 11–12 when the northern tribes inevitably rebel against this system. Thus "the quintessential

---

3. Walter Brueggemann, "The Social Significance of Solomon as a Patron of Wisdom,"
in *A Social Reading of the Old Testament*, p. 261.

4. Brueggemann, "Vine and Fig Tree," p. 103. Brueggemann (p. 100) suggests that it is "a
criticism couched in subtle and high irony, subtle enough to escape the vigilant censors and
high enough not to be missed by those who hold other visions."

5. Brueggemann, "Vine and Fig Tree," p. 100.

dream used by the promise-oracle to protest statism (that is, systems of swords and spears) is now co-opted by the propaganda of the state. The elemental dream of liberation from state usurpation is now preempted to support the very ideology of usurpation by the state. That is, the very same metaphor is now taken in a reverse way to support the system it was intended to criticize."[6] This is the new interpretation of the phrase "under one's own vine and fig tree" in 1 Kings 4.

The above differences in interpretation trace back to a divergent analysis of societal structures. Brueggemann's presupposition states that "The introduction of central power and economic surplus entails the systemic introduction of social inequality."[7] Solomon's social mutation is viewed as a complete overhaul from the covenantal-egalitarian social experiment that existed before the monarchy. However, a central government need not be interpreted as inherently negative, since such systems are a crucial part of God's good creation. For instance, this imagery of sitting under vines and fig trees is positively employed in 1 Macc 14:11-13:

> [11]He established peace in the land,
> and Israel rejoiced with great joy.
> [12]All the people sat under their own vines and fig trees,
> and there was none to make them afraid.
> [13]No one was left in the land to fight them,
> and the kings were crushed in those days.

This time of peace after the surrounding kings have been crushed, with Israel rejoicing because their central government has produced social security, sounds suspiciously similar to the descriptions in 1 Kings 4.[8] The fact that in 1 Macc 14:9 "the youths put on splendid military attire," demonstrates as well the presence of an army administered by a centralized state. Certainly Brueggemann's political interpretation should cause every reader to stop and evaluate the exegetical details of this passage once again. Sometimes our hermeneutical assumptions must be challenged. Therefore, it is an important enterprise to scour modern commentaries that offer new perspectives upon already interpreted texts. However, this does not eliminate a discern-

---

6. Brueggemann, "Vine and Fig Tree," p. 101.

7. Brueggemann, "Social Significance of Solomon," p. 252.

8. Brueggemann, "Vine and Fig Tree," p. 106, calls this a "victory narrative for an oppressed community recently liberated," but Simon Maccabee had established a central government complete with an army.

ment process that attempts to separate the exegetical wheat from the prover-bial straw. Frequently the traditional understanding will win out in the end.

2. Mark 12:41-44: The Widow's Mite

A NT exegetical example demonstrating the need to consult current schol-arly literature is the understanding of Mark 12:41-44, the widow's offering of two *lepta*. With electronic resources, the click of a mouse brings up such re-sources as Craig Evans's commentary on Mark in the Word Biblical Com-mentary series, which explains:

> The touching story of the widow's offering has often been cited in litera-ture, sermons, and Bible lessons as providing an exemplary model of sac-rificial giving. Many commentators have taken the passage in this sense, as most recently has Gundry. But the interpretation offered by A. G. Wright (*CBQ* 44 [1982] 256–65), which Gundry (730–31) questions but Fitzmyer (*Luke* 2:1320–21) accepts, to the effect that Jesus' word was not one of praise but one of lament, is in my opinion correct.[9]

Again the consultation of a contemporary commentary suggests an inter-pretation that might not have been visible after reading only the English ver-sions, grammars, and lexicons.

Evans contends that the context advocates a lament, since Jesus has just denounced the scribes for devouring widows' houses (Mark 12:40) and now this widow appears as a case in point of this condemnation. The scribes de-vour widows' houses by requiring this poor woman to contribute toward the temple treasury rather than receiving money through benevolence. Evans explains,

> Jesus apparently has taken up the cause of the marginalized, and widows were among the most marginalized in his society. Evidently he has leveled a prophetic complaint against the religious establishment for failing to live up to its Mosaic obligations. He has warned of the scribes whose religion devours the poor and enriches themselves. He has pointed to the poor widow who cast her last tiny coins into the temple's coffers as an example of one such person who has been consumed. We have here an important remnant of Jesus' criticisms against the temple establishment and what

---

9. Craig A. Evans, *Mark 8:27–16:20.* WBC 34B (Nashville: Nelson, 2001), p. 281.

motivated them. In the next passage (Mark 13:1-2) Jesus will prophesy the dreadful result, to which this oppressive policy will inevitably lead.[10]

If the temple was about to be destroyed as Jesus predicted in the next chapter, this offering to the temple fund was a waste of money. Therefore, Evans offers grammatical (the repetition of widow), historical (Jesus' concern for the leftovers), and contextual (both the previous and forthcoming contexts) evidence in favor of a new understanding of this text.

However, equally compelling arguments support an exemplary interpretation of the widow's action. The previous context can also be viewed as a contrast with the widow's behavior, the giving of a poor person versus the taking of the religious elite. The connection with the following context of Mark 13 centers on the disciples' offering of their lives in 13:9-13. The poor widow who gives everything she possessed becomes an example for the disciples as they face hardships. Mark is preparing for the Passion Narrative extensively throughout his book, and this pericope is another instance: the withered fig tree in Mark 11 alludes to the destruction of the temple, while the widow's sacrificial gift in Mark 12 points to Jesus' offering of his life. Grammatically, the word order of the story suggests that the climax is the ending, "but she, out of her poverty, put in everything — all she had to live on." She gave her life (ὅλον τὸν βίον αὐτῆς), just as Jesus and the disciples will be required to sacrifice their lives. The wording, therefore, supports a connection with discipleship, not condemnation of enemies. With regard to the historical situation, Jesus normally contrasts the marginalized with the establishment, which again supports a contrast in the context. Finally, women characters in Mark are regularly connected with discipleship, including the service of Peter's mother-in-law (1:31), the faith of the bleeding woman (5:34), the insight of the Syrophoenician woman (7:28-29), the sacrifice of the woman anointing Jesus' head (14:8-9), and the women disciples from Galilee following Jesus to the cross (15:40-41). Thus contextual, grammatical, historical, and literary evidence supports the traditional exemplary interpretation as well.

However, the normal supremacy of context in exegesis is trumped in this case by an attention to a Markan literary feature. Mark regularly employs frames to provide a theological perspective on the material located in between the two bookends.[11] These frames consist of two similar passages

10. Evans, *Mark 8:27–16:20*, p. 285.
11. See Appendix II, IC (pp. 360-61).

tied together thematically and grammatically. Thematically, here and in Mark 14:3-9 Jesus praises two women who demonstrate the way of extravagant self-giving. The widow giving her all matches the woman generously anointing Jesus' body for burial. Grammatically, the vocabulary connections are strong, including the repetition of "all" (ὅλος, 12:44; 14:9); sayings with "Amen, I say to you" (ἀμὴν λέγω ὑμῖν, 12:43; 14:9); and the stitch word "poor" employed twice in each story (πτωχός 12:42, 43; 14:5, 7). Furthermore, although the widow's mite is contrasted with the huge amount of money the nard is worth, both gifts are surprisingly better than the alternative options of enormous offerings placed by the rich in the temple treasury (12:41) and giving the money to the poor (14:5). Finally, both stories contain a stark contrast in the immediate context. The woman's generous act of anointing in support of Jesus as he prepares for death is contrasted with Judas's dastardly act of betrayal (14:10). Likewise, the negative example of the scribes' actions against widows (12:40, "you devour widows' houses") must be a contrast with the positive example of the widow.

Thus the literary journey of identifying an author's compositional style elicits the most significant exegetical data. These sacrificial acts of the two women enlighten how to watch and wait for the *parousia* of Jesus taught in Mark 13. They frame the eschatological discourse to offer a correct theological perspective. The proper posture for preparing oneself for the final woes and blessings is an act of discipleship where everything one possesses and holds dear is offered in the service of Jesus. Therefore, the actions of these women are exemplary, and the traditional interpretation is correct. Thus, although recent commentaries should be consulted, the most contemporary is not always the most correct.

3. Matthew 25:31-46: The Parable of the Sheep and the Goats

The traditional interpretation of the parable of the Sheep and the Goats in Matt 25:31-46 argues that the believer's benevolence to the needy, the hungry, stranger, sick, and imprisoned stands as the central theme. "Whatever you did for one of the least of these brothers of mine, you did for me" (25:40) is pictured as the action of the mature Christian toward the needy world. Unless you stay up to date by reviewing recent commentaries and studying periodical articles in the major biblical journals, you might imagine that this is the only interpretation. But Donald Hagner describes the present scholarly situation: "There is much disagreement about the meaning of the phrase 'the least of these my brothers.' From Gray's survey of the options, we may list the following, in descending order of popularity: (1) everyone, i.e. particularly the needy among humankind; (2) all Christians; (3) Christian missionaries; and (4) Jewish Christians."[12]

If you peruse theological periodicals, you realize that already in 1965 the theory was proposed that "the least of these my brothers" are Christian missionaries.[13] In evangelical circles, Robert Gundry has popularized this view in his commentary on Matthew by entitling this section "Demonstrating True Discipleship Through Doing Charity to the Persecuted Messengers of Jesus."[14] This new interpretation implies that ministers should preach on this passage during Mission Emphasis Week rather than on Hunger Sunday.

If we employ the exegetical techniques we have learned so far, the grammatical route primarily supports the new interpretation, while the context confirms the traditional reading, and the historical and cultural background evidence remains mixed. Confirmation that "the least of these" are Christian missionaries includes grammatical (1-3 below) and historical (4-6) backing:

1. "My brothers" in Matt 25:40 needs to be understood as fellow workers and disciples of Jesus as in 12:48-49; 28:19.

2. "The least of these" (τῶν ἐλαχίστων) means "little ones," which is a synonym for Christian disciple in other passages of Matthew (10:42; 18:6, 10, 14).

3. The closest parallels are in Matt 10:40, "He who receives you receives me," and 10:42, "to give a cup of cold water to one of these little ones because he is a disciple." These texts are found within the missionary discourse of Matthew 10.

4. This new interpretation fits a setting in the ministry of Jesus where he sends out the disciples who live very simply and depend upon others for their provisions (10:9-23).

5. The descriptions of Matthew 25 are similar to the experiences of Paul in preaching the gospel (1 Cor 4:11; 2 Cor 11:23-29).

6. 3 John 5 praises the churches for helping "the strangers" who are Christian missionaries.

---

12. Donald A. Hagner, *Matthew 14–28*. WBC 33B (Dallas: Word, 1995), p. 744.

13. J. R. Michaels, "Apostolic Hardships and Righteous Gentiles: A Study of Matthew 25:31-46," *JBL* 84 (1965): 27-37.

14. Robert H. Gundry, *Matthew: A Commentary on His Literary and Theological Art* (Grand Rapids: Eerdmans, 1982), p. 511.

Endorsement for the traditional interpretation that this passage speaks about what Christians do for others who are in need finds support in grammatical evidence (1-2 below) and historical background evidence (3-4), but especially in the context of Matthew 25 (5).

1. The use of "brothers" in Matthew can refer to all people, since Jesus is intentionally expanding the circle of "my brothers," as he does when he redefines "love your neighbor as yourself" to include the enemy (5:43-48).
   a. In Matt 23:10, where the speech is addressed to "the crowds and the disciples" (23:1), Jesus teaches, "you have only one Master and you are all brothers."
   b. Matthew 18:35 ("Forgive your brother from your heart") must refer to all people and 18:15 ("if your brother sins against you") as well as 18:21 ("how many times must I forgive my brother?") certainly do not refer to missionaries.
   c. Matthew 7:5 ("First take the plank out of your own eye, and then you will see clearly to remove the speck from your brother's eye") refers to human beings in general.
   d. Matthew 5:22 ("to be angry with your brother") means everyone's anger; 5:24 ("be reconciled to your brother") must apply to all people.
2. A disciple is referred to as a "little one" (μικρός) at least four times in Matthew (10:42; 18:6, 10, 14), but here the term "least" (ἐλάχιστος) is employed, a word given a negative connotation for disciples in 5:19.[15]
3. Care for the needy coheres with Jesus' concern for the socially marginalized in other Gospel passages (cf. Luke 14:13; parable of the Rich Man and Lazarus in Luke 16:19-31).
4. The traditional interpretation fits with Jewish teaching on the poor, as in Midrash *Tannaim* on Deut 15:9, where God says to Israel, "My children, when you gave food to the poor, I counted it as though you had given it to me."[16] Jesus is therefore God's representative, calling for a similar ministry of God's people to the needy.
5. The parable is not placed in Matthew 10, which concerns the treatment of missionaries, but in Matthew 25 and must be interpreted within that

---

15. Klyne Snodgrass, *Stories with Intent: A Comprehensive Guide to the Parables of Jesus* (Grand Rapids: Eerdmans, 2008), p. 556.

16. See Joachim Jeremias, *The Parables of Jesus*, 2nd rev. ed. (New York: Scribners', 1972), p. 207.

context. In the context, the oil of the five virgins symbolizes the good works instilled by the Holy Spirit in the lives of the church. The talents designate kingdom work done by church members. Therefore, performing benevolent acts for the hungry, etc. must be the work of the church, not the work of the nations with respect to suffering missionaries and church leaders.

In the exegesis of this passage, we experience the conundrum that grammatical exegesis slightly favors one view while the context supports another position. When this situation occurs in interpretation, caution rather than dogmatism provides the correct path. Therefore, although avoiding intransigence, I still believe that context trumps all other evidence and that the traditional interpretation thus remains the best understanding for the parable of the Sheep and Goats.

4. 2 Corinthians 5:21: Imputed Righteousness or Defense of Paul's Apostleship?

The traditional understanding of the verse "God made him who had no sin to be sin for us, so that in him we might become the righteousness of God" is that the subject matter is atonement theology. Christ exchanges our sins for his righteousness, so that the divine imputation of righteousness is the theme of the passage. N. T. Wright, however, in his book *Justification,* offers a new interpretation contending that Paul's message centers on his defense of his apostleship. Certainly the entire book of 2 Corinthians, but especially 2:14–6:13, is Paul's defense of his ministry to demonstrate that he is embodying the servant nature of the gospel and truly representing Jesus. From this, Wright argues that correct exegesis pays attention to the context "against all our traditions, however venerable their provenance and however pastorally helpful we find them."[17] He contends that the tradition from Martin Luther to John Piper has muzzled the text in favor of imputed moral righteousness, whereas Paul is defending his apostleship as an imitation of the righteousness of God. Wright discovers four texts in the context linking Christ's work on the cross and Paul's own ministry. These two-pronged statements tying together Christ

17. N. T. Wright, *Justification: God's Plan and Paul's Vision* (Downers Grove: IVP Academic, 2009), p. 158. Wright is opposed by John Piper, *The Future of Justification: A Response to N. T. Wright* (Wheaton: Crossway Books, 2007).

and us begin in 2 Cor 5:15 and climax in 5:21.[18] According to Wright, the "we" or "us" in each of these verses is limited to Paul and the apostolic team.

1. 5:15
   (a) Christ died for all;
   (b) we live for him, who died and was raised.
2. 5:18
   (a) God reconciled us to himself in the Messiah;
   (b) God entrusted to us the ministry of reconciliation.
3. 5:19
   (a) God was in the Messiah, reconciling the world to himself, not counting their trespasses against them;
   (b) entrusting to us the word of reconciliation.
4. 5:21
   (a) The one who knew no sin, God made sin for us;
   (b) so that in him we might become the righteousness of God.

These four dual statements climaxing in a defense of Paul's apostleship compel Wright to discard the theme of atonement theology as central to this text.

The righteousness of God, according to Wright, is God's covenant faithfulness that Paul is embodying in his ministry by including both Jews and Gentiles in the community of faith. Therefore, Wright takes the second part of each statement as applying only to a defense of Paul's own ministry. However, the more natural interpretation is to apply Paul's statements to all Christians who benefit from Christ's finished work. For example, in 6:1-2, which functions as the conclusion to this section, Paul exhorts all Christians through the Corinthians "not to receive God's grace in vain," since "now is the day of salvation." This general application to all believers is where Paul starts as well in 5:14-15. Whereas Wright applies the application of these verses to Paul's ministry, the subject "those who live" (οἱ ζῶντες) in 5:15 more appropriately applies Christ's work to all Christians, so that Paul draws the following conclusions:

5:14 (a) One died for all,
     (b) and therefore all died.
5:15 (a) He died for all,
     (b) that those who live should no longer live for themselves.

18. Wright, *Justification*, pp. 161-63.

If the passage begins and ends with a general application to all believers, then the middle section also likely speaks about Christ's atonement that is imputed to all Christians. Therefore, the reference to "us" in 5:18 must be consistent, so (a) "God reconciled us to himself through Christ" and (b) "thus gave us the ministry of reconciliation" must both refer to all Christians. The first "us" cannot refer to all Christians while the second "us" only applies to Paul and the apostolic team.[19] Then, in 5:19-20 Paul again references Christ's work followed by the task of all Christians to proclaim a message of reconciliation: (a) "Christ was reconciling the world to himself and not counting people's sins against them"; (b) Christians have a message of reconciliation and implore people to be reconciled to God. Consistency reigns thoughout the passage.

Finally, 5:21 follows the exact pattern: (a) God made Christ to be sin; (b) so that in him all believers ("we") might become the righteousness of God. Christ's finished work is applied to the believer throughout this passage. Therefore, Wright's insightful new look at the passage causes us to grapple deeper with the exegesis and grammar of the passage, but does not necessarily dislodge the traditional emphasis upon substitutionary atonement. Through every novel interpretation our exegetical tools are sharpened, but our theological grid is not necessarily altered.

5. Mark 9:42-47: A Sexual Interpretation of Hand, Foot, and Eye?

One of the most renowned and respected commentary series is Hermeneia, and one of the foremost interpreters within this collection is Adela Yarbro Collins from Yale University, who inscribed a detailed commentary on the Gospel of Mark.[20] Through her backing a scholarly approach is growing that supports what could be called an X-rated interpretation[21] of Mark 9:43-47, "if your hand, foot, or eye causes you to sin."[22] According to this view, when

---

19. Daniel B. Wallace, *Greek Grammar Beyond the Basics* (Grand Rapids: Zondervan, 1996), p. 399, admits that there is no linguistic basis for seeing a shift in referent, but because of Paul's rapid-fire, emotion-laden writing he posits a change in meaning.

20. Adela Yarbro Collins, *Mark.* Hermeneia (Minneapolis: Fortress, 2007).

21. Joel Marcus, *Mark 8–16,* AB 27A (New Haven: Yale University Press, 2009), p. 697, offers this title.

22. She accepts the research of Will Deming, "Mark 9.42–10.12; Matthew 5.27-32, and *B. Nid.* 13b: A First Century Discussion of Male Sexuality," *NTS* 36 (1990): 130-41. This interpretation is adopted by Dale C. Allison, *Jesus of Nazareth: Millenarian Prophet* (Minneapolis:

Jesus speaks about sinning against the "little ones" in 9:42, the molestation of actual children is meant.[23] Following this evil, Jesus speaks in 9:43-47 against adultery with the hand (masturbation) and with the foot (adultery in the normal sense, with the penis euphemistically called a foot), and against the erotic gaze of lust, which is interpreted as adultery in Matt 5:28.[24] This interpretation is based upon the parallel Jewish legislation in the Babylonian Talmud (*Niddah* 13b), which states, "It was taught in the school of Rabbi Ishmael, 'You shall not commit adultery' means there shall be in you no adultery neither with the hand nor with the foot. Our masters taught, 'The proselytes and those who play with children delay the messiah.'" All that is missing in this passage is adultery with the eye.[25]

This new interpretation certainly could result in some spicy (and legalistic) sermons. But the controversial nature of this exegesis is insufficient evidence to reject it, since Jesus did manage to find himself in the middle of many controversies. The main problem with this interpretation is that it is too specific. Jesus covers a variety of topics in this paraenetic sermon. His teaching in a house in Capernaum (9:33) begins with such diverse issues as hospitality and inclusion in the group (9:35-41), so that any legislation would speak generally concerning sin and not specifically about sexual sin. Since the context is connected by catchwords and not specific content, the "little ones" in verse 42 are not necessarily the same as the "little child" in verse 36. In fact, a close reading indicates that child abuse is not intended at all, since it is the little ones themselves that sin rather than their being sinned against. Furthermore, the passage ends (9:48) by quoting Isa 66:24, where wickedness in general ("those who have rebelled against me") and not specific sex-

---

Fortress, 1998), pp. 178-82; Robert H. Gundry, *Mark: A Commentary on His Apology for the Cross* (Grand Rapids: Eerdmans, 1993), p. 524; William Loader, *Sexuality and the Jesus Tradition* (Grand Rapids: Eerdmans, 2005), pp. 20-36; George Foot Moore, *Judaism in the First Centuries of the Christian Era* (1930; repr. New York: Schocken, 1971), 2:268.

23. Because the masculine form of the word "one" is employed, Deming, "Mark 9:42," p. 135, thinks that sexual relations between a man and a boy (pederasty) are in mind. See Loader, *Sexuality and the Jesus Tradition*, pp. 23-24, 59-60.

24. In the OT and Dead Sea Scrolls the hand is employed euphemistically for the penis (Isa 57:8; 11QT 46:13) as are the feet (Exod 4:25; Judg 3:24; Ruth 3:7; 1 Sam 24:3; 2 Sam 11:8; Isa. 6:2). See Yarbro Collins, *Mark*, p. 453.

25. Allison, *Jesus of Nazareth*, p. 179, calls attention to another quote from *Niddah* 13b that reports that the alternative to cutting off the hand is the pit of destruction similar to Mark 9:42: "Rabbi Tarfon said, 'If his hand touched the membrane, let his hand be cut off upon his belly. . . . It is preferable that his belly shall be split rather than that he should go down into the pit of destruction.'"

ual sins triggers the fire not to be quenched. It should be granted that Jesus refers to divorce as adultery in the following pericope in Mark 10 (especially verses 11-12), but the flow of material is interrupted with the mentioning of salt in 9:49-50, which cannot be easily applied to adultery.

General, not sexual sins, are the primary focus. As Joel Marcus explains, "the hand is the instrument for the commission of sin, the foot is the means of transport to the place of its commission, and the eye is the means by which the temptation to commit it enters in."[26] Furthermore, just as the command to cut off an organ is hyperbole, so the mentioning of specific parts of the body like the hand and the foot is not intended literally. This can be demonstrated by 9:45, where Jesus speaks of a preference for two feet over against being lame and so loses the euphemism of a foot for the penis. Instead, the excision of a hand would point to various sins, including stealing, sedition, and the secret forging of letters as was already true in Hellenistic literature.[27] In the same vein, Job 31 combines looking lustfully at a girl with walking in falsehood, so that my feet hurry after deceit; sexual sin is combined with injustice throughout (1-12 versus 13-40), supplying a reference to various dimensions of life. Finally, the real parallel passage in Matt 18:6-9 involves communal discord when read within the context of the entire chapter and need not be limited to sexual connotations.[28]

Therefore again, the consultation of the history of interpretation offers a possible interpretation that the reader in all likelihood never imagined possible. This new information, however, has to be carefully sampled and evaluated; some exegetical conclusions may provide substantial tasty nourishment, while other interpretations must be spit out as junk food. However, either way the reader benefits from a thorough investigation of the possible meanings of the text.

26. Marcus, *Mark 8–16*, p. 697.

27. See Josephus, *Life* 34 §169-73; *J.W.* 2.21.10 §642-45; *Life* 35 §177.

28. Loader, *Sexuality and the Jesus Tradition*, pp. 24-27, describes the arguments for the traditional position fairly before opting for a position that Matt 18:6-9 is consistently speaking about child abuse. However, 5:29-30 omits mentioning the foot, which seems the most important body part if the passage refers euphemistically to the penis. Loader (p. 28) admits that "'Left' or 'right' is inapplicable in an allusion to the penis." Finally, the order (hand, foot, eye) argues against a sexual interpretation, since the middle element is most frequently applied to the sexual organ.

6. The Centurion at the Cross:
A Gentile Voice from Heaven or a Negative Mocker?

How are we to interpret the centurion's confession in Mark 15:39, "Truly this man was the Son of God"? The traditional interpretation envisions the centurion as a proto-Christian who receives divine insight into the true identity of Jesus. Mark includes three prominent revelations of Jesus as the Son of God. At Jesus' baptism (Mark 1:11) the voice from heaven proclaiming the special identity of the Messiah is aimed at Jesus himself: "You are my beloved Son." Then, in the middle of the Gospel a voice from heaven at the transfiguration (Mark 9:7) broadcasts to the special disciples, "This is my beloved Son." Finally, at the end of the book the Gentile centurion declares like a voice from heaven for the whole world to hear that "this man was the Son of God." Previously when Jesus' true identity was exposed, Mark employed the messianic secret (see 9:9-10), but now at the cross the whole world is invited to perceive the true uniqueness of Jesus through the centurion's confession of faith.

Recently, serious arguments have been enlisted against the probability that a Roman soldier would produce a positive confession of belief. Some insist that the context of mockery in the crucifixion narrative paints the centurion as a negative character.[29] Therefore, the centurion simply continues this sequence of taunts alongside the other ironic statements at the foot of the cross:

15:26; cf. 15:2, 9	"King of the Jews" by Pilate's written notice of a charge
15:31	"Savior" by the chief priests and teachers of the law
15:32	"Christ, the King of Israel" by the chief priests, teachers of the law, and those crucified with him
15:36	"The one connected with the eschatological Elijah" by those standing near
15:39	"A son of a god" by the centurion

At a historical level, the centurion must be conceived of as a mocker who ironically speaks the truth like the other scoffers in the story. A Roman sol-

---

29. See Brian K. Blount and Gary W. Charles, *Preaching Mark in Two Voices* (Louisville: Westminster John Knox, 2002), p. 242; Mark Goodacre, *The Case Against Q: Studies in Markan Priority and the Synoptic Problem* (Harrisburg: Trinity Press International, 2002), p. 160, n. 28; Earl S. Johnson, "Is Mark 15.39 the Key to Mark's Christology?" *JSNT* 31 (1987): 14-16; Donald H. Juel, *A Master of Surprise: Mark Interpreted* (Minneapolis: Fortress, 1994), p. 74, n. 7.

dier's allegiance to the emperor was expected to be absolute, and such a confession would make him guilty of treason, an unlikely scenario.[30] In addition, the grammar of the sentence, which employs the imperfect tense[31] and omits the article before "Son of God," could produce a confession of Jesus as only "a son of God"[32] Therefore realistically, the centurion must have thought Jesus was heroic or a demigod at the very most. Finally, Mark would not allow a Roman soldier to be a positive figure if in the cultural background the emperor Nero had just persecuted the Christians and now the Romans were ready to destroy Jerusalem, the homeland of Christianity.

Deciding between these two opinions is one of the difficult choices that a preacher must make in the study before approaching the pulpit and proclaiming the word of God. Since it is important to have all the facts and the various arguments in favor of alternative interpretations, the history of interpretation road to the text must be traveled every time that a proclamation or discussion of God's word takes place.

Should the centurion be envisioned as a heroic truth-teller or a villainous ridiculer? My reflections give prominence to one of Mark's literary devices where he employs minor characters as the heroes of the story. Blind Bartimaeus is pictured as the paradigm disciple who sees clearly and follows along the way behind Jesus toward his crucifixion (10:52) whereas James and John in the immediate context desire glory and fame (10:35-37). Likewise, Simon of Cyrene who carries Jesus' cross replaces Simon Peter, who through his three denials proves unable to follow Jesus in his suffering. Here too, the centurion replaces the disciples at the cross and offers the ultimate Christian confession that Jesus is the Son of God. The title of Jesus that begins the Gospel in 1:1 climaxes the Gospel in 15:39. Importantly, a Gentile's confession betrays a prominent agenda in Mark's Gospel, namely the inclusion of Gentiles

30. Johnson, "Is Mark 15.39 the Key," 13.

31. Johnson, "Is Mark 15.39 the Key," 7, states that "it would be exceptional if Mark transmitted a Christological statement in the imperfect, since he consistently places confessional statements in the present tense (1.11,24; 2.28; 3.11; 8.29; 9.7; 12.35; 14.61f)." But with the death of Jesus, a past tense is natural. As Jack Dean Kingsbury, *The Christology of Mark's Gospel* (Philadelphia: Fortress, 1983), p. 134, explains, "Of course the centurion having just seen Jesus die says that Jesus 'was' the Son of God. But in the resurrection God overturns this 'was' so that it becomes 'is.'" Johnson himself admits that there is a close parallel to 15:39 in 11:32, where John the Baptizer is entitled a prophet in the imperfect tense (προφήτης ἦν) after his death. Therefore, the use of the imperfect tense is not awkward.

32. However, the articular noun right before this phrase (οὗτος ὁ ἄνθρωπος) makes it highly unlikely that Mark would repeat the article in order to establish a definite noun.

in the Christian church.[33] Finally, the build-up in Mark's Gospel consisting of architectonic acclamations of Jesus' identity from baptism, to transfiguration, to death argues for a positive affirmation by the centurion. Therefore, the crucifixion story places the centurion alongside the women after Jesus' death (15:40-41), not in conjunction with the mockers before that event.[34]

An investigation of the history of interpretation reveals two prominent interpretations of the centurion at the cross. Faced with difficult decisions we must attempt to unravel the exegetical possibilities and pay close attention to the arguments on both sides. This process might not result in a dogmatic conclusion to which all agree. But attention to grammar, structure, context, historical background, and literary features provides a road where we can travel through the jungle of interpretations and arrive at a firm conviction.

7. The Background Behind the Baptismal Ministry of John the Baptist

The use of commentaries sometimes complicates simplistic answers. Why did John begin to baptize? What was the background and current under-standing for such an action? First-time readers will probably connect John's baptism with Christian baptism, since according to Mark 1:4 it consisted of "a baptism of repentance for the forgiveness of sins" as in Acts 2:38. However, the disciples of John in Acts 19:4-6 have to be rebaptized into the name of Je-sus and receive the gift of the Holy Spirit before they become Christians. This information along with the fact that Josephus does not connect John's baptism with the Jesus movement (*Ant.* 18:117-19) demonstrates that Chris-tian baptism is not entailed. Therefore we must investigate a possible back-ground in the Qumran community, the OT, or the rite of proselyte baptism.

The discovery of the Dead Sea Scrolls at Qumran following the Second World War opened up a new window of exploration into the purpose of John's baptism.[35] John's ministry in the desert was geographically close to the Qumran community, and both appealed to Isa 40:3 to describe their

---

33. Already Jesus ministers in Gentile territory (5:1-20; 7:24–8:10), and in the eschatologi-cal discourse Mark proclaims that "the gospel must first be preached to all nations" (13:10). If this verse refers to Gentiles (εἰς πάντα τὰ ἔθνη) as evidenced by 13:8, then 14:9 implies Gentiles as well (εἰς ὅλον τὸν κόσμον), since the preaching of the gospel is again emphasized.

34. See Marcus, *Mark 8–16*, p. 1058.

35. See Everett Ferguson, *Backgrounds of Early Christianity.* 3rd ed. (Grand Rapids: Eerdmans, 2003), pp. 526-27; and Scot McKnight, *A Light Among the Gentiles* (Minneapolis: Fortress, 1991), pp. 82-85.

sense of identity as a voice calling in the wilderness preparing the way of the Lord (Mark 1:3; 1QS 8:13-14). Each is closely tied to an ascetic lifestyle and emphasized confession of sin. For instance, at Qumran "all those entering the covenant shall confess after them and shall say, 'We have acted sinfully, we have transgressed, we have sinned, we have acted irreverently, we and our fathers before us'"[36] (1QS 1:24-26). In addition, the cisterns unearthed at Qumran demonstrate the abundance of water employed for cleansing rites. The use of baptisms or lustrations for spiritual cleansing was so important that it was proclaimed that "flesh is cleansed by being sprinkled with cleansing waters and being made holy with the waters of repentance" (1QS 3:8-9).[37] However, one major difference suggests that John has already separated himself from membership in the Qumran community. The ritual cleanliness rites of Qumran were performed repeatedly every day by only members of the community, but the baptism of John was a onetime initiatory rite addressed to all Israel. John's baptism demonstrates that he had separated his mission and message from the Qumran community.

In her authoritative Hermeneia commentary, Yarbro Collins argues for a background in the Old Testament.[38] In the Pentateuch, the book of Leviticus reports numerous instances where ritual impurity is removed through cleansing with water.[39] Among the prophets, Ezekiel proclaimed a new day when God "will sprinkle clean water upon you, and you will be clean; I will cleanse you from all your impurities and from all your idols" (Ezek 36:25). Although an OT background fits coherently with Jesus' proclamation that "all the prophets and the law prophesied until John" (Matt 11:13), it clashes with the intense conflict and negative reactions from the Jewish religious establishment. If John was merely continuing an OT tradition, why would the most religious people of the day protest, "we don't need to be baptized, since we have Abraham as our father" (Matt 3:9)? Therefore, a background in the Old Testament as well as Qumran theology fails to do justice to all the exegetical and historical facts.

36. Florentino García Martínez, *The Dead Sea Scrolls Translated*, 2nd ed. (Grand Rapids: Eerdmans, 1996), pp. 3-4.

37. García Martínez, *Dead Sea Scrolls Translated*, p. 5.

38. Yarbro Collins, *Mark*, pp. 138-40. See also *Cosmology and Eschatology in Jewish and Christian Apocalyticism*. JSJSup 50 (Leiden: Brill, 1996), pp. 218-38, as well as Robert L. Webb, *John the Baptizer and Prophet: A Sociohistorical Study*. JSNTSup 62 (Sheffield: JSOT, 1991), pp. 123-29.

39. In note 25 Yarbro Collins calls attention to Lev 14:9; 15:13, 16, 18; 16:4, 24, 26, 27-28; 22:6; Num 19:7, 8.

John's baptism must have contained an element that challenged the very identity of Israel as the people of God in spite of their circumcision, temple worship, and the covenant with Abraham. John proclaimed a forgiveness of sins that would take place in the wilderness and not through temple sacrifices. The Jewish religious hierarchy objected that children of Abraham did not require baptism. The radicalness of John's message suggests a background in proselyte baptism. However, instead of the baptism being limited to converts to Judaism, now the rite is extended by John to include children of Abraham themselves. John was proclaiming that the entire nation of Israel was unclean and needed a new cleansing ceremony that involved returning to the wilderness before the new Israel could retake the promised land. Therefore, both John's baptism and proselyte baptism were initiatory rites performed only once that involved a call to repentance and appropriate obedient actions as well as a new definition of Israel.

Opponents of this position point out that historical evidence legitimatizing proselyte baptism as a procedure contemporary with Jesus is almost nonexistent.[40] Neither Philo nor Josephus mentions proselyte baptism. However, the Mishnah (*Pesaḥ.* 8:8; *b. Yebam.* 46a) records disputes between Hillel and Shammai concerning the immersion of newly circumcised proselytes, which indicates that rabbinic discussions were occurring contemporary with Jesus. Such a connection would establish the radicalness of John's baptism and reveal the necessity of a new covenant that Jesus would initiate. Therefore, a background in proselyte baptism offers a satisfactory explanation to the disputed significance of John's ministry in the Gospels.

Consulting the commentaries has opened up new vistas of interpretation. The backdrop to John's baptism could be the teaching of the Qumran community, the lustrations of the Old Testament, or the procedure of proselyte baptism. Since distinguished scholars offer cogent arguments for each position, my particular conclusion must be held tentatively and with the recognition that the exegetical evidence is divided. Therefore, our discovery of different background options to John's baptism has in the end made us less sure and dogmatic of our answers, but the wealth of knowledge we have obtained in the process compensates for all our loss of surety.

---

40. Compare Joachim Jeremias, *Infant Baptism in the First Four Centuries* (Philadelphia: Westminster, 1960), pp. 24-37; and H. H. Rowley, "Jewish Proselyte Baptism and the Baptism of John," *HUCA* 15 (1940): 313-34; or T. F. Torrance, "Proselyte Baptism," *NTS* 1 (1954): 150-54; with D. C. Smith, "Proselyte Baptism and the Baptism of John," *ResQ* 25 (1982): 13-32.

B. Different Periods in Church History

PROCEDURE

Recent commentaries can sometimes be shortsighted and only offer the latest interpretation of a particular passage. Church history, however, is rich in exegetical insights, so we should attempt to employ commentaries from different periods in the history of interpretation (church fathers, the Reformation, modern critical commentaries). Through such an exercise we can better grasp the flow of ideas throughout history. In addition, this conversation with our exegetical ancestors sharpens our ability to read contextually and to discover our cultural blinders. As John Thompson exclaims, "We may return from the past unpersuaded, but we will not return unchanged."[41] So we will take out our motion picture camera that has recorded the events of church history and attempt to retrieve footage from the many years of exegetical insights that have blessed the people of God.

Fortunately a contemporary renaissance of thinking is producing entire series of commentaries that concentrate upon the history of exegesis. Excellent reference works include the following (with many available electronically):

A. For different theological traditions (Catholic, Orthodox, Lutheran, and Evangelical): *The Bible in the Churches: How Various Christians Interpret the Scriptures,* ed. Kenneth Hagen (Milwaukee: Marquette University Press, 1994).

B. **For different periods of church history:**

  1. Series of commentaries include:

    a. *Ancient Christian Commentary on Scripture,* gen. ed. Thomas C. Oden (Downers Grove: InterVarsity)

    b. *The Church's Bible,* gen. ed. Robert Louis Wilken (Grand Rapids: Eerdmans), such as Wilken, *Isaiah: Interpreted by Early Christian and Medieval Commentaries* (2007)

    c. *Hellenistic Commentary to the New Testament,* ed. M. Eugene Boring, Klaus Berger, Carsten Colpe (Nashville: Abingdon, 1995)

---

41. John L. Thompson, *Reading the Bible with the Dead: What You Can Learn from the History of Exegesis That You Can't Learn from Exegesis Alone* (Grand Rapids: Eerdmans, 2007), p. 223.

2. Other works:
   a. John Thompson, *Reading the Bible with the Dead: What You
      Can Learn from the History of Exegesis That You Can't Learn
      from Exegesis Alone* (Grand Rapids: Eerdmans, 2007)
   b. *The Church Fathers on the Bible,* ed. Frank Sadowski (New
      York: Alba House, 1987)
   c. Stephen L. Wailes, *Medieval Allegories of Jesus' Parables*
      (Berkeley: University of California Press, 1987)
C. **For Reformational interpretations:**
   a. *The Reformation Commentary,* series forthcoming from
      InterVarsity
   b. *Calvin and the Bible,* ed. Donald K. McKim (Cambridge:
      Cambridge University Press, 2006)
   c. Anthony N. S. Lane, *John Calvin: Student of the Church Fa-
      thers* (Grand Rapids: Baker, 1999)
   d. *Calvin's Commentaries* (Grand Rapids: Eerdmans, 1948)
   e. Luther's commentaries and sermons in *Luther's Works* (St.
      Louis: Concordia, 1957–)

EXAMPLES

1. Matthew 3:11/Luke 3:16: Baptism with the Holy Spirit and Fire

The twentieth century has been hailed as the arrival of the age of the Spirit.
In previous generations the role of the Holy Spirit was minimized so that the
Apostles' Creed contains only one short matter-of-fact sentence, "I believe in
the Holy Spirit." Therefore, we might not expect the church fathers to discuss any of the controversial issues associated with the Holy Spirit. Take, for
example, what it means to be baptized with the Holy Spirit and fire. Do contemporary views trace back to the church fathers? Or should we turn just to
our age for enlightenment about these issues?

    In the last thirty years of the twentieth century, James Dunn was the
dominant theological writer on issues of the Holy Spirit in the English-
speaking world. His research and exegesis is exemplary because he recognizes the necessity of reviewing the history of interpretation. For example, in
the very first sentence of his article "Spirit-and-Fire Baptism," Dunn reports
that "In the history of the exegesis of this logion (i.e. Matt. 3:11; Luke 3:16)
scholarly opinion has usually settled on one of four interpretations — two

of them ancient, and two of them comparatively modern."[42] Both ancient and modern commentaries must be examined.

The positive view that both a baptism of the Holy Spirit and a baptism of fire are fulfilled by the Christian church at Pentecost traces back to the church father John Chrysostom[43] and is the Reformational interpretation of John Calvin. Calvin contends that the term "fire" is only an epithet to describe the Spirit's work of consecration, purging, and scouring off our dirt as gold is refined with fire.[44] The baptism of the Holy Spirit is witnessed in the mighty rushing wind at Pentecost and the baptism with fire in the flaming tongues that appear on the heads of the 120 believers. Today this is considered an anachronistic Christian interpretation that is difficult to harmonize with the message of judgment which dominates the preaching of the Baptist.[45]

In contrast stands the contemporary negative view that John the Baptizer only preached judgment, so that baptism in wind and fire is a hendiadys centering on the single theme of purification by the removal of evil. Supporters point to Isa 4:4, which predicts that the Lord "will cleanse the bloodstains from Jerusalem by a spirit of judgment and a spirit of fire." This view is especially advocated by scholars such as Vincent Taylor and T. W. Manson rather than preachers.[46] If you did a search of the Dead Sea Scrolls (available in some packages of Logos Bible Software), you would encounter evidence to support this view. 1QS 4:20-21 states, "God will purge by His truth every deed of man, refining for Himself the body of man by abolishing from the midst of his flesh every evil spirit, and by cleansing him through a holy spirit from all wicked practices and He will sprinkle on him a

---

42. James D. G. Dunn, "Spirit-and-Fire Baptism," *NovT* 14 (1972): 81.

43. *Homilia in Matt. 11:4,* in PG 7:154. Cf. Joseph A. Fitzmyer, *The Gospel According to Luke I–IX.* AB 28 (Garden City: Doubleday, 1981), p. 473.

44. John Calvin, *Institutes of the Christian Religion,* ed. John T. McNeill, trans. Ford Lewis Battles (Philadelphia: Westminster, 1960), 3:1:3, 4; and John Calvin, *A Harmony of the Gospels Matthew, Mark, and Luke,* ed. D. W. Torrance and T. F. Torrance, trans. A. W. Morrison (Grand Rapids: Eerdmans, 1994), 1:127-28.

45. See Namkuk Yang, "An Exegetical Study on Luke's Soteriological View of Spirit-Baptism: A Critical Response to Pentecostalism" (Th.M. diss., Calvin Theological Seminary, 2004), p. 24.

46. T. W. Manson, *The Sayings of Jesus* (Grand Rapids: Eerdmans, 1957), pp. 39-41; Vincent Taylor, *The Gospel According to Mark,* 2nd ed. (Grand Rapids: Baker, 1966), p. 157. For further bibliography, see Dunn, "Spirit-and-Fire Baptism," p. 82, n. 2; and Robert P. Menzies, *The Development of Early Christian Pneumatology with Special Reference to Luke-Acts.* JSNTSup 54 (Sheffield: JSOT, 1991), p. 136, n. 1.

spirit of truth as purifying fire."[47] Here the spirit and fire work together as one agent.

More popular is the double lustration view or double application view, with the baptism in the Holy Spirit applied to believers and baptism in fire experienced by nonresponders.[48] A form of this view was already advocated by Origen and is the earliest Christian interpretation that we possess.[49] Believers now receive the baptism of the Holy Spirit as Christ's gift to the church, and unbelievers will experience the baptism of fire at the final judgment. However, the original promise was a both/and prediction specifying that those who respond will be baptized both with the Holy Spirit and with fire.

Finally, there is the double-talk view of James Dunn and Max Turner,[50] where both the spirit and the fire apply to each group, a positive infilling Spirit and purifying fire to believers and a negative blowing away (the Spirit as wind) and consuming fire to nonbelievers. Support for this riddlelike nature of the Baptist's saying comes from the fact that "The idea of immersion in the river Jordan was itself one which was able to convey the ideas of both judgment and redemption."[51] In addition, Jesus seems to employ this type of play on words on a couple of occasions. A similar saying in Mark 9:49 ("Everyone will be salted with fire") means that the fire will be both purifying for the disciples like preserving salt and destructive for the wicked like the military use of salt (Gen 19:26; Judg 9:45; Wis 10:7).[52] In this same vein, Luke

47. Cf. Raymond E. Brown, *New Testament Essays* (Milwaukee: Bruce, 1965), pp. 135-36.

48. Supporters include Brown, *New Testament Essays*, pp. 134-36; Robert H. Stein, *Luke*. NAC (Nashville: Broadman, 1992), pp. 134-35; and Webb, *John the Baptizer*, pp. 261-306. For additional bibliography, see Dunn, "Spirit-and-Fire Baptism," p. 81, n. 2.

49. *Hom Luc 24*, in *Griechische christliche Schriftsteller* 35, 158. Origen distinguishes Spirit-baptism and fire-baptism without making them antithetical. Fire-baptism is not a punitive baptism for destruction of the unrepentant, but a gracious baptism for purification of those who already received water-baptism and Spirit-baptism but still need to be purified to enter paradise after death. See Yang, "Exegetical Study on Luke's Soteriological View of Spirit-Baptism," p. 22, n. 5.

50. James D. G. Dunn, *Baptism in the Holy Spirit: A Re-examination of the New Testament Teaching on the Gift of the Spirit in Relation to Pentecostalism Today* (Philadelphia: Westminster, 1970), pp. 11-14; Max M. B. Turner, "Holy Spirit," in *Dictionary of Jesus and the Gospels*, ed. Joel B. Green and Scot McKnight (Downers Grove: InterVarsity, 1992), p. 344. For additional bibliography, see Yang, "Exegetical Study on Luke's Soteriological View of Spirit-Baptism," p. 26, n. 18.

51. Dunn, *Baptism in the Holy Spirit*, p. 11.

52. See Dean B. Deppe, "The Imagery of Salt in the Sayings of Jesus: An Exegetical Study of Mark 9:49-50; Luke 14:34-35 and Matthew 5:13" (Th.M. diss., Calvin Theological Seminary, 1978), p. 81. This view is supported by Ezra P. Gould, *A Critical and Exegetical*

17:37 can be interpreted like a double-talk riddle describing both the eagles gathering where the body dwells and the vultures preying upon the carcass of the wicked.[53] I would support this modern view of Dunn and Turner as the correct interpretation, but research into the views of the early fathers and the Reformation giants is invaluable in understanding the possibilities of interpretation for this difficult concept.

2. Celebacy in the Church Fathers, Reformers, and Modern Commentaries

Different periods of church history sometimes interpret specific texts with strikingly divergent emphases. Therefore, the reading of commentaries from different eras requires an investigation of the ideology of the day, which may in turn challenge the presuppositions of the interpreter. We will consider Paul's teaching on sex in 1 Cor 7:1-9 as a case in point.

The teaching of the church fathers on specific Scripture passages is now easily accessible through two new series, the *Ancient Christian Commentary on Scripture* and *The Church's Bible*. Because of the prevalence of ascetic ideology in the early centuries, the commentaries on 1 Corinthians 7 are dominated by the supremacy of celibacy. As Judith Kovacs explains, "Patristic commentary on this chapter reflects the wide influence of the ascetic ideal in the early centuries of the Church, evident, for example, in the many treatises on virginity composed by fathers such as Athanasius, Ambrose, John Chrysostom, and Gregory of Nyssa."[54] In interpreting 1 Corinthians 7:1b ("It is good for a man not to marry"), Jerome concludes that "If it is good not to touch a woman, it is bad to touch one."[55] For these comments Jerome becomes the object of ridicule in Reformational and modern commentaries. When Paul permits married people to refrain from sexual relations for a

---

Commentary on the Gospel According to St. Mark. ICC (New York: Scribner's, 1896), pp. 176, 181; and James Moffatt, *A New Translation of the Bible, Containing the Old and New Testaments* (New York: Harper and Row, 1954), p. 56.

53. ὅπου τὸ σῶμα, ἐκεῖ καὶ οἱ ἀετοὶ ἐπισυναχθήσονται is translated "Where the body *is*, there the eagles will be gathered together" by the KJV, NKJV, ASV, RSV, and Young's Literal Translation, but with "Where the corpse is, there the vultures will gather" by the ESV, GNB, NASB, NET, NIV, NJB, NLT, NRSV, TNIV, and Holman Christian Standard Bible. Matthew 24:28 employs "corpse," whereas Luke 17:37 uses "body."

54. Judith L. Kovacs, ed., *1 Corinthians: Interpreted by Early Christian Commentators.* The Church's Bible (Grand Rapids: Eerdmans, 2005), p. 104.

55. Found in Kovacs, *1 Corinthians*, p. 111.

temporary time period (1 Cor 7:5), Origen concludes that the prayers of the celibate are purer than those of people who have conjugal relations.[56] Origen emphasizes how Israel purified herself from sexual relations at Mount Sinai (Exod 19:15) and that David and his band could only partake of the holy bread of the tabernacle if they had kept themselves from women (1 Sam 21:4-6).[57] The ascetic ideal is evident throughout the pages of patristic commentaries on 1 Corinthians 7.

Regarding marriage, Chrysostom asserts, "Paul permits marriage as a concession, but the very fact that it is designed to avoid fornication shows that he is really trying to encourage virginity."[58] Therefore, "the superior course" is "not to have any connection whatever with a woman."[59] Likewise, Jerome opposed Jovian, who said that "virgins, widows, and married women, once they have been cleansed by Christ, have equal merit as long as their other actions are similar." Jerome replies that "we must fight the enemy with all our might and marshall our battle lines to repulse the disorderly forces of the enemy."[60] Clement of Alexandria even contends that "the man who marries to have children must be continent, feeling no sexual desire for his wife. He ought to love her and beget children with a will that is holy and chaste."[61] These emphases are totally opposite of what we observe in modern commentaries. An analysis of the *Zeitgeist* of the culture is therefore a prerequisite for reading any biblical commentary.

The Reformers, on the other hand, react against centuries of emphasis upon the supremacy of celibacy and the monastic ideal. This changed cultural mileau creates a strikingly different atmosphere in the commentaries. Pointedly, Martin Luther declares about 1 Cor 7:1-2, "Consider how quickly he (i.e. Paul) breaks off in this statement, saying that it is well not to touch a woman, but he neither commands nor advises anybody to follow this but quickly goes over to talk of marriage."[62] Discussing the implications of this statement, Luther continues, "From this it follows that nobody can vow to be

56. Found in Kovacs, *1 Corinthians*, p. 105.

57. Found in Kovacs, *1 Corinthians*, p. 108.

58. *Hom. 1 Cor* 19.1, in *1-2 Corinthians*, ed. Gerald Bray. Ancient Christian Commentary on Scripture 7 (Downers Grove: InterVarsity, 1999), p. 60.

59. *Hom. 1 Cor* 19.1, in Anthony C. Thiselton, *The First Epistle to the Corinthians*. NIGTC (Grand Rapids: Eerdmans and Carlisle: Paternoster, 2000), p. 500.

60. Found in Kovacs, *1 Corinthians*, p. 110.

61. Found in Kovacs, *1 Corinthians*, p. 107.

62. Martin Luther, *Commentaries on 1 Corinthians 7; 1 Corinthians 15; Lectures on 1 Timothy*, in Luther's Works 28, ed. Hilton C. Oswald (St. Louis: Concordia, 1973), p. 9.

chaste, nor should he keep such a vow but rather break it . . . for such a vow is really contrary to God's command." Instead of applauding those committed to celibacy, now Luther chastises them, "They think that the bitterer chastity is for someone and the harder to endure, the more precious it will be to God."[63] Luther accuses the bishops of rejecting and perverting "the divine order so that St. Paul's words are no longer binding, 'each man should have his own wife,' but rather preach: 'some may have wives, some not have wives' thus making 'some' out of 'each.'"[64] Luther's conclusion on this matter states that "Such poor blinded people thought chastity could be put into people from without, whereas it is a gift from heaven and must come from within."[65] John Calvin too refutes the "foolish admiration of celibacy" but still wants to claim the church fathers as his own by concluding that Jerome's mistake was "not so much from ignorance, in my opinion, as from the heat of controversy."[66] In summary, Paul's teaching on celibacy and marriage seems to be employed for opposite purposes when we move from the church fathers to the Reformers.

Today, we live in a sex-crazed society that cannot imagine anyone committed to celibacy or even purity before marriage. We are bombarded hourly with sexual innuendoes from television sitcoms. This spirit inevitably infiltrates into the church, as evidenced by the abusive sexual acts performed by Roman Catholic clergy, supposedly content with the ideal of celibacy. Therefore, modern commentators tend to emphasize the beauty of sex as a prominent part of God's good creation. Paul, then, becomes a proponent of the God-given desire for sex. Regularly one reads in commentaries remarks such as David Garland's, that Paul is "not antimarriage, nor does he disparage sexuality."[67] Paul's theology then fits well with our contemporary views of human freedom: "He does not seek to make everyone conform to his own personal gifts and insists that the physical side of marriage not be curtailed by misguided spirituality."[68] Today commentaries emphasize that Paul's comment that people should get married because of temptations toward immorality (7:2) must not be wrongly construed. As Garland explains, "Paul

63. Luther, *Commentaries on 1 Corinthians 7*, p. 11.

64. Luther, *Commentaries on 1 Corinthians 7*, pp. 12-13.

65. Luther, *Commentaries on 1 Corinthians 7*, p. 10.

66. John Calvin, *Commentary on the Epistles of Paul the Apostle to the Corinthians,* trans. John Pringle (Grand Rapids: Eerdmans, 1948), 1:222. See also p. 232 for a second reason.

67. David E. Garland, *1 Corinthians*, Baker Exegetical Commentary on the New Testament (Grand Rapids: Baker Academic, 2003), p. 242.

68. Garland, *1 Corinthians*, p. 243.

does not devilize marriage only as a venereal safety valve for incontinent, noncharismatic people, providing them a lawful outlet for expressing their sexual urges."[69] Therefore, reading modern commentaries we find ourselves in a completely different cultural milieu that challenges many of the presuppositions of the church fathers.

Contemporary commentaries follow a historical and literary approach and attempt to bring to life the circumstances of first-century Corinth. Whereas the traditional opinion asserts that 1 Cor 7:1b comprises Pauline theology,[70] the dominant theory since David Smith in 1920[71] states that Paul is quoting a Corinthian saying that he insists on correcting.[72] Therefore, "it is good for a man not to have sexual relations with a woman" is now placed in quotation marks by the TNIV over against the NIV, the NRSV replacing the RSV, and the REB altering the NEB.[73] Ironically, Origen already advocated that 7:1b should be ascribed to a group at Corinth, so that a study of the history of interpretation brings up surprises to moderns who think their interpretations are novel.[74]

So today's commentaries attempt to protect Paul from being morbidly ascetic and advocating an embarrassingly jaundiced view of marriage. Following Brian Rosner, Anthony Thistleton contends that "Paul advocates 'a full conjugal life.'"[75] From these comments we can clearly perceive that each age of commentaries has its own individual emphases dependent upon the cultural issues of the day. To break out of our own presuppositions, it is important to investigate the entire history of interpretation. Maybe soon our

69. Garland, *1 Corinthians*, pp. 242-43.

70. Gordon D. Fee, *The First Epistle to the Corinthians.* NICNT (Grand Rapids: Eerdmans, 1987), p. 275, explains, "Traditionally it has been interpreted at face value as Paul's own position, in which he is seen to affirm not only celibacy but a basically ascetic position toward sex and marriage."

71. David Smith, *The Life and Letters of St. Paul* (New York: Doran, 1920), p. 262. Support for this thesis can be found in Thiselton, *First Epistle to the Corinthians*, pp. 298-99.

72. Fee, *First Epistle to the Corinthians*, 271, reconstructs the Corinthian situation: "on the basis of the slogan that it is *good* not to have sexual relations, they were arguing for abstinence within marriage; and since abstinence might be difficult for some, then divorce was being recommended as a viable alternative — most certainly so when the marriage partner 'one touches' is an unbeliever."

73. Interestingly, the New Jerusalem Bible identifies 7:1b as a quote which Paul endorses, "Yes, it is a good thing for a man . . ." disclosing the continual Roman Catholic preference for celibacy.

74. See Thiselton, *First Epistle to the Corinthians*, p. 498, for the Greek quotation.

75. Thiselton, *First Epistle to the Corinthians*, p. 501, following Brian S. Rosner, *Paul, Scripture and Ethics: A Study of 1 Corinthians 5–7.* AGJU 22 (Leiden: Brill, 1994), pp. 149-61.

age will again appreciate the beauty of a celibate life lived entirely for God. A renewed interest in the church fathers might lead our age in that direction.

3. John 1:34: "Son of God" or "Chosen One"?

Logos Bible Software contains a very useful searching device that can discern biblical texts in any document of your electronic library. Under Basic Search, type *Bible = "John 1:34"* and Libronix will supply every text in your entire library where this verse is mentioned. Or type *Bible in "John 1:34"* and it will include all intersecting verses such as John 1:34-35. Or you can include a topic like *Bible = "John 1:34" and "chosen one"* to determine if the reference works discuss the possibility that "chosen one" should be read rather than "Son of God." To save time, you can narrow the content of your library by defining unique collections of resources under the "Tools" bar. You can create a collection of the church fathers that includes the Anti-Nicene, Nicene, and Post-Nicene fathers. You can collect all the writings of the Reformation together, like Calvin's and Luther's commentaries, the *Institutes of the Christian Religion*, the Heidelberg Catechism, and Westminster confession and catechism. Furthermore, I have separated my commentaries into two separate collections so that I can search scholarly works in one category as well as more homiletical commentaries like the Pulpit commentaries and Barclay's *Daily Study Bible Series* with a different search.

Suppose while preparing a sermon on the titles of Jesus in John 1 you notice that one of the most recent English versions, the TNIV, reads "chosen one" rather than "Son of God" in John 1:34. You want to know whether this problem was discussed by the early church fathers, during the Reformation age, and in modern critical commentaries. In searching your collection of Anti-Nicene writings, you notice that the *Diatessaron* of Tatian has "Son of God" and that the reading "chosen one" is not recognized in any of the homilies of Chrysostom. Searching the Reformation documents, you discover the same phenomenon, no occurrences of "chosen one" in John 1.

If you search your scholarly modern commentaries, you discover that the problem is discussed in the *Anchor Bible Commentary*, the *New International Commentary on the New Testament*, the *New American Commentary*, and the *Word Biblical Commentary*. But these commentators are split upon which is the correct reading at John 1:34.[76] Has the textual alteration in the

---

76. Gerald L. Borchert, *John 1–11*. NAC 25A (Nashville: Broadman and Holman, 1996),

TNIV published in the twenty-first century resulted from a recent manuscript discovery? You finally ferret out that the deciding manuscript is papyrus 106, which was discovered in Oxyrhynchus, Egypt in the late nineteenth century but has finally been published in the last few years. Now the "earliest extent witness"[77] reads "chosen one," so that the external evidence of other papyri like $\mathfrak{P}^{66}$ and $\mathfrak{P}^{72}$ is now nullified by the papyri readings supporting "chosen one."[78] The external evidence as well emanates from several diverse geographical areas, being found in witnesses of Egypt, Syria, and the Latin-speaking West.[79] You can even read this Greek manuscript in Libronix with the add-on resource, *The Text of the Earliest New Testament Greek Manuscripts,* edited by Philip Comfort and David Barrett.[80] If you have opened a Greek text or commentary to John 1:34, Logos Bible Software will automatically bring up this verse when you click on $\mathfrak{P}$106 in the "Parallel Resource Sets" icon. Therefore, the publication of $\mathfrak{P}$106 will probably transform the English translation tradition, and the TNIV is the first English Bible to recognize the significance of this variant.

Another method of approach is to create a Layout in Logos Bible Software comprised of the Stuttgart Electronic Study Bible, the critical apparatus, and Metzger's *Textual Commentary.* If you tile these into three columns and link them together, you can examine this textual problem in another

---

p. 139; and G. R. Beasley-Murray, *John.* WBC 36 (Dallas: Word, 2002), p. 25, support "Son of God," while Raymond E. Brown, *The Gospel According to John.* AB 29 (Garden City: Doubleday, 1966), p. 57; and Leon Morris, *The Gospel According to John.* NICNT (Grand Rapids: Eerdmans, 1971), pp. 153-54, argue in favor of "chosen one" because it is the more difficult reading. The recent work by Andreas J. Köstenberger, *John.* Baker Exegetical Commentary on the New Testament (Grand Rapids: Baker Academic, 2004), p. 57, supports "chosen one" as well.

77. Peter M. Head, "Some Recently Published New Testament Papyri from Oxyrhynchus: An Overview and Preliminary Assessment," *TynBul* 51 (2000): 10. For a description of this manuscript, see pp. 10-11.

78. The reading ὁ ἐκλεκτός ("chosen one") fits better the length of the line in $\mathfrak{P}^5$, but Peter Head, "Recently Published Papyri," 11, n. 23, explains that "It is impossible to be certain about this reading as only the final sigma is visible, and although a *nomen sacrum* would result in a very short line, the manuscript may have had υἱός in full as reconstructed in W. J. Elliot and D. C. Parker, *The Gospel According to St. John: Volume One: The Papyri* (Leiden: Brill, 1995), p. 29."

79. Bart Ehrman, *The Orthodox Corruption of Scripture: The Effect of Early Christological Controversies on the Text of the New Testament* (Oxford: Oxford University Press, 1993), p. 69.

80. Philip W. Comfort and David P. Barrett, eds., *The Text of the Earliest New Testament Greek Manuscripts: A Corrected, Enlarged Edition* (Wheaton: Tyndale House, 2001).

format. Notice that Metzger's *Textual Commentary* still opts for "Son of God" in John 1:34 because it has not yet considered the weight of 𝔓106. But it also aids your research in revealing that Ambrose supported the reading "chosen one."[81] It is always important to realize the insufficiency of your library since you did not possess Ambrose's writings in your church fathers' collection. As more electronic resources become available as well as the new sets of commentaries on ancient texts, an investigation of the history of interpretation will become much easier and quicker to benefit from.

81. Bruce M. Metzger, *A Textual Commentary on the Greek New Testament*, 2nd ed. (Stuttgart: Deutsche Bibelgesellschaft, 1994), p. 172.

1. Jesus' words to Peter after his profession of faith in Jesus as "the Christ, the Son of the Living God" (Matt 16:16) have been interpreted differently by Catholics and Protestants. How do they understand Jesus' reply, "on this rock I will build my church, and the gates of Hades will not overcome it"? Does it refer to Peter himself or to Peter's confession? Offer arguments for each conclusion by investigating both Catholic and Protestant commentaries.

2. The New Testament narrates the beginning of the office of deacon in Acts 6:1-6. The poor were not being cared for financially by the church, so assistants to the apostles were chosen so that the apostles could devote themselves to prayer and the ministry of the word. Explore a theological dictionary and discover how Catholics and Protestants conceive of deacons differently. What are the tasks of deacons in these two traditions?

3. Various theological traditions emphasize different aspects of future eschatology. American evangelicals and fundamentalists cannot seem to get their fill of prophecy conferences. Detailed charts of future events, dogmatic assertions about biblical prophecies fulfilled in the events of the Middle East, decoded hidden messages from the Bible: these have become the symbols of vibrant Christianity in our time. On the other hand, Reformation thinkers have shied away from preaching about the future, probably continuing the tradition of John Calvin, who neglected to write a commentary only on the book of Revelation. What is the emphasis when the NT authors write about future events? Check out how Paul concludes his teaching about the coming of the Lord (1 Thess 4:18; 5:8-11; 2 Thess 1:11; 2:15; and 1 Cor 15:58). Then notice that Peter concludes with similar exhortations about everyday life in 1 Pet 4:7-11 and 2 Pet 3:11-14. To conclude his predictions about the end of the world in Matthew 24, what does Jesus teach in Matthew 25? Should our emphasis when we talk about the end of the world be on "How then shall we live?" or upon "What is going to happen in the future?" What was the angel's rebuke to the disciples at Jesus' ascension (Acts 1:11a), and what is the significance of this for how you answer the last question?

4. It is important to consult more than one contemporary commentary to receive the full breadth of interpretations. For instance, Mark 15:34 reports that "Jesus cried out in a loud voice, 'My God, my God, why have you forsaken me?'" and Mark 15:37 says "With a loud cry, Jesus breathed his last." Is

Jesus' cry one of abandonment and suffering or one of triumph and glory? Robert Gundry comments,

> To portray Jesus at his death as strong — strong in flesh and superhumanly so . . . — Mark mentions the loudness of Jesus' voice when he shouts, "'Eloi, Eloi, lema sabachthani?' . . . the mystique of an oriental foreign language carries the connotation of power. . . . Here, the power will turn out so superhuman that the breath-Spirit which Jesus exhales in shouting the Aramaic makes a wind strong enough to rend the veil of the temple.[82]

On the other hand, Donald Senior explains that

> Mark's death scene redefines what a "Christian death" must look like. To die in faith need not mean peaceful symmetry, or pious decorum. The Marcan Jesus struggles in death, crying out to God in a piercing lament, and breathing his last with a scream. Yet the God of Jesus is present even — and especially — in these moments when human dignity seems shredded.[83]

Is the emphasis in the Gospel of Mark upon the passion of Jesus or upon the triumph of Jesus? Offer exegetical evidence.

5. Does Jesus proclaim the end of the world in his eschatological discourse in Mark 13 or just the destruction of Jerusalem? Is the imagery in 13:24-25 describing the sun being darkened, the moon not giving its light, and the stars falling from the sky portraying the end of the world or the fall of a nation? See Isa 13:10 referring to Babylon in 13:1 and Ezek 32:7-8 referring to Egypt in 32:2. In Mark 13:26 is the Son of Man coming to earth on the clouds of heaven at his triumphant return, or is he ascending on the clouds to the Ancient of Days indicating Christ's ascension? See Dan 7:13-14. Are the angels who are gathering people from the four corners of the earth (Mark 13:27) the heavenly messengers gathering in the final harvest of souls or the Christian missionaries bringing the gospel to the ends of the earth? Should Mark 13:29 be translated "he is near," meaning Christ, or "it is near" speaking about the fall of Jerusalem? What does the one generation (13:30) refer to? You have to consult more than one commentary to receive the full range of opinions.

---

82. Gundry, *Mark*, pp. 947-48.

83. Donald Senior, *The Passion of Jesus in the Gospel of Mark* (Wilmington: Glazier, 1984), p. 147.

Three important commentaries on Mark are written by R. T. France, Robert Stein, and Joel Marcus. Go to your local library or add these commentaries to your Logos Bible Software collection and note how each commentator answers these questions.[84]

6. Revelation 16:16 asserts that the final battle between good and evil will occur at a place that in Hebrew is entitled Armageddon. Since this word literally means the "mountain of Megiddo," will the last battle occur in Palestine on this mountain? The problem is that the Bible talks about a city of Megiddo (Josh 17:11; Judg 1:27; 1 Kgs 4:12; 9:15; 2 Kgs 9:27; 23:29, 30), a king of Megiddo (Josh 12:21), a valley of Megiddo (2 Chr 35:22; Zech 12:11), and waters of Megiddo (Judg 5:19) but never speaks about a mountain of Megiddo. Search a Bible dictionary in Logos Bible Software and discover the possible meanings of this term. Were the plains around the city of Megiddo meant, since this was a notorious region of an ancient battleground? See the battle between Deborah and Sisera (Judg 5:19) and the scene of the fatal struggle between Josiah and Pharaoh Neco (2 Kgs 23:29, 30; 2 Chr 35:22). This was such a memorable event in Israel's history that the mourning for Josiah was recalled a hundred years later (Zech 12:11). Or does the mountain of Megiddo refer to Mount Carmel, with the dragon, beast, and false prophet being the latter-day counterparts of Ahab, Jezebel, and the prophets of Baal? Or should the reference in Hebrew be translated "his fruitful mountain," so that the final battle scene occurs in Jerusalem, as Joel 3:16-18, Zech 14:2-5, and Rev 20:7-10 prophesied? How does the genre of the book of Revelation affect how we interpret this imagery?

7. Many NT scholars contend that the miraculous feedings of the five thousand and four thousand derive from one original story, since Luke and John narrate only one multiplication event. Or is the traditional interpretation of two distinct feedings correct? Make a list of the similarities and differences between the feedings in Mark 6:34-44 and 8:1-9. Could one refer to the feeding of Jews and the other the miraculous nourishment of Gentiles? Notice that in the feeding of the five thousand the crowd is like sheep without a shepherd and there are twelve hampers full of pieces left over, whereas in the

---

84. R. T. France, *The Gospel of Mark*. NIGTC (Grand Rapids: Eerdmans and Carlisle: Paternoster, 2002), pp. 497-505; Robert H. Stein, *Mark*. Baker Exegetical Commentary of the New Testament (Grand Rapids: Baker, 2008), pp. 584-85, 610, 617; and Marcus, *Mark 8–16*, pp. 865-67.

feeding of four thousand the people come from afar and seven baskets full are left (see Deut 7:1; Acts 13:19). Or is there another reason why Mark records both miraculous feedings? Note, for instance, the two feedings during the time of Moses in Exodus 16 and Num 11:4-9. What would an allusion to these events in Moses' life say about Jesus? Consult various commentaries on the Gospel of Mark to visualize the different interpretations and arguments put forth.

8. What is the traditional interpretation of Rom 13:1-7 with regard to a Christian's view of the state? Now examine the recent view proposed by Warren Carter, *The Roman Empire and the New Testament: An Essential Guide* (Nashville: Abingdon, 2007), pp. 133-35. Which view do you prefer and why? (Afterwards, check chapter 7 below, footnote 50, for some of my conclusions.)

The Theological Exegesis Route

Developing the Finished Photo

Since theological exegesis concentrates upon the themes and concepts within a passage, it is usually portrayed as a concluding element in the exegetical process. While there is truth in this proposal, another crucial aspect of theological exegesis is an investigation of the reader's presuppositions. This may be necessary at the beginning of exegesis so that readers become aware of their theological perspectives as well as their social-economic environment and psychological make-up and disposition. A third element in theological exegesis is a comparison of the content of a passage within a particular book with the message throughout the whole Bible to determine the canonical meaning. To gain expertise in this skill, a firsthand knowledge of the history of doctrine is beneficial as well as an awareness of how these theological perspectives have influenced church history. Because the development of dogma is regularly contemporaneous with movements in cultural history, an understanding of the major schools of philosophy also proves advantageous. In this chapter we will first consider the interpretation of specific texts where theological presuppositions play a major role, then examine specific authors who have enumerated their presuppositions as they approach the Bible, and finally explore the role that the canonical meaning plays in the interpretation of specific Bible passages.

A. A Theological Analysis of the Biblical Text

PROCEDURE

Theological exegesis[1] contends that the Bible was written chiefly for theological purposes and not primarily as a political, moral, or even historical book. The Bible speaks infallibly about our relationship with God and how we are to live on earth in his presence. It is not a scientific textbook explaining all the laws of nature or a day-by-day chronicle of deeds, movements, and conversations reporting historiography with scientific precision. Therefore, in the final analysis the theological meaning of the text is normative.

However, our exegetical conclusions are frequently controlled by our theological presuppositions as well as the methodologies we employ upon the text. The first example below, which describes the apologetic purposes of Matthew, demonstrates that the biblical writers themselves had their own unique theological purposes in writing. The next two examples, which investigate political interpretations of Mark's Gospel and a polyvalent approach to the parables of Jesus, emphasize that our presuppositions as readers always color the interpretation of biblical passages. The primacy of the theological meaning of a text can easily get lost in the multiplicity of approaches to the biblical documents. Therefore, interpreters must always be careful not to allow their theological presumptions to trump a grammatical, literary, contextual, and cultural background approach to the text. Finally, the last two discussions argue for a careful investigation of alternative approaches before making an exegetical decision. The multiple approaches to the book of Revelation and one's theology of Spirit-baptism in Acts 8 can dramatically alter one's exegetical conclusions.

EXAMPLES

1. Apologetic Against the Pharisaic Synagogue in the Gospel of Matthew

The Gospel writers are not like front-page historians who attempt to preserve a day-by-day chronicle of the events of Jesus' life or the minutes of his speeches. They are not detached neutral observers reporting historiography;

---

1. Theological commentaries have become popular in recent years, including the series by Eerdmans entitled Two Horizons (OT ed. Gordon McConville and Craig Bartholomew; NT ed. Joel Green) and the Brazos Theological Commentary of the Bible (ed. R. R. Reno).

instead, they are theological editors who are proclaiming and persuading as well as supplying factual information. The appropriate manner to picture Matthew is as an apologist attempting to defend a Christian interpretation of the Jesus movement over against the Pharisaic synagogue across the street that has developed its own ideological defense against Jesus as the Messiah. In the Gospel of Matthew careful readers can discern the accusations attacking the convictions of the Christian movement as well as Matthew's theological defense against these innuendoes.

Already in the birth narrative two accusations against Jesus come to the forefront. The true Messiah would never have been born as a bastard child out of wedlock like Jesus. In response, Matthew constructs a genealogy of Jesus that surprisingly includes five women who could each be categorized as unrighteous, but whom God included in the line of David. In the Old Testament Judah wanted to burn Tamar (Matt 1:3) to death for her prostitution (Gen 38:24), but she proved to be more righteous than this forefather of David (38:26). Rahab was a renowned prostitute, but saved Israel from the people of Jericho and became a foremother of David (Matt 1:5). Uriah's wife, Bathsheba (Matt 1:6), committed adultery with David (2 Samuel 11), but God still granted her son Solomon the throne (1 Kgs 1:15-18). Ruth asked Boaz to spread the corner of his garment over her (Ruth 3:9), an expression intentionally ambiguous so that it can function as a euphemism for sexual intercourse, but Ruth joins the line of David (4:16-17). All suspicions about Mary the mother of Jesus carry the identical connotation; she is really more righteous than all her accusers. In fact, the child in her womb is from the Holy Spirit; God miraculously performs a virgin birth as foretold in Isa 7:14 (Matt 1:18-25).

The second accusation focused on Jesus' birthplace. Since Jesus was normally addressed as "Jesus of Nazareth" (Matt 26:71), he must have originated from that town, whereas the prophets predicted that the Messiah would be born in Bethlehem (Mic 5:2). So immediately following his defense of Jesus' virgin birth, Matthew narrates the story of the arrival of the magi and Jesus' nativity in Bethlehem as witnessed by King Herod and all of Jerusalem with him, including the chief priests and teachers of the law (Matt 2:3-4). The accusations of the Pharisaic synagogue are effectively countered.

Since Jesus' uniqueness as Son of God is closely connected with his baptism (Matt 3:17), the Pharisees initiate the allegation that Jesus must be a sinner because baptism implies the need to be washed. In addition, John baptizes Jesus, demonstrating his superiority and preeminence. In response, Matthew dictates a conversation between John and Jesus (3:14-15) whereby

John admits his inferiority and subservience: "But John tried to deter him, saying, 'I need to be baptized by you, and do you come to me?' Jesus replied, 'Let it be so now; it is proper for us to do this to fulfill all righteousness.' Then John consented." The other evangelists omit this detail because it specifically serves the purposes of Matthew, who as a theologian is defending the claims of his Christian synagogue over against the Jewish synagogue.

The Jewish leaders taught the people that Moses was the director and head teacher of their community (see John 9:28-29), not Jesus. Therefore, throughout his Gospel Matthew endeavors to prove that Jesus is greater than Moses and is God's elect representative who will lead Israel to the promised land. Similar to the Pentateuch written by Moses, Matthew's Gospel contains five "books" as well as a prologue and an epilogue. Matthew constructs five sermons of Jesus to remind the readers of the five books of Moses (note the common ending at 7:28; 11:1; 13:53; 19:1; 26:1).[2] Matthew's title, "the book of the genesis of Jesus Christ" (1:1), serves as a prologue reminiscent of the *Toledot* ("genealogy") structure of Genesis (2:4). Here Jacob the father of Joseph (1:16; Luke writes Heli) reminds the reader of OT history, where both Josephs interpret dreams and save their families by going to Egypt. Likewise, the Pentateuch ends with a covenant renewal and succession to Joshua (Deuteronomy 29–31) as well as the mysterious death of Moses (Deuteronomy 34), just as Matthew ends with a renewed covenant (Matthew 26), the passing of the baton to the disciples, and Jesus' mysterious death and resurrection (chs. 27–28).

Matthew employs typology to remind his audience of Israel's exodus experience. Just as Moses is more powerful than the sorcerers of Egypt (Exod 7:10-12), the magi kneel at the feet of the greater Moses (Matt 2:11). Both Moses and Jesus are delivered as a baby from Pharaoh's/Herod's slaughter (Matt 2:13; Exod 1:22; 2:5) so that, just as Pharaoh commanded every male of the Hebrews to be cast into the Nile (Exod 1:22), Herod massacres the boys of Bethlehem (Matt 2:16). Both Moses and Jesus come out of Egypt through divine intervention (Matt 2:15, 19; Exod 12). The people of Israel led by Moses cross through the waters of the Red Sea (Exod 14:26-31), and Jesus at his bap-

---

2. For a discussion of this interpretation, compare Benjamin W. Bacon, "The 'Five Books' of Moses against the Jews," *Exp* 15 (1918): 56-66; and *Studies in Matthew* (London: Constable, 1930), chs. 12-16; along with Dale C. Allison Jr., *The New Moses: A Matthean Typology* (Minneapolis: Fortress, 1993); against Jack Dean Kingsbury, "Form and Message of Matthew," in *Interpreting the Gospels*, ed. James Luther Mays (Philadelphia: Fortress, 1981), pp. 66-77; and J. M. Gibbs, "The Son of God as the Torah Incarnate in Matthew," *Studia evangelica* 4 (Berlin: Academie, 1963), pp. 38-41.

tism traverses the waters of the Jordan (Matt 3:13-17) as God's firstborn son (Exod 4:22-23; Matt 3:17). Both enter the wilderness for a period of testing that extends forty years or forty days. Jesus' ordeal becomes a reenactment of the temptations confronted in the wilderness by the Israelites, with the testing of manna corresponding to Jesus' turning stones to bread.

Furthermore, the Israelites receive the Ten Commandments on Mount Sinai, and Jesus delivers the new law in his Sermon on the Mount (Matt 5:21 = Exod 20:13; 5:27 = 20:14; 5:31 = Deut 24:1-4; 5:33 = Lev 19:12; 5:38 = Exod 21:24; Lev 24:20; Deut 19:21; 5:43 = Lev 19:18). Just as God performs ten miracles in the wilderness through Moses (Num 14:22), so Matthew combines ten of Jesus' miracles together in chapters 8–9. Both Moses and Jesus send out twelve messengers to prepare for the taking of the land (Numbers 13; Matthew 10). Therefore, although Moses brings Israel toward the rest of the promised land (Exod 33:14), they miss its blessings (Ps 95:11), whereas Jesus offers his community true rest (Matt 11:28-30). Just as the face of Moses shines as he comes down the mountain (Exod 34:29), Jesus is transfigured with divine glory. Whereas Mark 9:3 only describes Jesus' clothes, Matt 17:2 calls attention to Jesus' face shining like the sun similar to Moses' appearance. Finally, the twelve disciples will sit upon twelve thrones (19:28) judging the twelve tribes of Israel.[3] Therefore, Matthew pictures Jesus as the true leader of Israel who initiates a new exodus and retakes the promised land as the kingdom of heaven.

Furthermore, Matthew employs the Old Testament as an apologetic backdrop to provide proof-texts to use against his synagogue adversaries. On more than twenty occasions Matthew employs a standard introductory formula like "this was to fulfill the prophecy" to quote a text that Jesus fulfills as the Messiah. Furthermore, against the claim that Jesus' miracles are unverified since only one witness is cited, Matthew narrates the deliverance of two demoniacs (8:28) and the miraculous healing of two blind men (9:27; 20:30). Against the claim that Jesus did not interpret the Scriptures exactly and literally, Matt 21:4-7 offers a literal fulfillment of Zech 9:9 with both a donkey and colt, and the two drinks offered to Jesus on the cross (Mark 15:23, 36) become in Matthew wine mixed with gall and vinegar (27:34, 48), to match the vocabulary of Ps 69:21. Against the claim that Jesus completely lacked sovereign control at his death, Matt 26:53-54 adds that Jesus possessed at his disposal twelve legions of angels, but instead chose to fulfill the words of Scripture.

---

3. The best resource for parallels between Moses and Jesus is Allison, *The New Moses*.

An additional accusation by the synagogue concerned the fact that most Jews failed to become Christians. If Jesus was the Messiah, then God must have forsaken his people Israel, since the majority of Jews never followed him. To counter this claim, Matthew argues that God did not renounce his people, but disobedient Israel abandoned God and his chosen Messiah. In chapters 21–23 Matthew positions Psalm 118 at the beginning, middle, and conclusion of this section to demonstrate that Jesus rides triumphantly into Jerusalem as the Son of David (21:9 = Ps 118:26), becomes the stone which the builders rejected (21:42 = Ps 118:22), and is finally vindicated in his resurrection and will return in eschatological glory as the psalm prophesies (23:39 = Ps 118:26). Then the disobedience and rebellion of the Jewish people is demonstrated by three history-of-redemption parables in Matt 21:28–22:14. First the Jewish leaders reject God's message through John the Baptist (21:28-32), then they kill the beloved Son of the Lord of the vineyard (21:33-46), and finally they excuse themselves from the invitation to the wedding feast preached by Jesus' disciples so that their city is burned to the ground (22:1-10). God has not rejected his people; they have rejected him. Following this, Matthew narrates three debates with the Pharisees (22:15-22), Sadducees (22:23-33), and lawyers 22:34-40) where Jesus silences the Jewish leaders (22:46) and replaces them as the leader of Israel. At the end of this section Jesus offers seven woes against the Jewish leaders (23:1-36), followed by a compassionate plea for Jerusalem (23:37-39). They are the deceivers, not Jesus, but Jesus is longing for them to return to their Messiah.

Finally, Matthew's description of Jesus' death and resurrection provides a final defense against two accusations from the Pharisaic synagogue. As we know from the Talmud (*b. Sanh.* 43a[4]), the Jewish leaders claimed that the disciples of Jesus were deceiving the people (Matt 27:63). Jewish propaganda proclaimed that Jesus had not completely died in the short period of his crucifixion and that the disciples came and stole his body from the tomb and proclaimed that he had risen from the dead (Matt 28:13, 15). Matthew contradicts this report by describing how the guards kept close watch upon Jesus on the cross (27:36) and how the tomb was fortified with a seal as well as the posting of guards (27:62-66). The rumors against Jesus spread falla-

---

4. "On the eve of the Passover Yeshu was hanged. For forty days before the execution took place, a herald went forth and cried, 'He is going forth to be stoned because he has practiced sorcery and enticed Israel to apostasy. Any one who can say anything in his favour, let him come forward, and plead his behalf.' But since nothing was brought forward in his favour he was hanged on the eve of Passover"; *The Babylonian Talmud*, ed. I. Epstein (London: Soncino, 1938), p. 281.

ciously by the Jewish leaders were fostered by financial paybacks to keep the guards at the tomb silent (Matt 28:12-15). Therefore, Matthew triumphantly squashes the Jewish rumors.

Throughout his Gospel Matthew demonstrates that he is a gifted theologian who is employing the Jesus tradition to offer an alternative to the teaching of the Pharisaic synagogue. Therefore, we have to read the Gospels not only as a historical account of the life of Jesus but also as a theological interpretation of the significance of these events. Within the narrative of Jesus' life and death readers can discern the apologetic purposes of the author.

2. Political Readings of the Gospel of Mark

Recently, political interpretations of the Scriptures have abounded in popularity, especially in volumes published by Orbis Press.[5] In some circles high acclaim has been poured upon this movement. Walter Wink, for instance, categorizes Ched Myer's commentary on Mark, *Binding the Strong Man*, as "quite simply, the most important commentary on a book of Scripture since Barth's *Romans*."[6] He claims that this work "marks the watershed of a new theological era" and "the harbinger of a theological renaissance."[7] Myers defends a political interpretation of Mark by contending that "The 'battle for the Bible' today has increasingly less to do with theological divi-

---

5. See, e.g., Michel Clévenot, *Materialist Approaches to the Bible* (Maryknoll: Orbis, 1985); Warren Carter, *Matthew and the Margins: A Sociopolitical and Religious Reading* (Maryknoll: Orbis, 2000); Fernando Belo, *A Materialist Reading of the Gospel of Mark* (Maryknoll: Orbis, 1981); Richard J. Cassidy, *Jesus, Politics, and Society: A Study of Luke's Gospel* (Maryknoll: Orbis, 1978); *John's Gospel in New Perspective: Christology and the Realities of Roman Power* (Maryknoll: Orbis, 1992); Cassidy and Philip J. Scharper, eds., *Political Issues in Luke-Acts* (Maryknoll: Orbis, 1983).

6. Walter Wink, review of *Binding the Strong Man*, in *Christian Century* 106 (1989): 761. Christopher Rowland, in his review in *JTS* 60 (2009): 636, claims that "The result is a grasp of the Gospel of Mark which is without peer among contemporary commentaries, in which the wisdom of the modern interpreter is matched by an exegetical and historical sensitivity which could only come from a scholar immersed, as Ched Myers is, in the contemporary political struggle and with an eye on pedagogy."

7. Wink, review of *Binding the Strong Man*, pp. 761, 762. He categorizes the new movement as "one that has been gathering momentum for some time in liberation, feminist, and black theologies but which had not hitherto broken fully onto the American scene in a form indigenous to the mainline and evangelical white churches."

sions and allegiances and more to do with political and economic allegiances."[8] He adds that, since the reading site for most white North American Christians is empire, *"locus imperium,"* our eyes have been blinded to many aspects of the text of Mark.[9] Therefore, the proliferation of political interpretations opens the eyes of our myopic contemporary society.

Certainly the truth in these statements entails that the Gospel has political implications for the first century as well as now. However, if the Scriptures were written primarily as theological documents to reveal the nature of God and his relationship to the human community, does a political interpretation undermine the primary intention of the text? How can we be attentive to the political implications of biblical passages without surrendering the primacy of the theological character of Scripture? As far as I am concerned, the biblical narratives and scriptural teachings definitely have political, economic, and social ramifications in contemporary life, but to contend that these interpretations are original and primary can easily destroy the theological nature of the Bible. The dangers of political readings must be acknowledged.

Political interpretations can easily read current fashionable realities back into the text. In his review of Myers' book, Dwight Peterson demonstrates how the author "has created a Markan community in his own image." He explains that Myers's "construction of the Markan community looks suspiciously like the communities with which he himself has been associated in the 1970's and 1980's, and his 'discovery' of an alienated, non-aligned but politically engaged ideology looks suspiciously like that of these same communities."[10] Likewise, Dale Martin asserts that we must be "wary of attributing to ancient Palestinian authors a self-aware, post-Marxist analysis of the intricate realities between social structures and religious language."[11]

---

8. Ched Myers, *Binding the Strong Man: A Political Reading of Mark's Story of Jesus* (Maryknoll: Orbis, 1988), p. 10.

9. Myers, *Binding the Strong Man,* p. 5.

10. Dwight N. Peterson, *The Origins of Mark: The Markan Community in Current Debate* (Leiden: Brill, 2000), pp. 140, 143. He adds on p. 113, "Myers' own reading site has transparently governed his choice of a text to study. His extensive construction of an historical Markan community appears, then, to be an attempt to occlude his own political and theological commitments and those of his community and ascribe them instead to a highly hypothetical first century, rural-Galilean community of Christians."

11. Dale B. Martin, review of Myers, *Binding the Strong Man,* in *Modern Theology* 6 (1990): 409.

The politicalization of language is especially apparent in the anachronisms that Myers employs to describe the events in Jesus' life.[12] The Roman soldiers are described as "storm troopers" (414) who "drive the community underground" (419). The Jewish scribes are "government investigators from Jerusalem" (424). In turn, Jesus chooses the Twelve, creating a "vanguard revolutionary committee, a government in exile" (164), who through their missionary work establish a network of "safe houses" (214). The disciples' eating of grain on the Sabbath is an act of civil disobedience protesting the politics of food in Palestine (161), and Jesus' feeding of the five thousand is pictured as a mass organizing campaign (126). Jesus' entry into Jerusalem is described as a well-staged "street theater" (294); his temple action "shuts down the military industrial complex (352); and the betrayal by Judas occurs through governmental espionage (119). Finally, the subtle symbolism in the Gospel of Mark is explained by "the need for a coded discourse of resistance that could elude Roman censors and military intelligence" (419).

Let me use Ched Myers' other book, *Say to This Mountain,* to indicate how biblical terms are redefined so that a political connotation becomes primary.[13] The designation "crowds" becomes synonymous with the disenfranchised masses: the poor, the unemployed, the displaced, the sick, the unclean (p. 31). The term "kingdom" symbolizes the centralized state, while the "mystery of the kingdom" (Mark 4:11) conveys the fact that "jubilee justice is incongruous with the dominant social and economic system" (41). Parables are understood as metaphorical stories with thinly veiled political meanings (35). Finally, to "take up the cross" means to resist systems and structures that cause or perpetuate injustice (106).

Likewise, the genres of calling narratives, healings, exorcisms, and nature miracles are transformed into the genre of political action. The call of the disciples (1:16-20) is viewed as "summoning working folk to join in overturning the structures of power and privilege" (10). The healing of Peter's mother-in-law (1:29-31) is an overturning of patriarchal theology and the devaluation of women (15). Jesus' controversy with the Jewish leaders about Beelzebub (3:21-29) is "a homily from Jesus about revolution" (33). The casting out of the Decapolis demon (5:1-20) becomes "a political cartoon critical of Roman imperialism" (59). And the feeding of the five thousand (6:31-44)

---

12. For these examples, see Peterson, *The Origins of Mark,* pp. 118-19; and Martin's review, p. 408.

13. Ched Myers, *Say to This Mountain: Mark's Story of Discipleship* (Maryknoll: Orbis, 1996).

is a policy statement that the hungry masses cannot be fed through market economics but only through the redistribution of available resources, an "alternative economic model of cooperative consumption" (74).

These transformations to political language, imagery, genre, and content make for fascinating reading and lively discussion, but at the same time they can produce political meanings that push aside the theological intentions of the author. Maintaining a theological perspective while simultaneously enumerating the political, economic, and social implications of the narrative is the narrow road that the faithful interpreter must walk. In an effort to be relevant, exegetes need to be careful not to displace the theological nature of the narratives.

3. *Polyvalence in Interpreting the Parables*

Multiple meanings for a single text is nothing new in the church. The Alexandrian school in the early church was renowned for its allegorical interpretations. Just as a complete human was composed of body, soul, and spirit, so the full interpretation of a text included a literal, moral, and spiritual meaning. The literal told what happened; the allegorical explained what is to be believed; and the tropological or moral taught what is to be done. In the early Middle Ages the anagogical sense was added, offering an eschatological connotation in the future. This fourfold interpretation supplied a full and complete analysis of the text, so that Genesis 1:3 ("Let there be light") now meant (1) the creation in a literal sense; (2) "may we be illumined in mind and inflamed in heart through Christ" in the moral sense; (3) "let Christ be formed in the church" in the allegorical meaning; and (4) "may we be conducted to glory through Christ" in an anagogical sense.[14]

In the heyday of the Alexandrian school of exegesis, allegorical interpretations of the parables like the following chart incorporating the views of St. Augustine (*Quaestiones evangeliorum* 2:19) on the parable of the Good Samaritan ruled the religious market.[15]

---

14. See, e.g., Thomas Aquinas, *Commentary on Galatians* 4:7. For his defense of the fourfold sense, see *Summa Theologica*, part 1, question 1, article 10.

15. See the helpful charts summarizing the findings of the fathers and Reformational figures on this parable in Robert H. Stein, *The Method and Message of Jesus' Teachings*. Rev. ed. (Louisville: Westminster John Knox, 1994), pp. 46-50.

The man going down to Jericho	=	Adam
Jerusalem, from which he was going	=	The heavenly city
Thieves	=	The devil and his angels
Stripping him	=	Taking away Adam's immortality
Beating him	=	Persuading Adam to sin
Leaving him half dead	=	Adam was dead spiritually in sin but still retained the image of God
The priest	=	The OT law
The Levite	=	The OT prophets
The Good Samaritan	=	Christ
Binding of wounds	=	The restraint of sin
Oil	=	Comfort bringing good hope
Wine	=	Exhortation to spirited work
The animal ridden	=	The body of Christ
The inn	=	The church
Two denarii	=	Two commandments of love
The innkeeper	=	The apostle Paul
The return of the Good Samaritan	=	The *parousia* of Christ

The Reformation repudiated this fourfold sense of Scripture, so that Martin Luther describes the allegorizers as "clerical jugglers performing monkey tricks," whose conclusions are "worth less than dirt."[16] John Calvin, likewise, asserts that "Anyone may see that these speculations have been cooked up by meddlers, quite divorced from the mind of Christ."[17] In spite of the writings of the Reformers, allegorical interpretation of the parables was continually popular[18] until Adolf Jülicher's efforts to stifle this approach.[19] Under the influence of Joachim Jeremias,[20] a consensus formed that each parable comprised a single point of comparison *(tertium compara-*

16. See Stein, *Method and Message*, p. 48. Luther, however, did not deny outright the use of allegory. See Robert H. Stein, *An Introduction to the Parables of Jesus* (Philadelphia: Westminster, 1981), pp. 49, 155 n. 23.

17. John Calvin, *A Harmony of the Gospels Matthew, Mark, and Luke*, ed. D. W. Torrance and T. F. Torrance, trans. A. W. Morrison (Grand Rapids: Eerdmans, 1994), 3:39.

18. Archbishop Richard C. Trench, in his influential *Notes on the Parables of Our Lord* (1841; New York: Appleton, 1865), p. 36, claimed that Calvin's strictures "would leave the parables bare trunks, stripped of all their foliage and branches, of everything that made for beauty and ornament."

19. Adolf Jülicher, *Die Gleichnisreden Jesus* (Freiburg: Mohr, 1888, 1899).

20. Joachim Jeremias, *The Parables of Jesus* (New York: Scribner's, 1954; repr. 1972). Ironically, Jeremias has gone from the top of the exegetical ladder as the primary authority on parables to the dog house in subsequent decades.

tionis), whereas the additional details provided vivid coloring and background to this single meaning. Interestingly, with Jeremias's movement now waning, allegorizing is returning in new clothes in the polyvalence of reader-response criticism, as is evident in the designation of the first chapter of the book *The Challenge of Jesus' Parables*, entitled "From Allegorizing to Allegorizing."[21] Now, instead of allegorizing every detail of a parable, scholars promote a multiplicity of interpretations all bearing equal exegetical weight. Aesthetic, literary, historical, psychological, sociological, political, moralistic, and theological understandings are seen on equal par with each other if a group of readers discovers meaning in this interpretation.

Let's investigate how this new type of allegorizing is applied to one particular parable. For the parable of the Widow and the Judge (Luke 18:1-8), the plurisignificance of a multitude of interpretations is advocated by many today. Dan O. Via offers a Jungian approach, explaining that the parable teaches that the male ego (the judge) refuses to respond to the anima, the archetype of a woman in a man's unconscious.[22] Charles Hedrick argues for a social relationship model where the parable presents a thoroughly honest man who compromises his integrity for his own comfort.[23] Herman Hendrickx suggests a business model that applies the parable to the red tape and bureaucracy of today's society.[24] Bernard Scott focuses on the arena of conflict resolution, contending that the widow's continual wearing down of the judge means that the kingdom keeps battering down opposition.[25] William Herzog, on the other hand, chooses a sociological interpretation, since the presence of only one judge is a clear violation of Jewish legal practice, resulting in a condition where the oppressed must collide with authority figures for the system to work.[26] Finally, Robert Price supplies an ecclesiastical

---

21. Klyne R. Snodgrass, "From Allegorizing to Allegorizing: A History of the Interpretation of the Parables of Jesus," in *The Challenge of Jesus' Parables*, ed. Richard N. Longenecker (Grand Rapids: Eerdmans, 2000), pp. 3-29.

22. Dan O. Via, "The Parable of the Unjust Judge: A Metaphor of the Unrealized Self," in *Semiology and Parables: Exploration of the Possibilities Offered by Structuralism for Exegesis*, ed. Daniel Patte (Pittsburgh: Pickwick, 1976), pp. 1-32.

23. Charles W. Hedrick, *Parables as Poetic Fictions: The Creative Voice of Jesus* (Peabody: Hendrickson, 1994), pp. 187-207.

24. Herman Hendrickx, *The Parables of Jesus*, rev. ed. (San Francisco: Harper & Row, 1986), pp. 231-32.

25. Bernard Brandon Scott, *Hear Then the Parable* (Minneapolis: Fortress, 1989), pp. 175-87.

26. William R. Herzog II, *Parables as Subversive Speech: Jesus as Pedagogue of the Oppressed* (Louisville: Westminster John Knox, 1994), pp. 215-32.

setting where the parable attests the bitterness of widows who have been mistreated by church officials, so that justice is achieved through the terrorism of nuisance.[27]

These options exemplify a return to allegorizing where a parable is embedded within a new belief system foreign to the original. The theological meaning of a parable is placed on a par with every other meaning. We are contending in this chapter that the finished picture of the exegetical process should center upon the theological meaning. An emphasis upon the theological journey in exegesis means that the interpreter will not surrender to the cultural pressure of polyvalence, but will maintain the primacy of a theological understanding of the Bible that matches its original purpose.

4. Schools of Interpretation Regarding the Book of Revelation

Not only is the primacy of the theological interpretation of utmost importance; it is also crucial to investigate a variety of theological perspectives before we choose a particular interpretation, since no one particular tradition should be proffered as authoritative beyond question. In interpreting the book of Revelation, for instance, each section has been analyzed differently according to the theological approach one chooses.

The Preterist school opts for a contemporary-historical interpretation of Revelation that speaks to the specific situation at the end of the first century, where Rome under Domitian is persecuting Christians.[28] It understands the book as an apocalypse (Rev 1:1), in line with other apocalyptic literature of that period. The Continuous Historical approach pictures a continuous chronological flow to the book of Revelation that parallels the events of church history. The Apocalypse is a prophecy (Rev 1:3; 22:6, 10, 18, 19) of specific progressive events from the beginning of the church age until the end of the cosmos.[29] The Radical Futurist approach teaches that the saints are raptured into heaven in Rev 4:1 and the seals, trumpets, and bowls speak to the Jews during the seven-year tribulation period before the thousand-year

27. Robert Price, *The Widow Traditions in Luke-Acts: A Feminist-Critical Scrutiny.* SBLDS 155 (Atlanta: Scholars, 1997), pp. 191-201.

28. For an outline of the book according to this perspective, see Martin Hopkins, "The Historical Perspective of Apocalypse 1–11," *CBQ* 27 (1965): 42-47.

29. For an outline, see Albert Barnes, *Notes, Explanatory and Practical, on the Book of Revelation* (New York: Harper & Brothers, 1852), pp. lvi-lxii.

reign of Christ on earth taught in chapter 20.[30] On the other hand, the Moderate Futurist approach claims that the narration of the seals, trumpets, and bowls refers to events that will occur in the tumultuous last days.[31] Finally, the Idealist approach asserts that the visions reveal eternal spiritual principles rather than future events, successive visions of Christ rather than visions of successive events. Although the visions are chronological, the events represented in the visions are not, since through the literary device of progressive recapitulation the same landscape of the church age is repeated from different angles.[32] Thus the genre is pastoral exhortation rather than prophecy or apocalyptic.

This variety of theological approaches makes it imperative to see the big picture before concentrating upon a particular passage in the book of Revelation. Therefore, before settling upon an interpretation of Rev 11:11 ("But after three and a half days a breath of life from God entered the two witnesses"), the reader must perform theological exegesis and evaluate the evidence for the various approaches to the trumpets in Revelation 8–11. Did these events already occur at the time of the fall of Jerusalem, as the Preterist view advocates? Were they future to the seer but past events in church history, as the Continuous Historical approach proposes? Will they occur in the last days of earth, as the Moderate Futurist view promotes? Or are these events reserved for the Jews who will remain on earth after the church is raptured (Rev 4:1), as the Radical Futurist view teaches? Or finally, will these events occur again and again throughout our human experience so that Revelation offers a philosophy of history rather than a prophecy of specific events, as the Idealist approach suggests? The book *Four Views on the Book of Revelation* published in a series by Zondervan[33] can help readers develop an analytical comparison of these approaches. Whichever theological worldview of the book of Revelation you finally accept as true, theological perspectives certainly shape exegetical results.

---

30. For an outline, see the foreword of Tim LaHaye, *Revelation Illustrated and Made Plain* (Grand Rapids: Zondervan, 1973).

31. See George Eldon Ladd, *A Commentary on the Revelation of John* (Grand Rapids: Eerdmans, 1972).

32. See William Hendriksen, *More than Conquerors* (Grand Rapids: Baker, 1960).

33. C. Marvin Pate, ed., *Four Views on the Book of Revelation* (Grand Rapids: Zondervan, 1998). Since the popularity of the continuous historical view ended in the nineteenth century, this approach is not discussed, although it continues in Seventh Day Adventist circles. See Reimar Vetne, "A Definition and Short History of Historicism as a Method for Interpreting Daniel and Revelation," *Journal of the Adventist Theological Society* 14 (2003): 1-14.

5. Interpretations of Acts 8:4-25: A Second Blessing?

Theological presuppositions on the meaning of Baptism in the Holy Spirit also control the interpretation of Acts 8:4-25, the reception of the Spirit by the Samaritans. In Acts 8, Philip preaches Christ to the Samaritans (8:5, ἐκήρυσσεν αὐτοῖς τὸν Χριστόν) with signs following (8:6), so that as a result men and women believe (8:12, ἐπίστευσαν τῷ Φιλίππῳ) in the gospel of the kingdom as well as the name of Jesus (εὐαγγελιζομένῳ περὶ τῆς βασιλείας τοῦ θεοῦ καὶ τοῦ ὀνόματος Ἰησοῦ Χριστοῦ) and are baptized (ἐβαπτίζοντο). However, the Samaritans do not receive the Holy Spirit until Peter and John come down from Jerusalem and lay hands upon the new converts (8:14-17). How do we view this delayed reception of the Holy Spirit theologically? Are there Christians who have not received the Holy Spirit and need a second blessing? Or were the Samaritans not yet Christians? Or was this a unique experience that God used to teach his people an important truth? A theological commentary should set out the various options and present the exegetical evidence in favor of each possibility.[34]

The Pentecostal view states that Christians need a normative second blessing of the Holy Spirit accompanied by speaking in tongues. This is evidenced by a literal straightforward reading of Acts 8. However, the Pentecostal second blessing view lacks plausibility, since the remainder of Scripture closely ties together the presence of the Spirit with Christian initiation and identity. We cannot build a theology on one historical experience in the early church. Charles Talbert observes that it would be a mistake to take Acts 8 as a paradigm, since "The narrative of Acts seems to say that the gift of the Holy Spirit cannot be captured in any set procedure. . . . God is free; experience varies."[35]

On the other hand, James Dunn[36] argues that the Samaritans were not true Christians, similar to the disciples of John the Baptizer in Acts 19:1-7 who likewise did not receive the Spirit until Paul discovered them. Therefore, the Samaritans who expected a false Messiah called the *Taheb* (the "re-

---

34. Regarding the designated theological commentaries on the Book of Acts, Jaroslav Pelikan, *Acts* (Grand Rapids: Brazos, 2005) in the Brazos Theological Commentary on the Bible does not touch the issue before us, while Charles H. Talbert, *Reading Acts: A Literary and Theological Commentary on the Acts of the Apostles* (New York: Crossroad, 1997) in the Reading the New Testament series is especially helpful with literary issues.

35. Talbert, *Reading Acts*, p. 86.

36. James D. G. Dunn, *Baptism in the Holy Spirit* (Philadelphia: Westminster, 1970), ch. 5.

storer" or "returning one")[37] only possessed an intellectual agreement with Philip's proclamation. Supporters of this view point to the verbal form πιστεύω with the dative (8:12; 24:14; 26:27) as an indication for rational assent but not true faith. More importantly, advocates call attention to the fact that the narrative rotates back and forth between the Samaritans (8:5-8; 12, 14-17) and Simon the sorcerer (8:9-11, 13; 18-24), so that the same expressions are chosen for the response of the Samaritans to Simon the Magician as to Philip's preaching of Jesus. The crowds pay attention (προσεῖχον, 8:6, 11) to both Philip and Simon, who perform signs (τὰ σημεῖα, 8:6, 13) and mighty deeds (δύναμις τοῦ θεοῦ ἡ καλουμένη μεγάλη, 8:10). Simon believed and was baptized just as the rest (8:12-13), so that all the Samaritans were in the same condition as pre-Christians before Peter and John arrived.

Against Dunn's proposal, the expressions "accepted the Word of God" (8:14) and baptized "in the name of Jesus" (8:16) are constantly associated with true Christian identity in the book of Acts. Furthermore, the paralleling of the Samaritans with Simon can be interpreted as a literary device to distinguish their reactions. All heard and received the Word, but Simon proved to be apostate and double-minded in his motivation because of his love of power and money. Finally, the situation is different in Acts 19:3, where those who receive the Holy Spirit had been baptized into John (εἰς τὸ Ἰωάννου βάπτισμα) and were therefore John's followers, not Christians.

The answer to this theological predicament must be solved by Lukan usage of the miraculous manifestations of the Holy Spirit. At Pentecost, Luke narrates the normal three-step soteriological pattern to become a Christian: "Repent and be baptized, every one of you, in the name of Jesus Christ for the forgiveness of your sins. And you will receive the gift of the Holy Spirit" (Acts 2:38). What happens when this sequence is altered in later narratives? As we shall see, changes in the expected reception of the Holy Spirit contain missionary significance. The purpose of the book of Acts is to demonstrate that the gospel extends to the whole world (1:8). The mission summaries in Acts 6:7; 9:31; 12:24; 16:5; 19:20; 28:28, 31 divide the book into seven sections, where the reception of the gospel increases from Palestinian Jews (1:1–6:7), to Hellenistic Jews, Samaritans, and proselytes (6:8–9:30), to Gentiles who had been god-fearers (9:31–12:24), to Gentiles in Asia (12:25–16:5), Europe (16:6–19:20), and all the way to the emperor in Rome (16:21–28:31). To validate that God himself intended the gospel to be extended to all of these peo-

37. Cf. John Macdonald, *The Theology of the Samaritans* (Philadelphia: Westminster, 1964), pp. 74-75, 79-80, 359-71.

ple groups, Luke documents the extraordinary manifestations of the Holy Spirit. In each case they are different.

First of all, Luke creates the paradigm of repent, be baptized, and receive the Spirit through the extraordinary arrival of the Holy Spirit on Pentecost to the Aramaic-speaking Jews. Then to the Hellenistic Jews, God confirms his salvation through Stephen's miraculous deeds by means of the Holy Spirit (6:8) and his vision of Jesus himself in heaven (7:55-56). To the half-breed Samaritans, God waits to pour out the Holy Spirit until the apostles come down from Jerusalem to assure the Jewish-Christian church that the Samaritans as well are a part of the Spirit-led redemptive community.[38] With regard to Jewish proselytes, an angel miraculously leads Philip to the Ethiopian eunuch, who is reading Isaiah 53, and then the Holy Spirit picks him up and transports him to the next mission destination of Caesarea (8:26-40). To assure God's covenant blessings to Gentile God-fearers, the Holy Spirit comes upon Cornelius and his household with miraculous gifts even before they are baptized (10:44-46), again breaking the pattern of Acts 2:38 as in Acts 8. For the Gentiles in Asia, the Spirit miraculously speaks through divine prophecy, setting apart Paul and Barnabas to bring the gospel to these Gentiles (13:2). For the Gentiles in Europe, the Holy Spirit forbids Paul and Silas to visit certain destinations (16:6-7), until a miraculous vision finally directs them to the Gentiles in Europe (16:9-10). In conclusion, miraculous prophecies escort Paul to Jerusalem (21:10-11), where he appeals to Caesar, so the gospel finally arrives in Rome, the center of the known world. In each case, special manifestations of the Spirit demonstrate the inclusion of new people groups in the sovereign plan of God. This is what scholars entitle a history of salvation interpretation of Acts 8.[39]

Again, here a literary device employed throughout the book of Acts (the Lukan mission summary) directs the reader to a particular theological solution.[40] Through a careful investigation of possible theological interpretations, we have arrived at a satisfactory exegetical decision.

---

38. Talbert, *Reading Acts,* 86, points out that "In Acts, the Twelve in Jerusalem represent judges for a reconstituted Israel (Luke 22:29-30). As such they perform a supervisory role with reference to new developments in the Messianist mission. People either come to Jerusalem to report and receive approval (9:27; 11:2; 15; 18:22) or Jerusalem sends representatives to check on and supervise new enterprises (8:14; 17:22-24)."

39. Cf. Eduard Schweizer, "πνεῦμα," *TDNT* 6:412-13; W. Wilkens, "Wassertaufe und Geistempfang bei Lukas," *TZ* 23 (1967): 27.

40. See above Chapter 3, A3, "Conflict in the Early Church and the Structure of the Acts of the Apostles" (pp. 92-94).

B. An Investigation of the Reader's Presuppositions

PROCEDURE

In the examples above, we have witnessed how presuppositions can affect the particular route that is chosen in analyzing a text (for example, a political or theological approach) and the specific exegetical conclusions that are reached. Therefore, it is crucial to reflect deeply upon "my" presuppositions as an individual reader and "our" presuppositions as a denominational, cultural, or ethnic reader. Such a procedure can prohibit a prejudicial reading of the text.

1. An Analysis of Theological Presuppositions

Exegesis is predetermined by theological presuppositions. Readers are not simply innocent bystanders, sponges who soak up a text; all of us bring already formed conclusions into the exegetical process. For instance, precritical scholars tend to ignore differences and inconsistencies within the text by smoothing over the difficulties in light of the overall cohesion of the canon and the community's faith perspective. Critical scholars, on the other hand, create a gigantic gap between the Jesus of history and the Christ of faith. Or again, whereas followers of the historical-critical method suppose that they can discover the intention of the original author, advocates of reader-response criticism entitle this attempt a hermeneutic of reduction, since only one objective meaning is presupposed. Instead, they posit a hermeneutic of unfolding, which allows the text in dialogue with the reader to have a multiplicity of meanings. No single reading exhausts the possibilities of the text.

Attempts to eliminate theological presuppositions are futile; instead, it is crucial to admit and publish them. Therefore, even though the following presuppositions of Robert Funk and David Buttrick vary dramatically from my own assumptions about the text, I applaud the fact that they honestly inform their audiences about these presumptions. Robert Funk, the originator of the Jesus Seminar, published a series of his theological presuppositions on the internet under the title "The Coming Radical Reformation." Certainly these theological claims affect Funk's exegetical conclusions as the leader of the Jesus Seminar. Here is a sampling of his contentions, as listed on his website:[41]

---

41. *The Fourth R* 11:4 (July-August, 1998); http://www.westarinstitute.org/Periodicals/ 4R_Articles/funk_theses.html.

- #1 The God of the metaphysical age is dead. There is not a personal god out there external to human beings and the material world.
- #4 The notion that God interferes with the order of nature from time to time in order to aid or punish is no longer credible, in spite of the fact that most people still believe it. Miracles are an affront to the justice and integrity of God, however understood.
- #5 Prayer is meaningless when understood as requests addressed to an external God for favor or forgiveness and meaningless if God does not interfere with the laws of nature. Prayer as praise is a remnant of the age of kingship in the ancient Near East and is beneath the dignity of deity.
- #9 The doctrine of the atonement — the claim that God killed his own son in order to satisfy his thirst for satisfaction — is subrational and subethical. This monstrous doctrine is the stepchild of a primitive sacrificial system in which the gods had to be appeased by offering them some special gift, such as a child or an animal.
- #10 The resurrection of Jesus did not involve the resuscitation of a corpse. Jesus did not rise from the dead, except perhaps in some metaphorical sense. The meaning of the resurrection is that a few of his followers — probably no more than two or three — finally came to understand what he was all about. When the significance of his words and deeds dawned on them, they knew of no other terms in which to express their amazement than to claim that they had seen him alive.

David Buttrick, who teaches homiletics at Vanderbilt Divinity School, purposefully reveals his presuppositions in the preface of his book on parables. Certainly his volume on parables would look different from one written by Robert Funk, but it would also diverge from my writing because of our distinct presuppositions. Buttrick explains, "Do I suspect that the Gospel writers sometimes have misunderstood the parables of Jesus? Yes I do." Then he offers the following examples.

Matthew draws a reprehensible conclusion from the parable of the Unmerciful Servant after the fellow ends up being tortured: "So will my heavenly Father do to you unless everyone of you forgives your fellow human from your heart." Look out, Matthew has handed us dreadful theology. Later, by chaining together parables of the Treasure, the Pearl, and the Fishnet, I suspect Matthew has misunderstood all three. . . . I do not bother with the notion of "authority." We revere the Bible because it brings us good news of God and not because it is super perfect. The Bible is not an inerrant "Word of God." The idea is silly. . . . To want an inerrant Bible is an old temptation endorsed by the serpent in the Eden myth.[42]

Buttrick has identified his own suppositions and lets the audience know his contentions before he performs specific exegetical tasks. This procedure we should laud. One of the strengths of reader-response criticism is its contention that the author's presuppositions affect the meaning of the text.

Operating from a conservative Reformed perspective, I would offer the following list as my own presuppositional repertoire.

1. A supposition of trust in the scriptural record rather than a hermeneutic of suspicion.
2. The event character of revelation and the veracity of biblical teaching, so that one does not constantly challenge the Bible's historicity.
3. The normativity of Scripture as seen in the canon of the Old and New Testaments.
4. The coherence and harmony of the biblical books as evidenced in the covenantal relationship between the Old and New Testaments through concepts like corporate personality, the unity of the people of God in the covenant of grace, and typology.
5. Creation — Fall — Redemption — Consummation as a framework for viewing salvation history (rather than a proof-text approach).
6. God's intention in giving humanity his word is primarily theological in nature (vs. primarily scientific, political, moralistic etc.), so that a creedal and doctrinal interpretation of Scripture is foremost.
7. Prominence must be given to the doctrine of the sovereignty of God, so that the Bible emphasizes primarily the divine action and only secondarily the human response.
8. A view of the world as a controlled continuum (not a closed or open continuum), so that both God's in-breaking work of miracles and a scientific worldview are prized.
9. A presupposition of common grace (creation mercy) means that one will employ the best of scholarship without necessarily accepting all the presuppositions of the historical-critical method.

42. David Buttrick, *Speaking Parables: A Homiletic Guide* (Louisville: Westminster John Knox, 2000), pp. xi-xii.

2. An Analysis of Cultural and Psychological Presuppositions

All of us read a text on the basis of our own background and proclivities. For instance, Elisabeth Schüssler Fiorenza points out that "the so called 'first' world writers and readers place sexual-psychological problems in the foreground, whereas those from the so-called 'third' world focus on sociopolitical experience."[43] Therefore, a critical self-diagnosis is necessary with regard to one's cultural and psychological make-up as well as our theological assumptions. Readers always wear tinted glasses and make sense of a text according to the particular shade of the lenses. We see things not as they are, but as we are. We do not simply move from the Bible to theological assertions; all decisions are filtered through a network of tradition and preunderstanding. To separate exegesis (reading out of a text what is there) from eisegesis (reading into a text what one wants it to mean), every reader should indulge in a process of self-reflection. An awareness of our cultural and psychological presuppositions can occur through such experiences as personality tests, face-to-face conversations with opponents to investigate differences, racism seminars, and the reading of books that examine personal profiles based upon one's socio-economic background. Discerning readers should ask themselves the following questions:

1. How does the individualism of Western society control the way I read the biblical text?
2. How would I read the text differently if I grew up as an oppressed minority rather than as a member of the privileged majority?
3. How has my maturation process in a patriarchal or matriarchal family structure affected the manner in which I evaluate the stories in the Bible?
4. How do modern views of tolerance influence my interpretation of passages about judgment and punishment in the Bible?
5. How does membership in a mainline or sectarian denomination influence the issues that I pay attention to in the Bible?
6. How does my particular personality type color my interpretation of Bible passages?
7. What is my view of conflict? Do I relish conflict or run from strife? Am I

---

43. Elisabeth Schüssler Fiorenza, *Revelation: Vision of a Just World* (Minneapolis: Fortress, 1991), p. 14.

a peacemaker or a zealot for a cause, and what difference does this make in my choice of sermon topics on Sunday morning?

8. Do I possess countercultural assumptions or am I establishment-oriented, and how does this chosen worldview affect the way I use the Bible to justify my lifestyle choices?

9. How do the hurts in my childhood (abuse, racism, alcoholism, poverty, etc.) still live on in the religious convictions that I have chosen?

In conclusion, it should be emphasized that exegetical competence levels differ based upon our ability to recognize our own presuppositions in reading the biblical text. All of us should become more cognizant of the restraints placed upon the process of reading by our own theological, socio-economic, and psychological presuppositions as well as our ignorance of the linguistic, figurative, and ideological structures of the text. Put another way, knowledgeable and reflective readers are simply the best readers of the text.

C. Exploring the Canonical Meaning

PROCEDURE

The unity of Scripture is a foundational assumption behind a Christian canonical interpretation. As Jeannine Brown asserts, "While allowing for each author's distinctive purposes and message, the Christian affirmation is that the diversity of the sixty-six books fits within a broader theological and narrative unity."[44]

Determining the canonical meaning entails placing the particular passage under observation into the whole of Scripture. This is the process of comparing Scripture with Scripture to study the "whole counsel of God." If exegesis is laying the foundation, then this building upon the substructure is the process of forming a biblical theology. To continue the metaphor, this interpretive structure continues to grow with the additional floors of systematic theology, historical theology, and ethics or normative moral theology. Since the Bible is organized according to a Creation — Fall — Redemption — Consummation structure, determining the canonical meaning involves the use of this format as a filter to study various themes and doctrines.

---

44. Jeannine K. Brown, *Scripture as Communication: Introducing Biblical Hermeneutics* (Grand Rapids: Baker Academic, 2007), p. 229.

Therefore, each concept in Scripture such as the image of God, sin, our status before God, the kingdom of God, and even imagery like water, wilderness, and light needs to be investigated through the lens of these four organizing principles in the history of redemption. In the following examples we will employ canonical criticism to place specific passages within the themes of a biblical theology.

EXAMPLES

1. The Typology behind John the Baptizer

When the New Testament opens in Mark's Gospel, John the Baptizer is preaching in the wilderness, where Jesus temporarily joins him in order to be baptized before he crosses the Jordan and inaugurates his ministry in Galilee. What is the significance of this event within canonical theology? Why does Mark begin his account of the Gospel at this exact point and time?

To answer this question, we must investigate the imagery that ties this event to previous episodes in the history of redemption. Typologically, the wilderness experience traces back to Israel's journey through the desert for forty years before entering the promised land under Joshua. The presence of John the Baptizer in the wilderness calling Israel to repentance entails theologically that the land of Canaan has to be retaken.[45] Israel is living in a time of apostasy where Palestine is polluted and impure. Mark purposely places John in the wilderness to indicate that the promised land is again filled with ungodliness, moral pollution, and subjugation so that another conquest is necessary. John's message centers on repentance (Mark 1:4) as a prerequisite for Israel's restoration.[46] Therefore, confession of sins becomes a priority in the renewal of Israel (1:5). The situation parallels the time before Joshua brought God's kingdom to Canaan.

Similarly, in the reign of Ahab and Jezebel Baal worship dominated the land (1 Kgs 16:31-33; 18:18) and false prophets ruled the people (18:19, 22, 40), so that a new conquest of the land must be undertaken. Elijah calls down fire from heaven to consume the evil and purify God's people, just as John the

---

45. For the contemporary debate on this issue, see Craig A. Evans, "Jesus & the Continuing Exile of Israel," in *Jesus and the Restoration of Israel: A Critical Assessment of N. T. Wright's Jesus and the Victory of God*, ed. Carey C. Newman (Downers Grove: InterVarsity, 1999), pp. 77-100; and N. T. Wright's response on pp. 258-61.

46. See E. P. Sanders, *Jesus and Judaism* (Philadelphia: Fortress, 1985), pp. 107-13.

Baptizer broadcasts a message of judgment and fire (Luke 3:7-9). Like Moses, Elijah must travel to Mount Horeb in the wilderness to receive special commandments from God (1 Kgs 19:11-18). Significantly, Elijah also journeys back into the wilderness at the end of his life to be taken into heaven (2 Kgs 2:1-11). The narrator carefully recounts how Elijah journeys from Samaria to Bethel (2:2), Jericho (2:4), the Jordan River (2:6), and into the wilderness after drying up the Jordan. Then Elisha takes over Elijah's ministry in the wilderness and retraces his exact steps into Canaan (2 Kgs 2:13-25: wilderness, Jordan, Jericho, Bethel, Mt. Carmel, Samaria), since the land must still be retaken.

John the Baptizer takes on the role of Moses and Elijah in preparing the people of God for entering the promised land. Therefore Mark begins his Gospel with a quote from Mal 3:1 about a messenger who is identified as Elijah in Mal 4:5. John's clothing of camel's hair and his leather belt likewise remind the reader of Elijah in 2 Kgs 1:8.[47] Further confirmation that the land must be retaken comes from the special name "John" that the angel of the Lord assigned to Zechariah (Luke 1:13) and the commotion it caused among his relatives (1:59-63). The surnames Johanan and Jonas were used interchangeably at this time in Israel's history, as evidenced by the descriptions of Peter as Bar-Jonah in Matt 16:17 but Son of John in John 1:42. The theological significance of this nomenclature is that, just as Jonah went to the Gentiles at Nineveh with a message of repentance, so John goes to the Jews, treating them like Gentiles since the land is in exile. This radical message causes a stir throughout the entire Jewish community and accounts for the notoriety of John in the tradition.

After the destruction of Jerusalem and exile in Babylon, the Israelites again travel through the wilderness to reestablish the temple and replant themselves in a new Jerusalem (cf. Isaiah 40–66; Ezra-Nehemiah). Isaiah 40, for instance, begins with the voice of one calling for a road through the wilderness back to the promised land (40:3-4). This is followed by the coming of the Sovereign Lord in power (40:10a), who will enter the land and bring the gospel (good tidings) to Jerusalem and the towns of Judah (40:9) through the arm of his rule and reign (40:10b). The early church saw this as Jesus' proclamation of the kingdom of God to Jerusalem and the towns of Galilee, preceded by John's voice in the wilderness.[48] Thus the typology of

47. Mark 9:12-13 par.; Luke 1:17; and Matt 11:14 further confirm such an identity.

48. Likewise, the Qumran community chose the wilderness because the temple and the leaders of Canaan were polluted and impure. Similarly, they appealed to Isaiah 40 to identify their situation typologically (1QS 8:12-16). In all likelihood, John the Baptizer separated

Moses/Joshua; Elijah/Elisha; and Second Isaiah 40-55/Third Isaiah 56-66 is repeated in John the Baptizer/Jesus.[49] Moses, Elijah, and John the Baptizer first reform Israel through repentance, and then Joshua, Elisha, and Jesus lead God's people into the kingdom of God. Therefore, immediately following his baptism by John, Jesus crosses the Jordan and launches his ministry in Canaan to reestablish once and for all the reign and realm of God. Jesus is the new Joshua, as his name signifies. The narrative events have a theological and canonical meaning that can be investigated through typology.

2. A Biblical Theology of the State: Romans 13 and Revelation 13

If Romans 13 were the only text in the New Testament about the state, Christians would emphasize God's institution of the governing authorities (Rom 13:2) and the corresponding requirement of loyal submission to the state (13:1), since rulers provide beneficial oversight (13:3). Human rulers, who are assigned the identical Greek title as ministers of the gospel (διάκονος), are pictured as God's servants who dispense divine punishment (13:4).[50] However, if Revelation 13 were the only text in the New Testament about the state,

---

himself from the Qumran community, since he proclaimed a coming powerful one who would bring the presence of God back to the land. See Ben Witherington III, "John the Baptist," in *Dictionary of Jesus and the Gospels,* ed. Joel B. Green, Scot McKnight, I. Howard Marshall (Downers Grove: InterVarsity, 1992), pp. 384-85, who lists six similarities between John and Qumran.

49. See John H. Stek, "Elijah," *International Standard Bible Encyclopedia* (Grand Rapids: Eerdmans, 1979), 2:67; and Raymond Brown, "Jesus and Elijah," *Perspective* 12 (1971): 85-104.

50. For an alternative view of Romans 13, see Warren Carter, *The Roman Empire and the New Testament: An Essential Guide* (Nashville: Abingdon, 2006), pp. 133-35, who employs the issue of flattery in Romans 13 to minimize the command to be subject to the governing authorities as model citizens. He postulates that Paul is flattering Rome by declaring three times in Rom 13:1-2 that its governing authority is from God and then three times in the next four verses by calling the emperor God's servant. This flattery, according to Carter, does not cohere with Rom 12:2, where he instructs Christians not to be conformed to this world. Therefore, he concludes that this flattery must be caused by some particular circumstances the church is experiencing. He theorizes that some believers saw themselves as agents of God's judgment against the empire and were employing violence. But Carter does not develop a creation/fall paradigm here, which the Apostle Paul appears to have in mind. Because God's creation is good and government is an important part of God's good creation, Christians should submit themselves to the emperor's authority as God's servant. This type of thinking finds no place in Carter's appraisal of NT theology with regard to the relationship between church and state.

then the government compares to an ugly despicable beast (Rev 13:1-2) whom all the earth worships as divine (13:4), even though it breathes out blasphemous curses on God (13:5-6, 8) and persecutes the righteous citizens of God's kingdom as evildoers (13:7). Which portrait should we adopt as God's revelation?

In such decisions the acceptance of a canonical approach and the search after a biblical theology play a vital role in the interpretation of Scripture. God's revelation embodies both Romans 13 and Revelation 13. The Bible neither advocates escape from our responsibilities as human subjects in supporting the governing institutions nor does it advocate violent tactics to overthrow the empire. But within this middle ground one discovers a diversity of strategies in the New Testament documents with regard to the state. Warren Carter explains that "The strategies stretch from demonizing it (the Roman Empire), anticipating God's judgment on it, and opposing it with defiant (but self-protective) non-violent actions, to praying for it, submitting to it, and imitating it."[51] Therefore, we should not deploy a proof-text method to determine the Christian view of the state but instead employ a creation — fall — redemption — consummation framework.

God created political institutions for the well-being of human society. Therefore, we should respect our leaders and submit to their authority because of the creation order. But the fall into sin changed everything. The secular state can become a beast that crucifies God's people since the gospel message is politically threatening. Christ's redemption demonstrated that he alone is Lord of both heaven and earth and deserves ultimate allegiance. Jesus' resurrection anticipates the destruction of the ruling powers (1 Cor 2:8) and the establishment of God's empire over all (1 Cor 15:20-28). Finally, at the consummation God will terminate every unjust and idolatrous system in the final coming of Jesus Christ (1 Thess 2:19; 3:13; 4:15; 5:23; 1 Cor 15:23). But already now Jesus established a new community to live by a different set of values than those advocated by human empires. The new community demonstrates the shortcomings of the values of worldly empires through their practice of an extrarighteousness (Matt 5:20).

Therefore, the Christian stance toward the state demands both obedience and confrontation, depending upon whether the governing institutions are living out of their creation calling or demonstrating their fallen condition. Interestingly, the rhetoric that is employed in the New Testament about the lordship of Jesus parallels the terminology employed by Caesar and the

---

51. Carter, *Roman Empire and the New Testament*, p. 139.

society he governs. Jesus' central proclamation portrayed the coming of God's kingdom, whose reign and realm will endure forever (Luke 1:32-33). Likewise, Rome pictured itself as "an empire without end" (Virgil, *Aeneid,* 1:278-79). The term "good news" was employed "for the emperor's birth, military conquest, and accession to power" (Josephus, *J.W.* 4:618), but the Gospel writers apply "good news" as a summary of Jesus' liberating message (Mark 1:1, 14-15). Christian worship offered an alternative to the praise gatherings of the imperial cult as visualized in Revelation 4–5. Jesus is Savior and Lord, not the emperor (Josephus, *J.W.* 3:459). Jesus taught his followers to pray "Our Father who art in heaven," whereas Caesar was considered "Father of the Country" (*Acts of Augustus* 35; Suetonius, *Vespasian* 12). In his Roman trial Jesus touts his ability to summon legions of angels to his defense (Matt 26:53), which contrasts his power with the Roman legions that indwelt Jerusalem. The *Pax Romana* (Josephus, *War* 6:345-46) cannot offer the world true peace, since "while people are saying 'Peace and safety,' destruction will come on them suddenly" (1 Thess 5:3). Whereas Rome proclaimed its mission to bring justice to the world, "to crown peace with justice" (Virgil, *Aeneid,* 6:851-53; *Acts of Augustus* 34), Paul declared that the righteousness or justice of God is revealed in Jesus Christ (Rom 1:16-17). Finally, Jesus' coming is entitled the *parousia* (Matt 24:3, 27, 37, 39), a term that commonly denoted the arrival of the emperor or a prominent government official. Therefore, Christ's kingdom challenges Caesar's empire.

Certainly, the same government that serves God's creation ordinances (Romans 13) can become the beast of Revelation 13 when the empire takes over practices that are only appropriate to God. In such situations the beast needs to be challenged and disobeyed. This is the recognized position that the NT documents uniformly affirm: "Deliver to God the things that are God's" (Mark 12:17). But in the normal affairs of life, the state fulfils its creation mandate. Therefore, Christians must pray for (but not to) their leaders (1 Tim 2:1-2; Tit 3:1-2), support the state with their financial resources, and submit to its authoritative decisions. All the documents of the New Testament sing a harmonious chorus on this theme. Therefore, Christians should employ the rubric of creation — fall — redemption — consummation to apply the various NT texts in their critique of any governmental policy or political ideology.[52] These are the findings of a canonical approach to biblical theology.

---

52. I would advocate the approach of Seyoon Kim in his book *Christ and Caesar: The Gospel and the Roman Empire in the Writings of Paul and Luke* (Grand Rapids: Eerdmans, 2008).

3. Revelation 21:1: "No More Sea"

In the descriptions of the new heaven and renewed earth, Rev 21:1b concludes, "there was no longer any sea." A literal interpretation of this text would accept the remarks of Tim LaHaye, that "although it will have a river and an abundance of water, it will not have land surface wasted by seas."[53] However, our hermeneutical principles regarding the Apocalypse state that "we are to assume the symbolic character of the pictures unless it is clear that the expression must be taken literally, which is the opposite approach to the normal principle of interpretation."[54] How is the sea portrayed symbolically in the rest of the canon of Scripture?

The book of Revelation is placed last in the canon, since it parallels the beginnings of the first creation in the book of Genesis. Therefore, the symbolism of the sea in Revelation must correspond with water imagery in Genesis. The sea in the Old Testament symbolizes the primeval chaos, where the giant sea monster Leviathan or Rahab dwells.[55] When God separates the land from the chaotic sea, he creates the shoreline as a boundary, so that disorder and chaos can only extend its dominion so far.[56] Then when God destroys the earth at the time of Noah, the flood waters make the earth uninhabitable again. But God dries up the primeval flood to offer his chosen people a new creation. The sea symbolizes chaos.

Redemption at the exodus of Israel from Egypt is likewise portrayed with sea imagery. The hymn of Exodus 15 celebrates Yahweh's victory when "the deep waters congealed in the heart of the sea" (15:8). Likewise, the Jordan River parts when God through Joshua leads his people on dry land to their promised habitation, overcoming the authority of Baal who supposedly brought fertility to the land of Canaan. In Babylon the prophet Isaiah prays for a new exodus when God will again dry up the sea: "Awake, as in days gone by, as in generations of old. Was it not you who cut Rahab to pieces, who pierced that monster through? Was it not you who dried up the

53. LaHaye, *Revelation Illustrated and Made Plain*, p. 308.

54. See Appendix I, III.E.3 (p. 348).

55. God's victory over the sea monsters Rahab and Leviathan is recalled in Job 9:13; Ps 74:13-14; 89:10; Isa 27:1; 51:9, with the power of Leviathan described in Job 41. In the Canaanite myths found in the Ras Shamra tablets, the supreme god destroys the sea-god Lotan (= Leviathan), who is a seven-headed monster like the dragon of Rev 12:3. See G. B. Caird, *A Commentary of the Revelation of St. John the Divine*. HNTC (New York: Harper & Row, 1966), p. 66.

56. See Job 38:8-11; Ps 104:5-9; Prov 8:27-29.

sea, the waters of the great deep, who made a road in the depths of the sea so that the redeemed might cross over?" (Isa 51:9-10). Then when Jesus the Messiah arrives, he calms the sea (Mark 4:35-41) and on another occasion traverses the sea as if it is dry ground (6:45-53), fulfilling Job 9:8 and Ps 107:29-30. Redemption has arrived when chaos is overcome.

Now Revelation 21 pictures the new heaven and earth where no sea can be found; there is absolutely no chaos or disorder. As G. B. Caird explains, the imagery of Rev 21:1 must derive from "the primaeval ocean or abyss which is an alias for the dragon Leviathan, a home for the monster, and a throne for the whore (iv.6; xii.3; xiii.1; xvii.1)."[57] Thus the new creation is better than the original creation. No evil will ever again overcome the earth and its inhabitants. Along with the removal of the sea of chaos, the other elements of the old order including death, grief, crying, pain, God's curse, and night are completely destroyed (21:4; 22:3, 5).[58] The heavens and earth are forever perfect. Therefore instead of the storming terror of the sea, Rev 4:6 depicts a shiny lake of glass in front of the throne of God, indicating a divine transformation of all chaos.[59] Such is the canonical and theological meaning of Rev 21:1b.

4. The Tenses in Genesis 2:8 and 2:19

On several occasions in Genesis 2 the NIV employs a past perfect English translation. For instance, in Gen 2:8 the NIV states, "The LORD God <u>had</u> planted a garden in the east," whereas the NRSV reads, "And the LORD God planted a garden in Eden." Likewise at Gen 2:19 the NIV explains, "Now the LORD God <u>had</u> formed out of the ground all the beasts of the field," while the NRSV employs the simple past tense, "So out of the ground the LORD God formed every animal of the field."[60] Thus on both occasions the NIV implies

---

57. Caird, *Revelation*, p. 262.

58. G. K. Beale, *The Book of Revelation: A Commentary on the Greek Text*. NIGTC (Grand Rapids: Eerdmans, 1999), p. 1043, states that "the evil nuance of the sea metaphorically represents the entire range of afflictions that formerly threatened God's people in the old world."

59. Alternatively, the source of the imagery could be the counterpart basin in the earthly temple, which was called a sea (1 Kgs 7:23-25; 2 Kgs 16:17; 2 Chr 4:2, 4, 15; Jer 27:19).

60. The ESV employs the past perfect tense at Gen 2:19, but the TNIV is the only other major version that translates both verses with "had." John Calvin, *Commentaries on the First Book of Moses called Genesis*, trans. John King (Grand Rapids: Eerdmans, 1948), p. 113, supports a pluperfect sense.

that the actions involved had already taken place before the other incidents that are narrated, such as the creation of Eve. Both translations are possible with the fluidity of Hebrew tenses,[61] but which translation best presents a canonical meaning?

Whereas the NRSV employs the more frequent grammatical usage and therefore is most commonly followed,[62] the reason for the NIV's translation is theological in nature. The NIV reads Genesis 2 canonically and assumes that the two creation stories in Genesis 1–2 should be read together. Every translation is an interpretation; the NIV is based upon certain theological presuppositions whereby scriptural passages should not clash if at all possible.[63] Therefore, according to a canonical interpretation, the past perfect tense is more appropriate. With regard to theological exegesis, one Scripture is read in light of another. This is a valid principle of interpretation.

However, there is another solution. The assumption of the NIV is that the translation in 2:8 ("Now the Lord God planted a garden") contradicts the creation of the plants already narrated in Gen 1:12-13. But Claus Westermann points out that "2:8 is not a narrative about the creation of plants, but about the provision of nourishment for the human creatures."[64] Therefore, the establishment of the garden parallels the provision of food in 1:29, rather than the creation of the plants in 1:12–13. Kenneth Mathews adds that "The concluding clause, '[which] he had formed' (אֲשֶׁר יָצָר), as a pluperfect, shows that the formation of the man preceded the planting of the garden."[65] Therefore, the exegete is not required to employ translation heroics to establish a canonical reading; a careful reading of the final edition of the text reveals a consistent flow to the narrative.

In the examples above we have demonstrated the importance of arriving at theological conclusions in the process of exegesis. In the practice of theological exegesis the reader must explore his or her presuppositions and endeavor to build a biblical theology through the use of canonical criticism.

---

61. See above Chapter 2, F4, "2 Samuel 11:4 and Joel 2:18-19: Hebrew Tenses" (pp. 80-81).

62. The NIV is followed in Gen 2:8 by the TNIV and Holman Christian Standard Bible and at 2:19 by the TNIV, ESV, AV 1873, and Darby.

63. See, e.g., Chapter 2, F3, "Psalm 45:6/Heb. 1:8-9; Isaiah 7:14/Matt. 1:23: The Old in the New" (pp. 79-80), which explains how the NIV employs identical wording with regard to OT prophecies and NT fulfillment passages.

64. Claus Westermann, *Genesis 1–11* (Minneapolis: Augsburg, 1984), p. 208, supported by Gordon J. Wenham, *Genesis 1–15*. WBC 1 (Dallas: Word, 2002), p. 61.

65. K. A. Mathews, *Genesis 1–11:26*. NAC 1A (Nashville: Broadman & Holman, 1995), p. 199, n. 51.

In this manner the employment of grammatical, literary, structural, historical, and contextual exegetical tools will result in a finished photo album with
clear as well as nuanced theological integrity and beauty.

Study and Discussion Questions

1. Exegesis is the foundation of biblical interpretation. Using this analogy, the first floor could be described as Biblical Theology, the second story as Systematic Theology, and the top level as Normative Theology, which determines what truths of the Bible are normative for all places and times. To develop a Biblical Theology, it is important to ask, "What was the central theological concept that Jesus employed in his preaching and teaching?" Do a search of the term "kingdom" or "kingdom of God" and discover how frequently it is employed. What phrase takes its place in the Gospel of John? How are Jesus' death and resurrection related to this central concept? Paul, on the other hand, employs the phrase "in Christ" as the bedrock of his theology. Perform a search of this term and find out where it is employed by Paul. (In Logos Bible Software you type "in Christ" with the quotation marks in the Bible Search box). You can also try the phrases "in Him" and "in whom."

2. This book has argued for redaction criticism rather than harmonization as the correct approach to the task of exegeting the Gospels. When is harmonization not only legitimate but necessary in the process of interpretation? How is the development of a biblical theology different than exegesis? Think of Jesus' sayings on the cross. Which one is emphasized in Mark? But how can you place all seven sayings together into a biblical theology?

3. Biblical theologians speak about "the already but not yet" nature of the kingdom of God, which means that Jesus proclaimed both a realized and future eschatology. How does this relate to our recitation of the Lord's Prayer? Examine each line of the prayer and discuss how the praise and petitions relate both to the future age and to the Christian life already realized now because of Christ's work.

4. What is central to a biblical theology of Jesus' miracles? Is the issue of human compassion the primary emphasis? Gerard Mackrell concludes his book *The Healing Miracles in Mark's Gospel* with a chapter on the compassion of Jesus, indicating his opinion that compassion is prominent.[66] However, Alan Richardson asserts, "If we examine the miracle-stories of the Gos-

---

66. See Gerard Mackrell, *The Healing Miracles in Mark's Gospel: The Passion and Compassion of Jesus* (Slough: Daughters of St. Paul, 1987).

pels, we find few references to the compassion of Jesus, and we do not receive the impression that those stories have been included in the tradition because of the Evangelists' interest in the motives of the Lord."[67] In Logos Bible Software, search the word "compassion" or the lemma σπλαγχνίζομαι in the Gospels and discover when "compassion" is employed with Jesus' healing miracles. Do all the Synoptic Gospels ever use this term in the same story? So is Jesus' compassion central to a biblical theology of Jesus' miracles? What are some theological themes that the miracle stories are emphasizing?

5. Examine the issue of fasting in Jesus' teaching. Compare, for instance, Mark 2:18-20, where Jesus advocates partying rather than fasting, and Matt 11:19, where Jesus was known as a glutton and a drunkard, with passages like Matt 4:2 and 6:16-18. In a canonical interpretation of Scripture, how do you put these two sides together? For development in the history of salvation on the use of fasting in Israel, see Zech 8:18-19. For help in approaching this issue, you can consult the book *Jesus of Nazareth: Millenarian Prophet* by Dale Allison, chapter 3 on "Jesus as Millenarian Ascetic."[68]

6. Covenant is a comprehensive theological concept in the Scriptures. Perform a Bible Search of the NIV in Logos Bible Software using the designations "everlasting covenant" and "eternal covenant." Study the list of verses in context and determine with which biblical characters God established an everlasting covenant. What are the important turning points in biblical history where a covenant was enacted? What were the promises of the various covenants and the particular sign of those covenants?

7. Theological exegesis will not merely use proof-texts from the Bible to solve an issue but will employ the biblical framework of creation — fall — redemption — consummation. Employ this biblical scheme to argue for or against women becoming ordained ministers in the church. On creation, note both Gen 1:27-28 and 1 Tim 2:13. For the fall, consider both Gen 3:16 and 1 Tim 2:14. For redemption, look at both Matt 10:2-4 and Acts 2:17-18. Concerning the new creation, consider both Mark 12:25 and 1 Cor 11:3, since there will still be women and men in heaven. How does each side approach this contemporary issue differently?

---

67. Alan Richardson, *The Miracle Stories of the Gospels* (London: SCM, 1941), pp. 32-33.
68. Dale C. Allison, *Jesus of Nazareth: Millenarian Prophet* (Minneapolis: Fortress, 1998).

8. Each of us has personal, social, and theological presuppositions as we approach the interpretation of the Bible. Read the questions again in section B above and list some of your personal, social, as well as theological assumptions.

9. Some biblical historians contend that the stories about water coming from the rock in Exod 17:1-7 and Num 20:2-13 are duplicates. But if we approach these narratives canonically, the narrative of Exodus 17 would provide background for the actions of the characters in Numbers 20. What is the difference in the theme and message if these stories are viewed as duplicates or as two experiences in the life of the community? Compare Exod 17:6 with Num 20:8. What can we learn from the progression of these stories on how God works with his people?

10. 2 Samuel 24:1 states that "the anger of the Lord burned against Israel and he incited David against them, saying, 'Go and take a census of Israel and Judah.'" 1 Chronicles 21:1, on the other hand, asserts that "Satan rose up against Israel and incited David to take a census of Israel." With Logos Bible Software, place these two passages side by side on your computer screen and compare them. What was wrong with taking a census? If we understand these passages canonically, what do the differences say about the cause of evil in God's permissive will? See Ruth 1:20-21; Jas 1:13-15; and Job 1:12 for additional insights. What are some wrong ways to envision the relationship between God and Satan and their instigation of evil in our world?

CHAPTER 8

Exploring Spiritual Exegesis

Using an Exegetical X-Ray Camera

So far we have walked down seven roads toward a correct understanding of Scripture. Or using our second analogy, we have employed seven different types of cameras to develop a finished photo of the text. We have examined the literary features, grammar, structure, context, cultural and historical background, history of interpretation, and the theology involved in an analysis of the biblical text. This last chapter offers an approach that is normally not included in an exemplar for exegesis. We have entitled this chapter "Spiritual Exegesis." Here we will reflect upon the insufficiencies of the historical-critical method as well as the dangers of spiritual exegesis and then proffer examples of spiritual disciplines that can enable the reader to approach the text of Scripture with an attitude of trust and obedience to receive personal formation, practical applications, and the facilitation of an encounter with God. This process will center upon an x-ray of our personality, presuppositions, and spiritual makeup in order to certify that we are not deceiving ourselves and that this entire endeavor is not just an intellectual exercise completely separated from our life experience.

Over the past two centuries, the historical-critical method has dominated exegesis. From the methodologies developed, interpreters have gained an enormous wealth of knowledge and wisdom. Yet the arrival of postmodernism as well as the insights of generations of skillful exegetes in the precritical period should demonstrate the limits of the historical-critical method. Spiritual exegesis attempts to employ other skills than those employed by the historical-critical method and accordingly emphasizes such techniques as meditation, imaging, personalizing, listening prophetically, paradigm building, and imaginative application. These methods are geared not to studying Scripture as an object, but to placing one's self underneath the Bible so that the text exegetes the reader. In particular, spiritual exegesis investigates the attitudes of the reader to the text so that the study is undertaken in faith, reverence, honesty, and devotional vitality.

A. The Insufficiencies of the Historical-Critical Method

The assumptions of critical exegesis diverge from the precritical and postmodern approaches. The clear differences can best be diagnosed through a somewhat simplistic chart.

Exegesis	Precritical	Critical	Postmodern
Goal	A theological dogmatic understanding; purity of life and soundness of doctrine.	A historical understanding; the Bible as a record of ancient religious belief.	A contemporary meaning relevant to the reader.
Methodology	Faith seeking understanding through historical and grammatical means.	A disinterested reader approaches the text objectively to obtain verifiable information through scientific strategies.	The validation of readings is accomplished by demonstrating that the readings are consistent with an interpretative community.
Meaning	The reader finds meaning in the revelation of God.	Meaning is found in the historical and sociological circumstances of the origin of the work and the intention of the human author.	Meaning must be created by the reader, resulting in a multiplicity of meanings.
Authorship	God is the primary author.	Discovering the intention of the original human author is essential.	The reader collaborates with the text in producing a new work, so that the identity and circumstances of the original author are no longer important.

Exegesis	Precritical	Critical	Postmodern
Function of the reader	The reader applies the text to the contemporary situation.	The reader devises an objective method capable of establishing the original meaning of the text.	The reader as a subject acts upon the text to create meaning for the contemporary situation.
Text	The Bible is the source of ontological truth.	The Bible is viewed as an object directed from a sender to a receiver in a particular situation.	Texts are literature (not historical artifacts) that function in helping readers create worlds of meaning for themselves intellectually and behaviorally.
View of truth	Truth is transhistorical and authoritative for all times and places.	The supremacy of reason is viewed as the ultimate criterion for truth.	Truth only makes sense within a particular universe of meaning, so that there is no final and ultimate truth.
View of self	There is a separation of subject and object, with the subject responding to an objective text.	The claims of an autonomous self and an objective observer are both accepted.	The idea of an autonomous self is untenable; the self acts upon the text and is the object being acted upon by the text.
View of language	Words stand for realities within the transcendent order, causing repercussions in the natural order.	Language is descriptive of an objective, natural, temporal order.	Back to a precritical view of language as a metaphor with a quasi-physical power; the elevation of language from tool to master.

If we are intending to advocate exegetical disciplines other than those employed by the historical-critical method, the limits of that methodology must be explored. The primary criticism against the historical-critical method is that it is incommensurate with the intention of the biblical text. Whereas the biblical authors wrote "from faith to faith" (Rom 1:17), the very essence of modern scientific and historical inquiry is a detached neutrality in matters of faith. Listen to the claims of Leopold Immanuel Rückert (in his

1839 commentary on Romans), who wrote naively at a time when the historical-critical method was hailed as the solution to all our interpretative woes.

> The exegete of the New Testament as an exegete . . . has no system, and must not have one, either a dogmatic or an emotional system. In so far as he is an exegete, he is neither orthodox nor heterodox, neither supernaturalist nor rationalist, nor pantheist, nor any other -*ist* there may be. He is neither pious nor godless, neither moral nor immoral, neither sensitive nor insensible.[1]

Reader response criticism has now demonstrated that such neutrality is impossible and that any presumption of neutrality is in reality counterproductive to discovering the meaning of the text.

However, salesmen of the historical-critical method have promoted more than just disinterestedness; they practice a hermeneutic of suspicion, which purposely and systematically doubts the veracity of the manuscripts. Authors like Günther Bornkamm recognized this a generation ago and concluded, "Should we reduce the tradition critically to that which cannot be doubted on historical grounds, we should be left ultimately with a mere torso which bears no resemblance to the story set forth in the Gospels."[2] Walter Wink puts it this way: The historical-critical method "pretends to search for 'assured results,' 'objective knowledge,' when in fact the method presumes radical epistemological doubt, which by definition devours each new spawn of 'assured results' as a guppy swallows her children."[3]

Third, these historicist assumptions do not correspond with the ancient view of history writing. Biblical writers were not diarists who kept a day-by-day chronicle of deeds, movements, and conversations. Instead of demanding scientific precision concerning completeness of material, exactitude of historical detail, consistent chronology, and biographical interest, biblical authors were selective and wrote kerygmatically interpreted history. Rather than merely reporting historiography, their primary interest was theological. As Elizabeth Achtemeier explains, "because historical criticism approaches

---

1. Leopold Immanuel Rückert, *Commentar über den Brief Pauli an die Römer* (Leipzig: Boldmar, 1839), quoted in Werner Georg Kümmel, *The New Testament: The History of the Investigation of Its Problems* (Nashville: Abingdon, 1972), p. 110.

2. Günther Bornkamm, *Jesus of Nazareth* (New York: Harper, 1960), p. 15.

3. Walter Wink, *The Bible in Human Transformation: Toward a New Paradigm for Biblical Study* (Philadelphia: Fortress, 1973), p. 7.

the Bible solely as a historical document, the truth of the Bible has come to be identified with its facticity."[4]

In addition, through the historical-critical method biblical studies "increasingly fell prey to a form of technologism which regards as legitimate only those questions which its methods can answer."[5] Because of its employment of esoteric language, biblical criticism has become cut off from the church, for whose life its results are of utmost significance. As Richard Muller and John Thompson point out, "The text is of interest above all because it bears a divinely inspired message to an ongoing community of faith and not because it happens also to be a repository of the religious relics of a past age."[6] Wink insightfully reasons that "Historical criticism sought to free itself from the community in order to pursue its work untrammeled by censorship and interference. With that hard-won freedom it also won isolation from any conceivable significance."[7]

Another limitation of the historical-critical method centers upon its attempt to get behind the text instead of recognizing the canonical meaning. Speaking about the disconnect between the testaments, Elizabeth Achtemeier complains,

> Above all, there is nothing that necessarily binds the Old and New Testaments. In both Testaments we are dealing with disparate groups, from many different times and places, who produced their own unique literature and pursued their own unique religious practices, and there is no thread of divine activity and purpose that ties the whole story together.[8]

Finally and most importantly, Glen Scorgie points out formational, practical, and religious deficiencies with the historical-critical method, since it "completely ignores, deliberately underestimates, or cavalierly dismisses as peripheral" three crucial areas: (1) personal formation; (2) practical application; and (3) the facilitation of a direct encounter with God.[9] Scorgie con-

---

4. Elizabeth Rice Achtemeier, *Preaching from the Old Testament* (Louisville: Westminster John Knox, 1989), p. 30.

5. Wink, *The Bible in Human Transformation*, p. 8.

6. Richard A. Muller and John L. Thompson, "The Significance of Precritical Exegesis," in *Biblical Interpretation in the Era of the Reformation* (Grand Rapids: Eerdmans, 1996), p. 341.

7. Wink, *The Bible in Human Transformation*, pp. 10-11.

8. Achtemeier, *Preaching from the Old Testament*, p. 30.

9. Glen A. Scorgie, "Hermeneutics and the Meditative Use of Scripture: The Case for a Baptized Imagination," *JETS* 44 (2001): 273.

cludes, "The spiritual instincts of the people of God cannot be satisfied for long with a hermeneutical approach that minimizes personal formation, fades out when it comes to making practical applications, and fails to connect the reader directly to God in deeper and more meaningful ways."[10]

Historical-critical exegesis stands at a crossroads where it must recognize and incorporate other methods into its field of vision, including the insights of precritical exegesis.[11] These insufficiencies point out that additional paths of exegesis are both necessary and valuable in capturing "the faith dimension" of the biblical record. Therefore, spiritual exegesis has its place among the exegetical journeys toward a full understanding of the text. However, it is important to avoid certain dangers if this type of analysis is to be employed properly.

B. The Dangers of Spiritual Exegesis

Certainly we do not want to imply that spiritual exegesis replaces the historical-critical method of investigation. As Robert Stein points out, "All the prayer in the world cannot substitute for a Bible dictionary, if we do not know the meaning of a biblical word. For understanding the biblical text, meditation is no replacement for looking up how the author uses such terms elsewhere in his writings."[12] Furthermore, we need to be careful not to create a bifurcation between the historical-grammatical method of exegesis and spiritual exegesis so that one is accepted and the other excluded. Instead, we need to validate both in the exegetical process.

The presence of subjectivity in spiritual exegesis is a danger that must be recognized, although this should not disqualify its use. Scorgie points out that spiritual exegesis is frequently rejected, since "Imagination seems to connote the imaginary, the fanciful, the delusional, the false."[13] Therefore, we need to make sure that spiritual exegesis does not cross the border into magic or unbridled subjectivism. Distinctions must be drawn between the disciplines of spiritual exegesis and approaches to Scripture like Michael

10. Scorgie, *JETS* 44 (2001): 276.

11. See J. Todd Billings, *The Word of God for the People of God: An Entryway to the Theological Interpretation of Scripture* (Grand Rapids: Eerdmans, 2010), ch. 5, "Treasures in Jars of Clay: The Value of Premodern Biblical Interpretation."

12. Robert H. Stein, *Playing by the Rules: A Basic Guide to Interpreting the Bible* (Grand Rapids: Baker, 1994), p. 70.

13. Scorgie, *JETS* 44 (2001): 280.

Drosnin's *The Bible Code* and the infamous "open your Bible and point" method of biblical roulette.[14] To protect against such extremes, subjectivistic approaches to Scripture can be prevented by such practices as (1) a biblically-informed predisposition; (2) knowledge of the errors of church history; (3) a communal rather than individually autonomous quest for truth; and (4) a scientific disposition that lays a rigorous and responsible hermeneutical groundwork. In spite of this danger of subjectivity, we must not allow a fear of the unknown to prevent us from attempting to grow in our spiritual discernment of the text.

Finally, one must recognize that the illumination of the Holy Spirit in spiritual exegesis does not convey hidden information about the original meaning of the biblical text. Instead, the Spirit was given to advance the processes of sanctification and mission that are central to the gospel. Illumination rather than direct revelation is the work of the Holy Spirit today. This distinction can eliminate any fear or anxiety in employing spiritual exegesis.[15]

C. The Disciplines of Spiritual Exegesis

Spiritual exegesis is often presented very superficially. We need the Holy Spirit in order to interpret the Bible, since it was inspired by the Holy Spirit. And we stop there. We want to advance a step further and ask what disciplines are necessary for a spiritual approach to the Bible. We will outline with examples seven possible skills to develop.

1. A Humble, Receptive, Practicing Faith Perspective

PROCEDURE

Spiritual exegesis involves the preparation of the reader to hear the text in a correct manner. From the Holy Spirit we receive an attitude of expectation as we interpret the text. Rather than approaching the Bible with suspicious doubts and hardened skepticism, we come reverently and humbly, expecting

14. Michael Drosnin, *The Bible Code* (New York: Simon & Schuster, 1997). See the three wrong methodologies described by Dallas Willard, *Hearing God: Developing a Conversational Relationship with God* (Downers Grove: InterVarsity, 1999), pp. 57-62.

15. Cf. Clark Pinnock, "The Role of the Spirit in Interpretation," *JETS* 36 (1993): 493-94.

to receive a word from God. As Scorgie maintains, spiritual exegesis "sets a tone of humility and receptivity, rather than a tone of assertiveness and control."[16] No longer do we approach Scripture like a judge evaluating every claim. Instead, in a captivating, trustworthy voice, the Bible woos us to internalize its truth and leads us down a sure-footed path. The result is an attitude adjustment deep in our character, the same positive faith perspective that is portrayed throughout Scripture. When we practice spiritual exegesis, the words of Merrill Tenney come true. Exegesis is "not so much a technique as a spirit. It is the spirit of eagerness which seeks the mind of God; it is the spirit of humility which listens readily to the voice of God; it is the spirit of adventure which pursues earnestly the will of God; it is the spirit of adoration which rests in the presence of God."[17] Through spiritual exegesis, Bible study is transformed from just an analytical human-driven exercise to a divine encounter with the living God in Jesus Christ.

EXAMPLES

a. Scriptures about Creation In our twenty-first-century sophisticated scientific mindset we can read the creation story in Genesis 1 and scornfully poke fun of its idea of a three-storied universe with waters above and below the earth (Gen 1:6-7). We can read the description in Ps 19:5-6 about the sun running across the heavens and laugh at the Bible's conception of a flat earth. With such an analytical approach to these texts, we are unable to visualize divine natural revelation or fathom the mystery of creation. Instead, through spiritual exegesis we must recognize that God stoops in his revelation to meet us where we are in our understanding. Only then can we be overcome with wonder at the beauty and intricacy of God's world and read the creation story correctly.

b. Extrabiblical Literature Scholars and an increasing number of educated laypeople are studying the extrabiblical literature such as the *Gospel of Thomas* or the *Protoevangelium Jacobus*. There is a tendency in our postmodern world toward evaluating all literature alike. Whereas tolerance used to mean offering an attitude of respect to everyone's belief claims, our

---

16. Scorgie, *JETS* 44 (2001): 278.

17. Merrill C. Tenney, *Galatians: The Charter of Christian Liberty,* rev. ed. (Grand Rapids: Eerdmans, 1957), pp. 207-8.

"modern" conception of tolerance now states that one person's religious ideology is as correct as another's. Everyone's opinion is equally valid, so that truth is completely relative to one's cultural experience.

What is your response to this incident from the *Infancy Gospel of Thomas* 2?

> When this boy Jesus was five years old . . . He made soft clay and fashioned from it twelve sparrows. And it was the sabbath when he did this. And there were also many other children playing with him. Now when a certain Jew saw what Jesus was doing in his play on the sabbath, he at once went and told his father Joseph. . . . And when Joseph came to the place and saw (it), he cried out to him, saying: "Why do you do on the sabbath what ought not to be done?" But Jesus clapped his hands and cried to the sparrows: "Off with you!" And the sparrows took flight and went away chirping. The Jews were amazed when they saw this, and went away and told their elders what they had seen Jesus do.[18]

Second-century Christians wanted to fill in the gaps in the Gospel narratives, so they created various scenarios about Jesus' childhood. Their motivation was one of edification. Yet instead of marveling at the person of Jesus, today we are tempted to equate these apocryphal stories with the incident of Jesus in the temple at age twelve (Luke 2:41-52). "The Bible is full of fabricated tales to entertain us," conclude the skeptics. Spiritual exegesis equips us to discern the difference between apocryphal and biblical narratives and then to approach the text with reverence and awe.

c. **Experiencing Scripture through a Lifestyle of Obedience** In addition to creating an attitude of trusting expectation, spiritual exegesis also fosters a lifestyle of obedience. Promoters of spiritual exegesis recognize that lifestyle shapes exegetical insights. Stanley Hauerwas is fond of saying, "The lives of the saints are the hermeneutical key to Scripture," and Richard Hays explains that "the right reading of the New Testament occurs only where the Word is embodied."[19] Until we observe the text lived out, we cannot begin to conceive what it means. Therefore, to glean everything possible from the text we

18. Wilhelm Schneemelcher, ed., *New Testament Apocrypha,* rev. ed. (Louisville: Westminster John Knox, 1991), 1:392-93.

19. Both quotes from Richard B. Hays, *The Moral Vision of the New Testament: Community, Cross, New Creation: A Contemporary Introduction to New Testament Ethics* (San Francisco: HarperSanFrancisco, 1996), p. 305.

need to practice the scriptural exhortations and model our lives after its teaching. J. I. Packer defines evangelical Christians as those who "say that they should listen to Holy Scripture, and finally let its teaching guide them, however much reordering of their prior ideas and intentions this may involve, and however sharply it may set them at odds with the mind-set of their peers and their times."[20] This type of commitment is the breeding ground for a fruitful interpretation of the text.

Obedient Christian experience influences exegesis. For instance, what does 1 Cor 14:15b mean, "I will sing with my spirit, but I will also sing with my mind." This text comes alive with meaning when you as the exegete experience "singing in the Spirit" or creating a melody in an unknown tongue. When one experiences how praying in tongues bypasses the mind, this event enables one to understand Paul's earlier words in 1 Cor 14:15a, "I will pray with my spirit, but I will also pray with my mind." Experience shapes exegesis.

Similarly, the beatitude, "Blessed are you when people insult you, persecute you and falsely say all kinds of evil against you because of me" (Matt 5:11), will only expose its full meaning when you encounter insult and persecution and consider yourself truly blessed. Spiritual exegesis acknowledges that devotional vitality and a practicing faith are essential to exegesis. Dallas Willard goes so far as to state that "experience and understanding of God's voice can alone make the events of the Bible real to us and allow our faith in its truth to rise beyond mere abstract conviction that it *must* be true."[21] Experience confirms and personalizes the truths of Scripture.

2. Personalizing Scripture

PROCEDURE

The Scriptures present a historical and literary account of God's dealings with the human community. The reader as subject analyzes these documents as the object of his or her study. However, for a complete diet of the Scriptures the reverse procedure must also take place: the text must exegete the reader. Personalizing Scripture creates an environment where the text becomes the subject which reads the reader. Personalizing Scripture can occur

---

20. J. I. Packer, *Honouring the Written Word of God* (Carlisle: Paternoster, 1999), p. 150.
21. Willard, *Hearing God*, pp. 188-89.

through putting one's name into a passage or by creatively visualizing ourselves in the midst of a narrative.

a. Ephesians 1:1-11: "In Christ" Some people possess a naturally depressive personality and find it extremely difficult to praise and exalt God with thanksgiving. In my pastoral work, I remember an encounter with a young woman who could not receive any of God's blessings and the gifts of the Holy Spirit. All of the benefits of "being in Christ" found in Eph 1:1-11 were promises to other people but not reality for her. Honestly, I was completely baffled how to help her receive the riches of Christ until I suggested personalizing Scripture. The secret to appropriating the blessings described in Scripture is to place our own name into the text, as in the following quotation from Eph 1:3-4, "Praise be to the God and Father of our Lord Jesus Christ, who has blessed me, Dean Deppe, with every spiritual blessing in Christ even as he chose me, Dean Deppe, in him before the creation of the world so that I, Dean Deppe, would be holy and blameless in his sight." The ecstasy of exuberant praise and the experience of ethereal blessings like election become manifested reality when you personalize Scripture. The formerly constricted spiritual life of the young woman I was ministering to began to glow with the power of the Holy Spirit as she practiced the spiritual discipline of putting her name into the biblical text. At the same time, this practice increased her desire to memorize Scripture and meditate upon its meaning. In a word, personalizing Scripture produces experiences that confirm the power of the word of God.

b. An Example from Robert Mulholland Robert Mulholland advises the reader to imagine creatively the sights, sounds, smells, and voices in the narrative and personally relive the story. This creative visualization is another way to personalize Scripture. Listen how Mulholland describes this personal discipline of spiritual exegesis in his book *Shaped by the Word: The Power of Scripture in Spiritual Formation*:

> You imagine the things you would be seeing: what they would look like —
> their colors, their motion, their size; the appearance of the other people,
> the expressions on their faces, their clothing, their postures, their movements. You imagine the things you would be hearing: the sounds of na-

ture — the wind, birds, animals, the water lapping on the shore, boats creaking at their moorings; the sounds of human activity — talking, children playing, infants crying, people yelling or groaning, the sounds of work. You imagine the things you would be smelling: the scents of the surroundings — the flowers, the sea, the earth, fields, barnyards, a carpenter's shop, a fish market, a baker's shop; the human aromas — perfume, perspiration, freshly washed garments, dirty garments. You imagine the things you could feel: the wind blowing around you, the stillness of a room, the roughness of a path, the textures of clothing, the coolness of water or a marble pillar, the heat of the desert, the wetness of rain or sea spray. You use all your senses. You let your imagination loose to recreate the setting of the passage of scripture.

Once you have recreated the scene in your imagination and placed yourself in the scene, then begin to examine your thoughts and feelings about the situation. Here again you may experience harmony/dissonance. This can become a focus for your prayerful openness to God and your meditation on what the Word is saying to you in this experience. You may ask yourself what you identify with most comfortably in the scene and then prayerfully meditate on why you make this identification. Or you may ask yourself what you would avoid in the scene and meditate on what the Word is saying to you in that avoidance. What do your negative and/or positive feelings about the scene reveal to you about your inner dynamics of being and your outer dynamics of relationships and your patterns of reaction/response to life?[22]

A personal re-creation of the scenery and flow of the narrative as well as the practice of allowing the text to ask challenging questions of our character and Christian experience can enable the old stories to take on new meaning in our lives.

3. Praying Scripture

PROCEDURE

Prayer is communication and communion with God. In order to make exegesis also a process of communion with God, we can employ the technique

22. M. Robert Mulholland Jr., *Shaped by the Word: The Power of Scripture in Spiritual Formation* (Nashville: Upper Room, 1985), pp. 148-49.

of praying Scripture. In this spiritual discipline we turn the words of instruction aimed at us into a prayer aimed at God, in order that the content of the text enters our Christian experience. We pray the words of the Bible back to God in thanksgiving and intercession until they become a part of our being. Because the Scriptures were written in a spirit of prayer and contain prayers within their contents, this spiritual discipline creates within the heart of the reader the very same disposition as the original writers.

EXAMPLES

a. The Book of Psalms Because the book of Psalms was the prayer and praise hymnal of the Israelites, praying the psalms back to God is a natural spiritual exercise. Several books have been published on this theme, ranging in authorship from the Christian mystic Thomas Merton to the Old Testament scholar Walter Brueggemann, both with the identical title, *Praying the Psalms.*

Merton advocates this spiritual exercise because "Nowhere can we be more certain that we are praying with the Holy Spirit than when we pray the Psalms."[23] He chooses the book of Psalms in particular, since "There is no aspect of the interior life, no kind of religious experience, no spiritual need of man that is not depicted and lived out in the Psalms."[24]

Brueggemann advocates praying the Psalter because it offers us an eloquent and passionate voice to express all of the sentiments of the human heart: "When we turn to the Psalms, it means we enter into the middle of that voice of humanity and decide to take our stand with that voice. . . . We add a voice to the common elation, shared grief, and communal rage that besets us all."[25] Frequently in our human condition we are desensitized to God, inhibited in our relationships with others, and out of touch with our inner selves. We become dull, numb, repressed and in denial. Because self-knowledge and God-knowledge are all tied up with each other, as John Calvin proclaimed in his *Institutes of the Christian Religion,*[26] we lack one crucial element in interpreting the revelation of God. The Psalms provide the eloquent voice we need to liberate us in order to hear clearly and heed God's word. We carry within us

23. Thomas Merton, *Praying the Psalms* (Collegeville: Liturgical, 1956), p. 11.
24. Merton, *Praying the Psalms*, p. 31.
25. Walter Brueggemann, *Praying the Psalms* (Winona: Saint Mary's, 1982), p. 16.
26. John Calvin, *Institutes of the Christian Religion*, trans. Ford Lewis Battles (Philadelphia: Westminster, 1960), pp. 35-39.

feelings of abandonment, powerlessness, helplessness. But we discover our true selves in the Psalms because, as Brueggemann points out, "The Psalter is a collection over a long period of time of the eloquent, passionate songs and prayers of people who are at the desperate edge of their lives."[27]

Our gloom, anger, hopelessness, and disappointment are removed as we pray the Psalms. A new openness and vulnerability are created within us when we prayerfully recite back to God Ps 26:2-3, "Search me, O Lord, and try me, examine my heart and my mind; for your love is ever before me." A passion for God and his word is planted when we pray Ps 42:1-2, "As the deer pants for streams of water, so my soul pants for you, O God. My soul thirsts for God, for the living God." A foundation of confident trust is laid when we confess Ps 23:1, "The Lord is my shepherd, I shall not be in want." And an expectant reception of God's revelation is assured when we invoke Ps 29:4, "The voice of the Lord is powerful; the voice of the Lord is majestic." Praying the Psalms prepares us for the scholarly task of exegesis as our inner life is shaped by the language of the Psalms.

b. Internalizing Scripture through Prayer Other parts of the Bible can be internalized through prayers of petition as well. After reading a doctrinal portion from Romans, we can entreat God for a clearer understanding of these truths. As we confront an exhortation in the Paraenesis of James, we can request that God work this particular character quality into our personality. As we decipher the historical chronologies of 1 Chronicles 1–9, we can thank God for his faithfulness in history as well as construct a prayer list of people who have influenced our spiritual growth. After each scene in a historical narrative, we can intercede for people in our world who are undergoing similar experiences. We can digest the themes of the Old Testament prophets by imploring for justice to roll on like a river and righteousness like a never-failing stream (Amos 5:24). Wisdom literature like the book of Proverbs can invite us to invoke the Almighty for the fear of the Lord as well as practical wisdom in the everyday experiences of life. In praying the words of Scripture back to God we become more familiar with their power. The expressions of the Bible become a natural part of our vocabulary. We memorize the flow of words; we digest memorable phrases; we internalize the attitude of the text. Our personality and the text are wed. Scripture finds a home in our heart, and our heart finds a home in Scripture. A proper exegesis of the text will result.

---

27. Brueggemann, *Praying the Psalms*, p. 16.

4. Picturing Concepts through Meditation

PROCEDURE

Jerry Camery-Hoggatt, in his book *Irony in Mark's Gospel*, claims that "Scholarly reading is very much like natural reading, slowed to a snail's pace."[28] Meditating upon the Bible slows our reading even more dramatically, so that we carefully and deliberately attempt to form a picture in our mind of every important concept. The familiar proverb, "A picture is worth a thousand words," also applies to our reading the Bible. A large part of meditating upon Scripture consists in the picturing of concepts. I like to describe meditation as chewing one's cud. Just as a cow eats and digests a meal only to rechew it and swallow the food a second and third time, so we repeatedly and continually chew on the content of the Bible. Meditation is the type of reading that is recommended in the following passages: Josh 1:8; Deut 6:6-9; Prov 3:22-24; 6:22; 15:28; and Pss 19:14; 49:3; 119:15, 23, 48, 78, 97, 99, 148.

EXAMPLES

a. Romans 6:6: The Old Self Romans 6:6 reports that our old man (NKJV, NET) or old self has been crucified with Christ. How can we picture this concept of an old man or this deeply-rooted former sinful self? In his book *The Normal Christian Life*, Watchman Nee produces some very helpful portraits.[29] The early part of the book of Romans teaches that the problem of sins in the Christian life is taken care of through Christ's forgiveness. Whenever we commit sins, we prayerfully ask Jesus to forgive us and they are pardoned. However, the deeper problem of sin must also be resolved. We continue over and over again to commit the exact identical sins because of our sinful nature, the old person within us born of Adam. The solution to sin is not forgiveness, but crucifixion, death to our former self through Christ. Watchman Nee compares our situation to that of a housewife who determines to eliminate a spider web in the basement. Every day she removes the web and the next day another appears, over and over again. Finally, she dis-

---

28. Jerry Camery-Hoggatt, *Irony in Mark's Gospel: Text and Subtext*. SNTSMS 72 (Cambridge: Cambridge University Press, 1992), p. 89.

29. Watchman Nee, *The Normal Christian Life* (Carol Stream: Tyndale House, 1977), pp. 60-61.

covers the secret. Eliminating the web is not enough; the spider must be killed. Similarly, it is insufficient to continually ask forgiveness for our sins; the old self must be crucified.

Or suppose that a ruler wanted to eliminate all alcohol from his kingdom, suggests Watchman Nee. Would it be enough to break every bottle and empty every can of liquor in the whole realm? No, because the factories would simply produce more beer, wine, and strong drink. The factories must be destroyed. Christ has solved both problems for us. In Christ our sins are forgiven through his blood, and the sin-producing factory, our old self, has been crucified when Christ died on the cross. Meditation etches indelible pictures into the fabric of our soul.

b. The Office of Pastor-Teacher In our earlier investigation of Ephesians 4, we noticed the significant grammatical changes of prepositions in Eph 4:12 and performed a word study of the term καταρτισμὸν through a search of similar roots in the New Testament.[30] We concluded that the pastor-teacher equips the congregation, while the saints perform the work of ministry and upbuild the body of Christ. But why do we combine pastor and teacher together? Again, the Greek shows us the way. Although Eph 4:11 supplies five leadership terms — apostle, prophet, evangelist, pastor, teacher — only four pronominal articles occur in the Greek:

> τοὺς μὲν ἀποστόλους,
> τοὺς δὲ προφήτας,
> τοὺς δὲ εὐαγγελιστάς,
> τοὺς δὲ ποιμένας καὶ διδασκάλους.

So the pastor and teacher are viewed by Paul as one office.

Since the word "pastor" is an animal-farming term equivalent to a shepherd, and because teaching describes an educational function, we could draw from these cultural backgrounds to carve a picture into our consciousness. But suppose we wanted to sketch a more contemporary portrait of a pastor-teacher. As we meditate, the image of a player-coach is engraved upon our mind. As we chew our cud, several parallel functions of a player-coach and pastor-teacher are riveted into our consciousness.

A coach is a discoverer, developer, and trainer of the skills of other people. Likewise, the pastor-teacher discovers the gifts of people in the congregation

---

30. See above Chapter 2, B5, "Ephesians 4:12: One Single Comma" (pp. 46-47).

by planning activities where these Spirit-enriched abilities can come to the surface. Second, the pastor-teacher demonstrates skills that others can imitate and then develop within themselves. Third, like a player-coach, the pastor-teacher designs plays that work in the particular community where she or he is called to serve. Finally, the player-coach develops a team philosophy that encourages the full participation of the other team members. Tom Landry, former coach of the Dallas Cowboys, defined coaching as "making people do what they don't want so they can become what they want to be." Winning coaches set high demands upon themselves and their team. Likewise, pastors must not only sacrifice personal achievements for team goals, but they must place this requirement on others as well. Players are infused with confidence when the commitment of the pastor transforms a laissez-faire attitude into single-minded devotion to Christ and commitment to the church. Therefore, meditating upon the contemporary image of a player-coach enriches our understanding of a pastor-teacher.

Fred Smith, in an article in *Leadership* magazine, calls attention to a second picture of a pastor as an orchestra conductor.[31] From a fascinating interview with two first-chair players of the New York Philharmonic, Smith learned the attributes of an effective conductor. Number one, good conducting demands a reverence for the composer; second, the conductor must have an intimate knowledge of the score. Certainly these comments relate directly to the job description of a pastor. The congregation is called to devotion and consecration when they see their pastor exemplifying a reverence and awe for God, the composer. Likewise, an intimate knowledge of the score means daily saturation in the word of God so that fresh manna is always on the table. In addition, conductors set a meaningful beat for the orchestra and select a repertoire of music that the orchestra can play and the audience enjoy. Good conductors equip us to be better musicians. Effective pastors likewise provide the leadership needed to get the best sound from every instrument.

I am sure you have witnessed an orchestra warming up before the conductor makes an appearance. Musicians play whatever tune they wish, in any key, at whatever tempo. The result is a bedlam that is tolerated only because of what is to follow. Then the conductor steps to the podium, raps for silence, and now the same musicians and identical instruments thrill the audience with an inspiring concert. That picture illustrates the difference pastor-teachers can make when they are equipping the saints of God for ministry. These contemporary portraits of player-coach and orchestra conductor

31. Fred Smith, "The Minister as Maestro," *Leadership* 9 (1988): 130-37.

shine additional light upon the ancient biblical imagery of shepherd. The spiritual discipline of meditation provides the seedbed for such insights.

5. Listening Prophetically

PROCEDURE

Because this type of spiritual exegesis can be thoroughly abused, prophetic listening is the most controversial of the recommended spiritual disciplines. Caught up with their own egos, some preachers can say "Thus says the Lord" in almost any situation. Other "spiritual" people regularly repeat the chorus, "The Lord told me such and such," but nothing ever comes of it. But one false proclamation does not erase the office of prophet from existence. Although the canon of Scripture is closed, the history of salvation continues, and so God continues to speak his word prophetically in order to lead and guide individuals and the church. As Willard explains, "There is nothing in Scripture to indicate that the biblical modes of God's communication with humans have been superseded or abolished by either the presence of the church or the close of the scriptural canon."[32] Most commonly God respeaks the words that he already spoke in Scripture. Therefore, as we read the Bible meditatively, we can listen to the Holy Spirit within us prophetically applying these words to our experience.

This process is described in 1 Cor 2:10-16, where Paul concludes that we have the mind of Christ. "The Spirit searches all things, even the deep things of God," and "we speak, not in words taught us by human wisdom but in words taught by the Spirit, expressing spiritual truths in spiritual words." Therefore, as we read Scripture we need to practice spiritual discernment so that we can detect the difference between our own thoughts, feelings, and personality and the movements and insights of the Holy Spirit as well as the tempting devices of the devil. To develop this ability, we need to learn to live in constant communion with God as we carry on the normal human day-to-day activities. As Thomas Kelly perceptively affirms in his classic study of spirituality,

---

32. Willard, *Hearing God*, p. 103. He clarifies this statement by stating, "The close of the scriptural canon marks the point in the (still ongoing) divine-human conversation where the principles and doctrines that form the substance of Christian faith and practice are so adequately stated in human language that nothing more need be said *in general.*"

There is a way of ordering our mental life on more than one level at once. On one level we may be thinking, discussing, seeing, calculating, meeting all the demands of external affairs. But deep within, behind the scenes, at a profounder level, we may also be in prayer and adoration, song and worship and a gentle receptiveness to divine breathings. . . . For the religious man is forever bringing all affairs of the first level down into the Light, holding them there in the Presence, reseeing them and the whole of the world of men and things in a new and overturning way, and responding to them in spontaneous, incisive and simple ways of love and faith. Facts remain facts, when brought into the Presence in the deeper level, but their value, their significance, is wholly realigned. Much apparent wheat becomes utter chaff, and some chaff becomes wheat.[33]

God continues to guide his people in specific circumstances. Our speaking God whispers to the human spirit through a still small voice within carried by the Holy Spirit. Dallas Willard thinks that "the interior or inner voice, as it is also called — is the preferred and most valuable form of individualized communication for God's purposes. God usually addresses individually those who walk with him in a mature, personal relationship using this inner voice, proclaiming and showing forth the reality of the kingdom of God as they go."[34] Therefore, as I thoughtfully read the Bible, I should be aware how a word, phrase, concept, or passage is speaking to something in my life or the world around me. This prophetic application of the word does not always take into consideration the context or historical situation of the original author. But as long as we do not make improper claims about the original meaning of the text, God can use this prophetic listening to guide our lives and ministries.

EXAMPLES

a. **"Immediately"** A deliberate scholarly reading of the text demands a pause at every important term, phrase, and clause for an investigation of the original meaning and background of the passage. A slow prophetic listening to the text requires rather an openness to the Spirit of God to bring to our consciousness thoughts and ideas from the passage that will guide our

---

33. Thomas R. Kelly, *A Testament of Devotion* (New York: Harper & Brothers, 1941), pp. 35-36.

34. Willard, *Hearing God,* p. 89.

Christian life and speak to our everyday experience. The stop-and-start method of research is no longer employed, but instead we read until we are struck by a particular insight, convicted by a character's response, or encouraged by a development in the narrative. Rather than asking questions of the text, we discover that the text interrogates us. We are confronted with our shortcomings, stopped in our tracks with regard to our selfish planning, and supplied direction for our future endeavors.

I remember reading chapter 1 of Mark's Gospel while I was pondering the timing of a particular decision. I was positive about my future direction, but I was holding back from making a decision out of fear and insecurity. As I listened prophetically to the text, one little adverb caught my attention: "immediately" (εὐθὺς): Mark 1:10, "immediately"; Mark 1:12, "immediately"; Mark 1:18, 20, 21, 23, 28, 29, 30, 42, 43, "immediately." I could not avoid this one word, "immediately." As a result I could not procrastinate either. My decision was no longer a future action; it had to be done immediately. This was not the original meaning of the text, of course, but God had personally respoken this word to provide light to my path.

b. Marriage and the Imagery of a Fig Tree I was meeting with a couple to discuss their future wedding plans. Tim's life had been turned upside down by a divorce several years before. The interpersonal battles and bewildering personality clashes with his former wife had eaten his soul like a grasshopper plague. With three growing boys now in his custody, all his energy and attention were directed to his children and his daily employment. He experienced weekly contact with Carol, but had never really "noticed" her. Then on one occasion, to pass the time of day more quickly, Tim asked Carol to accompany him while he cared for the fig trees he was nourishing. A fig tree brought them together.

As I listened to their story, the picture of nourishing fig trees grew into a prophetic metaphor in my mind. Their marriage relationship would have to be cultivated in the same manner that they spend hours nurturing and sustaining the fig trees. They chose Joel 2:22 as their wedding text: "The trees are bearing their fruit; the fig tree and the vine yield their riches." As I listened prophetically to this text in preparation for the wedding message, I noticed that Joel 1:7 and Joel 1:12 also employ this imagery. The invasion of grasshoppers had laid waste the vines and ruined the fig trees (1:7); any hope of a fruitful harvest was completely destroyed because the fig tree had withered (1:12). These texts spoke powerfully to Tim's experience of a broken relationship and fractured marriage. The enemy had destroyed the previous crop, but now the fig tree would again yield fruit. Just as this imagery was important in Israel's history, so now it became significant for Tim and Carol as well.

At the high point of Israel's history during Solomon's reign, *shalom* and prosperity were pictured with the imagery of everyone dwelling in security under their own vine and fig tree (1 Kgs 4:25). Likewise, in biblical times the worst curse involved the unforgettable experience of finding no grapes on the vine and no figs on the tree (Jer 8:13). The fig tree imagery had become forever embedded in the experience of Israel. Now this biblical imagery was prophetically becoming an intricate part of Tim and Carol's life. Their first date nourishing the fig trees was no accident. Their whole life together would involve the nurturing of the fig tree of their relationship. Listening prophetically to Scripture shaped and molded the lives of Tim and Carol.

6. Paradigm Building through Mirroring

PROCEDURE

A mirror reflects back to us an image of what we look like, who we are. The spiritual discipline of paradigm building likewise constructs a model, proto-type, or archetype of our identity, character make-up, or vocational vision. God uses the Scriptures as a prism through which to understand our unfolding life experience, the future pattern of our ministry, or the cultural happenings around us. This is what we call Scriptural mirroring. We discover connections between the great story of God's redemptive work in the Bible and our life stories here and now.

EXAMPLES

a. Images of the Church The New Testament is saturated with images of the church that provided the first generation of Christians with a mirror to evaluate themselves and their community. Paul Minear has written a three-hundred-page book describing these *Images of the Church in the New Testament*.[35] These "picture mirrors" include the familiar "Body of Christ" and "Family of God" metaphors but also the more unique images of "boat"

---

35. Paul S. Minear, *Images of the Church in the New Testament* (Philadelphia: Westminster, 1960; repr. 2004).

(Matt 8:23-27; 14:22-27) and "pillar and buttress of the truth" (1 Tim 3:15). These helpful scriptural paradigms can offer us hours of reflection and captivating conversational starters as we discover together what type of community we would like to form in our estranged and individualistic culture.

Suppose that as a communicator to the "now generation" you are not satisfied with first-century images of the church but aspire to introduce a contemporary mirror for congregational members to see themselves. Because your community contains a multitude of broken people, struggling immature converts, and people who have emerged from a past plagued by addiction, depression, and co-dependence, you want to emphasize that the church is a healing community of unpretentious human beings.

As you meditate, the paradigms of a washing machine, lightning rod, and recycling center are frozen into your consciousness. The church is the organization in society that gathers everyone's dirty laundry and allows itself to be the container wherein the detergent of Christ's blood cleanses each and every piece. The church is like a lightning rod that incapacitates the power of evil within society and each separate human being. Or maybe the most compelling image is the church as a recycling center. More important than the recycling of glass, paper, and plastic is the transformation of people's lives. The church is the institution upon earth that is in the business of recycling people from alienation with God to communion with their Creator, from broken relationships to reconciliation, and from meaningless work to fruitful labor in building God's kingdom on earth. Such paradigms of the church visualized in the eye of our soul become a mirror to visualize our identity in Christ.

b. Rebuilding the City in the Book of Nehemiah After the devastating hurricane in Homestead, Florida, in the 1990s, I escorted a busload of Christian school kids to spend their spring vacation rebuilding this town. Searching for a relevant Bible study theme, I settled upon the OT book of Nehemiah where the Israelites rebuilt the walls of Jerusalem. These narratives became a paradigm that mirrored our experience in Homestead. Originally the text narrated the prayerful vision of Nehemiah in a distant city of Persia, described his trips to Jerusalem to rebuild the fortress of Jerusalem, and portrayed the opposition without and within the residents of Israel. Now this story would become a mirror for a group of young people to picture their mission in a hurricane-damaged town of Florida.

Nehemiah's work was instigated by a pain in his heart as he personally felt the distress of his beloved Jerusalem, where "the wall is broken down and its gates have been burned with fire" (Neh 1:3). In distant Minnesota we were likewise confronted by the television pictures portraying the wreckage of Homestead and the commentary describing the plight of the homeless; we felt their pain. Nehemiah's heartache produced a vision that brought him to Jerusalem, where he analyzed the present needs of the city and constructed a picture of its anticipated future. Likewise, we toured the devastation in Homestead, Florida, and began to envision what we would like to see transformed in the week ahead. Arriving in Jerusalem, Nehemiah organized the workforce to increase productivity and community. We divided into teams to tackle our separate projects. Nehemiah's enemies proved to be both outside opposition as well as inner demoralization. We discovered as well that the physical work was strenuous, but our own discouragement and interpersonal conflicts and disagreements proved to be the greater obstacles to overcome. When the Jerusalem residents finished rebuilding the wall, Nehemiah called everyone together to celebrate their completed project and to offer praise to God for his guidance and strength (Nehemiah 8). At the end of our visit to Florida, we planned a celebrative worship service where we glorified God for his sovereign care and shared our personal stories of God's faithfulness and guidance over the past week.

Each morning and evening the Bible studies on the book of Nehemiah provided insights and encouragement for our day of labor. The spiritual exegesis of Scripture supplied a mirror to guide our experience.

7. Imaginative Application

PROCEDURE

A final discipline of spiritual exegesis involves the imaginative applications we extract from a passage of Scripture. Peter Toon explains that spiritual reading is "a particular way of receiving the revealed and dynamic Word of God into the heart from the mind so as to direct the will in the ways of God's guidance."[36] We shorten that long distance from the head to the heart, from our intellect to our experience, from the abstract to the concrete, by contemplating the possibilities that the Holy Spirit may want to bring into existence.

Mulholland distinguishes an informational reading from a formational

---

36. Peter Toon, *From Mind to Heart: Christian Meditation Today* (Grand Rapids: Baker, 1987), p. 10.

reading of the Bible.[37] Informational reading dictates that the reader cover as much material as possible in as quick a time period as achievable, while formational reading resists quantifying the amount and concentrates on the depth of the content. With informational reading, the text is an object that the reader attempts to master and control, whereas in formational reading, the reader becomes the object who is exegeted and interpreted by the text. If we seek information, we approach the Bible with a problem-solving mentality, whereas if we read for formation, we desire to be shaped by an encounter with the divine mystery we call God. Therefore, informational reading is functional, while formational reading is relational. In summary, formational reading practices an imaginative application of Scripture into our context and milieu.

EXAMPLES

a. Moses and Pharaoh The technique of discerning harmony or dissonance between the text and our experience is especially beneficial in imaginative application. Frequently, God wants to affirm our convictions and actions through an experience of harmony with the text. At other times God desires to break the callous crust of our lives by convicting us through dissonance with the text. This dissonance or alienation from the content of the Bible can involve our perceptions, attitudes, habits, personal and corporate relationships, defense mechanisms, and patterns of response to the world. Robert Mulholland describes an instance of imaginative application while he was meditating upon the encounter between Moses and Pharaoh in the beginning of the book of Exodus.

> During this period of reading, however, I would read the daily portion assigned by the lectionary and then I would sit before it and say, "Lord, what are you seeking to say to me through this? What is your Word of address to me?" All sorts of thoughts would be going through my mind — Moses said this and Pharaoh did that, Pharaoh's resistance, God's hardening of Pharaoh's heart — all thoughts I had been through many, many times. I knew everything that was there, and I really seemed to be getting nothing from it. There seemed to be no "Word from the Lord." However one important (but uncomfortable) thing about a lectionary is that if you make it a spiritual discipline, you cannot move beyond it. You can't just move

37. Mulholland, *Shaped by the Word*, ch. 5.

on and get to the "good parts" or the sections which appeal to you or seem to speak to you. You have to stay with the portion assigned. Well, I had been wrestling with this portion of Exodus for a week or more. Each day the lectionary moved me to a new portion of the plagues, sort of a "plague a day." Each day I would stop and ask, "Lord, what are you seeking to say to me in this passage?" Each day I was met with silence — or the noise of my own understanding of the passage.

One morning, as the lectionary moved me toward the end of the plagues, I read the portion and then asked the same question I had asked each day, "Lord, what are you seeking to say to me here?" This time the answer came, "You are Pharaoh!"

"What?" I replied. "Me, Pharaoh? Moses perhaps, even one of the Hebrew people, but Pharaoh? Perhaps one of the servants, one of the slaves, perhaps a taskmaster, Lord?"

"You are Pharaoh!"

Then, with that Word, things began to open up — in the text and in me.[38]

After being convinced through imaginative application that he was like Pharaoh, Mulholland continues and describes how the word of God convicted him in unexpected ways and reformed his reading perspective. So often we study the Bible simply for information rather than for application. We apply the Scriptures to others but not to ourselves. The spiritual exercise of imaginative application refuses to ignore the contextualization of the text into one's own experience.

b. Mark 6:45-51: Jesus Walks on the Sea For our concluding example, we will attempt to read the account of Jesus walking on the sea both with an eye to conventional exegesis and another eye focused on imaginative application. In reading historical narratives, the meditative reader will focus on unexpected twists in the sequence of events, surprising vocabulary, startling introductions and conclusions, as well as allusions to other familiar literature and helpful background material. As an example of spiritual exegesis, we will place ourselves in the middle of the story of the Sea-walking Miracle of Jesus found in Mark 6:45-51 and experience the unexpected twists in the narrative that give this account its thematic punch.

Immediately following the powerful miracle of the feeding of the five

---

38. Mulholland, *Shaped by the Word*, pp. 55-56.

thousand, Jesus forces (ἠνάγκασεν) his disciples to climb into the boat (Mark 6:45a). Normally, miracle stories conclude with an acknowledgement of awe on the part of the audience as well as a confession regarding the celebrity nature of the healer. Neither occurs in the conclusion of the feeding of the five thousand. Regularly, after important events in Jesus' ministry Mark narrates a period of rest and renewal in communion with Jesus and their master's instruction (Mark 1:29; 3:7, 13; 4:10; 6:31-32). However, instead of the familiar celebration after a powerful miracle or a time of restful communion with their master, Jesus has something else in mind for his followers. The disciples are compelled by Jesus to face the stormy winds and the uncontrollable waves all by themselves without his presence. Apparently, God has divinely preordained struggles for us when we would rather celebrate the bountiful blessings of life, when we would rather rest in comfort.

Meanwhile, Jesus retreats to a mountain to pray. The disciples are alone on the ship; Jesus is absent. Certainly the readers of Mark pictured themselves in this scene. Their experience mirrored the situation of the disciples. For them Jesus had ascended above the highest mountain to heaven and was sitting at the right hand of God, praying for them. With Jesus' absence their Christian life could be compared to a trip from one seashore to the other. They must somehow find their own way through the night, fighting the tormenting winds and rough seas to reach their destination. In the midst of distress they are straining at the oars but accomplishing nothing. It is the fourth watch of the night; the end is near, with the morning of the new age about to dawn, but they are still in the middle of the lake. Will they complete the discipleship journey that began when Jesus forced them into the boat? Will we make it through our struggles safely to the other side?

The disciples are miles away from Jesus. With the Sea of Galilee twenty-one kilometers long and eleven kilometers broad, they are all by themselves in the thick of a storm. However, the text reports that Jesus sees them (Mark 6:48a). No human being could fix his eyes on a boat in the heart of the sea, miles away in the middle of the night, but Jesus like God observes everything. Not only does Jesus observe their every movement, but he is praying for them on that heavenly mountain. Not only is he thinking about their welfare, but he acts by coming to their rescue, traversing the waves. According to the Old Testament, only God can walk on water (Job 9:8b; Hab 3:15; Ps 77:19; Isa 43:16; Wis 14:1-4). In our deepest distress, we can picture God himself in the person of Jesus approaching us in our time of need. Jesus as God himself is praying for us, thinking about us, but also ready to act and deliver us. In addition, the Scriptures explain that it is God's prerogative alone to control the forces of nature (Pss 89:10-11; 74:13-14; 107:23-30; Job 9:13; Isa 51:9-10). Only Yahweh can command the sea to obey (Job 26:11-13; Ps 104:7; Isa 51:9-10; Pss 18:15; 106:9; Isa 50:2). We discover in Jesus one who is more powerful than any earthly circumstance and sovereign over all danger and unforeseen catastrophe.

But right in the middle of these divine actions, Mark tells us that Jesus "was about to pass them by" (Mark 6:48c). I am sure the disciples' hearts sank; maybe their master was no longer their friend. Perhaps Jesus would now continue his life journey without them. No! Here is where you need historical-grammatical exegesis. The terminology "to pass by" alludes back to the Old Testament narratives of Moses and Elijah. The imagery reveals a divine epiphany as indicated in Exod 33:19, 22; 34:6; and 1 Kgs 19:11-13. On Mount Sinai God positions Moses in the cleft of a rock and passes by so that Moses can glimpse the Almighty One and not die. On Mount Horeb God speaks in a still small voice to Elijah as he passes by in a divine epiphany. Likewise, here in the middle of the night with the contrary wind halting any forward progress for the discipleship community, God himself is passing by and displaying his glory in the person of Jesus. Jesus greets them, "it is I" (ἐγώ εἰμι). Again these words contain more than meets the eye. Jesus employs the solemn and sacred divine name (Exod 3:14). It is Yahweh, God himself, the "I am."

In our imaginative application, we can apply this story to our precarious feelings of abandonment by God, tortured by the winds of adversity, unable to achieve our destination, and living the longest night of our lives. But our human frailty must always be contrasted with Jesus' divine sovereignty. The emphasis falls upon divine action. Christ is praying for us in heaven; he always sees us, no matter the distance; and he controls the winds and the sea. The night may be long and filled with torment, but we will reach the kingdom of God through the grace of a divine rescue. God may wait until the fourth watch of the night, but Jesus always enters our boat and the winds cease.

But surprisingly, the narrative continues. The response of the disciples is not adoration and awe but a negative fear, for "they had not understood about the loaves; their hearts were hardened" (Mark 6:52). On the surface, the genre appears to be a miracle story, but this final incident transforms the passage into a discipleship narrative.[39] By compelling his disciples to enter the boat by themselves, Jesus endeavors to teach them how to endure the

---

39. Notice the different application in Matt 14:33, which maintains the genre of miracle story: "Then those who were in the boat worshiped him, saying, 'Truly you are the Son of God.'"

coming dark night of torture and persecution without a consciousness of his presence. But Jesus' followers still do not understand. What don't they understand? The uncomprehended miracle of the loaves points to another feeding miracle, the Last Supper, where Jesus will multiply himself through his death on the cross to feed Jew and Gentile alike. But the disciples remain hardhearted. They prefer a miracle to meet their every need over a torturous boat ride through a stormy sea without the presence of Jesus. They do not want a multiplication that includes denying themselves, taking up their cross, and losing their life to find it. They would prefer that the central symbol of Christianity be a miracle rather than a cross. The inconclusive and unsatisfactory ending to this pericope requires that we keep reading the Gospel. In fact, the reader must finish the story. We must learn from the disciples' mistakes so that we can become the faithful disciples who place both the sacrificial cross and the miraculous resurrection at the middle of our lives. The ending of the story is left open so that we, the readers, can complete the application of the narrative.

In addition to the practices of spiritual exegesis, such as personalizing Scripture and paradigm building through mirroring, a full-embodied interpretation of this text employs the techniques of grammatical-historical analysis. Grammatically, we must interpret the phrase "straining at the oars" (βασανιζομένους ἐν τῷ ἐλαύνειν, Mark 6:48), which an interlinear Bible literally translates as "tortured in the drive." While searching the lemma reference, we discover that Mark also employs βασανίζω in Mark 5:7 for the torturing experience of a demonic exorcism. In fact, this term is employed most prominently in the last book of the Bible, where it describes the horrors of eschatological tribulation (Rev 9:5; 11:10; 12:2, etc.). Significant as well is its regular use in martyrdom narratives (2 Macc 7:13; *4 Macc* 6:5; *Mart. Pol.* 2:2). Mark is employing imagery to allude to the stressful circumstances of persecution and struggle in the Christian life.

This surprising imagery of being tortured on the sea fits in well with a literary analysis of the Gospel of Mark as a persecution tract. The historical background of Mark's audience is spelled out by Alan Richardson, who reports that this story is "a word of special encouragement to St. Mark's first readers, if (as is usually supposed) they were the Christians living in Rome during the days of Nero's persecution. It might seem to the faint-hearted that the Lord was asleep and indifferent to their peril; but in truth He is present in the Church and will arise and cast out the demon of the storm."[40] Pro-

---

40. Alan Richardson, *The Miracle Stories of the Gospels* (London: SCM, 1941), p. 92.

posals about the cultural background of the Gospel of Mark shine light
upon the text of Jesus' storm-stilling.

Examining other ancient writings, we discover in the literary background that the covenant community was commonly compared to a boat.
Listen to this interesting parallel from the *Testament of Naphtali* 6.

> [1]And again, after seven days, I saw our father Jacob standing by the sea of
> Jamnia, and we were with him. [2]And behold, there came a ship sailing by,
> without sailors or pilot; and there was written upon the ship, The Ship of
> Jacob. [3]And our father said to us: Come, let us embark on our ship. [4]And
> when he had gone on board, there arose a vehement storm, and a mighty
> tempest of wind; and our father, who was holding the helm, departed
> from us. [5]And we, being tossed with the tempest, were borne along over
> the sea; and the ship was filled with water, (and was) pounded by mighty
> waves, until it was broken up. [6]And Joseph fled away upon a little boat,
> and we were all divided upon nine planks, and Levi and Judah were to-
> gether. [7]And we were all scattered unto the ends of the earth. [8]Then Levi,
> girt about with sackcloth, prayed for us all unto the Lord. [9]And when the
> storm ceased, the ship reached the land as it were in peace. And, lo, our fa-
> ther came, and we all rejoiced with one accord.[41]

Documents from the cultural background indicate that the image of a ship
was understood symbolically in the Jewish exegetical tradition to apply to
the community. Thus Mark would naturally have applied this story to the
trials of his community as well.

In the history of interpretation, the church fathers offer the initial exegesis of the biblical narratives, and we encounter in Tertullian's writings (*On
Baptism* 12:5) a recognition of the ship as symbolic of the church.

> That little ship did present a figure of the Church, in that she is disquieted
> "in the sea," that is, in the world, "by the waves," that is, by persecutions
> and temptations; the Lord, through patience, sleeping as it were, until,
> roused in their last extremities by the prayers of the saints, He checks the
> world, and restores tranquility to His own.[42]

---

41. R. H. Charles, *Apocrypha and Pseudepigrapha of the Old Testament in English* (Oxford: Clarendon, 1913), 2:338. This can be found electronically in Logos Bible Software. The
Testament of the Twelve Patriarchs contains Christian additions but is usually seen as a Jewish document, so that the boat would here refer to the Jewish covenant community.

42. In *The Ante-Nicene Fathers: Translations of the Writings of the Fathers down to* A.D. *325,*

The history of interpretation, therefore, confirms our reading of the passage. This story is intended to apply to the entire church and not just to the twelve who experienced the storm.

We have demonstrated that grammatical, literary, and historical exegesis as well as the history of interpretation support the conclusions of spiritual exegesis. Therefore, if we listen prophetically to the text and place ourselves into the story through imaginative application, we can visualize ourselves unable to reach the desired destination of the kingdom of God. But right before morning dawns, suddenly Christ appears walking on the water. We think he will pass us by, but no! The "passing by" turns out to hold a divine epiphany. We thought we were alone, but Christ was praying for us in heaven, saw our every move from his perch in the sky, and came to rescue us. This story then becomes a paradigm mirroring our life experience. We are never alone; Christ in his divine sovereignty is the "I am."

Finally, the text concludes with the disciples in a state of fear, misunderstanding, and hardness of heart (Mark 6:52). Here we employ the spiritual discipline of praying Scripture and intercede for ourselves. We pray that, through our meditation upon the disciples' experience, we will never fall into the same state of faithlessness that plagued them. This spiritual reading of the text enables us to maintain a humble, receptive, practicing faith perspective in all of life's circumstances.

This example drawn from Mark 6:45-51 demonstrates how the reader can employ all the exegetical journeys of grammatical-historical exegesis as well as the techniques of spiritual exegesis to appropriate a full understanding of the text.

---

ed. Alexander Roberts, James Donaldson, and A. Cleveland Coxe (Oak Harbor: Logos Research Systems, 1997), 3:675.

Study and Discussion Questions

1. What insufficiencies of the historical-critical method described in this chapter stick out to you? How would you evaluate the statement by Gordon Fee in his book *Listening to the Spirit in the Text,* "I would argue that the exegetical process is not completed until we return to the proper posture of objects being addressed by the subject"?[43]

2. What types of spiritual exegesis have you employed in the past? Offer examples. What methods of spiritual exegesis are completely new?

3. What dangers of spiritual exegesis are you particularly aware of and concerned about?

4. What is the difference between an informational reading of the Bible and a formational reading of Scripture? Give an example of each.

5. What do you consider to be the role of the Holy Spirit in the production, interpretation, application, and proclamation of Scripture? What is the testimony of the Holy Spirit? What is true and untrue about Robert Stein's statement, "Christians with the Spirit of God are unlikely to have any advantage of insight over non-Christians laboring without the Spirit of God when it comes to unpacking the meaning of a biblical text."[44]

6. Stanley Hauerwas is fond of saying, "The lives of the saints are the hermeneutical key to Scripture," and Richard Hays explains that "the right reading of the New Testament occurs only where the Word is embodied." How do you evaluate these statements? Offer examples where disobedience to a biblical imperative has resulted in a wrong interpretation of Scripture. Where have positive examples of modeling the word of God resulted in significant insights into the Bible?

7. Robert Mulholland advises his readers to imagine creatively the sights, sounds, smells, and voices in the narrative and personally relive the story. Read the story about Jesus and the Samaritan woman at the well (John 4:4-

---

43. Gordon D. Fee, *Listening to the Spirit in the Text* (Grand Rapids: Eerdmans, 2000), p. 14.
44. Stein, *Playing by the Rules*, pp. 69-71. See Scorgie, *JETS* 44 (2001): 274.

42). Imagine a close contact between a man and a woman in a Near Eastern culture, a Jew and a Samaritan, a celibate and a person married at least five times. Now offer parallels in our own culture. Finally, what does it feel like to be thirsty, and who is thirsty in the story and in our world?

Some additional questions to ponder include: What is the look upon the faces of Jesus' disciples when they return? Why does the author notice that the woman left her water jug at the well (4:28)? How do the descriptions of Jesus deepen throughout the narrative (4:9, 12, 14, 19, 25, 29, 42)?

8. Personalizing Scripture and theology is an important spiritual discipline. It is customary in discussions of eucharistic theology to outline the various views of transubstantiation, consubstantiation, and "nonsubstantiation." Instead, to develop a practice-oriented exegesis, attempt to discern what understandings of divine presence and absence are at work within you and your congregation or spiritual community. In the same way, discussions about baptism regularly rehearse the standard arguments for and against infant baptism or believer baptism. Instead, reflect on how you can more deeply claim and celebrate your baptismal identity.

9. What are the blessings and responsibilities of meditating upon Scripture as outlined in some of the following passages: Josh 1:8; Deut 6:6-9; Prov 3:22-24; 6:22; 15:28; and Pss 19:14; 49:3; 119:15, 23, 48, 78, 97, 99, 148.

10. Discover connections between your life story and the great stories of God's redemptive work in the Bible. This discipline of spiritual exegesis is called paradigm building. Think of such imagery as the exodus, the wilderness, the retaking of the promised land, the rediscovery of the law in the temple during the time of Josiah, the rebuilding of the walls of Jerusalem, and the metaphors of death and resurrection that Paul employs in such passages as Rom 6:3-7; Eph 4:22-24; and Col 2:20–3:4. How does this imagery provide vision for your life?

11. Practice praying the Scripture back to God. Take one of the praise psalms like Psalm 100 and re-express the sentiments of the Psalmist back to God in your own words. Now turn to a lament like Lam 3:1-20 ending with 3:21-26 to practice expressing your negative emotions and struggles to the Lord. Or again transform the words of Paul's theology as in Col 2:11-15 into a prayer of praise and intercession to God as well as a hortatory section like Eph 6:10-17.

Conclusion

Our journey of learning exegesis has led us down eight different paths. We have traveled the road of literary, grammatical, structural, contextual, historical, traditional, theological, and spiritual exegesis. But in the process we have discovered that each road directs and guides us toward the identical destination, the meaning of the text. Through the use of an abundant array of scriptural examples rather than a theoretical analysis of hermeneutics, we have demonstrated how each of these methods of exegesis can shine new light upon our current understandings of the biblical text.

After assembling the results obtained through each of these methods of exegesis, the reader is now ready to draw conclusions about the content of a passage. This could be entitled content analysis, a synthetic approach employed near the end of the exegetical process. Then conclusions about the central content of a passage lead to the practice of application whereby we address a particular audience through a sermon or Bible study. Several steps in the process of application can be distinguished:

1. Ascertain the major thematic idea of the pericope.
2. Integrate the major theme into the overall structure and total message of the book.
3. Exegete your audience just as you did the text until you are confident that your message will be both meaningful and relevant. Here we must recognize that it is insufficient to exegete the text and the ancient culture unless our audience is exegeted as well.

4. State the need that you are addressing and describe your intended audience.

5. Prepare applications that speak to the varied needs and challenges of your total audience.

6. Construct an outline of your message or Bible study, including an introduction that speaks to the needs of your audience and a conclusion that summarizes your main point.

7. Finally, you are ready to write your message. Gordon Fee offers the helpful advice that "What the passage treats as significant is probably what the sermon should treat as significant; what you feel is most helpful and important to you personally is probably what the congregation will find most helpful and important to them."[1]

Frequently the young preacher or Christian leader feels compelled to include in one's message everything that is in the text. Instead, the more profitable procedure is to be selective in our application and pointed in our message. In addition, rather than organizing one's thoughts into a homily that exactly follows the flow of the passage, it is frequently more appropriate to reconstruct the text creatively in order to organize the message according to the needs of the audience. Now we have moved from text to sermon, from exegesis to application. We have employed various types of exegetical cameras to capture the multidimensional angles of the text. But now we have an opportunity to film a sequel to the biblical narratives by re-speaking and re-enacting the ancient text in our lives and in our ministries to our contemporary audience. Now the camera is aimed at us.

1. Gordon D. Fee, *New Testament Exegesis: A Handbook for Students and Pastors,* 3rd ed. (Louisville: Westminster John Knox, 2002), p. 152.

Genres

I. A Morphology of Genre

The biblical genre can be specified in a number of ways. The unique presupposition in our approach states that the categorization of genre traces back to real life people with specific vocations in the culture where the genres arose. Thus the narrative literature was personified in the life work of storytellers and scribes and the prophetic literature in those who played the role of prophet or apocalyptic seer; the liturgical literature was developed by the priest and worship leader; the legal literature was personified in the king, ruler, or judge; and the instruction was carried out by the wise man, philosopher, and pastor-teacher. Therefore, the following distinctions of genre are based upon the distinctive roles that different leaders played in their various cultures.

A. Narrative personified by the storyteller and scribe

   1. Narrated History
      a. Historical Account
         A historical account for the ancients consisted of actions *(praxeis)* and speeches *(logoi)*.[1] Standardized paradigms include:
         1) Call Narratives[2]

1. Cf. Gerhard von Rad, *The Problem of the Hexateuch* (London: SCM, 1984), pp. 192, 201.
2. See Norman Habel, "The Form and Significance of the Call Narrative," *ZAW* 77 (1965): 297-323.

        a) Divine confrontation

        b) Introductory word

        c) Commission

        d) Objection

        e) Reassurance

        f) Sign

            Examples: Gen 1:28-30; 12:1-4a; 17:1-14; Exod 3:1–4:16; Num 22:22-35; Deut 31:14-15; Josh 1:1-11; 1 Sam 3:1–4:1a; Isaiah 6; Jer 1:1-10; Ezekiel 2; Matt 28:1-8; 28:16-20; Luke 1:5-25; 1:26-38; 2:8-20; 24:36-53; John 20:19-23; Acts 9:1-9; 9:10-17; 10:1-8; 10:9-23; 22:6-11; 22:17-21; 23:11; 26:12-20; 27:21-26; Rev 1:12-20; 10:1–11:2.

    2) Annunciation Scenes[3]

        a) The appearance of an angel of the Lord or the Lord himself

        b) Fear or prostration of the visionary confronted by this supernatural presence

        c) The divine message

            a. A visionary is addressed by name.

            b. A qualifying phrase describes the visionary.

            c. The visionary is urged not to be afraid.

            d. A (barren) woman is with child or about to be with child.

            e. She will give birth to a (male) child.

            f. The name by which the child is to be called is revealed.

            g. An etymology interpreting the name is given.

            h. The future accomplishments of the child are narrated.

        d) An objection by the visionary as to how this can be or a request for a sign

        e) The giving of a sign to reassure the visionary

            Examples: Gen 18:1-15; Judges 13; 1 Samuel 1; 2 Kgs 4:8-37; Luke 1:11-20; Matt 1:20-21.

    3) Betrothal Scenes: a prospective bridegroom or his representative journeys to a foreign land, where he en-

---

3. See Raymond E. Brown, *The Birth of the Messiah* (Garden City: Doubleday, 1979), p. 156, for the five steps.

counters a young woman at a well. After an initial
meeting where one of them draws water, the woman
hurries home to share the news followed by a common
meal and betrothal.

Examples: Gen 24:10-61; 29:1-20; Exod 2:15b-21; Ruth;
spiritually, John 4:1-42.

  b. Saga and Legend

According to G. B. Caird, "Saga is the name we give to
historical memories which antedate written records. . . .
Legend is the embellishment of the story of genuine persons and events with anecdotes or details supposed to be
illustrative of their character or significance."[4]

Examples: Moses is assigned authorship of not only the
whole written Torah but also the oral tradition of rabbinic
interpretation (*Pirke Aboth* 1:1). Cf. *Life of Adam and Eve;
Lives of the Prophets; Jannes and Jambres; History of the
Rechabites; Eldad and Modad; History of Joseph; Joseph and
Aseneth; Martrydom and Ascension of Isaiah; Jubilees;
Pseudo-Philo.*

  c. Myth

According to Rudolf Bultmann, "Mythology is the use of
imagery to express the otherworldly in terms of this world
and the divine in terms of human life, the other side in
terms of this side."[5] Stanley Saunders demonstrates the
practical application of myth by stating that "Myth is the
organization of 'mystery' and 'muttering' in the form of
primary stories . . . by which we communicate with one
another, make sense of life, and form our social contracts."[6] Caird applies this definition to employing history
to establish one's identity by contending that "the thought
world of myth . . . was rather a fund of powerfully emo-
tive language on which creative thinkers could draw 'along

4. G. B. Caird, *The Language and Imagery of the Bible* (Grand Rapids: Eerdmans, 1980),
pp. 204-5.

5. Rudolf Bultmann, *Kerygma and Myth: A Theological Debate* (New York: Harper and
Brothers, 1961), p. 10, n. 2.

6. Stanley P. Saunders, "Revelation and Resistance: Narrative and Worship in John's
Apocalypse," in *Narrative Reading, Narrative Preaching,* ed. Joel Green and Michael
Pasquarello III (Grand Rapids: Baker, 2003), p. 132.

morally persuasive lines', to lead their people into ever deepening appreciation of the significance of their national history."[7] He enumerates three characteristics that transform a story into a myth: "it must be told in order to explain facts, practices, beliefs, or experiences of the present; it must embody some ultimate truth about human existence or some universal aspiration; and it must provide imagery by which men in every generation can interpret and express their own experience."[8]

Examples: the combat myth in Revelation 12; see Bailey and Vander Broek, *Literary Forms in the New Testament*, 208.

   d. Etiological Tale

The etiological story ties a biblical name with the origination of a place, custom, or tradition.[9]

> Examples: Gen 32:22-32; 35:9-14; Judg 6:11-24, 25-32; within Gen 1-11 and the Elijah-Elisha cycle. See Gerhard von Rad, *Problem of the Hexateuch*, 168-76.

   e. Fable

This genre humanizes the world of animals in order to mirror human behavior.

Examples: Judg 9:7-15 (fable of Jotham); 2 Kgs 14:9 (fable of Jehoash).

   f. Covenant Renewal

     1) Rehearsal of Yahweh's saving acts in the past

     2) Announcement of blessings and curses in formulated antithetical conditions

     3) Apodictic commands for obedience

     4) Concluding threat of curse if obedience is not rendered

       Examples: Gen 9:1-17; 15:1-21; 17:1-27; 22:1-18; Deuteronomy 27–30; 2 Samuel 7.

        Royal Grant Covenant

        a) Preamble (Deut 1:1-5)

        b) Historical prologue recounting the previous his-

---

7. Caird, *Language and Imagery*, p. 232; see pp. 220-23 for seven categories.

8. G. B. Caird, *A Commentary on the Revelation of St. John the Divine*. HNTC (New York: Harper and Row, 1966), p. 66.

9. See von Rad, *Problem of the Hexateuch*, pp. 168-72.

tory of the relationship between the two parties
of the covenant (Deut 1:6–3:29)

c) Statement of the relationship (Deuteronomy 4–11)

d) Stipulations of the covenant (Deuteronomy 12–
26)

e) List of gods as witnesses (Deut 27:2-3; 30:19; 31:19,
21, 26, 28, 30; 32:1, 46)

f) Curses and blessings (Deut 27:11-26; 28)

g. Lists (annals, chronicles, genealogies, catalogues)
Paul Achtemeier perceptively captures the purpose of genealogies when he explains, "Genealogies are not marked
by strict biological accuracy, but serve instead to structure
history, to mediate status and power" and "serve important social roles since they provide the basis for membership in particular groups of kin."[10]

Examples: Gen 5:1-32; 10:1-32; 36:9-43; 46:8-27; Exod
6:14-25; Num 1:5-46; 2:3-33; 26:4-62; 33:3-49; 34:19-28;
Joshua 12; 14-21; Ruth 4:18-22; 2 Sam 23:8-39; 1 Kgs 4:1-
19; 1 Chr 1-9; 11:26-47; 23:7-23; 24:7-30; 25:9-31; 26:1-11;
26:23-32; 27:1-34; Ezra 2; 8:1-14; 10:18-43; Neh 7:8-73;
10:1-27; 11:1–12:26; Matt 1:1-17; Luke 3:23-38.

2. Biography
Biography can be defined as "a discrete prose narrative de-
voted exclusively to the portrayal of the whole life of a particular individual perceived as historical."[11] In biography, a
person's achievements illustrate character, while in history
achievements are part of the broad historical framework. Included in biography are such subgenres as *chreiai* (anecdotes), *gnomai* (maxims), and *apomnemoneumata* (reminis-
cences).

a. Examples of biblical *novella*: Ruth, Judith, Easter, Tobit,
parts of Job and Daniel, Jonah.

b. Greco-Roman biographies

1) First surviving examples, fourth century B.C. (Isocrates,

10. Paul J. Achtemeier, Joel B. Green, and Marianne Meye Thompson, *Introducing the
New Testament: Its Literature and Theology* (Grand Rapids: Eerdmans, 2001), p. 75.
11. David E. Aune, *The New Testament in Its Literary Environment* (Philadelphia: Westminster, 1987), p. 29.

Evagoras; Xenophon, *Agesilaus, Memorabilia, Education of Cyrus*)

2) No biographies from the third and second centuries are preserved except papyrus fragments of Satyrus, *Life of Euripides* (P.Oxy. 1176)

3) First century B.C. (some biographies from the Roman writer Cornelius Nepos)

4) First to fourth centuries A.D. Plutarch's *Lives* (statesmen); Suetonius (emperors, *Lives of the Caesars;* literary figures, orators); Diogenes Laertius, *Lives of the Ancient Philosophers;* Lucian, *Demonax;* Philostratus, *Life of Apollonius of Tyana;* Porphyry, *Life of Pythagoras; Life of Plotinus;* Iamblichus, *Life of Pythagoras.*

   a) Anonymous lives of poets: *Life of Pindar* (P.Oxy. 2438); Pseudo-Hesiod, *Life of Homer*

   b) Anonymous biographies: Secundus the Silent Philosopher; *Life of Aesop*

   c) Twenty-five fictional imperial biographies of the *Historia Augusta* (ca. 395 A.D.)

5) Finally called *biographia* by Damascius, *Life of Isidore* in fifth century A.D.

c. Encomiastic biography (advocate various virtues): Philo, *Life of Abraham; Joseph; Moses;* Xenophon, *Agesilaus;* Plutarch, *Alexander* 1:1-3; *Pompey* 8:6

   1) Abraham is viewed as wisdom through study; Isaac is wisdom through nature; Jacob is wisdom through practice (*On Joseph* 1).

   2) Enos is seen as hope (*Abr.* 7-16; Gen 4:26 LXX), Enoch as repentance (*Abr.* 17-26; Gen 5:24), Noah as justice (*Abr.* 27-46; *Praem.* 11-17; Gen 6:9).

d. Early church history: "Life of Origen" in Eusebius, *EH* 6

3. Gospel

Gospel can be categorized as a subset of biography, but its uniqueness consists in being kerygmatic history or preached biography.

Examples:

1) Canonical gospels: Matthew, Mark, Luke, John.

2) Apocryphal gospels: *Gospel of the Nazaraeans, Ebionites, Hebrews; Secret Gospel of Mark.*

3) Nag Hammadi gospels: *Gospel of Truth* (philosophical discourse), *Thomas* (sayings of Jesus), *Judas* (contrast with other disciples), *Philip* (teaching on the sacraments and ethics), *Egyptians* (life and redemptive activity of Seth), and *Mary* (revelation discourse of the risen Jesus with his disciples)

Sub-genres include:

a. Parable

A short narrative fiction to reference a transcendent symbol that is subdivided into:

1) Simile (explicit comparison) or metaphor (implicit comparison) with three parts:

   a) The illustration half *(Bildhälfte):* topic or item illustrated by the image

   b) The actuality half *(Sachhälfte):* the image itself

   c) *Tertium Comparationis:* the point of similarity or comparison

   Examples:

   Similes: Mark 10:15 par?; 14:48 par; Matt 6:29 par; 10:16; 12:40; 13:40, 43; 18:17; 23:27; 24:27, 37; 25:32-33; Luke 17:6 par; 13:34; Luke 10:18; 11:36; 17:28-30; 21:34-35; 22:31.

   Metaphors: Mark 1:17 par; 2:17, 19-20; 3:34-35; 7:26-27; 8:15, 34; 9:49-50; 10:38-39; 14:22, 24, 36; Matt 5:13-16; 6:22 par; 7:6, 13-14, 15, 16-20; 9:37-38; 10:6, 16, 34; 11:7, 29-30; 12:34; 15:13; 16:18; 19:12; 23:33; Luke 9:62; 12:35, 49; 13:31-32; 15:32; 23:31.

2) Similitude: a simile expanded into a picture; a brief, straightforward picture narrative using one or more verbs in the present tense to apply some commonly recurrent typical event to a greater spiritual reality

3) Parable: a simile expanded into a story; a narrative that juxtaposes reality with a transcendent symbol to develop a comparison with metaphorical character, vivid realism, surprising, and often ambiguous features that prompt active participation

4) Example Story: a similitude describing characters who serve as examples, as in the Good Samaritan (Luke

10:29-37), the Rich Fool (Luke 12:16-21), and the Rich
Man and Lazarus (Luke 16:19-31)

    5) Allegory: a series of metaphors strung together, establishing an extended and systematic comparison at a number of points

  b. Miracle Story

A miracle story includes the following subdivisions:

    1) Exorcism[12]

      a) Confrontation

        a. Meeting of exorcist and possessed

        b. The demon's warding-off formula

        c. The exorcist's rebuke and silencing

      b) Expulsion

        a. Command to exit

        b. Demon's violent exit

      c) Acclamation

        a. Choral formula

        b. Propagation of cure

          Examples: Mark 1:23-28; 5:1-20; 9:14-29; Luke 11:14; Matt 9:32-33.

    2) Healing Story which has three characteristics with a variety of possible formulations:[13]

      a) Exposition of Healing

        a. Arrival of healer and sick person

        b. Staging of a public forum (onlookers)

        c. Explication of sickness

        d. Request for help

        e. Public scorn or skepticism

      b) Performance of Healing

        a. Utterance of healing formula

        b. Healing gestures

        c. Statement of cure

      c) Confirmation of Healing

        a. Admiration/confirmation formula

---

12. This material comes from Werner H. Kelber, *The Oral and the Written Gospel: The Hermeneutics of Speaking and Writing in the Synoptic Tradition, Mark, Paul, and Q* (Philadelphia: Fortress, 1983), p. 52.

13. Kelber, *Oral and Written Gospel*, p. 46.

          b. Dismissal of the healed person

          c. Injunction of secrecy

          d. Propagation of healer's fame

          Examples: Mark 1:29-31 (Peter's mother-in-law); 1:40-45 (leper); 2:1-12 (paralytic); 3:1-5 (paralyzed hand); 5:21-43 (bleeding woman and dead girl); 7:24-30 (Syrophoenician's daughter); 7:31-37 (deaf-mute); 8:22-26 (blind man); 10:46-52 (blind Bartimaeus); Luke 7:11-17 (widow of Nain's son); 13:10-17 (crippled woman); 14:1-6 (man with dropsy); 17:11-19 (ten lepers); John 2:1-11 (water turned to wine); 4:46-54 (official's son); 5:1-11 (lame man at Bethesda); 9:1-11 (man blind from birth); 11:1-44 (raising of Lazarus).

     3) Provision Story

        Examples: feedings (Mark 6:30-44; 8:1-10; John 6:1-14), safety in a storm (Mark 4:35-41), money for taxes (Matt 17:24-27); freedom from imprisonment (Acts 12:1ff.; 16:16ff.).

     4) Epiphany (revelation miracle; sign)

        Examples: Mark 6:45-52/Matt 14:22-33; Luke 5:1-11; signs in John.

  c. Controversy Dialogue

    Other terms for this genre include pronouncement story (Taylor); apophthegm (Bultmann); paradigm (Dibelius); and *chreia* (Robbins, Mack).

     1) Definition of a pronouncement story: a brief story about a well-known person that culminates in a short, striking saying that is applicable to continuing situations.

     2) Types of Controversy Dialogues

        a) Bultmann distinguishes three types: controversy dialogues, scholastic dialogues, and biographical apophthegms.[14]

        b) Robert Tannehill advocates six types:[15]

---

14. Rudolf Bultmann, *History of the Synoptic Tradition* (New York: Harper & Row, 1963), pp. 39-61.

15. Robert C. Tannehill, "Introduction: The Pronouncement Story and Its Types," *Semeia* 20 (1981): 1-13; and "Varieties of Synoptic Pronouncement Stories," pp. 101-19.

a. Correction story: ends with the main character correcting one or more individuals (Mark 1:35-38; 9:33-37).

b. Commendation story: ends with the main character commending (Matt 13:51-52; Mark 10:13-16; Luke 10:17-20; 17:12-19).

c. Objection story: an objection calls forth the response of the main character (Matt 3:13-15; 18:21-22; Mark 2:15-17; Luke 11:27-28).

d. Quest story: depicts a secondary character's quest for success and the response of the main character (Matt 8:5-13; Mark 7:24-30 par.; Mark 10:17-22; 12:28-34; Luke 7:36-50; 19:1-10).

e. Inquiry story: response to an inquiry (Mark 7:17-23; Luke 3:10-14)

f. Description story: ends with a description of the situation by the main character (Luke 14:15-24).

c) The categories identified by Vernon Robbins include:[16]

a. Two kinds of aphoristic pronouncement stories, the description and the inquiry.

b. Two basic types of adversative pronouncement stories, the correction and the dissent.

c. Two basic types of affirmative pronouncement stories, the commendation and the laudation.

3) <u>Constituent Elements</u>

a) Three Essential Ingredients

a. Situation initiating a conversation or debate

b. Question or accusation

c. Pronouncement saying

b) Werner Kelber envisions the following five constituent parts:[17]

a. *Mise en scène*

b. Raising of (provocative) question

c. Protagonist's counterquestion

---

16. Vernon Robbins, "Classifying Pronouncement Stories in Plutarch's Parallel Lives," *Semeia* 20 (1981): 29.

17. Kelber, *Oral and Written Gospel*, p. 56.

  d. Response by inquirer(s)

  e. Protagonist's answer: memorable saying

 c) Five Frequent Elements in the Canonical Gospels
(see Appendix I, Section II below, pp. 333-44)

  a. Description of a conflict situation

  b. Question by Jesus' opponents

  c. Jesus' return question (and sometimes an answer
to this question or a response)

  d. The pronouncement saying

  e. Response by the crowd or additional concluding
saying

4) <u>Examples</u> have been conveniently assembled by Burton L. Mack, who recites the lists of Tannehill, Bultmann, and Taylor; Arland Hultgren, who combines the lists of Albertz, Bultmann, Dibelius, and Taylor; and Bailey and Vander Broek.[18]

Eleven pure examples are frequently enumerated: Mark 2:15-17; 2:18-22; 2:23-28; 3:31-34; 10:13-16; 10:17-22; 10:35-40; 12:13-17; 12:18-27; 14:3-9; Luke 14:1-6.[19]

See Appendix I, Section II below for our list.

5) The <u>Function</u>: A theological, christological, and social function is exemplified in the five controversies of Mark 2:1–3:6:

 a) A Kingdom Theology Function

  a. Forgiveness of sins becomes a present reality (saying in Mark 2:9)

  b. The marginalized leftovers are welcomed to the feast (saying at Mark 2:17a)

  c. The marriage party has begun with joy (saying at Mark 2:19a)

  d. The eternal rest of the Sabbath is here (saying at Mark 2:27)

---

18. Burton L. Mack, *A Myth of Innocence: Mark and Christian Origins* (Philadelphia: Fortress, 1988), pp. 379-84; Arland J. Hultgren, *Jesus and His Adversaries: The Form and Function of the Conflict Stories in the Synoptic Tradition* (Minneapolis: Augsburg, 1979), pp. 203-5; James L. Bailey and Lyle D. Vander Broek, *Literary Forms in the New Testament: A Handbook* (Louisville: Westminster John Knox, 1992), p. 121.

19. James L. Bailey, "Genre Analysis," in *Hearing the New Testament: Strategies for Interpretation,* ed. Joel Green, 2nd ed. (Grand Rapids: Eerdmans, 2010), p. 152.

  e. Bodies are healed (saying at Mark 3:4a)

 b) A Christological Function (Jesus' authority as king of the kingdom)

  a. Mark 2:10: "The Son of Man has authority on earth to forgive sins"

  b. Mark 2:17b: "I have not come to call the righteous, but sinners"

  c. Mark 2:19: "How can the guests of the bridegroom fast while he is with them?"

  d. Mark 2:28: "The Son of Man is Lord even of the Sabbath"

  e. Mark 3:4: The Messiah's actions replace his person: "to do good" and "to save life"

 c) A Socially Demarcating Function[20]

  a. Mark 2:1-12: The Christian community proclaims forgiveness now through Jesus vs. the Jewish expectation of a future salvation or forgiveness now through sacrifices at the temple.

  b. Mark 2:13-17: The marginalized are included in the Christian community vs. being seen as impure sinners to be excluded from the Jewish community.

  c. Mark 2:18-22: The Christian community has created new wineskins and is the new garment since the joy of the kingdom has come: the incompatibility of old and new.

  d. Mark 2:23-28: A legalistic maintenance of Sabbath regulations is replaced by an emphasis on the benefits of the resurrection (new eternal Sabbath) in the Christian community.

  e. Mark 3:1-6: The Christian community is the group that "does good and saves life" vs. the Jewish community that has killed the Messiah.

d. Call to Discipleship Story (especially in the Gospel of Mark)

---

20. Gerd Theissen, *The Gospels in Context: Social and Political History in the Synoptic Tradition* (Minneapolis: Fortress, 1991), p. 116, explains that "in the synoptic apophthegms one group affirms its own convictions and behavior by differentiating itself from other surrounding groups."

1) The constituent elements include:
   a) Jesus sees the person (instead of the normal seeking of a rabbi by a disciple)
      1:16: Jesus saw Simon and Andrew
      1:19: Jesus saw James and John
      2:14: Jesus saw Levi sitting at his tax booth
      8:34a: Jesus summoned the crowd with his disciples
   b) Jesus calls the person
      1:17: "Come, follow me"
      1:20: "Without delay he called them"
      2:14: "Follow me"
      8:34b: "If anyone would come after me"
   c) The potential disciple leaves something behind
      1:18: Left their nets
      1:20: Left their father Zebedee
      2:14: Levi got up = left tax collecting
      8:34c: "Let him deny himself and take up his cross"
   d) The disciple follows Jesus
      1:18, 20; 2:14: Followed him
      8:34d: "And continue to follow me"
2) Genre become mixed, so that a healing narrative becomes a discipleship story: Mark 10:46-52 contains the elements of both a miracle and discipleship story.
   a) Jesus sees him: 10:49a: Jesus stopped traveling toward Jerusalem
   b) Jesus calls the blind man: 10:49b: "On your feet, he's calling you"
   c) Something is left behind: 10:50: "throwing his cloak aside" = leaves his begging blanket behind
   d) The disciple follows Jesus: 10:52: "He followed Jesus along the road"
e. The Symposium
   Paul Achtemeier points out that "In contemporary practice and literature, the symposium was the second course of a banquet, a drinking-and-talking party."[21] The characters include the host renowned for his wealth, the special guest notable for his wit and wisdom, and others who

---

21. Achtemeier, Green, and Thompson, *Introducing the New Testament*, p. 76.

participate in the discussion with proper etiquette concerning social status to win the favor of the host.

Examples: Luke's meal gatherings should be read against this background: Luke 5:27-32; 7:36-50; 14:1-24; 22:24-27.

f. Passion Narrative

A passion narrative is the story of the suffering and vindication of a righteous person.

Examples:

The Gospels devote a significant amount of material to Jesus' suffering and death (Matt 26–27; Mark 14–15; Luke 22–23; John 12–19).

Precedents for this material include: the accounts of Joseph in Genesis 37–42; Jeremiah's persecutions (Jeremiah 26; 37–38); Daniel 1–6; the Servant Songs of Isaiah (Isa 52:13–53:12), the psalms of the innocent sufferer, e.g., Psalm 22; 2 Maccabees 7; Wisdom 1–2, 4.

4. Fiction

The novel was not written to rehearse history but to entertain.

Examples:

1) In Greco-Roman Literature: Chariton's *Chaereas and Callirhoë* is dated between the first century B.C. and first century A.D.; surviving examples from the second century A.D. include Xenophon's *Ephesiaka;* Iamblichus's *Babyloniaka;* Longus's *Daphnis and Chloe;* Achilles Tatius's *Leucippe and Clitophon.*

2) The apocryphal gospels and acts developed about the same time as the high point of the novel.[22]

B. Prophetic Literature personified by the prophet/seer

1. Prophecy

a. Oracles of Judgment

1) Threat or Indictment *(Gerichtswort)*

a) Elements[23]

---

22. Aune, *The New Testament in Its Literary Environment,* pp. 151-53.

23. Cf. Claus Westermann, *Basic Forms of Prophetic Speech* (Philadelphia: Westminster, 1967), pp. 142ff., 169ff., esp. 174-75, for examples, with a list of oracles of judgment against individuals on p. 137.

    a. Introduction and summons to hear

    b. Accusation and its development

    c. Messenger formula (thus says the Lord)

    d. Intervention by God with a prediction of disaster

b) Three Types of Threats:

    a. An indictment against Israel

Examples: Cf. Westermann, *Basic Forms of Prophetic Speech,* 169-76: Jeremiah has extended judgment sermons followed by laments in Jer 8:4–10:25: Sermon no. 1: Babylonians are coming (8:4-17) and lament (8:18–9:1); Sermon no. 2: Jerusalem will be destroyed (9:2–10:18); lament (10:19-25).

    b. Judgment against the nations

Examples: Isaiah 13–23; Jeremiah 46–51; Ezekiel 25–32; Amos 1–2; Obadiah; Zeph 2:4-15; Nahum.

    c. A disputation speech *(Streitgesprach):*

      i. Description: the prophet uses the people's own statements to reveal their errors.

      ii. Elements:

        1. An introductory formula or initial statement

        2. A quotation of one's opponent to show their errors

        3. A refutation that points out the error of their reasoning

Examples: Isa 28:14-19; 28:23-29; Jer 31:29-30; 33:23-26; Ezek 18:1-20; Mic 2:6-11 (cf. Westermann, *Basic Forms of Prophetic Speech,* p. 201).

      iii. Malachi is organized into six controversies or disputations:

        1. God and Israel contend over the extent to which Yahweh is committed to his people (1:2-5)

        2. Discussion with priests about giving God his due (1:6–2:9)

        3. Dispute over people who commit divorce (2:10-16)

        4. Calling good what is evil (2:17–3:5)

        5. Withholding tithes is robbing God (3:6-12)

6. Evildoers seem to prosper, but the day of
the Lord approaches (3:13–4:3)
2) Covenant Lawsuit (judicial debating)
a) Description: a summons to the divine law court
with a trial setting where witnesses are called, leading to an indictment of guilt upon Israel or the nations and the sentence due.
b) Elements in the genre[24]
a. Introduction calling the audience to hear, with a
frequent appeal to the heavens and earth as witnesses.
b. Statement of the accusation along with a ques-
tioning of the witnesses.
c. The prosecuting attorney addresses the court,
contrasting the sins of the people with the saving
acts of God.
d. The inability of cultic rituals to atone for these
wrong acts.
e. A warning followed by a call to return to God
and obey his commands.
Examples: Mic 6:1-2; Hos 4:1-17; Isa 3:13-26; 41:21-
24. Yahweh's judgment upon the gods of the nations: Isa 41:1-5; 41:21-29; 43:8-15; 44:6-8 or upon
Israel: Isa 42:18-25; 43:22-28; 50:1-3.
3) Woes
Description: a judgment prophecy that contains "woe"
(hôy) followed by a series of participles detailing the
subject, transgression, and judgment.
Examples: Six in Isa 5:8-24 (also 10:1); six in Isaiah 28-
31; five in Hab 2:6-19; Amos 5:18-20; Mic 2:1-4; Nah 3:1-
7 (cf. Westermann, *Basic Forms of Prophetic Speech,* pp.
190-94).
4) Funeral Dirge: a lamentation because of destruction
Examples: Isa 14:4-21; 23:1-14; Jer 9:17-22; Ezek 19:1-14;
26:19-21; 27:2-11; Amos 5:1-2; Rev 18:1-24, esp. 2-3.

24. Cf. Trent C. Butler, "Announcements of Judgment," in *Cracking Old Testament Codes: A Guide to Interpreting Literary Genres of the Old Testament,* ed. D. Brent Sandy and Ronald L. Giese Jr. (Nashville: Broadman and Holman, 1995), p. 163.

5) Taunts and Curses
   Taunt examples: Mic 2:4; Nah 3:8-17.
   Curse examples: Judg 5:23; Gen 49:5-7; 9:25; Deut 27:15-26 (cf. Westermann, *Basic Forms of Prophetic Speech*, 194-98).

b. Announcements of Salvation *(Heilswort)*[25]
   Definition: a deliverance due to the intervention of God.

   1) Type one: Oracles of salvation, blessing, and restoration
      Examples: Cf. Westermann, *Prophetic Oracles of Salvation*, chs. 2-7 (pp. 39-191), with 157 texts described (35 examples in Deutero-Isaiah; 29 for Isaiah 1-39; 34 for the minor prophets; 38 for Jeremiah; 15 for Ezekiel; and 6 for Trito-Isaiah).
      Oracle collections include Isaiah 40-55; parts of Isaiah 56-66 (60-62); parts of Isaiah 32-35; Jeremiah 30–33; 3:6–4:4; Ezekiel 33-37 (38-39; 40-48); Amos 9:11-15; Micah 4-5; Zeph 3:11-20 (cf. Westermann, *Prophetic Oracles of Salvation*, 18).

   2) Type two: A twofold proclamation whereby the judgment on the enemy is followed by the deliverance of Israel. Westermann, *Prophetic Oracles of Salvation*, ch. 8, offers 39 texts. The finished prophetic books are frequently organized into cycles:
      a) Three cycles of accusation, punishment, restoration in Hosea
         a. Cycle 1 (4:1–6:3)
            i. Accusations: 4:1–5:2 (against the land, 4:1-3; priest, 4:4-10; cult, 4:12-19; and royal house, 5:1-2)
            ii. Punishment (5:3-15)
            iii. Restoration (6:1-3)
         b. Cycle 2 (6:4–11:12)
            i. Accusations (6:4–7:16)
            ii. Punishment (8:1–11:7)
            iii. Restoration (11:8-12)
         c. Cycle 3 (chs. 12–14)

---

25. The examples are taken from Claus Westermann, *Prophetic Oracles of Salvation in the Old Testament* (Louisville: Westminster John Knox, 1991).

              i. Accusation (12:1-2)

              ii. Punishment (12:3–13:16)

              iii. Call to restoration (14:1-9)

    b) Three oracles of judgment followed by oracles of salvation in Micah

        a. Cycle 1 (chs. 1–2)

             i. Judgment about Judah based on judgment of Israel (1:2–2:11)

             ii. Future salvation (2:12-13)

        b. Cycle 2 (chs. 3–5)

             i. Judgment against Judah's rulers (ch. 3)

             ii. Future salvation (chs. 4–5)

        c. Cycle 3 (chs. 6–7)

             i. Judgment (6:1–7:7)

             ii. Future salvation (7:8-20)

    c) Three cycles of punishment and restoration in Isa 2:6–11:16

        a. Cycle 1 (2:6–4:6)

             i. Problems and punishment (2:6–4:1)

             ii. Restoration through the Branch (4:2-6)

        b. Cycle 2 (5:1–9:7)

             i. Punishment (5:1-30)

             ii. The Syria-Ephraim War (6:1–9:6)

             iii. Restoration through a child (8:21–9:7)

        c. Cycle 3 (9:8–11:16)

             i. Punishment of Samaria and Judah (9:9–10:4)

             ii. Woes on Assyria (10:5-34)

             iii. Restoration through the Branch (11:1-16).

    d) Zephaniah is organized with:

        a. A threat against Judah (1:2–2:3)

        b. Oracles against the nations (2:4–3:7)

        c. Restoration to the nations (3:8-10)

        d. Restoration to Jerusalem (3:11-20)

3) <u>Type three</u>: Conditional oracles of salvation. Examples: Westermann, *Prophetic Oracles of Salvation,* ch. 9, lists 34 examples.

4) <u>Type four</u>: Passages that contrast the fate of the ungodly with that of the godly

Examples: Westermann, *Prophetic Oracles of Salvation,*
ch. 10, describes 16 texts.

c. Prophetic Actions
OT examples include Hosea marrying a harlot (Hos 1:2-9;
3:1-5); Ahijah tearing his new robe into ten pieces for
Jeroboam (1 Kgs 11:30); Isaiah walking around stripped of
his clothes and barefoot (Isa 20:1-6); Jeremiah smashing
the potter's jar (Jer 18:1-11), carrying a yoke bar through
the city (Jer 27:1-22; 28:10-11), and buying a field (Jer 32:6-
25); and Ezekiel eating a scroll (Ezek 3:1-9) and shaving
his head (Ezek 5:1-17).

See also Amos 7:7-9; 8:1-3; 9:1; Isa 7:1-9; 8:1-4; Jer 1:11-12;
1:13-16; 13:1-11; 16:1-4; 19:1-15; 24:1-10; 25:15-29; Ezek 3:24-27;
4:1-17; 12:1-20.[26]

NT examples include Jesus claiming his kingship at Jerusalem in a triumphal entry (Mark 11:1-11), cleansing the
temple (11:12-19), cursing the fig tree (11:20-26), and having a covenant meal with his disciples (14:12-31), and
Agabus binding his own feet and hands with Paul's girdle
(Acts 21:10-14).

d. Divine-Human Dialogue or Conversation
Examples: Jeremiah 12; 14:11-16; 15:1-4; 16:10-13; 24.

e. Narrative Accounts of the Prophets
Examples: Isaiah 36-39; Jeremiah 26-29; 32-45; 52; Haggai
1-2; Daniel 1-6.

f. Parable and Allegory
Examples: 2 Sam 12:1-7; Isa 5:1-7; Ezek 16:1-43; 17:1-21; 23:1-
27; 31:1-18.

g. Wisdom Sayings and Prophetic Torah
Examples of Torah: Isa 1:10-17; 8:11-15; Jer 7:21; Mic 6:6-8
(cf. Westermann, *Basic Forms of Prophetic Speech,* 203-4).
Examples of wisdom sayings: Amos 3:3-6; Isa 28:23-29;
Ezek 18:2.

h. Liturgical Elements

---

26. See also Edwin K. Broadhead, *Teaching with Authority: Miracles and Christology in
the Gospel of Mark.* JSNTSup 74 (Sheffield: Sheffield Academic, 1992), p. 173, n. 1.

Examples of <u>laments</u>: Amos 5:1-3; Jer 2:31-32; 8:4-7; 9:16-21; 10:19-20; 13:18-19, 23; Lament of Yahweh over his land: Jer 2:31-32; 12:7-13; 15:5-9; 18:13-17 (cf. Westermann, *Basic Forms of Prophetic Speech*, 202-3).

Examples of <u>doxologies</u>: Amos 4:13; 5:8-9; 9:5-6.

Examples of <u>songs</u> (usually concluding a section of prophecy): Isa 12:1-6; 24:14-16; 25:1-5; 26:1-21; 27:2-6; 42:10-13; 44:23; 45:8; 52:9-12.

2. Apocalyptic Literature
   a. Differences from Prophecy[27]
      1) Prophecy carries with it a contingency so that its outcome depends upon the actions of a certain group of people. The apocalyptist comforts the reader with the eschatological future.
      2) The prophetic future is a continuation of the present, whereas in apocalyptic there is a decisive break with the present age.
      3) Prophecy is poetic while apocalypse is prose, although highly figurative. Prophecy presents its message as direct speech from God, but apocalyptic employs graphic images, visions, and symbols.
      4) Prophecy urges people to repent from their sin, but apocalyptic considers that the only solution to the present wickedness is total destruction.
      5) Prophecy reveals God's displeasure with his chosen people, but apocalyptic assumes that the readers are themselves displeased with the evil around them, and so they are comforted by God.
   b. Characteristics of Apocalyptic Literature
      1) Employs symbolic language for socio-political realities.
      2) Filled with revelations of divine secrets that God makes known to elect individuals through extraordinary means.
      3) Takes over the themes of Old Testament prophecy.

---

27. Taken from W. Randolph Tate, *Biblical Interpretation: An Integrated Approach* (Peabody: Hendriksen, 1991), p. 139; and D. Brent Sandy and Martin G. Abegg Jr., "Apocalyptic," in Sandy and Giese, *Cracking OT Codes*, pp. 178-79.

4) Written in times of trouble and hopelessness to strengthen believers.

5) The awaited time of salvation is expected to dawn momentarily, so the documents are filled with eschatological fervor and calculate an imminent end.

6) A dualistic view of reality emphasizing the blessings of the future ideal age.

7) Offers a rational and systematic approach to history in order to demonstrate that God is in control of the present situation (periodization).

8) Describes past events of history as if future *(vaticinia ex eventu),* since it is written from the point of view of a previous age.

9) This study of history passes over into a prophecy and the immediate end of the world.

10) Pseudonymity (supposedly written by a person of a previous age) to provide authority.

c. Subgenres within Apocalyptic Literature

1) Eschatological oracles of judgment and renewal in the last times. These are prophetic precursors to apocalyptic or alternative works that are really prophecy with the inclusion of cryptic symbols.
Examples: Isaiah 24–27; Zechariah 12–14; Joel 2; Mark 13; 1 Corinthians 15; 2 Thessalonians 2; 2 Peter 3. The *Sibylline Oracles* lack the distinctive apocalyptic form of mediated revelation and an interest in the angelic world.

2) Visions
Examples: Daniel 7–12; Revelation; Ezekiel 1; 10–11; 37–48; Zechariah 1–6; *1 Enoch* 83–90; *Shepherd of Hermas* (Visions); seven visions in *4 Ezra* 3:1–5:20; 5:21–6:34; 6:35–9:25; 9:26–10:59; 11:1–12:51; 13:1-58; 14:1-48 and *2 Baruch* 6–7, 10:1-3; 13–20, 22–30, 36–43, 48–51, 53–76.

3) Otherworldly Journeys
Examples: *3 Enoch; Apocalypse of Paul; Apocalypse of Abraham* 10; *Gospel of Mary;* Allogenes; Aostrianos; Marsanes; *Three Steles of Seth;* tours by angels (Exodus 40; Rev 11:1-2; Zechariah 1); ascent into heaven (Rev 4:1; *1 Enoch* 14; *Apocalypse of Abraham* 19).

4) Historical Surveys (*ex eventu* prophecy)

Examples: Dan 2:24-43; 7:15-25; 8:19-25a; Dan 9:24-27a;
11:2-39; Revelation 6–11; *1 Enoch* 85–90; Apocalypse of
weeks in 91:12-17 and 93:1-10; *4 Ezra* 11–12; *Apocalypse of
Abraham* 27-28; *The Demotic Chronicle;* Persian *Zand-i
Vohuman yasn* or *Bahman Yasht; Potter's Oracle; Sib.
Or.* 4:49-101.

5) Revelation Dialogues

Examples: *Apocryphon of James, Epistle of the Apostles,
Thomas the Contender, First Apocalypse of James, Dialogue of the Savior, Sophia, Gospel of Mary, Letter of Peter to Philip, Apocalypse of Peter* (in part); Zostrianos;
Hypostasis of the Archons.

6) Redeemer Myth

Examples: *Paraphrase of Shem, Trimorphyic Protennoia;*
Hypiphrone, *Second Apocalypse of James; Tripartite
Tractate;* Sethite literature.

7) Calendologia

Example: *1 Enoch* 72–82.

8) Parables and Allegory

Examples: Ezek 17:2-24; *Shepherd of Hermas* (Similitudes); *1 Enoch* 37–71 (Similitudes).

9) Ethical Instruction

Examples: *Shepherd of Hermas* (Mandates); *1 Enoch* 94–
106 or *the Epistle of Enoch; 2 Baruch* 78–87.

3. Testaments

  a. Four Main Components

    1) Prediction of one's death

Examples: 2 Pet 1:13-15; John 13:33; 14:2-3; 16:16; *T. Moses* 1.

    2) Reminiscences of the past relationship

Examples: 2 Pet 1:17-18; John 13:33; 14:10; 15:3, 20; 17:4-8;
T. Moses 2–9.

    3) Prediction of what will happen afterward, especially
hard times and apostasy

Examples: 2 Pet 2; 3:3-7; John 15:18, 20; 16:2-3; *T. Moses* 10.

    4) Eschatological ethics

Examples: 2 Pet 3:11-18; *T. Levi* 13; *T. Dan* 5:1-3; 6:1ff.;
T. Naph. 8; to keep the commandments: John 14:15, 21,

23; 15:10, 14 and to keep unity among themselves: John
17:11, 21-23.

b. Nine Characteristics of a Testament[28]

    1) Announcement of approaching death
    2) Paraenetic sayings or exhortations
    3) Prophecies or predictions
    4) Retrospective accounts of the individual's life
    5) Determination of a successor, which is the paraclete in
       John
    6) Final instructions
    7) Prayer
    8) Not included are instructions about burial (since Jesus'
       burial occurs in John 19:38-42)
    9) Not included are promises and vows requested of the
       gathering (because of the disciples' failure to under-
       stand until the Spirit comes).

c. Biblical Examples:
    Jacob in Gen 47:29–49:33; Moses in Deuteronomy 33;
    Joshua in Joshua 23–24; Samuel in 1 Samuel 12; David in
    2 Sam 23:1-7; 1 Kgs 2:1-9; 1 Chronicles 28-29; Jesus in John
    13–17; Paul in Acts 20:17-38; 2 Tim 3:1–4:8; 2 Peter is a tes-
    tament of Peter.

d. Intertestamental Literature
    Examples: Tobit 4; 14; 1 Macc 2:49-70: testament of
    Mattathias; *1 Enoch* 91–104; *2 Enoch* 2, 56–63 (14–18
    T. Enoch); *2 Baruch* 44-46; *Jubilees* (Noah, 10; Abraham,
    20–22; Rebekah and Isaac, 35–36); Eve's testament in *Lives
    of Adam and Eve* 49–50; *Book of Biblical Antiquities* (Mo-
    ses, 19; Joshua, 23–24; Deborah, 33); 4Q*Visions of Amram*
    (Qumran); 4Q*Testament of Qahat* (Qumran); Aramaic
    Testaments of Judah, Levi, Naphtali (Qumran).

e. Full Testaments
    Examples: *Testaments of Adam; Abraham; Isaac; Jacob; the
    Twelve Patriarchs; Moses; Solomon; the Apocalypse of Moses*
    (Adam as main character); *T. Asher* is missing the histori-

---

28. Fernando F. Segovia, *The Farewell of the Word: The Johannine Call to Abide* (Minneapolis: Fortress, 1991), pp. 308-9, identifies nine characteristics, with seven found in the testament of John 14–17.

cal retrospective; *T. Job* has no future prediction and a direct exhortation in only two brief passages.[29]

C. Liturgical Literature <u>personified in the priest or worship leader</u>
  1. Homily
    1) Entire books as sermons: Five sermons are combined in Hebrews 1–12, labeled a word of exhortation (λόγου τῆς παρακλήσεως) in 13:22; see Acts 13:15)
      a) Christ's Superiority to Angels (Heb 1:1–2:18)
      b) Christ, Superior to Moses and Joshua (3:1–4:13)
      c) Christ, Superior to the Aaronic Priesthood (4:14–7:28)
      d) Christ, Mediator of a Better Covenant (8:1–10:31)
      e) True Faith and Faithfulness (10:32–12:29)
        Examples: also *2 Clement:* Interpretation of Knowledge and Testimony of Truth, Gnostic tractates from Nag Hammadi.
    2) Examples within books: Five discourses of Jesus in Matthew (standard ending in Matt 7:28; 11:1; 13:53; 19:1; 26:1)
      a) Sermon on the Moral Life (Sermon on the Mount): chs. 5–7
      b) Missions Discourse (ch. 10)
      c) Kingdom Parables (ch. 13)
      d) A Primitive Church Order (ch. 18)
      e) Eschatological Discourse (chs. 24–25)
    3) Discourses within the Gospel of John include
      a) The new birth (3:1-21)
      b) The water of life (4:1-42)
      c) The divine Son (5:19-47)
      d) The bread of life (6:22-66)
      e) The life-giving Spirit (7:1-52)
      f) The light of the world (8:12-59)
      g) The good shepherd (10:1-42)
    4) Sermons from The Acts of the Apostles
      Also Apocryphal *Acts of Thomas* 28, 33-36, 39, 82-86, 94; *Acts of John* 29, 67-69, 103-104, 106-7; *Acts of Peter* 2, 7, 20.
      a) Preaching Centered in the Kerygma
        a. Peter's Pentecost message (Acts 2:14-40)

---

29. See James H. Charlesworth, ed., *The Old Testament Pseudepigrapha* (Garden City: Doubleday, 1983), vol. 1, for the complete texts.

           b. Peter's message in Solomon's portico (Acts 3:12-26)

           c. Peter's message to Cornelius (Acts 10:34-43)

        b) Preaching Rehearsing the History of Salvation

           a. Stephen's dying message, with subtle kerygma in vv. 51-52 (center on Moses) (Acts 7:2-53)

           b. Paul's message at the synagogue in Antioch of Pisidia, with Acts 13:23-41 as kerygma (center on David) (13:16-41)

        c) Preaching Centered on Natural Revelation

           a. Paul to turn the people of Lystra from idols (Acts 14:15-17)

           b. Paul at Athens to the Areopagus (Acts 17:22-31)

2. Prayers

    1) Entire genre: *Prayer of Manasseh; Prayer of Nabonidus* (Qumran).

    2) Within narratives in intertestamental literature: Prayer of Azariah, between Dan 3:23 and 3:24; Tob 3:2-6; 3:11-15; 8:5-6; 8:15-17; 13:1-18; 1 Macc 4:30-33; 2 Macc 1:2-5, 24-29; *3 Macc.* 2:1-20; 6:1-15; *Joseph and Aseneth* 12-13; Add Esth 13:8–14:19; Bar 2:6–3:8; 4:36–5:9.

    3) Within apocalyptic literature: *2 Bar.* 21:1-26; 28:1-20; 54:1-14; *4 Ezra* 8:20-36; 11QPs^a Zion (Apostrophe to Zion); *The Words of the Luminaries.*

    4) At the beginning of the Pauline Epistles, where it is combined with a thanksgiving.

    5) For victory and help in battle: 1 Macc 7:40-42; 4:30-33; 2 Macc 8:2, 14-15, 18-20; 10:16; 11:6; 12:15; 14:15; 14:35-36; 15:9; 15:21-24, 34; Judith 8–9.

3. Songs and Psalms

    1) Entire volumes: the OT book of Psalms; DSS *Hodayot; Psalms of Solomon; Odes of Solomon.*

    2) Possible songs (or creedal statements) within NT literature: Phil 2:6-11; Col 1:15-20; Eph 1:3-14; 1 Tim 3:16; Luke 1:46-55; 1:67-79; 2:29-32; John 1:1-18; Rev 4:8, 11; 5:9-10, 12, 13; 15:3-4.

    3) Other songs: *Acts Thom.* 6-7 (Wedding hymn), 108-13 (Hymn of the Pearl); the *Naassene Psalm* (NT Apocrypha).

Subgenres:

a. Laments
   1) The normal elements include:
     a) Declaration of innocence
     b) Prayer for deliverance
     c) Complaint
       a. About the enemy: Pss 5:9; 10:2-11; 17:10-12; (22:12-18; 35:11-16, mixed); 36:1-4; 55:10-14; 56:1-2; 56:5-6; 57:4, 6; 58:1-5; 59:6-7; 59:14-15; 64:3-6; 69:7-12; 71:10-11; 83:2-8; 86:14; 94:4-7; 109:2-5; 119:85-87; 123:3b-4; 129:1-3; 137:1-4; 139:19-20; 140:2-3, 4b-5; 142:3-4; 143:3-4.
       b. About oneself: Pss 22:6-8; 42:6-10; 55:2b-5; 69:1-4; 77:1-4; 88:3-5; 102:3-11; 109:22-25; 119:81-84.
       c. About God: Pss 22:1-2; 60:1-3; 77:5-9; 80:4-6; 88:6-18; 89:38-45.
     d) Imprecation: Pss 5:10; 6:10; 12:3-4; 17:13?; 28:4-5; 35:1-8; 35:26-27; 36:11; 40:14-15 = 70:2-3; 54:5; 55:9, 15; 56:7; 58:6-8; 59:5; 59:12-13; 68:1-2; 69:22-29; 79:6, 12; 83:9-18; 94:2; 109:6-20; 129:5-8; 140:9-11; 141:10; 143:12.
     e) Song of confidence
   2) Community Laments: Psalms 12; 44; 60; 74; 79; 80; 83; 90; 94; 123; 137; Lamentations.
   3) Individual Laments: Psalms 3-7; 10; 13; 14 (= 53); 17; 22(pt); 25(pt); 26; 28; 31; 35; 39?; 40:14-18 = 70; 42; 54-59; 61; 64; 69; 71(pt); 77; 86; 88; 102; 109; 120; 139-43; 2 Sam 1:17-27; 3:33-34.

b. Songs of Confidence
The difference from Thanksgivings is that Songs of Confidence are usually about the future.
   1) Community Songs of Confidence: Psalms 85; 115; 125; 126.
   2) Individual Songs of Confidence: Psalms 11; 16; 23; 25(pt); 43; 62; 71(pt); 94:12-23; 121; 131.

c. Thanksgivings
   1) Community Thanksgivings: Psalms 65–67; 107; 108 (change lament of Psalms 57; 60); 124; 129; 136; some of the Qumran psalms from 1QH.

2) Individual Thanksgivings: Pss 9; 22:23-31; 30; 31:19-22; 40:1-13; 41; 63; 69:30-36; 92; 111; 116; 138; Jonah 2:2-9; many of the Qumran psalms from 1QH.

d. Hymns

   1) Enthronement Hymns: Psalms 47; 93; 96–99; 146; 149 (Yahweh reigning as judge; Pss 47:9; 93:1; 96:10; 97:1; 98:6; 99:1; as king: Pss 146:10; 149:2); Rev 11:15, 11:17-18; 19:1-2; 19:6-8; Song of the Angels (Luke 2:14; Hosanna cry: 19:38).

   2) Zion Hymns: Psalms 46 (security of Zion); 48 (beauty); 76 (destruction); 84 (pilgrimage); 87 (universal citizenship); 122 (pilgrimage and prayer for peace).

   3) Hymns of Nature: Psalms 8; 19:1-7; 29; 33; 77:17-20; 104; 147; 148.

   4) Hymns of the Character of God (and Christ): Psalms 36, esp. 5-9; 77:13-15; 89:1-19; 103; 111; 113; 114; 117; 135; 145; 150; Rev 4:8; 5:9-10, 12, 13; 15:3-4.

e. Penitential Psalms

   Examples: Psalms 25 (pt); 32:1-5; 38; 51; 130; 155 (Syriac Psalm 3).

f. Entrance Liturgies

   Examples: Psalms 15; 24; 47; 68; 95; 100; 118; 120–22; 134.

g. Prophetic Words

   Examples: Psalms 50; 75; 81; 82; 89:19-37; 95:8-11; Deut 32:1-43.

h. Wisdom Psalms

   Examples: Psalms 1; 49; 52; 112; 127; 128; 133; Ps 154 (Syriac Psalm 2).

i. Didactic Psalms

   Examples: Pss 19:8-15; 32; 34; 37; 62:9-12; 73; 78; 90:3-12; 91; 105; 106; 119. *Heilsgeschichte* (history of salvation): 78; 105; 106 (almost a subgenre).

j. Royal Psalms

   Examples: Psalms 2; 110; 132 (coronation); 18; 21; 118; 63? (thanksgiving for victory); 20; 27 (war preparations); 72; 144; 61? (prayer); 89 (lament); 101 (vow); 45 (marriage); 1 Sam 2:1-10.

k. War (Victory) Songs

   Examples: Exod 15:1-18; Judges 5; Num 21:27-30; possibly

the Magnificat (Luke 1:46-55); Benedictus (1:68-79); Nunc
Dimittis (2:29-32) (also call to arms: Exod 17:16; Judg 7:18,
20; Num 10:35-36; cry about military prowess: 1 Sam 18:7;
21:11; 29:5; and dismissal of troops: 1 Kgs 12:16).

l. Love Songs
Example: Song of Songs.

4. Salutations, Benedictions, and Doxologies
Examples: the beginning and end of the Epistles; Rom 11:33-
36; 1 Thess 3:12-13; 2 Thess 2:16-17; Rev 4:11; 7:10, 12; 1QS^b;
Eighteen Jewish Benedictions.

5. Penitential Liturgy or Confessions of Sin
Examples: Dan 9:4-19; Bar 1:15–3:8; Qumran Words of the
Heavenly Luminaries.

6. Liturgies
   1) Anointing with oil (*Acts of Thomas* 27, 121, 132, 157)
   2) Eucharist (*Didache* 9–10; *Acts of Thomas* 50, 133, 158; *Acts of Peter* 5; *Acts of John* 109ff.)
   3) Baptism (*Acts of Thomas* 157)
   4) Used at sacrifices: (4QShirShabb: The Angelic Liturgy)

D. Legal Literature personified in a king/ruler/judge
Legal literature has been subdivided into three types of speech.
As Jeffrey Weima points out,

> Judicial (or forensic) rhetoric belongs to the setting of a court-
> room where the audience functions as judges who must make
> a decision of guilt or innocence concerning some past event.
> Deliberative rhetoric belongs to the setting of a public assem-
> bly where the audience must make a decision about the best
> course of action concerning some future activity. Epideictic
> (or demonstrative) rhetoric belongs to the setting of the pub-
> lic marketplace or civic event where the audience, rather than
> making a judgment about some past or future activity, ob-
> serves the skill of the orator as he seeks to persuade them to
> adopt or reaffirm some point of view in the present, whether
> it be the praise or blame of some person or quality.[30]

30. Jeffrey A. D. Weima, "What Does Aristotle Have to Do with Paul?" *CTJ* 32 (1997):
460.

1. Juridical Speech
   Juridical speech fits a courtroom setting and is defined by
   David Aune as "strategies of defense or accusation to persuade an audience to make a decision about past events or
   circumstances."[31]
   Subgenres:
   1) Juridical Defense
      Examples: Acts 22:1-21; 24:10-21; with an evangelistic
      message: 2:14ff.; 3:12ff.; 4:8ff; Acts 5:29ff.; 10:34ff.;
      13:16ff.; 14:14ff.; 17:22ff.
   2) Apodictic Laws
      Examples: Exodus; Leviticus; Deuteronomy; Jewish
      Halakah; Temple Scroll; Pseudo-Phocylides.
   3) Blessings and Curses
      Examples: Genesis 49; Deuteronomy 33; beatitudes;
      Matthew 23/Luke 11.
   4) Vice and Virtue Lists
      Examples: Jeremiah 7:9; Prov 6:17-19; Hos 4:2; Rom
      1:29-31; 13:13; 1 Cor 5:10-11; 6:9-10; 2 Cor 6:6-7; 12:20-21;
      Gal 5:19-23; Titus 1:7-10; 1 Tim 3:2-7; 6:4-5; Eph 4:31-32;
      6:14-17; Phil 4:8; Heb 7:26; Jas 3:17; 1 Pet 4:3; 2 Pet 1:5-8;
      Rev 9:20-21; 14:4-5; 21:8, 27; Wis 14:22-31.
   5) Contract or Oaths
      Examples: Qumran 1QS, CD.
2. Deliberative Speech
   Deliberative speech is persuasive literature that advocates
   some appropriate future action. The following are the constituent parts of rhetorical analysis that were a part of Greco-
   Roman rhetorical training.
   1) *Exordium (prooemium):* introduction
      a) Establishes rapport between speaker and audience
      b) Creates interest in the subject matter
      c) Sometimes foreshadows the major topics
   2) *Narratio (prothesis)*
      a) States the proposition
      b) Provides background information

31. Aune, *The New Testament in Its Literary Environment*, p. 35.

      c) Provides rationale for the point to be made

      d) Later a *partitio* was added as a separate part which enumerated the opponent's arguments as well as the author's countering arguments

   3) *Probatio (pistis* or *confirmatio)*

      a) Includes a presentation of arguments

      b) Elicits quotations of supportive authorities

      c) Adds citations of parallels and favorable examples appealing to the audience

      d) Later a *refutatio* was added that refutes opposing views and includes digressions of added information

   4) *Peroratio (epilogos* or *conclusio)*

      a) Summarizes the major points and appeals to the audience's reason

      b) Arouses emotions in support of the proposition as well as the speaker

Subgenres:

   1) Apologetic

   Examples: 1 Corinthians 15; 2 Corinthians 1–7; Romans 9–11; cultural polemics in Josephus, *Antiquities* or *Against Apion;* Philo, *Against Flaccus* and *Embassy to Gaius;* Eupolemus's works in the second century B.C.E.

   2) Diatribe

   A diatribe consists of a dialogue with an imaginary interlocutor or objectioner as representative of the typical error in order to enlighten the audience about typical errors and pitfalls. The various elements of diatribe include:

      a) Dialogue with a fictive opponent (imaginary interlocutor): Rom 2:1-5; 2:17-24; 9:19-21; 11:17-24; 14:4, 10; Jas 2:18-22

      b) Rhetorical questions

      c) Strong statements of rejection and exclamation Examples of b) and c): Rom 3:1-9; 3:31–4:2a; 6:1-3, 15, 16; 7:7, 13-14; 9:14-15, 19-20; 11:1-3, 11, 19-20.

      d) Frequent inclusion of satire, irony, and paradox

3. Epideictic Speech

Epideictic speech consists of motivational literature that attempts to persuade an audience to adopt or maintain a par-

ticular point of view in the present by means of assigning
honor or blame or giving one's authoritative opinion on a
particular subject.[32]

Subgenres:

    1) Encomium (Praise)

        Examples: 1 Corinthians 13 (love); Hebrews 11 (faith);
        Wisdom (wisdom); Josephus, *Against Apion* 2:145-220
        (encomium on the Jewish law or Mosaic constitution);
        2:291-96 (on the Jewish laws).

    2) Midrash (biblical commentaries)

        a) Continuous commentary: Wisdom 11–19 is based
           on the account of the plagues in Exodus 7–12; Reve-
           lation 6, on Mark 13; some authors contend the
           birth narratives of the Gospels are largely midrash
           from OT stories of Hannah and Abraham and
           Sarah; *Jubilees; Genesis Apocryphon;* Philo's com-
           mentaries; Pseudo-Philo's *Biblical Antiquities;* rab-
           binic midrashim *(Mekilta, Sifra, Rabba);* rabbinic
           targumim.

        b) Pesharim

           a. A Pesher is a prophetic midrash applying the fulfill-
              ment of Scripture to the contemporary situation.

           b. Examples: Qumran pesharim on Isaiah, Hosea,
              Micah, Nahum, Habakkuk, Zephaniah, Malachi,
              Psalms, and Genesis.

           c. Possible NT examples: 2 Cor 3:12-18; 1 Cor 15:54-
              55; Rom 10:6-13; Luke 4:16-21; Matt 1:23; 2:6, 15, 18,
              23, etc.[33]

        c) Typology

           a. Walther Eichrodt defines typology as "persons,
              institutions, and events of the Old Testament
              which are regarded as divinely established models

---

    32. For a description of its characteristics, see Maurice Gilbert, "Wisdom Literature," in
Jewish Writings of the Second Temple Period, ed. Michael E. Stone. CRINT 2 (Philadelphia:
Fortress, 1984), p. 307.

    33. See Richard Longenecker, *Biblical Exegesis in the Apostolic Period* (Grand Rapids:
Eerdmans, 1975), pp. 70-75, for an extensive list assigned to Jesus; pp. 129-32, for a list of
pesher interpretations from Paul; and pp. 200-204, for examples from 1 Peter.

or prerepresentations of corresponding realities in the New Testament salvation history."[34]

    b. Examples[35]: Rom 5:12-21; 1 Cor 10:1-5; Gal 4:21-31; Matt 12:39-40; John 6.

  d) Church order

    Examples: *Didache* 7–15; Matthew 18; Luke 16:16-18; 17:1-4; 1 Timothy.

E. Instruction[36] personified in a wise man/philosopher/teacher/pastor

  1. Wisdom Literature

    a. Proverb or Aphorism[37]

    Examples: Prov 10:1–22:16 (Solomon); 22:17–24:22 (influenced by Amen-en-Opet); 24:23-34; 25-29 (collected by the men of Hezekiah); Eccl 9:17–10:20; Sumerian: *Instructions of Shuruppak;* Egyptian: *Instructions of Ptah-hotep, Meri-ka-Re, Ani, and Amen-en-Opet; Wisdom of Ahikar.*

    1) Proverbs in other types of literature:

      a) Historical narratives: Judg 8:2, 21

      b) Psalms: Ps 34:11-14

      c) Prophetic literature: Jer 13:12-14

      d) Gospels: Mark 10:25, 31

      e) Epistles: Jas 4:6; 1 Pet 4:8

    2) Types or subgenres of Proverbs:[38]

      a) Observation: a sentence in the indicative where an observable phenomenon is described to further a given course of conduct

      Examples: Prov 11:24; 13:12; 14:20, 13; Jer 23:28; 31:29-30; Ezek 18:1-2.

      b) Precept: a sentence or observation, usually in the in-

34. Walther Eichrodt, "Is Typological Exegesis an Appropriate Method?" in *Essays on Old Testament Hermeneutics,* ed. Claus Westermann (Richmond: John Knox, 1963), p. 225.

35. For a very helpful survey of the dangers, characteristics, rules, and examples of typology, see Sidney Greidanus, *Preaching Christ from the Old Testament: A Contemporary Hermeneutical Method* (Grand Rapids: Eerdmans, 1999), pp. 249-61.

36. For a glossary of terms, see John G. Gammie, "Paraenetic Literature: Toward the Morphology of a Secondary Genre," *Semeia* 50 (1990): 67-71.

37. See Theodore A. Hildebrandt, "Proverbs," in Sandy and Giese, *Cracking Old Testament Codes,* p. 240, for eleven different forms in which proverbs appear.

38. The following definitions are taken from Gammie, "Paraenetic Literature," p. 58.

dicative, which instructs and contains an implied or
obvious directive for conduct
Examples: Prov 21:5; Exod 23:8; Judg 8:21; 15:16;
1 Sam 16:7; 24:13; Gal 5:9; 1 Cor 15:33; 2 Pet 2:22.

c) Exhortation: an imperative that invites the addressee
to a given course of action
Examples: Prov 9:9; 20:18; 25:21-22; Eph 5:16.

d) Prohibition: a warning to the addressee against taking a given course of action or displaying a particular attitude
Examples: Prov 22:24-25; 24:17-18.

b. Didactic Instruction
Didactic instruction consists of longer didactic discourses,
frequently in the second person where a father gives a
personal address to his son: "Listen, my son."
Examples: Proverbs 1-9; 22:17–24:22; 31:1-9; wisdom
psalms; *Instruction of Vizier Ptah-hotep; Instruction for
King Meri-ka-Re; Instructions of Amen-em-Opet; Instructions of Shuruppak; Counsels by Wisdom, Words of Ahiqar;
Sentences of Menander.*

c. Personified Sophia
Examples: Matt 11:28-30; Prov 1:20-33; 3:13-18; 4:1-9; 8-9;
Job 28; Sirach 24; Wisdom 7-8; Baruch 3:9–4:4, esp. 4:1.

d. Praises (Encomia)
For OT examples, see *Semeia* 50 (1990): 61-63; Prov 31:10-
31; Sir 51:13-30; 1:11-20; 24; 44–50; 51:1-2; *Meri-ka-Re* 124-38;
Amen-em-het 2:1-111; *Ahiqar* 7:103-10.

e. Riddles
Examples: Judg 14:10-18; disintegrated riddles: Prov 5:1-6;
5:15-23; 6:23-24; 16:15; 20:27; 23:27; 23:29-35; 25:2-3; 27:20;
Matt 10:34; 11:12; 13:52; 19:12; Mark 2:19; 9:12-13; 14:58; Luke
13:32b-33; 22:36 (see *Semeia* 50 [1990]: 64 for examples).

f. Numerical Sayings
Examples: Job 5:19-22; Prov 6:16-19; 30:11-33; Sir 25; 50:25-
26.

g. Confessions
Through a personal experience the sage drives home the
truthfulness of the argument.

Examples: Job 29-31; 40:4-5; 42:1-6; Prov 4:3-9; 24:30-34;
Eccl 1:12–2:26.

  h. Beatitudes and Abomination Sayings or Curses

    Beatitude examples: Prov 3:13; 8:32-34; 14:21; 16:20; 20:7;
28:14; Pss 1:1; 112:1; Eccl 10:17.

    Abomination sayings: Prov 15:8.

2. Philosophical Literature

  a. Reflection

    Examples: Ecclesiastes; *Epistle of Aristeas* 172-300;
4 Maccabees.

  b. Disputation

    Examples: Job; imagined opponent: Prov 1:11-14; 1:22-23;
5:12-14; 7:14-20; 8:4-36; Wis 2:1-20; 5:3-13.

  c. Symposium or *Deipnon* (dinner dialogue)

    Common Elements:

    a) Invitation to dinner including the host, a chief guest
philosopher, the invited guests, and an uninvited
guest

    b) Announcement of an issue for debate like seating
arrangements or guest lists

    c) Dialogue in the form of table talk

      Examples: Plato, *Symposium;* Lucian, *Symposium;*
Xenophon, *Symposium;* Plutarch, *Table Talk; Aristeas*
172-81; Methodius, *The Banquet of the Ten Virgins;*
Luke 14:1-24; 7:36-50; 11:37-54 (see gospel).

3. Epistles

  Examples: Pauline and Catholic Epistles; Acts 15:23-29; 23:25-
30; 2 Sam 11:15; 1 Kgs 21:9-10; 2 Kgs 5:6; 10:2-3, 6; 19:10-13 (Isa
37:10-13); Jer 29:4-23, 26-28; 2 Chr 2:11-15; 21:12-15; Ezra 4:7-16;
4:17-22; 5:6-17; 7:11-26; Neh 6:6-7; 1 Macc 10:3-5; 10:25-45;
11:30-37; 12:6-18; 15:2-9; *1 Clement;* Ignatius's epistles; *Epistle of
Barnabas; Epistle of Polycarp; Epistle to Diognetus.*

  a. Standard Components of a New Testament Letter

    1) Greeting

      Description: includes the writer or author, recipient or
addressee, salutation or greeting with a wish for good
health, a prayer-wish, or information about the writer
or addressee.

    2) Thanksgiving and Prayer

Description: includes the mentioning of the author's circumstances, the purpose of the letter, or some favorable remembrance of the addressee.

3) Body of the Letter
Description: the various types of letters are described below.

4) Paraenesis
Description: includes a series of short commands or imperatives on a variety of subjects.

5) Farewell
Description: includes such things as the travelogue, greetings, doxology, benediction, personal signature, and date.

b. Various Types of Letters[39]

1) Problem-solving = a Pastoral Epistle
Examples: 1 Corinthians; 2 Thessalonians; *1 Clement;* 1-3 John; Pastoral Epistles; Philemon; Ignatius's epistles; Dionysius; Acts 15.

2) The teaching of religious concepts = a Doctrinal Epistle
Examples: Romans; Eph 1:1–4:16; Col 1–2; *Barnabas.*

3) Correspondence of activities and information
Pauline Examples: Philippians; Philemon;
1 Thessalonians 1–3; 1 Cor 1:10-17; Phil 1:12-26; Gal 1:10–2:21; 2 Cor 1:8–2:12; travel plans: Rom 15:22-33; 1 Cor 4:14-21; 2 Cor 12:14–13:13; Gal 4:12-20; Phil 2:19-24; 1 Thess 2:17–3:13; Phlm 21-22.
Other Examples: Ignatius, *To the Romans;* 1 Maccabees quotes 11 letters (5:10-13; 12:6-18; 10:18-20, 25-45; 11:30-37, 57; 13:36-40; 15:2-9; 12:20-23; 14:20-22; 15:16-21); 2 Maccabees contains 5 letters (9:19-27; 11:23-26, 27-33; 11:17-21, 34-38); *3 Macc.* has 2 letters (3:12-29; 7:1-9); *Epistle of Aristeas* 35-40 with reply, 41-46; *Paralipomena Jeremiah* 6:17-23, with reply 7:23-29; Josephus cites 37 letters, 13 from texts we already know.[40]

---

39. For a wider variety of letters, see Stanley K. Stowers, *Letter Writing in Greco-Roman Antiquity* (Philadelphia: Westminster, 1986); and Hans-Josef Klauck, *Ancient Letters and the New Testament: A Guide to Context and Exegesis* (Waco: Baylor University Press, 2006).

40. See P. S. Alexander, "Epistolary Literature," in Stone, *Jewish Writings of the Second Temple Period,* p. 580, n. 5, for examples.

    4) Apologetic Defense

        Examples: Galatians; 2 Corinthians; Jude; *Diognetus;*
        Epistle of Jeremiah (tract against idolatry); possibly
        Ignatius's epistles should be placed here.

    5) Paraenetic Epistle (deliberative rhetoric)

        Examples: 1 Thessalonians 4–5; Eph 4:17–6:24;
        Colossians 3–4; Polycarp, *To the Philippians; 1 En.*
        100:6?

    6) Other Genres Placed into the Form of Epistles

        a) Apocalypse: Revelation 2–3; *2 Baruch* 78–87

        b) Testament: 2 Peter; *Epistles of Enoch* (92–105);
           2 Baruch (78–87)

        c) Homily: *2 Clement* and Hebrews; *2 Baruch* 78–87

        d) Called a narrative in the first sentence: *Aristeas*

        e) Paraenesis: James; Hebrews 13

        f) Postresurrection dialogues: *Apocryphon of James;*
           Epistle of the Apostles

        g) Philosophical or ethical treatise: Quintilian's *Institutes;* Plutarch, *On Tranquility*

        h) Hymns: Phil 2:6-11; Col 1:15-20; Eph 1:3-14; 5:14;
           1 Tim 3:16; 2 Tim 2:11-13

        i) Confessions, creeds: Rom 1:3-4; 4:24-25; 10:9; 1 Cor
           12:3; 15:3-5; 2 Cor 13:4; 1 Tim 2:5; 6:11-16; 1 Pet 3:18,
           22; Gal 3:20; Eph 5:2

4. Paraenetic Literature

  a. General Paraenesis

    Description: Short ethical exhortations on a variety of
    topics

    Examples: James 1; 5:7-20; Rom 12:9-21; 1 Thess 5:12-22;
    2 Cor 13:11; *Did.* 1–6; *Barn.* 18-21.

    Rom 12:9-13, e.g., includes the topics of love, hate, evil,
    good, brotherly affection, the bestowal of honor, zeal, spir-
    itual aliveness, service, hope, patience, constancy in prayer,
    liberality in giving, and hospitality.

  b. Extended Paraenetic Discourse *(topoi)*

    Description: *Topoi* are standardized responses to
    frequently-asked questions on certain topics or extended
    exhortations on particular themes.

Examples: three examples in Jas 2:1–3:12; Rom 13:1–14:23;
1 Thess 4:9–5:11; 1 Cor 13.

c. Disciplinary Exhortations and Prophetic Denunciations
   Examples: Jas 3:13-18; 4:1-10; 4:13-17; 5:1-6.

d. Household Codes *(Haustafeln)*
   Examples: Rom 13:1-7; Eph 5:21–6:9; Col 3:18–4:1; 1 Pet
   2:11–3:7; 1 Tim 2:1-15; 5:1-2; 6:1-2; Titus 2:1-10; 3:1-7; *Did.*
   4:9-11; *1 Clem.* 1:3; 21:6-8; *Pol. Phil.* 4:1–6:2.

e. Overlap with Other Genres
   1) Vice or Virtue Lists from Legal Literature: Gal 5:19-23;
      Col 3:5-17
   2) Eschatological Ethics from Apocalyptic Literature: Jas
      5:7-11; Rom 13:11-14; 1 Thess 4:13–5:11; *Did.* 16
   3) Ethical Application Portion of Testaments: 2 Pet 3:11-18;
      T. Levi 13; *T. Dan* 5:1-3; 6:1ff.; *T. Naph.* 8
   4) Wisdom Sayings: *Gospel of Thomas;* Q; Jas 1:12; 2:13

II. Canonical Examples of Controversy Dialogues[41]

I will attempt to demonstrate how the following five component elements are regularly found in the canonical gospels.

1. Description of a conflict situation.
2. Question by Jesus' opponents.
3. Jesus' return question (and sometimes an answer to this question or a response).
4. The pronouncement saying.
5. Response by the crowd or additional concluding saying.

A. Mark 1:35-39: What Is the Purpose of Jesus' Mission?
1. 1:35-36: Jesus is in a solitary place praying and the disciples attempt to find him.
2. 1:37: Not a question but an exclamation: "Everyone is looking for you!"
3. None.
4. 1:38: "Let us go somewhere else — to the nearby villages — so I can preach there also. That is why I have come."
5. 1:39: Jesus traveled throughout Galilee, preaching in their synagogues and driving out demons.

B. Mark 2:1-12: Can a Human Agent Forgive Sins? (mixture with a healing narrative)
1. 2:1-5: Jesus forgives the sins of a paralytic.
2. 2:6-7: Thoughts of the teachers of the law: "He's blaspheming! Who can forgive sins but God alone?"
3. 2:8-9: "Why are you thinking these things? Which is easier: to say to the paralytic, 'Your sins are forgiven,' or to say, 'Get up, take your mat and walk'?"
4. 2:10: "The Son of Man has authority on earth to forgive sins."
5. 2:12: "This amazed everyone and they praised God, saying, 'We have never seen anything like this!'"
Added element: 2:11 the healing.

---

41. Robert C. Tannehill, "Varieties of Synoptic Pronouncement Stories," *Semeia* 20 (1981): 101-19, is unique in recognizing Mark 1:35-38; 6:1-6; 9:9-13; others that I do not recognize include Mark 7:24-30; 9:33-37; 8:31-33; 11:15-17, 20-25. See the convenient chart in Mack, *Mark and Christian Origins*, pp. 379-84.

C. Mark 2:15-17: Why Would Jesus Have Table Fellowship with Sinners?
1. 2:15: Tax collectors and sinners eating with Jesus at Levi's house.
2. 2:16: Pharisaic scribes ask, "Why does he eat with tax collectors and 'sinners'?"
3. 2:17a: "Is it the healthy who need a doctor or the sick?" (most frequently translated as a proposition and not a question).
4. 2:17b: "I have not come to call the righteous, but sinners."
5. No response.
Versus Matthew 9:10-13
New 4. "But go and learn what this means: 'I desire mercy and not sacrifice.'"
4 becomes 5.

D. Mark 2:18-22: Why Do Jesus and His Disciples Not Fast?
1. 2:18a: The disciples of John the Baptizer and the Pharisees are fasting.
2. 2:18b: "How is it that John's disciples and the disciples of the Pharisees are fasting, but yours are not?"
3. 2:19: "How can the guests of the bridegroom fast while he is with them?"
4. 2:20: "The time will come when the bridegroom will be taken from them, and on that day they will fast."
5. 2:21-22: General principle of incompatibility.

E. Mark 2:23-28: Was Picking Grain on the Sabbath Equivalent to Working?
1. 2:23: Jesus' disciples pick heads of grain as they are walking through the grain fields.
2. 2:24: The Pharisees ask, "Why are they doing what is unlawful on the Sabbath?"
3. 2:25: "Have you never read what David did?"
4. 2:27: "The Sabbath was made for man, not man for the Sabbath."
5. 2:28: Conclusion: "So the Son of Man is Lord even of the Sabbath."
Versus Matthew 12:1-8

Added question to 3. 12:5-6: "Or haven't you read in the Law that on the Sabbath the priests in the temple desecrate the day and yet are innocent? I tell you that one greater than the temple is here."

Skip 4 (Mark 2:27) and replace it with Matt 12:7: "If you had known what these words mean, 'I desire mercy, not sacrifice,' you would not have condemned the innocent."

F. Mark 3:1-6: Should Jesus Heal on the Sabbath? (mixture with a healing narrative)
   1. 3:1: A man with a shriveled hand is in the synagogue on the Sabbath.
   2. 3:2: Not a question but a silent accusation: some are looking for a reason to accuse Jesus.
   3. 3:4a: "Which is lawful on the Sabbath: to do good or to do evil, to save life or to kill?"
   4. 3:5: Same as 3 above.
   5. 3:6: Pharisees plot with the Herodians how to kill Jesus. Added elements from a miracle story: 3:3: Jesus asks the man to stand up in front of everyone; 3:4b: Response to Jesus' question (they remained silent); 3:5: Jesus' anger and healing gesture ("Stretch out your hand").

   Versus Matt 12:9-12, which is an example of a more complete controversy dialogue:
   1. Description of a conflict situation (12:9-10a).
   2. Question by Jesus' opponents (12:10b): "Is it lawful to heal on the Sabbath?"
   3. Jesus' return question (12:11): "If any of you has a sheep and it falls into a pit on the Sabbath, will you not take hold of it and lift it out?"
   4. The pronouncement saying (Matt. 12:12a): "How much more valuable is a man than a sheep!"
   5. Response by the crowd or an additional concluding saying (12:12b): "Therefore it is lawful to do good on the Sabbath." In Mark we only have Jesus' return question (3:4), which is worded differently: "Which is lawful on the Sabbath: to do good or to do evil, to save life or to kill?"

G. Mark 3:22-30: Does Jesus Cast Out Demons by the Prince of the Demons?

1. 3:22a: The teachers of the law come from Jerusalem.
2. 3:22b: A double accusation rather than a question: "He is possessed by Beelzebub! By the prince of demons he is driving out demons."
3. 3:23: "How can Satan drive out Satan?"
4. 3:27: "No one can enter a strong man's house and carry off his possessions unless he first ties up the strong man. Then he can rob his house."
5. 3:28-30: An additional saying about blasphemy against the Holy Spirit.

Additional element: 3:24-26: 3. if . . . then sayings about a kingdom divided against itself.

H. Mark 3:20-21, 31-35: Who Are Jesus' True Family?
   1. 3:20-21: Jesus' family thinks he is out of his mind because of his hectic lifestyle.
   2. 3:31-32: Not a question but a request: Jesus' family is standing outside asking for him.
   3. 3:33: "Who are my mother and my brothers?"
   4. 3:34-35: "Whoever does God's will is my brother and sister and mother."
   5. No response.

I. Mark 4:10-12: Why Does Jesus Speak in Parables?
   1. 4:10a: Jesus is alone with his disciples after speaking a parable.
   2. 4:10b: The disciples ask Jesus about speaking in parables.
   3. 4:13: "Don't you understand this parable? How then will you understand any parable?" (the question's position is reversed to place it before the application of the parable).
   4. 4:11-12: "The secret of the kingdom of God has been given to you. But to those on the outside everything is said in parables" with a quote from Isa 6:9-10.
   5. 4:14-20: Jesus' application of the parable to the disciples.

J. Mark 6:1-6a: Why Was Jesus Rejected by His Own People at Nazareth?
   1. 6:2a: Jesus teaches on the Sabbath in the synagogue at Nazareth, his hometown.
   2. 6:2b: "Where did this man get these things?"

6:2c: "What's this wisdom that has been given him, that he even does miracles!"

6:3: "Isn't this the carpenter? Isn't this Mary's son and the brother of James, Joseph, Judas and Simon?"

6:3b: "Aren't his sisters here with us?"

3. None.

4. 6:4: "Only in his hometown, among his relatives and in his own house, is a prophet without honor."

5. He could not do many miracles there.

K. Mark 7:1-23: Why Do Jesus' Disciples Eat with Unwashed Hands?

1. 7:2: The disciples are eating with unwashed hands.

2. 7:5: "Why don't your disciples live according to the tradition of the elders?"

3. 7:6-8: Accusation with a quote from the prophets (Isa 29:13) rather than a question.

7:9-13: Accusation with a quote from the law (Exod 20:12; Deut 5:16) rather than a question.

4. 7:15: "Nothing outside a man can make him 'unclean' by going into him. Rather, it is what comes out of a man that makes him 'unclean.'"

5. 7:17-19, 20-23: Explanation of this parable to the disciples.

L. Mark 8:11-21(12): Will Jesus Give a Sign?

1. 8:11a: The Pharisees arrive to discuss theology.

2. 8:11b: The Pharisees demand a sign, putting him to the test (rather than a question).

3. 8:12a: "Why does this generation ask for a miraculous sign?"

4. 8:12b: "Truly I say to you, a sign will not be given to this generation."

5. 8:14-21: Application to discipleship.

M. Mark 9:9-13: Will Elijah Come before the Fulfillment?

1. 9:9-10: Discussion about the Transfiguration, where Elijah appears with Jesus.

2. 9:11: The disciples ask, "Why do the teachers of the law say that Elijah must come first?"

3. 9:12: "Why is it written that the Son of Man must suffer first?"

4. 9:13: "Elijah has come and they have done to him everything they wished."

5. No response.

N. Mark 9:38-40: Who Is Permitted To Do Miracles in Jesus' Name?

    1. No conflict situation (placed into a sermon on discipleship).

    2. 9:38: John inquires about how they should view an outsider who employs Jesus' name to cast out demons.

    3. 9:39a: Instead of a question, Jesus responds: "Do not stop him."

    4. 9:39b-40: "No one who does a miracle in my name can in the next moment say anything bad about me, for whoever is not against us is for us."

    5. Added logia in 9:41 with the catchword "in my name."

O. Mark 10:1-9: Is It Lawful to Divorce? or When Is It Lawful to Divorce?

{Mark 10 is constructed by Mark into the traditional *Haustafeln* with marriage and divorce (1-12), children (13-16), possessions (17-22), and household and farm (23-31). Mark 10:23-28 is similar to a healing narrative with a powerful saying (23, 25) followed by astonishment by the disciples (24, 26) in a twofold cycle.}

    1. 10:2a: The Pharisees tested Jesus.

    2. 10:2b: "Is it lawful for a man to divorce his wife?"

    3. 10:3: "What did Moses command you?"

    4. 10:6: "But at the beginning of creation God made them male and female."

    5. 10:9: "Therefore what God has joined together, let man not separate."

Added elements: dialogue in 10:4-5; quotation from Scripture in 10:7-8; discipleship saying in a house in 10:10-12.

P. Mark 10:13-16: What Is the Place of Children in the Kingdom?

    1. 10:13a: People are bringing children to Jesus to touch them.

    2. 10:13b: No question: instead a rebuke by the disciples (no words given).

    3. 10:14a: No return question: instead Jesus is indignant.

    4. 10:14b: "Let the little children come to me, and do not hinder them, for the kingdom of God belongs to such as these."

5. 10:15: Added saying on receiving the kingdom like a child
(omitted in Matthew and placed in 18:5 with controversy
over who is greatest).

Added elements: 10:16: the blessing of the children would be expected at the beginning as the introduction of the conflict.

Q. Mark 10:17-22: How Does One Inherit Eternal Life? (constructed
into a dialogue and similar to a miracle story with responses of
amazement)
1. 10:17a: A man falls on his knees before Jesus.
2. 10:17b: "Good teacher, what must I do to inherit eternal life?"
3. 10:18-19: "Why do you call me good?"
4. 10:21: "One thing you lack," he said. "Go, sell everything you
have and give to the poor, and you will have treasure in
heaven. Then come, follow me."
5. 10:22: The man's face fell and he went away sad.

Added element: 10:20: Response of an inquirer ("all these I have
kept since I was a boy"), so that Mark makes it into a dialogue.
Jesus' saying in 10:18b, "No one is good except God alone," follows
the question and could be seen as the pronouncement saying.

R. Mark 10:23-27: Can the Rich Be Saved? (again constructed into a
dialogue)
1. A second issue in the encounter with the rich man.
2. A question is assumed from the radicality of Jesus' pronouncement saying (10:24: the disciples are amazed).
3. 10:23-24: Instead of a question, an exclamation: "How hard it
is for the rich to enter the kingdom of God!"
4. 10:25: "It is easier for a camel to go through the eye of a nee-
dle than for a rich man to enter the kingdom of God."
5. 10:26-27: Jesus' response to the disciples' amazement: "With
man this is impossible, but not with God; all things are possible with God."

S. Mark 10:35-45: Who Is Exalted in the Kingdom of God? (again
constructed into a dialogue)
1. James and John want position in the kingdom of God.
2. Instead of one question, there is a dialogue:
10:35: James's and John's request ("We want you to do for us
whatever we ask").

3. 10:36: Jesus' first question ("What do you want me to do for you?").

10:37: James's and John's answer ("Let one of us sit at your right and the other at your left in your glory").

10:38a: Jesus' comment on their answer ("You don't know what you are asking").

10:38b: Jesus' second question ("Can you drink the cup I drink or be baptized with the baptism I am baptized with?").

10:39a: James's and John's answer ("We can").

4. 10:39b-40: Jesus' pronouncement ("To sit at my right or left is not for me to grant").

5. 10:41-45: Application from the future eschaton to the present time: Whoever wants to become great must be the slave of all.

T. Mark 11:27-33: Where Does Jesus Get His Authority, from Heaven or Men?

1. 11:27: The Sanhedrin confronts Jesus after his cleansing of the temple.

2. 11:28: "By what authority are you doing these things? And who gave you authority to do this?"

3. 11:29-30: "John's baptism — was it from heaven, or from men?"

4. 11:33: "Neither will I tell you by what authority I am doing these things."

5. No response.

Additional element: 11:31-33a: The opponents' answer to Jesus' question that they do not know.

U. Mark 12:13-17: Should One Pay Taxes to Caesar?

1. 12:13: The Pharisees and Herodians attempt to trap Jesus.

2. 12:14: "Is it right to pay taxes to Caesar or not?"

3. 12:15-16a: "Whose portrait is this? And whose inscription?"

4. 12:17a: "Give to Caesar what is Caesar's and to God what is God's."

5. 12:17b: "They were amazed at him."

Added element: answer to Jesus' return question 12:16b ("'Caesar's,' they replied.")

V. Mark 12:18-27: Will There Be a Resurrection from the Dead, and What Will It Be Like?

1. 12:18: The Sadducees come with a question.
2. 12:19-23: "At the resurrection, whose wife will she be?"
3. 12:24: "Are you not in error because you do not know the Scriptures or the power of God?"
4. 12:25: "When the dead rise, they will neither marry nor be given in marriage; they will be like the angels in heaven."
5. 12:27b: An accusation rather than reaction: "You are badly mistaken!"

Additional elements: repeat of 3 and 4: 12:26: a second question by Jesus ("have you not read in the book of Moses") and 12:27a: a second pronouncement saying ("He is not the God of the dead, but of the living").

W. Mark 12:28-32: What Is the Greatest Commandment?
1. 12:28a: Another teacher of the law enters the debate.
2. 12:28b: "Of all the commandments, which is the most important?"
3. 12:29: No counterquestion by Jesus.
4. 12:28-31: The Shema and the Love Command.
5. 12:34b: "And from then on no one dared ask him any more questions."

Additional elements: More dialogue; 12:32-33: the response of the teacher of the law that love is more important than all burnt offerings and sacrifices; and 12:34a: the response by Jesus that he is not far from the kingdom of God.

vs. Luke 10:25-28: How to Inherit Eternal Life?
1. 10:25a: A scribe tests Jesus.
2. 10:25b: "What must I do to inherit eternal life?"
3. 10:26: "What is written in the law? How do you read it?"
4. 10:27: The scribe's pronouncement saying rather than Jesus': The double-love command.
5. 10:28: "'You have answered correctly,' Jesus replied. 'Do this and you will live.'"

Additional elements: the dialogue continues after this controversy with the scribe's question, "Who is my neighbor?" and Jesus' Parable of the Good Samaritan.

X. Mark 12:35-38: How Is the Christ the Son of David?
1. 12: 35a: Jesus is teaching in the temple.
2. 12:35b: Jesus asks a question rather than the opponents:

"How is it that the teachers of the law say that the Christ is
the son of David when he calls him Lord?"
3. No counterquestion.
4. 12:37a: An additional question by Jesus after quoting Ps 110:1
(12:36) rather than a normal pronouncement saying, "David
himself calls him 'Lord.' How then can he be his son?"
5. 12:37b: "The large crowd listened to him with delight."
Matthew places an answer to Jesus' question in the mouth of
the audience, 22:42: "'The son of David,' they replied."

Y. Mark 13:1-2: What Place Does the Temple Have within the New
Israel?
   1. 13:1a: The disciples view the beauty of the temple.
   2. 13:1b: Instead of a question, an exclamation: "What massive
      stones! What magnificent buildings!"
   3. 13:2a: "Do you see all these great buildings?"
   4. 13:2b: "Not one stone here will be left on another; every one
      will be thrown down."
   5. 13:3ff.: The eschatological discourse.

Z. Mark 14:3-9: To Whom Do We Give Our Money?
   1. 14:3: A woman pours expensive perfume on Jesus.
   2. 14:4-5: "Why this waste of perfume?"
   3. 14:6: "Why are you bothering her?"
   4. 14:7: "The poor you will always have with you, and you can
      help them any time you want. But you will not always have
      me."
   5. 14:10-11: Judas goes to the chief priests to betray Jesus.

Additional element: 14:8-9: the relationship to Jesus' burial and
the future gospel preaching.
Additional Examples from Other Gospels

Luke 13:10-17: Healing on the Sabbath (mixture with a healing
narrative)
   1. 13:10-13: Jesus heals a crippled woman on the Sabbath.
   2. 13:14: The synagogue ruler's accusation rather than question
      ("There are six days for work. So come and be healed on
      those days, not on the Sabbath.")
   3. 13:15: "Doesn't each of you on the Sabbath untie his ox or
      donkey from the stall and lead it out to give it water?"

4. 13:16: The pronouncement is really a question ("Then should not this woman, a daughter of Abraham, whom Satan has kept bound for eighteen long years, be set free on the Sabbath day from what bound her?")
5. 13:17: "His opponents were humiliated, but the people were delighted."

Luke 14:1-6: Healing on the Sabbath (mixture with a healing narrative)
1. 14:1a: It is the Sabbath.
2. 14:1b: No question, but the Pharisees are watching Jesus.
3. 14:3: "Is it lawful to heal on the Sabbath or not?"
4. 14:5: The pronouncement is really a question ("If one of you has a son or an ox that falls into a well on the Sabbath day, will you not immediately pull him out?"). In every controversy about healing on the Sabbath the pronouncement is a question (Mark 3:4; Luke 13:16; 14:5).
5. 14:6: "And they had nothing to say."
Additional elements: 14:2 and 4b contain the healing of the man; 14:4a: there is a lack of response to Jesus' question so that the Pharisees are silent.

Matthew 17:24-27: Who Should Pay the Temple Tax?
1. 17:24a: The collectors of the two-drachma tax come to Peter.
2. 17:24b: "Doesn't your teacher pay the temple tax?"
3. 17:25: "From whom do the kings of the earth collect duty and taxes — from their own sons or from others?"
4. 17:26-27: "Then the sons are exempt. But so that we may not offend them, go to the lake and throw out your line. Take the first fish you catch; open its mouth and you will find a four-drachma coin. Take it and give it to them for my tax and yours."
5. There is no crowd or disciple response.

John 8:1-11: The Adulterous Woman.
1. 8:1-3: The teachers of the law and Pharisees bring in a woman caught in adultery.
2. 8:4-5: "In the Law Moses commanded us to stone such women. Now what do you say?"
3. 8:6: Instead of a counterquestion Jesus writes in the sand.

4. 8:7: "If any one of you is without sin, let him be the first to throw a stone at her."
5. 8:9 The accusers leave from oldest to youngest.
   Additional elements: 8:8: a second writing on the sand, which is symbolic of the two givings of the law; 8:10: a dialogue between Jesus and the woman, with
   a. Jesus' question ("Woman, where are they? Has no one condemned you?").
   b. Her answer ("No one, sir").
   c. Jesus' pronouncement ("Then neither do I condemn you. Go now and leave your life of sin").

III. **Principles of Interpretation for the Main Genre Types**
   For more information and examples of principles of interpretation organized by genre, see:

   • Gordon Fee and Douglas Stuart, *How to Read the Bible for All Its Worth*
   • D. Brent Sandy and Ronald L. Giese Jr., *Cracking Old Testament Codes: A Guide to Interpreting Literary Genres of the Old Testament*
   • Thomas G. Long, *Preaching and the Literary Forms of the Bible*
   • Walter C. Kaiser, Jr., *Preaching and Teaching from the Old Testament: A Guide for the Church*

   A. Interpreting Narratives
      1. The interpreter should identify each scene of the narrative, analyze the plot, determine the point of view from which the narrative is recorded, and pay close attention to the sensory details of the scene.
      2. Frequently the author employs dialogue to narrate the story, so that special attention should be paid to where dialogue is introduced into the narrative and how the author moves back and forth between dialogue and narrative.
      3. Because the biblical historians are not simply recorders of events, interpreters should seek to determine the motive for the author telling a story and choosing the details involved in the story.
      4. Narratives record what happened — not necessarily what should have happened or what ought to happen.
      5. There is usually no identifiable moral in a narrative. Readers are not normally informed at the conclusion of a narrative whether what happened was good or bad.
      6. A narrative does not directly teach a doctrine. Narratives were not written to answer all our theological questions. Instead, narratives illustrate a doctrine taught propositionally elsewhere.
      7. In the final analysis, God is the hero of all the biblical narratives.
      8. "History writing is not primarily the accurate reporting of past events. It also considers the reason for recalling the past and the significance given to past events. History writing examines the causes of present conditions and circumstances.

In antiquity these causes are primarily moral — who is responsible for a certain state of affairs?"[42]

B. Interpreting the Gospels
  1. Divine providence furnished four different gospels, not a
     harmonized version.
     a. Therefore, we must reject Tatian's attempt to fuse the four
        gospels into one continuous account, making the theme
        of a particular story the same in each gospel.
     b. Furthermore, we must reject Marcion's attempt to criti-
        cally sift the material according to one dogmatic perspec-
        tive, to retain only portions of the gospel tradition, or to
        subordinate one gospel to another.
  2. Some gospel stories have been arranged in chronological or-
     der, while others favor a logical order of content depending
     upon the purpose of the evangelist. One method of arrange-
     ment should not dominate gospel studies.
  3. The evangelists selected and shaped the material to meet the
     needs of their particular audiences.
  4. The genre of the gospels is kerygmatic history or preached bi-
     ography. This entails that the gospels are written at two levels
     to rehearse the life and teachings of Jesus as well as to retell
     the story to meet the existential needs of later communities.

C. Interpreting Parables
  1. What we frequently entitle parables can be helpfully subdivided
     into similes (explicit comparisons), metaphors (implicit com-
     parisons), similitudes (simile expanded into a picture), para-
     bles (simile expanded into a story), example stories (parable
     providing an example), and allegories (a series of metaphors).
  2. The identification of the main characters will determine the
     comparison or comparisons that are being developed to real-
     life experiences. After exploring the levels of identification
     with real-life experience, the reader should decide what sin-
     gle decision or response the audience is pressed to make.
  3. The interpreter must distinguish between details of local color
     and theologically loaded details that carry theological meaning.

42. John Van Seters, *In Search of History: Historiography in the Ancient World and the
Origins of Biblical History* (New Haven: Yale University Press, 1983), pp. 4-5.

4. The surprise in the parable is normally the main point of the message.

5. The narrative retelling of the story should never be lost in the seeking for some theological point to the parable. On the other hand, the "earthly story" should not so dominate the discussion that no "heavenly meaning" is thought appropriate.

6. The interpretation is affected by the audience, structure, and context so that parables can have different meanings in various contexts of the gospels.

7. The parable must be interpreted within the particular emphases of the gospel writer.

8. The parable should be related to Jesus' kingdom teaching and the particular emphases of Jesus' ministry.

9. Since memorization of material requires repetition, Jesus in all likelihood spoke the parables on more than one occasion to different audiences.

D. Interpreting Prophetic Literature

1. The prophet should be understood within his historical context before an application is made to the New Testament or to contemporary life. Douglas Stuart argues that less than 2 percent of Old Testament prophecy is Messianic, less than 5 percent relates to the new covenant age, and less than 1 percent covers events still future.[43]

2. The prophet was a "forth-teller" before he was a "foreteller." The edification and instruction to the original audience should be studied first.

3. Prophecies can have more than one fulfillment. There is a scoping of time so that prophecies can be viewed from a perspective of two mountain ranges of fulfillment with a valley in between whose length is difficult to perceive.

4. Old Testament prophecies should be seen as futuristic to our present time only if they are repeated in the New Testament.

5. Prophecies that were unfulfilled should be seen as conditional prophecies that were originally based upon the people's response.

43. Gordon D. Fee and Douglas Stuart, *How to Read the Bible for All Its Worth: A Guide to Understanding the Bible,* 2nd ed. (Grand Rapids: Zondervan, 1993), p. 166.

E. Interpreting Apocalyptic Literature

 1. The apocalyptic seer has written primarily for the edification
    of the people of his own time. As far as possible, the symbols
    must be explained in terms of persons, events, trials, dangers,
    and triumphs related to the original audience.
 2. Although the apocalyptic symbols and events refer to the au-
    thor's day, their meaning is not exhausted in this fulfillment,
    but in prophetic fashion they point beyond the initial fulfill-
    ment to issues that arise in every age in the conflict between
    God's kingdom and the kingdom of this world.
 3. Apocalyptic literature such as the book of Revelation consists of
    a divine picture book that should be interpreted symbolically.
    We are to assume the symbolic character of the pictures unless it
    is clear that the expression must be taken literally, which is the
    opposite approach to the normal principle of interpretation.
 4. Apocalyptic takes over the themes of Old Testament proph-
    ecy so that the Old Testament is the first place we look to de-
    termine the meaning of the symbols.
 5. Since the genre of apocalyptic was popular mainly between
    200 B.C. and A.D. 200, the study of other extracanonical liter-
    ature from this time is essential for a proper control in
    studying the canonical material.
 6. "An apocalyptic author is like a political cartoonist, sketching
    the course of world events and the prominent leaders of the
    world in figurative, graphic, and even bizarre ways."[44]
 7. An interpretation of the whole book is more important than
    a concentration upon the minute details.
 8. "Though for prophecy the function of pronouncing God's
    hatred of disobedience and harsh judgment of those who
    disobey is a call to repentance, in apocalyptic the coming
    judgment is written to encourage the saints who are caught
    up in the crises of living in an evil world; they are encour-
    aged to persevere and not give up hope, for God is truly in
    control and will 'soon' intervene into world events in the
    person of the Son of Man."[45]

44. Sandy and Abegg, "Apocalyptic," p. 179.
45. Ronald L. Giese Jr., "Literary Forms of the Old Testament," in Sandy and Giese, *Cracking Old Testament Codes*, p. 22.

F. Interpreting Liturgical Literature
   1. The literary feature of parallelism must be particularly recognized and explored.
   2. A determination of the subgenre of a psalm (lament, descriptive praise, declarative praise, penitential sections, etc.) is crucial to its interpretation.
   3. Since psalms are poems that were sung, chanted, or recited over and over again in worship, the cultural background of the role of worship in the life of Israel must be thoroughly studied in any interpretation of the psalms.
   4. The historical background of the psalms (if available) is important, although the superscriptions themselves frequently derive from a later time and are not necessarily helpful to determine the original intention of the author.
   5. Before a christological interpretation is attempted, a psalm should be understood in its original setting in the history of redemption.

G. Interpreting Legal Literature
   1. With regard to law, we must make a distinction between laws that unconditionally and categorically assert right and wrong (apodictic law, like the Ten Commandments) and laws that define specific cases and prescribed legal consequences (case or casuistic law, like "if . . . then" legislation).
   2. To understand the role of legal literature within Israel, the reader should study the role of this genre in the whole of ancient Near Eastern literature. After comparing laws in the biblical text with one another, we must look for parallels with the ancient Near Eastern literature.
   3. God's covenant of grace begins in the Old Testament, so that New Testament believers participate in the same covenant, although the form of the covenant has changed.
   4. Regarding the normativity of Old Testament legal literature, New Testament believers are still required to keep the principles established in the Old Testament law, but not necessarily the specific regulations.
   5. The Old Testament law in its moral, ceremonial, and social dimensions is not abolished but fulfilled in Jesus Christ.

H. Interpreting Wisdom Literature

1. Each genre has its own rules of interpretation. For Wisdom literature, the context is not as important as with other genres, since each aphorism has a life of its own.

2. Proverbs are not laws or even promises, but general observations learned from a wise and careful look at life.[46] Proverbs arise out of recurring story lines, so that a proverb is larger than one case, but not large enough to embrace all cases.[47]

3. A proverb is a "short, salty, concrete, fixed, paradigmatic, poetically-crafted saying."[48] Each of these elements has exegetical consequences.

4. The literary feature of parallelism is of utmost importance in interpreting proverbial literature. A frequent mistake in interpreting parallel poetry lies in seeking a difference in meaning between two words employed as synonyms.

5. The cultural importance of the sage must be investigated before a proper understanding of this literature can be mastered. Since most proverbs originated in family life, schools, royal courts, and scribal circles, the meaning of individual proverbs should be investigated in these settings.

6. "Without being a narrative, the proverb implies a story — actually a set of stories. The proverb calls forth a series of everyday vignettes which are varied on the surface but bundled together by a deep harmony discerned through the proverb itself."[49]

7. Wisdom literature consists of timeless pieces of advice that function to help devotees develop skills in handling everyday decisions.

8. Although wisdom is primarily pragmatic and practical in orientation, the theological dimension should never be underestimated, since "the fear of the Lord is the beginning of wisdom" (Prov 1:7).

9. A helpful method in interpreting Wisdom literature is to collate similar proverbs according to their subject matter, interpreting them together.

---

46. Robert H. Stein, *Playing by the Rules: A Basic Guide to Interpreting the Bible* (Grand Rapids: Baker, 1994), p. 85.

47. Cf. Thomas Long, *Preaching and the Literary Forms of the Bible* (Philadelphia: Fortress, 1989), p. 55.

48. Hildebrandt, "Proverbs," p. 234.

49. Long, *Preaching and the Literary Forms*, p. 57.

I. Interpreting Paraenetic Literature
   1. The simplest form of paraenesis is the command or summons making the imperative a dominant feature.
   2. Paraenesis consists of a fusion of eclectic material from diverse origins and multiform traditions, including allusions to everyday natural events, wisdom sayings, popular maxims, sayings of Jesus, and ecclesiastical moral reflection.
   3. This conglomerate of admonitions is loosely strung together, especially through the device of catchword. This accounts for the difficulty exegetes encounter in unearthing a logical structure for paraenesis.
   4. Paraenesis is composed primarily of traditional material. This explains why the background questions pertinent to the documents are so difficult to answer.
   5. Paraenetic precepts have universal applicability. Therefore, one encounters exhortations in favor of general virtues and against various vices whose specific circumstances remain vague and nonspecific.
   6. The primary function of paraenesis is the socialization of the audience. To accomplish this purpose, norms and values are rehearsed to enable members of the group to realize and perform their proper role and function. Renowned human paradigms of virtue and vice are repeatedly referred to for emulation and avoidance respectively.[50]
   7. Paraenesis provides little opportunity for the development and elaboration of religious preconceptions and theological substructures. Consequently, the human side of the sanctification process is emphasized.

J. Interpreting the Epistles
   1. The epistles within the biblical record are intended for instruction.
   2. A letter should be read historically so that the situation of the author and readers can be reconstructed.
   3. Before exegeting an epistle verse by verse, the whole book should be read in one sitting in order to develop the literary meaning of the text.

50. See Leo G. Perdue, "The Social Character of Paraenesis and Paraenetic Literature," *Semeia* 50 (1990): 24-25.

4. The reader should identify the epistolary function of the letter opening, thanksgiving, body, and letter closing.

5. The reader of a letter should think in paragraphs and study
   the logical development of the argument in order to receive
   the full context and content of every text.

6. "Letters are another — and different — way of being
   there. . . . They are a unique blend of closeness and distance."[51] Therefore, the expositor and preacher should endeavor to develop a closeness between the author, text, and
   the contemporary reader.

---

51. Long, *Preaching and the Literary Forms*, p. 109.

Literary Techniques

Literary Devices Employed as Organizational Techniques

A. Envelope Technique *(Inclusio)*
Definition: The repetition of a concept, clause, or sentence at the beginning and end to tie a message together like bookends.
Examples by book:
1. In Matthew,
   a. Alternating Joseph (1:18-25; 2:13-15; 2:19-23) and Herod (2:1-12; 2:16-18) narratives in the birth narrative are balanced by an alternating pattern of the disciples (27:55-61; 28:1-10; 28:16-20) and the opposing forces of the Jewish leaders and Pilate (27:62-66; 28:11-15) in the resurrection narrative.
   b. "Immanuel, God with us" in 1:23 is paralleled by "I will be with you to the end of the world" in 28:20.
   c. The mission to the Gentiles (28:18-20) is foreshadowed in the arrival of the magi and the fact that Jesus is a descendent of Abraham (1:1, 2, 17) to bless the nations.
   d. Herod's lie (2:8: "so that I too may go and worship him") parallels the lie at the resurrection (28:13: "His disciples came during the night and stole him away while we were asleep").
   e. Jesus' ministry begins with baptism (3:13-17) and ends with a commission to baptize (28:19).

     f. The implicit trinity at Jesus' baptism (3:16-17) is made ex-
plicit in the commission to baptize in the Trinitarian formula (28:19).

    2. In Mark, the proclamation of Jesus as the Son of God at his
call to ministry and his death (1:1; 15:39) corresponds with
the tearing of heaven as a revelation at Jesus' baptism and
crucifixion (1:10; 15:38).

    3. In Luke-Acts, the narrative begins and ends with the em-
peror in Rome (Luke 2:1 and Acts 28), so that the whole
known world hears the gospel.

    4. In John, Jesus is proclaimed as God in 1:1 and 20:28.

    5. Examples by pericope:
Acts 5:29-32: obey God; Matt 10:26, 31: do not be afraid; Johan-
nine prologue with Jesus as God: John 1:1, 18; also: John 9:2, 41;
Pss 3; 8; 28:2, 6; 35:4, 26; 37:1, 8, 9, 34?; 103; 104; 118; 128:1, 4.

B. Chiasm
Definition: Words or events inversely repeated in order to shape
episodes, speeches, or cycles of stories.

    1. Macrochiasms of Entire NT Books Are Questionable
      a. An Entire Gospel
        1) Matthew (supported by Combrink, Fenton, Gaechter,
Green, Lohr[1])
        2) Mark (Humphrey, Scott, Van Iersel[2])
        3) Luke-Acts (Wolfe[3])
        4) John (Deeks, Ellis, Wyller[4])

1. H. J. Bernard Combrink, "The Structure of the Gospel of Matthew as Narrative,"
TynBul 34 (1983): 61-90; J. C. Fenton, *The Gospel of St. Matthew* (Baltimore: Penguin, 1964),
pp. 15-16; H. Benedict Green, "The Structure of St. Matthew's Gospel," *SE* IV (1968): 47-48;
Paul Gaechter, *Das Matthäus Evangelium* (Innsbruck: Tyrolia, 1963), p. 17; C. H. Lohr, "Oral
Techniques in the Gospel of Matthew," *CBQ* 23 (1961): 403-35.

2. Hugh M. Humphrey, *"He Is Risen!" A New Reading of Mark's Gospel* (New York:
Paulist, 1992), p. 4; M. Philip Scott, "Chiastic Structure: A Key to the Interpretation of
Mark's Gospel," *BTB* 15 (1985): 18-19, 25; Bas M. F. van Iersel, *Mark: A Reader-Response Com-
mentary.* JSNTSup 164 (Sheffield: Sheffield Academic, 1998), p. 84.

3. Kenneth R. Wolfe, "The Chiastic Structure of Luke-Acts and Some Implications for
Worship," *SwJT* 22 (1980): 60-67.

4. David Deeks, "The Structure of the Fourth Gospel," *NTS* 15 (1968): 107-29; Peter F.
Ellis, *The Genius of John: A Composition-Critical Commentary on the Fourth Gospel*
(Collegeville: Liturgical, 1984), pp. 14-15; Egil A. Wyller, "In Solomon's Porch: A Henological
Analysis of the Architectonic of the Fourth Gospel," *ST* 42 (1988): 151-67.

b. The Travel Narrative in Luke (Baarlink, Bailey, Blomberg, Farrell, Goulder[5])
c. The Upper Room Discourse of John 13–17 (Brouwer, Zorilla[6])
d. Acts 3–28 as well as 11:19–15:40 (Di Marco[7])
e. 1 Corinthians (Bailey[8])
f. 2 Corinthians 1–7 (Blomberg[9])
g. Galatians (Bligh[10])
h. Philippians (Luter and Lee, Porter and Reed[11])
i. 1 Timothy (Gibson[12])
j. 2 Timothy (Luo[13])
k. James (Crotty[14])
l. Jude (Bandstra, Wendland[15])

5. Heinrich Baarlink, "Die zyklische Struktur von Lukas 9.43b–19.28," *NTS* 38 (1992): 481-506; Kenneth E. Bailey, *Poet and Peasant* (Grand Rapids: Eerdmans, 1976), pp. 80-82; Craig L. Blomberg, "Midrash, Chiasmus, and the Outline of Luke's Central Section," in *Studies in Midrash and Historiography*, ed. R. T. France and David Wenham. Gospel Perspectives 3 (Sheffield: JSOT, 1983), pp. 217-61; Hobert K. Farrell, "The Structure and Theology of Luke's Central Section," *TJ* 7 (1986): 33-54; Michael D. Goulder, "The Chiastic Structure of the Lucan Journey," *SE* II (1964): 195-202.

6. Wayne Brouwer, *The Literary Development of John 13–17: A Chiastic Reading*. SBLDS 182 (Atlanta: Society of Biblical Literature, 2000), ch. 7; Hugo Zorilla, "A Service of Sacrificial Love," *Direction* 24 (1995): 74-85.

7. Angelico di Marco, "Der Chiasmus in der Bibel," *LB* 39 (1976): 37-85.

8. Kenneth E. Bailey, "The Structure of 1 Corinthians and Paul's Theological Method with Special Reference to 4:17," *NovT* 25 (1983): 152-81.

9. Craig L. Blomberg, "The Structure of 2 Corinthians 1–7," *CTR* 4 (1989): 3-20.

10. John Bligh, *Galatians in Greek: A Structural Analysis of St. Paul's Epistle to the Galatians* (Detroit: University of Detroit Press, 1966), who offers 48 chiastic patterns.

11. A. Boyd Luter and Michelle V. Lee, "Philippians as Chiasmus: Key to the Structure, Unity and Theme Questions," *NTS* 41 (1995): 89-101; Stanley E. Porter and Jeffrey T. Reed, "Philippians as a Macro-Chiasm and Its Exegetical Significance," *NTS* 44 (1998): 213-31.

12. Richard J. Gibson, "The Literary Coherence of 1 Timothy," *RTR* 55 (1996): 53-66.

13. Ling Luo, "The Structure of 2 Timothy: An Epistolary Analysis" (Th.M. diss., Calvin Theological Seminary, 2004).

14. Robert B. Crotty, "The Literary Structure of the Letter of James," *ABR* 40 (1992): 45-57.

15. Andrew J. Bandstra, "Onward Christian Soldiers — Praying in Love, with Mercy: Preaching on the Epistle of Jude," *CTJ* 32 (1997): 136-39; Ernst R. Wendland, "A Comparative Study of Rhetorical Criticism, Ancient and Modern: With Special Reference to the Larger Structure and Function of the Epistle of Jude," *Neot* 28 (1994): 193-228.

m. Revelation (Beale, Fiorenza[16])
2. Macrochiasms of Entire OT Books Are Questionable
   a. Genesis (supported by Prewitt[17])
   b. Numbers (Radday[18])
   c. Ruth (Bertman, Gow, Luter and Rigsby, Radday and Welch[19])
   d. Judges (Gooding[20])
   e. I and II Kings (Savran[21])
   f. Esther (Radday[22])
   g. Job (Dahood[23])
   h. Chiastic Psalms (Alden[24])
   i. Song of Songs (Shea, Webster[25])

16. G. K. Beale, *The Book of Revelation: A Commentary on the Greek Text.* NIGTC (Grand Rapids: Eerdmans, 1999), p. 131; Elisabeth Schüssler Fiorenza, *Revelation: Vision of a Just World* (Minneapolis: Fortress, 1991), pp. 35-36.

17. Terry J. Prewitt, "Story Structure and Social Structure in Genesis: Circles and Cycles," in *Semiotics, 1981,* ed. John N. Deely and Margot Lenhart (New York: Plenum, 1983), pp. 529-43.

18. Yehuda T. Radday, "Chiasmus in Hebrew Biblical Narrative," in *Chiasmus in Antiquity: Structures, Analysis, Exegesis,* ed. John W. Welch (Provo: Research, 1999), p. 89, following S. R. Hirsch.

19. Stephen Bertman, "Symmetrical Design in the Book of Ruth," *JBL* 84 (1965): 165-68; Murray D. Gow, "The Significance of Literary Structure for the Translation of the Book of Ruth," *BT* 35 (1984): 309-20; A. Boyd Luter and Richard O. Rigsby, "An Adjusted Symmetrical Structuring of Ruth," *JETS* 39 (1996): 16-29; Yahuda T. Radday and John W. Welch, "Chiasmus in the Scroll of Ruth," *Beth Mikra* 77 (1979): 180-87.

20. D. W. Gooding, "The Composition of the Book of Judges," *ErIsr* 16 (1982): 70-79.

21. George Savran, "I and II Kings," in *The Literary Guide to the Bible,* ed. Robert Alter and Frank Kermode (Cambridge, MA: Harvard University Press, 1987), p. 148.

22. Radday, "Chiasmus in Hebrew Biblical Narrative," p. 54.

23. Mitchell J. Dahood, "Chiasmus in Job: A Text-Critical and Philological Criterion," in *A Light unto My Path; Old Testament Studies in Honor of Jacob M. Myers.* ed. Howard N. Bream, Ralph D. Heim, and Carey A. Moore (Philadelphia: Temple University Press, 1974), pp. 119-30.

24. Robert L. Alden, "Chiastic Psalms: A Study in the Mechanics of Semitic Poetry in Psalms 1–50," *JETS* 17 (1974): 11-28; "Chiastic Psalms: A Study in the Mechanics of Semitic Poetry in Psalms 51-100," *JETS* 19 (1976): 191-200; "Chiastic Psalms: A Study in the Mechanics of Semitic Poetry in Psalms 101–150," *JETS* 21 (1978): 199-210.

25. William H. Shea, "The Chiastic Structure of the Song of Songs," *ZAW* 92 (1980): 378-96; Edwin C. Webster, "Pattern in the Song of Songs," *JSOT* 22 (1982): 73-93.

      j. Jeremiah (Rosenberg[26])

      k. Amos (Noble[27])

      l. Nahum (Bliese[28])

      m. Habakkuk (Walker and Lund[29])

      n. Zechariah (Payne[30])

  3. A Few Examples of Pericope Chiasms[31]

      Examples: Exod 20:21–24:3;[32] Num 11:11-15: questions and re-
sponse;[33] 1 Kings 3–11[34]; 1 Chronicles 1–9;[35] Isaiah 40–55;[36]
Ezekiel 40–48;[37] Amos 5:1-17;[38] Matthew 11-12;[39] ch. 13;[40]

26. Joel Rosenberg, "Jeremiah and Ezekiel," in Alter and Kermode, *The Literary Guide to the Bible*, pp. 190-91.

27. Paul R. Noble, "The Literary Structure of Amos: A Thematic Analysis," *JBL* 114 (1995): 209-26.

28. Loren F. Bliese, "A Cryptic Chiastic Acrostic: Finding Meaning from Structure in the Poetry of Nahum," *Journal of Translation and Text Linguistics* 7 (1995): 48-81.

29. Henry H. Walker and Nils W. Lund, "The Literary Structure of the Book of Habakkuk," *JBL* 53 (1934): 355-70.

30. Philip Payne, "Chiastic Structure in the Book of Zechariah," in *Interpreting the Book of Revelation: Hermeneutical Guidelines, with Brief Introduction to Literary Analysis*, ed. Kenneth A. Strand (Worthington: Ann Arbor, 1976), pp. 81-85.

31. For lists, see Nils Wilhelm Lund, *Chiasmus in the New Testament: A Study in the Form and Function of Chiastic Structures* (Chapel Hill: University of North Carolina Press, 1942); Angelico di Marco, "Der Chiasmus in der Bibel," *LB* 36 (1975): 21-97; 37 (1976): 49-68; 39 (1976): 37-85; 44 (1979): 3-70; Ian H. Thomson, *Chiasmus in the Pauline Letters*. JSNTSup 111 (Sheffield: Sheffield Academic, 1995). For literature, see John W. Welch and Daniel B. McKinlay, eds., *Chiasmus Bibliography* (Provo: Research, 1999).

32. Joe M. Sprinkle, *"The Book of the Covenant": A Literary Approach*. JSOTSup 174 (Sheffield: JSOT, 1994).

33. W. Randolph Tate, *Biblical Interpretation: An Integrated Approach* (Peabody: Hendriksen, 1991), p. 90.

34. Bezalel Porten, "The Structure and Theme of the Solomon Narrative (1 Kings 3–11)," *HUCA* 38 (1967): 93-128.

35. Raymond B. Dillard, "The Literary Structure of the Chronicler's Solomon Narrative," *JSOT* 30 (1984): 85-93.

36. Antti Laato, "The Composition of Isaiah 40–55," *JBL* 109 (1990): 207-28; Leon J. Liebreich, "The Compilation of the Book of Isaiah," *JQR* 46 (1956); 259-77; 47 (1956): 114-38.

37. Steven Shawn Tuell, *The Law of the Temple in Ezekiel 40–48*. HSM 49 (Atlanta: Scholars, 1992).

38. Jan De Waard, "The Chiastic Structure of Amos V 1-17," *VT* 27 (1977): 170-77.

39. Daniel Boerman, "The Chiastic Structure of Matthew 11–12," *CTJ* 40 (2005): 313-25.

40. D. A. Carson, Douglas J. Moo, and Leon Morris, *Introduction to the New Testament* (Grand Rapids: Zondervan, 1992), p. 65; David Wenham, "The Structure of Matthew XIII," *NTS* 25 (1979): 517-18.

Mark 2:1–3:6;[41] 3:13-35;[42] 4:1-34;[43] 4:26-29; 8:22–10:52;[44] 11:1–12:40;[45] ch. 13;[46] Luke 1:6-25;[47] 4:16-30;[48] ch. 15;[49] 18:18-30;[50] John 18:28–19:16;[51] Heb 6:19–10:39.[52]

4. Sentence or Subsection Chiasms[53]

Amos 5:4b-6a; Matt 3:14; 3:8-10; 5:43-47; 6:9-13, 24; 7:6; 10:28; 11:4-5; 13:24-30; 17:25-26; 23:16-22; Mark 1:19-20; 2:14-16, 22, 27; 8:35; 9:43, 47; 10:31; Luke 4:16-21a; Luke 6:44; 8:40-56; 16:25; 23:2-25; John 6:36-40; Acts 1:4-8; 20:18-35; 28:26-27; Rom 2:6-11; 11:20, 33-35; 1 Cor 4:10; 5:2-6; 9:19-22; 11:8-12; 13:8-13; Eph 5:8-11; Phil 1:15-17; 2:5-11; Col 1:14-22a; 1 Tim 3:16.

5. Rules for Discerning a Chiasm

a. There must be a problem with the structure of the text that conventional outlines fail to resolve.

41. Joanna Dewey, "The Literary Structure of the Controversy Stories in Mark 2:1–3:6," *JBL* 92 (1973): 394-401.

42. Jan Lambrecht, "The Relatives of Jesus in Mark," *NovT* 16 (1974): 252.

43. Joanna Dewey, *Markan Public Debate: Literary Technique, Concentric Structure, and Theology in Mark 2:1–3:6.* SBLDS 48 (Chico: Scholars, 1980), pp. 149-50; Greg Fay, "Introduction to Incomprehension: The Literary Structure of Mark 4:1-34," *CBQ* 51 (1989): 81.

44. Humphrey, *"He Is Risen!"* p. 79.

45. Stephen H. Smith, "The Literary Structure of Mark 11:1–12:40," *NovT* 31 (1989): 104-24; repr. in *The Composition of Mark's Gospel,* ed. David Orton (Leiden: Brill, 1999), pp. 171-91.

46. Dean Deppe, "Charting the Future or a Perspective on the Present? The Paraenetic Purpose of Mark 13," *CTJ* 41 (2006): 93; Jan Lambrecht, *Die Redaktion der Markus-Apokalypse: Literarische Analyse und Strukturuntersuchung.* AnBib 28 (Rome: Päpstliches Bibelinstitut, 1967), pp. 273-74.

47. James L. Bailey and Lyle D. Vander Broek, *Literary Forms in the New Testament: A Handbook* (Louisville: Westminster John Knox, 1992), p. 179.

48. Jeffrey S. Siker, "'First to the Gentiles': A Literary Analysis of Luke 4:16-30," *JBL* 111 (1992): 73-90.

49. Bailey, *Poet and Peasant,* pp. 144, 156, 159-60.

50. Kenneth E. Bailey, *Through Peasant Eyes: More Lucan Parables, Their Culture and Style* (Grand Rapids: Eerdmans, 1980), p. 158.

51. Raymond Brown, *The Gospel According to John XIII-XXI.* AB 29A (Garden City: Doubleday, 1970), pp. 858-59.

52. George E. Rice, "The Chiastic Structure of the Central Section of the Epistle to the Hebrews," *AUSS* 19 (1981): 243-46.

53. The examples are taken from Bailey and Vander Broek, *Literary Forms in the New Testament,* pp. 49-54, 178-83; Di Marco, *LB* 37 (1976): 37-85; 44 (1979): 3-7; Joachim Jeremias, "Chiasmus in den Paulusbriefen," *ZNW* 49 (1958): 145-56; and Robert H. Stein, *The Method and Message of Jesus' Teachings,* rev. ed. (Louisville: Westminster John Knox, 1994), p. 31.

b. There must be clear examples of multiple sets of parallelism.

c. There must be verbal and grammatical repetitions that are
   widespread, central to the passage, and unique to the passage.

d. The chiastic outline should follow the natural breaks of
   content in the text as evidenced by the majority of commentators.

e. The center or climax of the chiasmus should be recogniz-
   ably significant for its theological or ethical import.

f. Balanced elements are normally of similar length.

g. Rather than rearranging the text, interpreters should use
   the text as it stands so that the symmetrical elements are
   in precisely inverted order.

h. The chiasm should begin and end at natural textual
   boundaries.

6. Principles of Interpretation for a Chiasm

a. "There is often a change in the trend of the argument in
   the center, and an opposite idea is introduced, before the
   original trend is resumed. Lund names this 'the law of the
   shift at the centre.'"[54]

b. The center can play "any of three functions: forming the
   climax of the argument, indicating its purpose, or acting
   as a apophthegmatic summary of its contents."[55]

c. Similar ideas are often distributed so as to be found in the
   extremes and the center of a concentric system and nowhere else within it.[56]

d. "The symmetries that emerge in a chiasmus have the effect of making the combined impact of element X with its
   chiastic partner X′ more than the impact of X and X′ in
   isolation."[57]

e. "A concentric structure may serve to integrate additional
   dimensions or emphases into a chronological or linear
   narrative." Therefore, "symmetry hardly suppresses the

54. Dewey, *Markan Public Debate*, p. 36.
55. Thomson, *Chiasmus in the Pauline Letters*, p. 43.
56. Thomson, *Chiasmus in the Pauline Letters*, p. 41.
57. Thomson, *Chiasmus in the Pauline Letters*, p. 39.

chronological development; rather it adds depth or another dimension."[58]

C. Markan Intercalation (Sandwich) and Markan Frame
   Definition of a Markan intercalation: A literary device whereby one story is bifurcated into two sections and a second story is inserted in between, indicating that the two stories are somehow similar in nature. Both the intercalations and the frames in the Gospel of Mark call attention to a suffering Messiah and the cost of discipleship in following this Messiah. On two occasions the intercalation demonstrates how this Messiah fulfils Jewish ceremonial regulations.

Examples	Passage	Theme
Accusations against Jesus	3:20-34(35)	Suffering Messiah + Discipleship
The Bleeding Woman and Dead Girl	5:21-43	Jewish Regulations
The Mission of the Twelve and John's Death	6:7-30	Suffering Messiah + Discipleship
The Fig Tree and the Temple Action	11:12-26	Jewish Regulations
Those Plotting vs. the Woman Preparing	14:1-11	Suffering Messiah + Discipleship
Peter's Denial and Jesus' Jewish Trial	14:53-72	Suffering Messiah

Definition of a Markan frame: Two similar passages serve as bookends *(inclusio)* to a section of narrative to focus the content and offer an interpretation of the material in between.

Examples	Passage	Theme
The Gospel of the Suffering Son	1:1, 14-15	Suffering Messiah
Successful Preaching Ministry	1:14-15, 39	Contrast with Passion
Secrecy frame around Controversies	1:40-45; 3:7-12	Suffering Messiah
Insider/Outsider frame	3:13-19, 33-34	Discipleship
Seed Parables frame	4:1-2, 33-36	Discipleship
Sea Trips frame	4:35-41; 8:13-21	Discipleship

58. Dewey, *Markan Public Debate*, p. 37.

Examples	Passage	Theme
Blind Men Healed frame	8:22-26; 10:46-52	Discipleship
Royal Psalms frame	11:9-11; 12:36 + 13:1	Suffering Messiah
Woman's Sacrificial Action frame	12:41-44; 14:3-9	Discipleship
Burial Actions frame	14:3-9; 16:1-8	Suffering Messiah

D. Catchwords

Definition: Words that tie together a section that is not closely connected by similar content and theme in order that the reader can more easily memorize the material.

Examples:

1. Matt 18:1-13: kingdom of God, child, cause to sin, little one.
2. Mark 9:35-50: in your (my) name, cause to sin, it is better, fire, salt.
3. Luke 15:13 (διεσκόρπισεν) and Luke 16:1 (διασκορπίζων): squander wealth.
4. Luke 16:19-31 (The parable of the Rich Man and Lazarus) is tied to the parable of Lost Son (15:11-32) by catchwords: celebrating, εὐφραίνω (15:23, 24, 29, 32; 16:19); longing to eat, ἐπιθυμῶν χορτασθῆναι (15:16; 16:21); father in the vocative (15:12, 18, 21; 16:24, 27, 30); the address to a son with τέκνον (15:31; 16:25).
5. Luke 16:10-12: mammon (μαμωνᾶ), 16:9, 11, 13; unrighteous (ἀδικίας, ἄδικος): 16:8, 9, 10.
6. Soul (ψύχη) in L at Luke 12:19, 20 and in Q at 12:22, 23.
7. Luke 13:4, 11: eighteen who died at the tower of Siloam and eighteen years as a cripple.

E. Parallelism

1. Synonymous Parallelism

Definition: The second verset restates the thought of the first verset in a different way.

Examples: Two strophe (Mark 3:24-25); three strophe (Matt 7:7-8); four strophe (Luke 6:27-28).

OT examples: throughout Wisdom literature and the Psalms; Gen 49:11b; Prov 3:14; 20:1; Isa 53:5.

NT examples: Mark 2:21-22 par.; 3:4, 28; 4:22, 30; 8:17, 18; 9:43-

47; 10:38, 43-44; 13:24-25; Matt 5:39-40 par.; 5:46-47; 6:25; 7:6;
10:24-25, 41; 12:30, 41-42; 13:16; 23:29; Luke 2:46-47; 6:37, 38;
12:48b; 13:2-5; 15:32; 17:26-29 par.; 19:43-44; 23:29; cf. John 3:11;
6:35, 55; 12:31; 13:16.

Movement in the second couplet:

 a. Complementary movement

 Examples: Ps 103:3 (forgive sins, heal diseases); 103:7 (ways,
 deeds); 103:11-12 (heaven and earth, east and west); Prov
 3:16 (long life, riches and honor).

 b. Toward intensification

 Examples: Ps 2:2a (take stand, gather together = treaty); Ps
 2:3 (break chains, throw off); Ps 8:4 (think, care); Ps 62:11
 (once, twice); Prov 20:1 (wine, strong drink); Jer 50:19b
 (pasture, satisfied); Mic 5:5b (seven, eight).

 c. Toward specification

 Examples: Ps 19:1 (glory, work of his hands); Amos 8:10
 (feasts, songs).

2. Antithetical Parallelism

 Definition: the same idea is expressed in a negative manner.

 Examples: more numerous than all the other types combined:
 Mark 2:19-20 par.; 3:28-29; 4:25; 7:8, 15; 8:35; Matt 5:19; 6:2-3, 5-
 6, 22-23, 24 par.; 7:17, 18; 10:32-33; 13:16-17; 22:14; Luke 1:52;
 6:21a, 25a, 21b, 25b; 7:44-47; 16:10; cf. John 3:6, 12, 17, 20-21.

 Movement in the second couplet:

 a. From correct to incorrect: Prov 1:7 (fear of the Lord,
 fools); 10:1 (wise and foolish children).

 b. From incorrect to correct: Ps 20:7 wrong trust, right trust;
 Prov 3:1 forget, keep.

3. Synthetic Parallelism

 Definition: The second verset complements the first by clarification or explanation so that it supplements the first or
 brings it to completion.

 Examples: Amos 1:7; Matt 23:5-10; Luke 12:49-51; cf. John
 8:44.

 Movement in the second couplet:

 a. From cause to effect (step parallelism): Pss 1:3; 18:3; Mark
 2:27-28; 9:37 par.; Matt 5:17; 6:22-23 par., 34; 10:34, 40;
 12:28?, 29?; Luke 10:16 par.; cf. John 6:37; 8:32; 10:11; 11:25;
 13:20; 14:2-3, 21; 16:7, 22.

b. Repetition and addition (climactic parallelism): Ps 29:1.
4. Movement from One Type to Another (an example from Isa 55:6-10)
   a. 55:6-7: Synonymous Parallelism (AABBCC)
   b. 55:8-9: Antithetical Parallelism (ABC [the heavens are higher than the earth] BA)
   c. 55:10-11: Step Parallelism (ABCDABCD)

F. Repetition
   1. A *Leitwort* (Keyword)
      Examples: Rom 8:18-27 (groaning); Rom 5:1-11 (we rejoice); Eph 4:4-6 (one); Rev 22:6-20 (Behold, I am coming soon: 22:7, 12, 20).
   2. Word Chains
      Examples: Rom 5:3-5; 8:38-39; 2 Pet 1:5-7.
   3. A Motif or Picture
      Example: 1 Pet 2:4-8 (stone or rock).
   4. Formulas
      Examples: the prophetic imprecation formula in Amos 1:3–2:16 ("for three sins of _____, even for four, I will not turn back my wrath").
   5. A Refrain or Chorus
      Examples: Pss 42–43; 46; 49; 57; 67; 80; 99; 107; 136.
   6. A Form Letter: Revelation 2–3
      a. Address: "To the angel . . ."
      b. Christ's Self-designation: "The Words of him . . ."
      c. Their Present Condition: "I know your works . . ."
      d. Correction: "But I have this against you . . . (except the last three and Smyrna)
      e. Command
      f. Warning or Encouragement
      g. Standard Concluding Exhortation: "He who has an ear, let him hear . . ."
      h. Eschatological Promise: "To him who conquers I . . ."

A Glossary of Literary Techniques and Grammatical Terms

Alliteration   A series of words with the identical sound.

Examples: This can include (1) acrostic passages like Psalms 9–10; 25; 37; 111; 119; 145; Prov 31:10-31; Lamentations 1–4; (2) the use of consonants as, e.g., in Heb 1:1 with five Greek terms beginning with p, five occurrences of l, and two adverbs ending in -ōs; and (3) assonance (usually vowel sounds) as in the hymn at 1 Tim 3:16 or in the description of wisdom from above in Jas 3:17.

For further examples, see Bullinger, *Figures of Speech Used in the Bible*, pp. 171-79.[1]

Anacoluthon   The breaking off of a sentence partway through while a new sentence is begun without finishing the first one.

Examples: See *BDF* 466-70.

Anthropomorphism   When God is described with earthly features.

Examples: shepherd (Ps 23:1); warrior (35:2); singer (Zeph 3:17); very common are the images of rock, king, father. Cf. Bullinger, *Figures of Speech Used in the Bible*, pp. 871-97.

Apophthegm   A short and pointed saying, commonly supported by a narrative framework and also called a pronouncement saying in a controversy dialogue.

---

1. Ethelbert W. Bullinger, *Figures of Speech Used in the Bible: Explained and Illustrated* (1898; repr. Grand Rapids: Baker, 1968).

Aposiopesis   The suppression of part of a sentence because of emotion, an unpleasant conclusion, or because the writer wants to gain a certain rhetorical effect.

Examples: Cf. Bullinger, *Figures of Speech Used in the Bible,* pp. 151-54.

Apostrophe   An exclamatory address to an object or person.

Examples: gates (Ps 24:7); mountains (68:16); sea (114:5-6); barren woman (Isa 54:1-3); cows of Bashan (Amos 4:1); Jerusalem (Matt 23:37); Cf. Bullinger, *Figures of Speech Used in the Bible,* pp. 901-5.

Asyndeton   The omission of an element of the sentence (esp. a conjunction) in order to add solemnity or emphasis.

Examples: Matt 5:3-17; 5:24; 8:4; John 1:23, 26, 29; 2 Tim 3:2; 1 Pet 4:3; Jas 2:13; 5:13-14. For further discussion and examples, see Bullinger, *Figures of Speech Used in the Bible,* pp. 137-48.

Chiasmus   An extended concentric structure with an introverted parallelism of words, clauses, or content.

For examples, see Appendix II, B above (pp. 354-60).

Divine Passive   The use of a verb in the passive voice as a circumlocution for God's action ("it has been given" instead of "God has given"), since the divine name was too holy to speak.

Epizeuxis   The repetition of the same word(s) for emphasis.

Examples: Cf. Bullinger, *Figures of Speech Used in the Bible,* pp. 189-98.

Euphemism   Substituting a less distasteful word or phrase for a more shocking one.

Examples: sex (Lev 18:6-8; Matt 1:25); toiletry duties (Judg 3:24; 1 Sam 24:3); death (John 11:11); Gentiles (Acts 2:39). Cf. Bullinger, *Figures of Speech Used in the Bible,* pp. 684-88.

Hendiadys   Two words are used but one concept is meant.

Examples: See Bullinger, *Figures of Speech Used in the Bible,* pp. 657-673.
Disputed Examples:

> Gen 1:26: Let us make man in our image, after our likeness.
> Matt 3:11: Baptized with the Holy Spirit and fire.
> John 3:5: Born of water and the Spirit.
> John 4:21, 24: Worship God in spirit and in truth.

Hyperbole   Employing deliberate exaggeration to produce effect.

Examples: Gen 22:17; Exod 32:13; Deut 28:62 (as many children as stars in the sky and sand on the seashore); 1 Kgs 1:40 (the ground shook from the playing of flutes); Mark 9:42-47 (cutting off a member of your body). Cf. Bullinger, *Figures of Speech Used in the Bible,* pp. 423-28.

Inclusio   A literary bracket or bookends; the purposeful repetition of a word or phrase at the beginning and end of a passage signifying a rhetorical unit.

    For examples, see Appendix II, A above (pp. 353-54).

Irony

    Verbal Irony   Saying something other than what one means. Camery-Hoggatt distinguishes the following subcategories: "There are four forms of verbal irony which may be uttered with the speaker's full consciousness: deliberate ambiguity, sarcasm, hyperbole, and meiosis."[2]

    Examples of deliberate ambiguity (cf. also Bullinger, *Figures of Speech Used in the Bible,* pp. 807-18):

    a. Eglon says to Ehud, "I have a word from God for you" (Judg 3:20).
    b. David tells Uriah, "Stay the night, tomorrow you will be dispatched" (2 Sam 11:12).
    c. The sign on the cross is true, even though it was said in mockery: "King of the Jews" (Mark 15:26).
    d. The Jews mock Jesus, saying, "Save yourself" (Mark 15:30), when in reality Jesus is saving the whole world by dying.
    e. Characters unconsciously state the truth in John 3:2; 4:12; 6:42; 7:27, 35, 42; 8:22; 9:40-41; 11:50; 12:19; 19:5, 15, 19.

    Dramatic Irony   Two levels of meaning exist within a certain situation where the readers possess knowledge that the characters do not have.

    Examples:

    a. In Job 1–2 the readers are aware of the wiles of Satan, while the characters know nothing about the heavenly engagement.
    b. The moment Jesus is being mocked by the Sanhedrin as a false prophet, his prophecy that Peter will deny him is happening (Mark 14:53-72).
    c. Although Jesus is mocked for proclaiming that he would destroy the temple (Mark 15:29), it occurs in the ripping of the curtain (15:38).

Lemma   The root or lexical form of a word in Hebrew or Greek.

---

2. Jerry Camery-Hoggatt, *Irony in Mark's Gospel: Text and Subtext.* SNTSMS 72 (Cambridge: Cambridge University Press, 1992), p. 85.

Meiosis   A deliberate understatement used to call attention to something; the opposite of hyperbole.
> Examples: Cf. Bullinger, *Figures of Speech Used in the Bible*, pp. 155-58.

Metaphor   A comparison where one thing represents another without the use of the word "like" or "as."
> Examples: Cf. Bullinger, *Figures of Speech Used in the Bible*, pp. 735-43.
> Examples in Parables: See Appendix I, A 3 a 1): Parable (p. 302).

Metonymy   Two objects are closely associated so that one substitutes for the other.
> Examples: a throne for kingship (1 Chr 17:12); a sword for judgment (Isa 51:19); a key for authority (Isa 22:22; Matt 16:19); Moses for the Torah (Luke 16:29; 24:27); circumcision for the Jews (Phil 3:3). Cf. Bullinger, *Figures of Speech Used in the Bible*, pp. 538-608.

Morphology   A description of a word's grammatical form and function.

Onomatopoeia   Where the sound of the word parallels the phenomenon in real life.
> Examples: Isa 17:12 ("the thundering of the sea" and "the sound of roaring waves"); Gen 1:2 ("without form or void," *tōhû wābōhû*).

Parataxis/Hypotaxis   Parataxis occurs when phrases, clauses, or sentences of equal structural rank are placed side by side without coordinating conjunctions. On the other hand, hypotaxis occurs when subordinating conjunctions connect dependent clauses to independent units.

Paronomasia   A pun with similar sounds but different meanings.
> Examples (cf. Bullinger, *Figures of Speech Used in the Bible*, pp. 307-20):
> a. Amos 8:2: "summer fruit" *(qāyiṣ)* sounds like "end" *(qēṣ):* "The end has come upon my people."
> b. Jer 1:11-12: "almond branch" *(šāqēd)* and "watching over" *(šōqēd).*
> c. Isa 5:7: "justice" *(mišpāṭ)* and "bloodshed" *(miśpāḥ);* "righteousness" *(ṣĕdāqāh)* and "weeping" *(ṣĕʿāqāh).*

Pericope   A self-contained unit or passage of Scripture, which derives from the Greek for "cut around."

Personification   An inanimate object or group of persons assumes human properties.
> Examples (Cf. Bullinger, *Figures of Speech Used in the Bible*, pp. 861-69):
> a. Death and destruction (Job 28:22).

    b. The heavens (Ps 19:1-2).

    c. Wisdom (Prov 1:20-33; 3:13-20; 4:1-9; 8:1-11; 8:12-36).

    d. Israel (Hos 11:1).

    e. The body (1 Cor 12:15-21).

    f. Sin (Jas 1:15).

    g. Animals in the book of Revelation: eagle (8:13), locusts (9:3-11), dragon (12:3-17), beasts (13:1-17).

Prominence   The focus or emphasis of a paragraph.

    Marked Prominence   Various devices in the structure, like word order or repetition, that highlight portions of a discourse.

    Natural Prominence   Those elements that are more significant for the development of a discourse because they are the backbone of the episode or reveal the development of the theme.

Redaction   The work of editing especially employed to describe the evangelist's adaptations of the traditions, e.g., the redaction by Matthew and Luke of the Gospel of Mark.

Simile   A declaration that one thing represents another through the use of "like" or "as."

    Examples: Cf. Bullinger, *Figures of Speech Used in the Bible,* pp. 726-33.

    Examples in Parables: See Appendix I, A 3 a 1): Parable (p. 302).

Synecdoche   The practice of using a part to refer to a whole or vice versa.

    Examples: the gates for the entire city (Ps 87:2; Isa 3:26; 14:31); the human body for the whole person (1 Cor 6:15). Cf. Bullinger, *Figures of Speech Used in the Bible,* pp. 613-56.

Select Bibliography

Achtemeier, Elizabeth Rice. *Preaching from the Old Testament.* Louisville: Westminster John Knox, 1989.

Achtemeier, Paul J., Joel B. Green, and Marianne Meyer Thompson. *Introducing the New Testament: Its Literature and Theology.* Grand Rapids: Eerdmans, 2001.

Albertz, Martin. *Die synoptische Streitgespräche: Ein Beitrag zur Formgeschichte des Urchristentums.* Berlin: Trowitzsch & Sohn, 1921.

Alter, Robert. *The Art of Biblical Narrative.* New York: Basic Books, 1981.

Aune, David E., ed. *Greco-Roman Literature and the New Testament: Selected Forms and Genres.* SBLSBS 21. Atlanta: Scholars, 1988.

———. *The New Testament in Its Literary Environment.* LEC 8. Philadelphia: Westminster, 1987.

Bailey, James L., and Lyle D. Vander Broek. *Literary Forms in the New Testament: A Handbook.* Louisville: Westminster John Knox, 1992.

Bailey, Kenneth E. *Poet and Peasant: A Literary-Cultural Approach to the Parables in Luke.* Grand Rapids: Eerdmans, 1976.

Baltzer, Klaus. *The Covenant Formulary in Old Testament, Jewish, and Early Christian Writings.* Trans. David E. Green. Philadelphia: Fortress, 1971.

Berger, Klaus. "Hellenistische Gattungen im Neuen Testament." *ANRW* 2.25.2 (1984), pp. 1031-1432.

Berkhof, Louis. *Principles of Biblical Interpretation.* Grand Rapids: Baker, 1950.

Betz, H. D. "The Early Christian Miracle Story: Some Observations on the Form Critical Problem." *Semeia* 11 (1978): 69-81.

Black, David Alan. *Linguistics for Students of New Testament Greek.* 2nd ed. Grand Rapids: Baker, 1995.

———. *Using New Testament Greek in Ministry: A Practical Guide for Students and Pastors.* Grand Rapids: Baker, 1993.

Blackwelder, Boyce W. *Light from the Greek New Testament*. Anderson, Indiana: Warner, 1958.

Bornkamm, Günther. *Jesus of Nazareth*. New York: Harper, 1960.

Breck, John. *The Shape of Biblical Language: Chiasmus in the Scriptures and Beyond*. Crestwood: St. Vladimir's Seminary Press, 1994.

Broadhead, Edwin K. *Teaching with Authority: Miracles and Christology in the Gospel of Mark*. JSNTSup 74. Sheffield: Sheffield Academic, 1992.

Brouwer, Wayne. *The Literary Development of John 13–17: A Chiastic Reading*. SBLDS 182. Atlanta: Society of Biblical Literature, 2000.

Brown, Raymond E. *Biblical Exegesis and Church Doctrine*. New York: Paulist, 1985.

———. *The Birth of the Messiah*. Garden City: Doubleday, 1993.

———. *The Death of the Messiah*. 2 vols. ABRL. New York: Doubleday, 1994.

———. *New Testament Essays*. Milwaukee: Bruce, 1965.

Brueggemann, Walter. *Praying the Psalms*. Winona: Saint Mary's, 1982.

Bullinger, E. W. *Figures of Speech Used in the Bible: Explained and Illustrated*. London: Eyre & Spottiswoode, 1898; repr. Grand Rapids: Baker, 1968.

Bultmann, Rudolf. *The History of the Synoptic Tradition*. Trans. John Marsh. New York: Harper & Row, 1963.

Buttrick, David G. *Speaking Parables: A Homiletic Guide*. Louisville: Westminster John Knox, 2000.

Caird, G. B. *The Language and Imagery of the Bible*. Grand Rapids: Eerdmans, 1980.

Camery-Hoggatt, Jerry. *Irony in Mark's Gospel: Text and Subtext*. SNTSMS 72. Cambridge: Cambridge University Press, 1992.

Carson, Donald A. *Exegetical Fallacies*. 2nd ed. Grand Rapids: Baker, 1996.

Charlesworth, James H., ed. *The Old Testament Pseudepigrapha*. 2 vols. Garden City: Doubleday, 1983-85.

Chisholm, Robert B. *From Exegesis to Exposition: A Practical Guide to Using Biblical Hebrew*. Grand Rapids, Baker, 1998.

Clark, D. J. "Criteria for Identifying Chiasm." *LB* 35 (1975): 63-72.

Collins, John J., ed. *Apocalypse: The Morphology of a Genre*. Semeia 14 (1979).

Cotterell, Peter, and Max Turner. *Linguistics and Biblical Interpretation*. Downers Grove: InterVarsity, 1989.

Dewey, Joanna. "The Literary Structure of the Controversy Stories in Mark 2:1–3:6." *JBL* 92 (1973): 394-401. Repr. in *The Interpretation of Mark*. ed. W. R. Telford. Minneapolis: Fortress, 1995, pp. 141-51.

———. "Mark as Aural Narrative: Structures as Clues to Understanding. *STRev* 36 (1992): 45-56.

———. "Mark as Interwoven Tapestry. Forecasts and Echoes for a Listening Audience." *CBQ* 53 (1991): 221-36.

———. *Markan Public Debate: Literary Technique, Concentric Structure, and Theology in Mark 2:1–3:6*. SBLDS 48. Chico: Scholars, 1980.

———. "Oral Methods of Structuring Narrative in Mark." *Int* 43 (1989): 32-44.

Dibelius, Martin. *From Tradition to Gospel*. Trans. Bertram Lee Woolf. Cambridge: Clarke, 1971.

Di Marco, Angelico. "Der Chiasmus in der Bibel." *LB* 36 (1975): 21-97; 37 (1976): 49-68; 39 (1976): 37-85; 44 (1979): 3-70.

Doty, William G. *Letters in Primitive Christianity.* GBS. Philadelphia: Fortress, 1973.

Droge, A. J. "Call Stories in Greek Biography and the Gospels." *SBLSP* 22. Atlanta: Scholars, 1983, pp. 245-57.

Drosnin, Michael. *The Bible Code.* New York: Simon & Schuster, 1997.

Dunn, James D. G. *Baptism in the Holy Spirit.* Philadelphia: Westminster, 1970.

———. "Spirit-and-fire Baptism." *NovT* 14 (1972): 81-92.

Edwards, James R. "Markan Sandwiches: The Significance of Interpretations in Markan Narratives." *NovT* 31 (1989): 193-216.

Fee, Gordon D. *New Testament Exegesis: A Handbook for Students and Pastors.* 3rd ed. Louisville: Westminster John Knox, 2002.

———, and Douglas Stuart. *How to Read the Bible For All Its Worth: A Guide to Understanding the Bible.* 2nd ed. Grand Rapids, Zondervan, 1993.

Fiorenza, Elisabeth Schüssler. *Revelation: Vision of a Just World.* Minneapolis: Fortress, 1991.

Funk, Robert W. "The Form of the New Testament Healing Miracle Story." *Semeia* 12 (1978): 57-96.

Gerstenberger, Erhard. "The Woe-Oracles of the Prophets." *JBL* 81 (1962): 249-263.

Giese, Ronald L., Jr. "Literary Forms of the Old Testament." In Sandy and Giese, *Cracking Old Testament Codes,* pp. 5-27.

Good, Edwin M. *Irony in the Old Testament.* Philadelphia: Westminster, 1965.

Green, Joel B. *Hearing the New Testament: Strategies for Interpretation.* 2nd ed. Grand Rapids: Eerdmans, 2010.

———, and Michael Pasquarello III, eds. *Narrative Reading; Narrative Preaching: Reuniting New Testament Interpretation and Proclamation.* Grand Rapids: Baker Academic, 2003.

Hagen, Kenneth, ed. *The Bible in the Churches: How Various Christians Interpret the Scriptures.* Milwaukee: Marquette University Press, 1994.

Hays, Richard B. *The Moral Vision of the New Testament: Community, Cross, New Creation: A Contemporary Introduction to New Testament Ethics.* San Francisco: HarperSanFrancisco, 1996.

Hedrick, Charles W. *Parables as Poetic Fictions: The Creative Voice of Jesus.* Peabody: Hendrickson, 1994.

Hendrickx, Herman. *The Parables of Jesus.* San Francisco: Harper & Row, 1986.

Herzog, William R. *Parables as Subversive Speech: Jesus as Pedagogue of the Oppressed.* Louisville: Westminster John Knox, 1994.

Hultgren, Arland J. *Jesus and His Adversaries: The Form and Function of the Conflict Stories in the Synoptic Tradition.* Minneapolis: Augsburg, 1979.

Kaiser, Walter C., Jr. *Preaching and Teaching from the Old Testament: A Guide for the Church.* Grand Rapids: Baker Academic, 2003.

———, and Moises Silva. *An Introduction to Biblical Hermeneutics: The Search for Meaning.* Rev. ed. Grand Rapids: Zondervan, 2007.

Kelber, Werner H. *The Oral and the Written Gospel: The Hermeneutics of Speaking and Writing in the Synoptic Tradition, Mark, Paul, and Q.* Philadelphia: Fortress, 1983.

Lane, A. N. S. *John Calvin: Student of the Church Fathers*. Grand Rapids: Baker, 1999.

Lindsell, Harold. *The Battle for the Bible*. Grand Rapids: Zondervan, 1976.

Lohr, C. H. "Oral Techniques in the Gospel of Matthew." *CBQ* 23 (1961): 403-35.

Long, V. Philips. "Toward a Better Theory and Understanding of Old Testament Narrative. *Presbyterian* 13 (1987): 102-109.

Long, Thomas G. *Preaching and the Literary Forms of the Bible*. Philadelphia: Fortress, 1989.

Longenecker, Richard N. *Biblical Exegesis in the Apostolic Period*. Grand Rapids: Eerdmans, 1975.

————, ed. *The Challenge of Jesus' Parables*. McMaster New Testament Studies. Grand Rapids: Eerdmans, 2000.

Lund, Nils Wilhelm. *Chiasmus in the New Testament: A Study in the Form and Function of Chiastic Structures*. Chapel Hill: University of North Carolina Press, 1942.

Luter, A. Boyd, and Michelle V. Lee. "Philippians as Chiasmus: Key to the Structure, Unity and Theme Questions." *NTS* 41 (1995): 89-101.

MacDonald, John. *Theology of the Samaritans*. Philadelphia: Westminster, 1964.

Mack, Burton L. *A Myth of Innocence: Mark and Christian Origins*. Philadelphia: Fortress, 1988.

Marshall, I. Howard, ed. *New Testament Interpretation: Essays on Principles and Methods*. Grand Rapids: Eerdmans, 1977.

McKim, Donald K. *Calvin and the Bible*. Cambridge: Cambridge University Press, 2006.

Merton, Thomas. *Praying the Psalms*. Collegeville: Liturgical, 1956.

Minear, Paul S. *Images of the Church in the New Testament*. Philadelphia: Westminster, 1960.

Mulholland, M. Robert, Jr. *Invitation to a Journey: A Road Map for Spiritual Formation*. Downers Grove: InterVarsity, 1993.

————. *Shaped by the Word: The Power of Scripture in Spiritual Formation*. Nashville: Upper Room, 1985.

Muller, Richard A., and John L. Thompson. "The Significance of Precritical Exegesis." In *Biblical Interpretation in the Era of the Reformation*. Grand Rapids: Eerdmans, 1996, pp. 335-45.

Muto, Susan Annette. *Approaching the Sacred: An Introduction to Spiritual Reading*. Denville: Dimension, 1973.

————. *The Journey Homeward: On the Road of Spiritual Reading*, Denville: Dimension, 1977.

————. *A Practical Guide to Spiritual Reading*. Rev. ed. Petersham: St. Bede's, 1994.

————. *Steps along the Way: The Path of Spiritual Reading*. Denville: Dimension, 1975.

Myers, Ched. *Say to This Mountain: Mark's Story of Discipleship*. Maryknoll: Orbis, 1996.

Nee, Watchman. *The Normal Christian Life*. Carol Stream: Tyndale House, 1977.

Osborne, Grant R. *The Hermeneutical Spiral: A Comprehensive Introduction to Biblical Interpretation*. Downers Grove: InterVarsity, 1991.

Packer, J. I. *Honouring the Written Word of God*. Carlisle: Paternoster, 1999.

Patte, Daniel, ed. *Semiology and Parables: Exploration of the Possibilities Offered by Structuralism for Exegesis.* Pittsburgh: Pickwick, 1976.

Pinnock, Clark H. "The Role of the Spirit in Interpretation." *JETS* 36 (1993): 491-497.

Porter, Stanley E. *Idioms of the Greek New Testament.* 2nd ed. Sheffield: Sheffield Academic, 1995.

Porter, Stanley E., and Jeffrey T. Reed. "Philippians as a Macro-Chiasm and Its Exegetical Significance." *NTS* 44 (1998): 213-31.

Price, Robert. *The Widow Traditions in Luke-Acts: A Feminist-Critical Scrutiny.* SBLDS 155. Atlanta: Scholars, 1997.

Puhl, Louis J., trans. *The Spiritual Exercises of St. Ignatius.* New York: Vintage, 2000.

Rad, Gerhard von. *The Problem of the Hexateuch.* Trans. E. W. Trueman Dicken. Edinburgh: Oliver and Boyd, 1966; repr. London: SCM, 1984.

Ramm, Bernard L. *Protestant Biblical Interpretation: A Textbook of Hermeneutics.* 3rd rev. ed. Grand Rapids: Baker, 1970.

Ramsay, William M. *The Letters to the Seven Churches of Asia and Their Place in the Plan of the Apocalypse.* London: Hodder and Stoughton, 1904.

Richardson, Alan. *The Miracle Stories of the Gospels.* London: SCM, 1941.

Rojas, Carmen. *Daily Prayer Companion: A Catholic Guide to Reading and Praying the Bible.* Ann Arbor: Redeemer, 1989.

Russell, Walter B., III. "Literary Forms in the Hands of Preachers and Teachers." In Sandy and Giese, *Cracking Old Testament Codes,* pp. 281-98.

Sadowski, Frank, ed. *The Church Fathers on the Bible,* New York: Alba House, 1987.

Sandy, D. Brent, and Ronald L. Giese Jr., eds. *Cracking Old Testament Codes: A Guide to Interpreting Literary Genres of the Old Testament.* Nashville: Broadman and Holman, 1995.

Schneemelcher, Wilhelm, ed. *New Testament Apocrypha.* 2 vols. Louisville: Westminster John Knox, 1991-92.

Scorgie, Glen A. "Hermeneutics and the Meditative Use of Scripture: The Case for a Baptized Imagination." *JETS* 44 (2001): 271-84.

Scott, Bernard Brandon. *Hear Then the Parable.* Minneapolis: Fortress, 1989.

Scott, M. Philip. "Chiastic Structure: A Key to the Interpretation of Mark's Gospel." *BTB* 15 (1985): 17-26.

Segovia, Fernando F. *The Farewell of the Word: The Johannine Call to Abide.* Minneapolis: Fortress, 1991.

Shepherd, Tom. *Markan Sandwich Stories. Narration, Definition, and Function.* Andrews University Seminary Doctoral Dissertation Series 18. Berrien Springs: Andrews University Press, 1993.

———. "The Narrative Function of Markan Intercalation." *NTS* 41 (1995): 522-40.

Smith, Martin L. *The Word Is Very Near You: A Guide to Praying with Scripture.* Cambridge, MA: Cowley, 1989.

Stein, Robert H. *Playing by the Rules: A Basic Guide to Interpreting the Bible.* Grand Rapids: Baker, 1994.

Stone, Michael E. *Jewish Writings of the Second Temple Period: Pseudepigrapha, Qumran, Sectarian Writings, Philo, Josephus.* Philadelphia: Fortress, 1984.

Stowers, Stanley K. *Letter Writing in Greco-Roman Antiquity.* Philadelphia: Westminster, 1986.

Stuart, Douglas K. *Old Testament Exegesis: A Handbook for Students and Pastors.* 4th ed. Louisville: Westminster John Knox, 2009.

Talbert, Charles. *Luke and the Gnostics: An Examination of Lucan Purpose.* Nashville: Abingdon, 1966.

Tannehill, Robert C. "Attitudinal Shift in Synoptic Pronouncement Stories." In *Orientation by Disorientation: Studies in Literary Criticism and Biblical Literary Criticism in Honor of William A. Beardslee,* ed. Richard A. Spencer. Pittsburgh: Pickwick, 1980, pp. 182-98.

————. "Types and Function of Apophthegms in the Synoptic Gospels." *ANRW* 2.25.2 (1984), pp. 1792-1829.

Tate, W. Randolph. *Biblical Interpretation: An Integrated Approach.* Peabody: Hendrickson, 1991.

Theissen, Gerd. *The Gospels in Context: Social and Political History in the Synoptic Tradition.* Trans. Linda M. Maloney. Minneapolis: Fortress, 1991.

————. *The Miracle Stories of the Early Christian Tradition.* Philadelphia: Fortress, 1983.

Thompson, John L. *Reading the Bible with the Dead: What You Can Learn from the History of Exegesis That You Can't Learn from Exegesis Alone.* Grand Rapids: Eerdmans, 2007.

Thompson, Marjorie, *Soul Feast: An Invitation to the Christian Spiritual Life.* Louisville: Westminster John Knox, 1995.

Thomson, Ian H. *Chiasmus in the Pauline Letters.* JSNTSup 111. Sheffield: Sheffield Academic, 1995.

Toon, Peter. *From Mind to Heart: Christian Meditation Today.* Grand Rapids: Baker, 1987.

Trumbull, Henry Clay. *The Covenant of Salt as Based on the Significance and Symbolism of Salt in Primitive Thought.* New York: Scribner's, 1899.

VanderKam, James C. "Intertestamental Pronouncement Stories." In *Pronouncement Stories,* ed. Robert Tannehill. Semeia 20 (Chico: Scholars Press, 1981), 65-72.

Van Iersel, Bas M. F. "Concentric Structures in Mark 2,1–3,6 and 3,7–4,1: A Case Study." In *The Synoptic Gospels: Source Criticism and the New Literary Criticism,* ed. Camille Focant. Leuven: Leuven University Press, 1993, pp. 521-30.

Van Oyen, Geert. "Intercalation and Irony in the Gospel of Mark." In *The Four Gospels 1992: Festschrift Frans Neirynck,* ed. F. van Segroeck. BETL 100. Leuven: University Press, 1992, pp. 949-74.

Via, Dan O., Jr. *Kerygma and Comedy in the New Testament: A Structuralist Approach to Hermeneutic.* Philadelphia: Fortress, 1985.

Waltke, Bruce K., and M. O'Connor. *An Introduction to Biblical Hebrew Syntax.* Winona Lake: Eisenbrauns, 1990.

Webb, Joseph M., and Robert Kysar. *Greek for Preachers.* St. Louis: Chalice, 2002.

Weinfeld, Moshe. "The Covenant of Grant in the Old Testament and in the Ancient Near East." *JAOS* 90 (1970): 184-203.

Welch, John W., and Daniel B. McKinlay, eds. *Chiasmus Bibliography*. Provo: Research, 1999.

Westermann, Claus. *Basic Forms of Prophetic Speech*. Trans. Hugh Clayton White. Philadelphia: Westminster, 1967.

————. *Prophetic Oracles of Salvation in the Old Testament*. Trans. Keith Crim. Louisville: Westminster John Knox, 1991.

————. *The Psalms: Structure, Content, & Message*. Trans. Ralph D. Gehrke. Minneapolis: Augsburg, 1980.

Windham, Neal. *New Testament Greek for Preachers and Teachers: Five Areas of Application*. Lanham: University Press of America, 1991.

Wink, Walter. *The Bible in Human Transformation: Toward a New Paradigm for Biblical Study*. Philadelphia: Fortress, 1973.

Woodard, Branson L., Jr., and Michael E. Travers. "Literary Forms and Interpretation." In Sandy and Giese, *Cracking Old Testament Codes*, pp. 29-43.

Wright, George Al, Jr. "Markan Intercalations: A Study in the Plot of the Gospel." Ph.D. diss., Southern Baptist Theological Seminary, 1985.

Wright, N. T. *Justification: God's Plan and Paul's Vision*. Downers Grove: IVP Academic, 2009.

Wuest, Kenneth S. *The Practical Use of the Greek New Testament*. Rev. by Donald L. Wise. Chicago: Moody, 1982.

Index of Names

Achtemeier, Elizabeth Rice, 265, 266
Africa, Thomas, 167n.15
Aland, Kurt, 25n.31, 75, 142, 156, 170, 186n.61
Allen, Leslie C., 104n.20, 105
Allison, Dale C., 205n.22, 206n.25, 231n.2, 232n.3, 260
Ambrose, 217, 223
Anderson, A. A., 11n.10
Anderson, Francis I., 58n.15
Athanasius, 217
Aune, David E., 95n.10, 170, 184

Bacon, Benjamin W., 103n.19, 145n.15, 231n.2
Bailey, James L., 20
Balz, Horst R., 164n.10
Bandstra, Andrew J., 128n.51
Barclay, William, 221
Barnes, Albert, 240n.29
Barrett, David, 222
Bartchy, Scott S., 179, 180n.38, 180n.42, 181n.46
Barth, Karl, 234
Bartholomew, Craig, 229n.1
Bauckham, Richard J., 128n.51
Beale, Greg K., 164n.11, 170, 183n.49, 256n.58
Beasley-Murray, G. R., 222n.76
Belo, Fernando, 234n.5

Berger, Klaus, 213
Best, Ernest, 19, 114n.35, 185n.60
Billings, J. Todd, 267n.11
Black, David Alan, 121
Black, Matthew, 76n.32
Blass, Friedrich, 52, 67, 74n.29
Blount, Brian K., 208n.29
Boesak, Allan A., 102
Borchert, Gerald L., 221n.76
Boring, M. Eugene, 213
Bornkamm, Günther, 265
Bosma, Carl J., 103n.16, 136n.3
Boyer, James L., 70n.24
Brisco, Thomas V., 159
Brown, Jeannine K., 158n.1, 249
Brown, Raymond E., 36, 91, 150, 174, 216n.48, 216n.47, 222n.76, 252n.49
Bruce, F. F., 140n.9, 170n.21
Brueggemann, Walter, 12, 153, 195, 196-97, 274, 275
Burns, John Barclay, 151n.21
Burton, Ernest DeWitt, 67
Buttrick, David G., 174, 175n.29, 245, 246-47

Cadbury, Henry J., 94
Caird, G. B., 255n.55, 256
Calvin, John, 215, 219, 221, 224, 238, 256n.60, 274
Camery-Hoggatt, Jerry, 276

Carnegie, D. R., 23n.30
Carson, D. A., 164n.11, 180n.43
Carter, Warren, 227, 234n.5, 252n.50, 253
Cassidy, Richard J., 234n.5
Chadwick, Harold J., 159
Chapman, Benjamin, 67
Charles, Gary W., 208n.29
Charles, R. H., 103n.18, 290n.41
Charlesworth, James H., 160n.2, 177n.32
Childs, Brevard S., 103n.15
Chrysostom, John, 215, 217, 218, 221
Clement of Alexandria, 218
Clévenot, Michel, 234n.5
Colpe, Carsten, 213
Comfort, Philip, 222
Cotterell, Peter, xiv
Cranfield, C. E. B., 76n.32, 86

Debrunner, Albert, 52, 67, 74n.29
Delekat, Lienhard, 10
Deming, Will, 205n.22, 206n.23
Deppe, Dean B., 7n.1, 58n.15, 78n.36,
    106n.25, 146n.17, 189n.64, 216n.52
de Solages, Bruno, 188n.63
deVos, Craig S., 180
Dewey, Johanna, 15n.17
Drosnin, Michael, 268
Dunn, James D. G., 55n.13, 214, 215n.42,
    215n.46, 216, 217, 242, 243
du Toit, A. B., 159

Edersheim, Alfred, 159
Ehrman, Bart, 222n.79
Elliot, W. J., 222n.78
Elliott, Raymond, 71n.27
Endres, John C., 151n.21
Epp, Eldon Jay, 38, 39n.1
Evans, Craig A., 90n.2, 198-99, 250n.45

Farris, S. C., 173n.26
Fee, Gordon D., 105n.23, 143n.13,
    220n.70, 220n.72, 292, 295
Ferguson, Everett, 210n.35
Fiorenza, Elisabeth Schüssler, 101,
    102n.13, 248
Fitzmyer, Joseph A., 198, 215n.43

Fleddermann, Harry, 78n.35
Forbes, A. Dean, 58n.15
Fowl, Stephen E., 23n.30
France, R. T., 90n.2, 178, 226
Freeman, James M., 159
Funk, Robert W., 52, 67, 74n.29, 245,
    246

García Martínez, Florentino, 192n.65,
    211n.36, 211n.37
Garland, David E., 219, 220n.69
Gaster, T. H., 161n.4
Gerstenberger, Erhard S., 14n.15
Gibbs, J. M., 231n.2
Gibson, Shimon, 159
Goodacre, Mark, 208n.29
Gorman, Michael J., 138
Gould, Ezra P., 216n.52
Gray, S. W., 201
Green, Gene L., 139n.7
Green, Joel B., 130
Gregory of Nyssa, 217
Gundry, Robert H., 29n.32, 90n.2, 198,
    201, 206n.22, 225
Guthrie, George H., 106n.24, 121, 130

Haacker, Klaus, 162n.7
Haenchen, Ernst, 140n.9
Hagen, Kenneth, 213
Hagner, Donald A., 200, 201n.12
Halpern, Baruch, 153
Harris, Murray J., 180n.40
Hauerwas, Stanley, 270, 292
Hawkins, John C., 103n.17
Hayes, John H., xiii
Hays, Richard B., 54, 55n.13, 270, 292
Head, Peter M., 222nn.77-78
Hedrick, Charles W., 239, 239n.23
Heil, John Paul, 163n.8
Hemer, Colin J., 170n.21
Hendrickx, Herman, 239
Hendriksen, William, 91n.4, 241n.32
Hertzberg, Hans Wilhelm, 12
Herzog, William R., II, 239
Holladay, Carl R., xiii
Holmes, Michael W., 165n.12

Hooker, Morna D., 89n.1
Hopkins, Martin, 240n.28
Hultgren, Arland J., 171n.23

Isachar, Hanan, 159

Jeremias, Joachim, 202n.16, 212n.40,
   238-39
Jerome, 217, 218
Johnson, Earl S., 208n.29, 209nn.30-31
Johnston, Robert M., 193n.66
Jones, David A., 79n.39, 172
Joubert, Stephan, 159
Juel, Donald H., 208n.29
Jülicher, Adolf, 238

Kaiser, Walter C., Jr., 81n.42
Kelly, Thomas R., 279-80
Keys, Gillian, 10, 12
Kim, Seyoon, 254n.52
Kingsbury, Jack Dean, 145n.15, 146n.17,
   209n.31, 231n.2
Klein, Ralph W., 151, 152
Knowles, Michael J., 171n.23
Köstenberger, Andreas J., 222n.76
Kovacs, Judith, 217-18
Kümmel, Werner Georg, 265n.1

Ladd, George Eldon, 241n.31
LaHaye, Tim, 241n.30, 255
Lane, Anthony N. S., 214
Langton, Stephen, 3
Lightfoot, R. H., 89
Lindsell, Harold, 148
Loader, William, 206nn.22-23, 207n.28
Lohfink, Gerhard, 140n.10
Longacre, Robert, 130
Longenecker, Richard N., 111n.31, 113n.32
Longman, Tremper, III, 163n.9
Louw, Johannes P., 61n.17, 127n.48
Lukaszewski, Albert L., 52, 55n.14, 58n.15
Luther, Martin, 54, 203, 214, 218-19, 221,
   238
Luttikhuizen, G. P., 23n.30

MacDonald, John, 243n.37

Mackrell, Gerard, 259
Malherbe, Abraham J., 184n.51
Malina, Bruce, 159
Manson, T. W., 215
Marcus, Joel, 18, 19n.23, 177, 178n.33,
   205n.21, 207, 210n.34, 226
Marshall, I. Howard, 185n.60
Martin, Dale B., 235, 236n.12
Martin, Ralph P., 23
Mathews, Kenneth A., 257
Mays, James Luther, 103n.16
McArthur, Harvey K., 193n.66
McCarter, P. Kyle, Jr., 10n.5
McConville, Gordon, 229n.1
McKenzie, Steven L., 151n.22
McKnight, Scot, 210n.35
Menzies, Robert P., 215n.46
Merton, Thomas, 274
Metzger, Bruce M., 26, 40, 41, 222-23
Michaels, J. R., 201n.13
Millar, William R., 151n.21
Miller, Cynthia L., 130n.56
Minear, Paul S., 282
Moffatt, James, 217n.52
Montgomery, James A., 161n.5
Moo, Douglas J., 180n.43
Moore, George Foot, 206n.22
Morris, Leon, 91n.4, 222n.76
Mowry, L., 23n.30
Mulholland, M. Robert, Jr., 272, 273n.22,
   284, 285-86, 285n.37, 286n.38, 292
Muller, Richard A., 266
Myers, Ched, 234-35, 236

Nee, Watchman, 276-77
Negev, Avraham, 159
Nida, E. A., 61n.17
Nineham, Dennis E., 18n.22
Norris, D. Thaine, 159
Noth, Martin, 151, 151n.22
Nunn, H. P. V., 67, 67n.22

O'Connor, M., 85
Oden, Thomas C., 213
O'Donnell, Matthew Brook, 58n.15
Olbricht, Thomas H., 113n.32

Olsson, Birger, 130
Origen, 216, 220
O'Rourke, John J., 23n.30
Osborne, Grant R., xv
Osburn, Carroll D., 70, 71nn.26-27,
    76n.32
O'Toole, Robert F., 168nn.18-19
Ourisman, David J., 145, 146n.18

Packer, J. I., 271
Papias, 164-65
Parker, D. C., 222n.78
Parsons, Mikeal C., 94n.7
Pater, C. Marvin, 241n.33
Pelikan, Jaroslav, 242n.34
Pervo, Richard I., 94n.7
Peterson, Dwight N., 235, 236n.12
Peterson, Eugene H., 75-76, 82-84
Philipps, H. David, 79, 172
Phillips, J. B., 83
Pinnock, Clark, 268n.15
Piper, John, 203
Plutarch, 166, 168
Porter, Stanley E., 58n.15, 74n.28
Price, Robert, 239, 240n.27

Rackham, Richard B., 99
Ramsay, William Mitchell, 159, 170n.20
Rapske, Brian, 181n.44
Reed, Jeffrey T., 58n.15, 130
Ribbens, Benjamin, 183n.48, 183n.50,
    184nn.51, 184nn.55-57, 185n.58
Richardson, Alan, 259, 260n.67, 289
Robertson, A. T., 67
Robinson, James M., 23n.30
Rosner, Brian, 220, 220n.75
Rost, Leonhard, 10n.5
Rowland, Christopher, 234n.6
Rowley, H. H., 212n.40
Rückert, Leopold Immanuel, 264, 265n.1
Runge, Steven, 106, 106n.26
Russell, Walter B., III, 8
Ryken, Leland, 163n.9

Sanders, E. P., 250n.46
Sanders, Jack T., 23n.30

Saunders, Stanley P., 100n.12
Scanlin, Harold P., 159
Schneemelcher, Wilhelm, 270n.18
Schneider, Gerhard, 164n.10
Schürmann, Heinz, 185n.60
Schweizer, Eduard, 244n.39
Scorgie, Glen A., 266, 267, 269, 292n.44
Scott, Bernard Brandon, 239
Senior, Donald, 225, 225n.83
Sheppard, Gerald T., 103n.15
Shogren, Gary S., 67
Silva, Moisés, 54n.11, 130
Smith, Charles, W. F., 177n.31
Smith, David, 220
Smith, D. C., 212n.40
Smith, Fred, 278
Smith, Robert H., 23n.30, 94, 95n.8
Snodgrass, Klyne R., 171n.23, 174n.28,
    202n.15, 239n.21
Snyman, Andries H., 130
Standaert, Benoît, 113, 114n.35
Stein, Robert H., 19n.25, 90n.2, 91n.3,
    216n.48, 226, 237n.15, 238n.16, 267, 292
Stek, John H., 135n.2, 252n.49
Stuart, Douglas, 105n.23, 143n.13
Suetonius, 254

Talbert, Charles H., 95n.9, 143, 144, 242,
    244n.38
Tan, Randall, 58, 58n.15
Tate, Marvin E., 172
Tate, W. Randolph, xiv, xvnn.6-7
Taylor, Kenneth N., 75, 82
Taylor, Vincent, 215
Tenney, Merrill C., 269
Thiselton, Anthony C., 218n.59, 220
Thomas Aquinas, 237n.14
Thompson, John L., 213, 214, 266
Throntveit, Mark A., 152, 153
Toon, Peter, 284
Torrance, T. F., 212n.40
Torrey, Charles Cutler, 78n.38
Travers, Michael E., 8
Trench, Richard C., 238n.18
Trumbull, Henry Clay, 78n.37
Turner, C. H., 92, 93n.6

Turner, Max M. B., xiv, 216, 217

van der Watt, Jan, 159
Van Seters, John, 10
Vetne, Reimer, 241n.33
Via, Dan O., Jr., 7, 239
Virgil, 254

Wailes, Stephen L., 214
Wallace, Daniel B., 39, 52, 54, 67,
    124n.47, 205n.19
Walters, Patricia, 94n.7
Waltke, Bruce K., 85
Wanamaker, Charles A., 185
Warfield, Benjamin B., 139n.6
Webb, Robert L., 211n.38, 216n.48
Wegener, Mark, 24n.30
Weima, Jeffrey A. D., 113n.33, 114n.37,
    181n.45, 182, 183, 184
Wellhausen, Julius, 89
Wendland, Ernst, 130n.56
Wenham, Gordon J., 257n.64

Westermann, Claus, 103n.15, 257
Wheaton, D. H., 168n.17
Whybray, Roger N., 10
Wilken, Robert Louis, 213
Wilhoit, James C., 163n.9
Wilkens, W., 244n.39
Willard, Dallas, 268n.14, 271, 279, 280
Wink, Walter, 161n.6, 234, 265n.3, 266
Winter, Bruce W., 114, 184
Witherington, Ben, III, 90n.2, 114,
    115n.40, 140n.9, 252n.48
Woodard, Branson L., 8
Wright, A. G., 198
Wright, N. T., 54, 55n.13, 203-5, 250n.45
Wuellner, Wilhelm H., 177n.31

Yang, Namkuk, 215n.45, 216nn.49-50
Yarbro Collins, Adela, 114, 205, 206n.24,
    211

Zodhiates, Spiros, 61n.18

Index of Scripture and Other Ancient Literature

OLD TESTAMENT

Genesis

1–2	257
1:3	237
1:6-7	269
1:12-13	257
1:27-28	260
1:29	257
2:4	129, 231
2:8	256-58
2:19	256-58
3:16	260
4:24	176
12:3	85
19:26	216
24:10-61	162
26:12	176
29:1-12	162
38:16	230
38:24	230
40:22	167n.16

Exodus

1:22	231
2:5	231
2:16-21	162
3:5	163
3:14	288
4:22-23	232
4:25	206n.24
7:10-12	231
12	231
14:26-31	231
15	255
16:29	71n.26
17:1-7	261
18:21	11
19:15	218
20:13	232
20:14	232
21:24	232
24:39	232
30:35	189
33:14	232
33:19	288
33:22	288
34:6	288

Leviticus

2:11	175
2:13	78, 189
14:9	211n.39
14:18	211n.39
15:13	211n.39
15:16	211n.39
15:19-33	66, 129
16:4	211n.39
16:24	211n.39
16:26	211n.39

16:27-28	211n.39
19:12	232
19:18	232
22:4	66
22:6	211n.39
24:20	232
24:7	189

Numbers

6	172
6:4-5	110
13	232
14:22	232
18:19	78, 189
19:7	211n.39
19:8	211n.39
19:11-22	66, 129
20:2-13	261
24:17	174

Deuteronomy

1:15	11
6:6-9	276, 293
7:1	227
10:21	232
12:32	35
13:18	35
18:15	190
24:1-4	232
29–31	231

34	231	11:4	80-81	7:23-25	256n.59
		11:8	206n.24	8:20	12
Joshua		11:25	10	9:15	226
1:8	276, 293	11:27	10, 12	10:28–11:40	152
3:13-17	191	12:24	10, 12	11–12	196
6:10	71n.26	12:25	12	11:1	12
10:26	167n.16	13:1-2	11	11:5	12
12:21	226	13:14	11	11:10	12
17:11	226	13:28	11	16:31-33	250
		15:1	11	18:18	250
Judges		15:6	11	18:19	250
1:27	226	15:7	11	18:22	250
3:24	206n.24	16:3	9	18:40	250
5:19	226	17:14	10, 11n.11	19:11-13	288
9:45	216	17:23	167n.16	19:11-18	251
		18:9	167n.16		
Ruth		18:18	11	**2 Kings**	
1:20-21	261	24:1	261	1	37
3:7	206n.24			1:8	251
3:9	230	**1 Kings**		2:1-11	251
4:16-17	230	1–2	9, 152	2:13-25	251
		1:5	11	9:27	226
1 Samuel		1:6	11	10:19	70
5:5	163	1:13	9	16:17	256n.59
8:6-7	196	1:15-18	230	17	151
8:11-15	196	1:17	9	17:24-41	161
8:18	11	1:20	9	17:29-34	161
9:2	11	1:24	9	18:4	153
15:11	11	1:27	9	18:9–20:19	153
15:19	11	1:30	9	23:29	226
15:23	11	1:35	9	23:30	226
15:26	11	1:46	9		
16–2 Sam 5:5	13	1:48	9	**1 Chronicles**	
16:7	12	2:12	9	1–9	275
16:14	11	2:46	195n.1	12:39-40	152
18:14	12	3:2-6	152	17:13-14	152
21:4-6	218	3:3	12	17:15	152
24:3	206n.24	3:6	12	21:1	261
		3:14	12	22:9-10	152
2 Samuel		4:12	226	28:10	152
2:3-4	11	4:20-28	196	28:6-7	152
3:2-5	11	4:21	195		
5:1	11	4:25	194-98, 282	**2 Chronicles**	
5:14-16	11	4:26	195	1:3-6	152
9–20	9	4:28	195	2:1–8:16	152
11	37, 230	5:5	195n.1	4:2	256n.59

4:4	256n.59	5:1	135	86	102
4:15	256n.59	6:1	135	87–88	102
10:19	151	7:1	135	89:10	255n.55
13:5	78, 189	7:17	135-36	89:10-11	288
13:8-9	151	8	134-36	90–106	102
16:1-2	151	8:4	190	95:11	232
16:7	151	8:7	88	100	293
18:5-7	151	9	135-36	101	102
20:35	151	9:13	135	103	102
21:13	151	10:1	135	104:5-9	191, 255n.56
21:18-19	165	10:18	136	104:7	288
28:2	151	11:2-3	135	106:9	288
29–31	153	12:1	135	106:48	102
32	153	13:1	88, 135	107–150	102
35:22	226	15–24	136n.3	107:23-30	288
36:22-23	153	18:15	288	107:29-30	256
		18:28	88	108	13-14
Ezra		19	136n.3	109	102
1:1-3	153	19:5-6	269	109:8	167
4:14	77-79	19:14	276, 293	110	102
6:9-10	189	23:1	275	111–118	102
		26:2-3	275	118:22	149, 233
Nehemiah		29:4	275	118:26	233
1:3	283-84	31:5	143	118:32	233
5:13	164n.11	41:13	102	119:11	136
8	284	42–43	13	119:15	276, 293
		42–72	102	119:16	136
Esther		42:1-2	275	119:23	276, 293
4:14	12	45:6	79-80	119:48	276, 293
7:9-10	167n.16	49:3	276, 293	119:78	276, 293
		57	14	119:97	276, 293
Job		57:1-4	14	119:99	276, 293
1:12	261	57:5	13	119:148	276, 293
9:8	256, 287	57:7-11	14	119:176	136-37
9:13	255n.55, 288	57:11	13	120–122	104-105
26:11-13	288	60	14	120–134	102
31	207	60:5-12	14	122	102
38:8-11	255n.56	67	172	124	102
41	255n.55	67:6	87	124:1	104
		68:9-10	88	124:8	104
Psalms		69:21	232	125:5	104
1–41	102	69:25	167	128:1	104
2:6-7	103	73–83	102	128:5	104
2:7	108, 142	74:13-14	255n.55, 288	128:6	104
3:1	135	77:19	287	129:1	104
4:1	135	84–85	102	131	102

131:3	104	63:18	163	**Joel**	
132:9	104	66:24	206	1:7	137n.4, 281
133	102			1:12	281
134:3	104	**Jeremiah**		2:12-13	81
138–145	102	5:17	137n.4	2:18-19	80-81
145:13	192	8:13	137n.4, 282	2:22	281
146–150	102	19:1-13	167	3:13	163
150	103	23:5	173-74	3:16-18	226
		24:1-10	137n.4		
Proverbs		25:30	163	**Amos**	
3:22-24	276, 293	27:19	256n.59	1–2	129
6:22	276, 293	29:17	137n.4	5:24	275
8:27-29	255n.56	31:15	2	9:11-15	129
15:28	276, 293	32:6-9	167	9:13	92
23:6	154				
28:22	154	**Lamentations**		**Micah**	
		1:15	163	1:2–2:11	130
Ecclesiastes		3:1-20	293	2:12-13	130
1:1	36	3:21-26	293	3	130
12:9-14	36			3:12	157
		Ezekiel		4–5	130
Isaiah		2:1	190	4:1-5	157
1–12	130	3:1	190	4:3	195
2:1-5	157	4:1	190	4:4	194-98
2:6	157	5:1	190	5:2	2, 230
4:4	215	6:1	190	5:5-6	163
5:1-7	190	17:20	177	6:1–7:7	130
6:2	206n.24	23:7-8	225	7:1	137n.4
7:14	2, 79-80, 230	31	175	7:8-20	130
9:1-6	129	31:1-9	174		
11:1	2	32:2	225	**Habakkuk**	
13:1	225	33:1-9	164n.11	3:15	287
13:10	225	34:6	176	3:17	137n.4
27:1	255n.55	34:11-12	176		
28:4	137n.4	36:25	211	**Zechariah**	
36–37	80	43:24	189	3:8	173-74
40–66	251-52			6:12	173-74
40:3	190, 210	**Daniel**		7:10	70
42:1	108, 142	4:12	174	8:18-19	260
43:16	287	7:13	31	9:9	232
50:2	288	7:13-14	190, 225	11:12-13	167
51:9	255n.55	8:13	163	12:11	226
51:9-10	255-56, 288			14:2-5	226
53	93	**Hosea**		14:4-5	155
55:6-13	129	2:12	137n.4		
57:8	206n.24	9:10	137n.4		

Malachi		4:21	47	11:28-30	232
3:1	251	5–7	15, 103	12:17-21	35
4:5	251	5:3	76	12:27	72-73
		5:11	271	12:48-49	201
		5:13	52n.10, 188	13	103
NEW TESTAMENT		5:14	52n.10	13:31-32	174
		5:19	202	13:33	175
Matthew		5:20	253	13:35	35
1–2	173	5:21	232	13:47	177
1:1	231	5:22	202	13:53	231
1:3	73, 230	5:24	202	14:22-23	191
1:5	73, 230	5:27	232	14:22-27	283
1:6	73, 230	5:28	206	14:33	74, 288n.39
1:16	231	5:31	71n.27, 232	15:14	87
1:18-19	156	5:33	232	15:24	176
1:18-25	230	5:38	232	16:12	155
1:18–2:23	2	5:43	232	16:13-20	145
1:20	73	5:43-48	202	16:16	224
1:23	35, 36, 79-80	6:1-18	154	16:17	251
2:1	156, 174	6:12	154	16:21	145
2:2	174	6:16-18	260	16:21–28:20	145
2:3-4	230	6:19-21	154	17:1-8	17-18
2:8	36	6:20	154	17:2	232
2:9	174	6:22-23	154	17:20	137, 155
2:11	231	6:24	154	18	103
2:13	231	6:25-34	154	18:6	201, 202
2:15	35, 231	7:3	83	18:6-9	207n.28
2:16	231	7:5	202	18:10	201, 202
2:18	35	7:6	163	18:10-14	31-32
2:19	231	7:7	44	18:12	176
2:23	35, 156	7:24-27	170-71	18:14	201, 202
3:9	211	7:28	231	18:15	202
3:11	214	8–9	15-16, 232	18:15-17	138
3:13-15	156	8:13	71n.27	18:18	82, 138
3:13-17	232	8:17	35	18:21-22	175-76
3:14	87	8:23-27	191, 283	18:21-35	138
3:14-15	142, 230	8:28	232	18:23-27	176
3:16-17	36	9:27	232	18:35	202
3:17	142, 230, 232	10	103, 232	19:1	231
4:2	260	10:2-4	260	19:28	232
4:3	67-68	10:9-23	201	20:1-16	193
4:5	87	10:40	201	20:15	154
4:8	87	10:42	201, 202	20:30	232
4:9	67-68	11:13	211	21–23	155, 233
4:15-16	35	11:14	251n.47	21:4-7	232
4:17	145	11:19	260	21:9	155, 233

21:21	137, 155	27:46	186	2:1–3:6	14-15, 16
21:28-32	156, 233	27:48	232	2:13-17	14-15
21:28–22:14	233	27:51-53	150	2:14	17
21:33-46	156, 233	27:62-66	233	2:18-20	260
21:42	233	27:63	233	2:18-22	14-15
22:1-7	156	28:6-9	207	2:21-22	37
22:1-10	233	28:12-15	234	2:22	129
22:15-22	233	28:13	233	2:23–3:6	35
22:23-33	233	28:15	233	2:24-28	14
22:34-40	233	28:16-20	36	2:28	209n.31
22:46	233	28:19	173, 201	3:1-6	14-15
23	155			3:6	90
23:1	202	**Mark**		3:7	287
23:1-36	233	1:1	35, 41-42, 209, 254	3:11	209n.31
23:10	202			3:11-12	145
23:37	156	1:1-13	113	3:13	287
23:37-39	233	1:3	211	3:13-19	90
23:39	155, 233	1:4	250	3:16	177
24	224	1:5	250	3:17	177
24–25	103	1:9-11	108	3:20-33	5-6
24:3	191, 254	1:10	281	3:21-29	236
24:27	254	1:11	42, 208, 209n.31	3:34-35	6
24:28	88, 217n.53	1:12	281	4	160n.3
24:35	88	1:14-15	41, 254	4:1-9	154
24:37	254	1:14–6:13	113	4:3	71
24:39	254	1:16	17	4:8	176
25	224	1:16-18	90	4:9	71
25:6	43	1:16-20	236	4:10	154, 287
25:24	87	1:16–8:21	142	4:11	87, 236
25:31-46	200-203	1:17	176-78	4:13	90
26	231	1:18	281	4:14-20	154-55
26:1	231	1:19	17	4:20	176
26:53	254	1:19-20	90	4:24	82
26:53-54	232	1:20	281	4:26-29	27-28
26:71	230	1:21	281	4:35-41	256
27–28	231	1:23	281	5:1-20	210n.33
27:1-10	186	1:24	209n.31	5:7	289
27:3-10	156, 164-67	1:24-25	145	5:19	190
27:9-10	35	1:28	281	5:21-24	66
27:13-15	156	1:29	281, 287	5:25-27	65-66, 129
27:17	85	1:29-31	236	5:25-34	66
27:19	156	1:30	281	5:28	129
27:24	156, 167, 186	1:31	199	5:30	129
27:25	156, 167, 186	1:42	281	5:31	129
27:34	232	1:43	281	5:34	199
27:36	233	2:1-12	14-15	5:35-43	66

5:41	129	9:49	82, 88, 216	13:30	225
6:1-6	90, 147	9:49-50	188-89, 207	14–15	142
6:7-30	90	10:11-12	207	14:3-9	200
6:11	163-64	10:33	186	14:8-9	199
6:14–10:52	113-14	10:33-37	146	14:9	210n.33
6:16	155	10:35-37	209	14:10	200
6:31-32	287	10:46-52	16-17	14:31	88
6:31-44	236	10:52	209	14:40	18n.22
6:34-44	226	11–13	142	14:43-45	90
6:45-51	286-91	11	199	14:49	149
6:45-53	256	11:1–15:47	113	14:50	91
6:52	288, 291	11:12-14	137	14:50-52	90
7:24–8:10	210n.33	11:12-19	149	14:58	149, 150
7:28-29	199	11:12-26	5-6	14:61	209n.31
8:1-9	226	11:13	87	14:66-72	90
8:11	155	11:14	88	14:68	87
8:15	155	11:15-16	149	14:72	148
8:17	87	11:15-19	91, 137	15:2	208
8:17-21	90	11:20-21	137	15:9	208
8:19-21	177	11:22-23	137-38	15:23	87, 232
8:21–10:52	36	11:22-25	155	15:26	208
8:22–10:52	142	11:23	155	15:29	150
8:22-26	17, 42, 146	11:27–12:40	149	15:31	208
8:27	17	11:32	209n.31	15:32	208
8:27–10:45	19	12:1-12	190	15:34	186, 187, 224
8:27–10:52	90	12:11	149	15:36	208, 232
8:29	42, 90, 190,	12:17	254	15:37	224
	209n.31	12:25	260	15:38	150
8:31	186	12:33	155	15:39	42, 191, 208, 209,
8:33	145, 146	12:35	149, 209n.31		209n.31
8:33-34	190	12:40	198, 200	15:40-41	90, 199, 210
8:34	90, 189	12:41-44	198-200	15:47	144
9:1	190	13	149, 200	16:1-8	113
9:2-8	17-19	13:1-2	199	16:7	146
9:3	232	13:1-3	149	16:8	89-91
9:6	18n.22	13:2	88	16:9-20	89-91, 186
9:7	42, 190, 208,	13:8	210n.33		
	209n.31	13:9	189	**Luke**	
9:12-13	190, 251n.47	13:9-13	199	1–2	96, 107
9:14-29	18	13:10	210n.33	1:1–28:31	95
9:31	186	13:12	189	1:5-25	37
9:31-34	146	13:12-13	146, 189	1:9	96
9:33	206	13:24-25	225	1:10	96, 143
9:35-41	206	13:26	225	1:11-17	109-10
9:35-50	188	13:27	225	1:11-20	36
9:42-47	205-7	13:29	225	1:13	251

1:15	96	6:40	47	16:19-31	202
1:17	251n.47	6:47-49	170-71	17:11-17	97
1:26-38	37, 110	7:1-10	97	17:11-18	148
1:28-38	36	7:32	82	17:12	162
1:32-33	254	8:39	190	17:18	162
1:35	96	8:54	97	17:19	162
1:41	37, 96	9	97	17:37	88, 216-17,
1:57-80	37	9:18	143		217n.53
1:59-63	251	9:18-22	146	18:32	98
1:67	96, 110	9:22	98	18:34	98
1:76	110	9:28	143	19:28-44	147-48
1:78	173-74	9:28-36	97	19:37	98
2:1	95	9:37-43	35	19:41-48	95
2:1-40	37	9:44	98	19:45-48	98
2:9-12	96	9:45	98	21	97
2:22-35	110-11	9:49-50	97	21:8	191
2:32	96	9:51-53	97	21:9-10	191
2:36	111	9:51-55	95, 97, 148	21:12-13	97
2:38	111	9:51–19:44	95	21:18	99
2:41	87	9:54	177	21:24	163
2:41-49	96	10	97	21:25	191
2:41-52	270	10:25-37	160-62	21:37	96
3:1-20	130	10:38-42	193	22:4	98
3:3	96	11:1	143	22:29-30	244n.38
3:4	190	11:4	154	22:31-32	45-46
3:7-9	251	11:37-54	155	22:32	143, 146
3:16	88, 214	12:1	155, 175	22:39-46	25-27
3:19-20	143	12:2	155	22:41-44	143
3:21	143	12:32	175	22:42	98
3:21-22	96, 107-8	13:10-17	35	22:43	99
3:22	143	13:18-19	174	22:66	99
4:1-2	96	13:18-21	35	23:1	99
4:1-13	108	13:20-21	175	23:1-2	98
4:9	96	13:22-35	97, 148	23:2	98, 191
4:14	96	13:31	97	23:4	191
4:14-30	95, 147	13:31-33	99	23:5	98
4:16-30	96	13:33	98	23:8	99, 155
4:18-19	107-8	13:35	155	23:10	98
4:31-37	97	14:1-6	35	23:13	99
5:24-26	97	14:13	202	23:14	191
5:29–6:11	96	14:26	82	23:15	99
6:12	143	14:34-35	188	23:16	99
6:13	63n.19	15	136	23:18	98
6:14-16	96	15:1-10	35	23:18-19	98
6:16	96	15:3-7	31	23:19	191
6:39	48-49	15:4-10	32-34	23:20	99

23:21	98	2–4	91	19:28	187
23:22	99, 191	2:13-22	91	19:38-39	3
23:23	98	2:21	31, 92	19:39-40	4
23:26-34	186	2:24–3:21	3-4	20	154
23:28	99	3:1-12	92	20:17	69-70
23:32	98	3:7-12	45-46	20:28	5, 30
23:34	99, 143	3:30	92	20:31	29-30, 188
23:35-43	187	4:2	54	21:15	154
23:43	99	4:4-42	292-93		
23:44-49	187	4:12	46	**Acts**	
23:45	149, 150	4:14	88	1–2	96
23:46	99, 143, 150	4:20-22	46	1:1–6:7	34, 243
23:47	191	4:22	162	1:2	96
23:50-56	99	4:25	46	1:3	96
23:55	144	4:34	187	1:4	77-79, 189
24:11	146	4:35-38	92	1:5	96
24:30	99	4:42	46, 92	1:8	79, 95, 96, 243
24:32	99	4:53	92	1:9-11	95, 144
24:34	146	5–10	30, 91	1:10	96
24:39	144	6:35	88	1:11	224
24:41-43	99	7:27	87	1:13	96
24:43	144	7:50	3	1:14	96, 187
24:44-45	99	7:51	4	1:15	96
24:47	95, 99	8:19	86	1:16	96
24:48	95	8:48	162	1:18-19	164-67
24:49	95	9:1–10:21	4-5	1:22	95
24:50-51	95, 144	9:28-29	231	1:24	96
24:53	96	9:34	30	2	95
		9:38	30	2:1-4	96
John		10:3	30	2:14-40	96, 114
1:1	30	10:9	71-72	2:17-18	260
1:1-18	23	10:22	4	2:28	244
1:8-9	3	10:33-36	30	2:32	95
1:18	30, 74-75	11:29	87	2:38	51, 71, 95, 96, 210,
1:19-28	144	11:32	87		243
1:29-34	144	11:33	87	2:45	87
1:32	144	11:47-57	92	2:46	96
1:33	144	12:27	187	3:6	97
1:34	221-23	12:32	87, 187	3:12-26	114
1:35-42	144	12:42-43	4	4:1–8:3	96
1:36	144	13:17	86	5:1-11	97, 168
1:42	251	16:2	30	5:14	169
1:43-51	144	16:21	87	5:35	87
1:47-49	92	18:11	187	5:38-39	67-68
1:50-51	45-46	18:36	86	6–8	97
1:51	30	19:26-27	187	6:1-6	93, 168, 224

6:7	93, 243	13:46	97	21:4	98
6:8	93, 244	13:51	164	21:10-11	244
6:8–9:30	243	14:11-18	156, 169	21:11	98
6:15	97	15	244n.38	21:12-14	98
7:2-53	114	15:1-41	168	21:14	98
7:55	97	15:37-41	94	21:17-20	98
7:55-56	93, 244	16:5	94, 169, 243	21:26-30	98
7:60	187	16:6-7	94, 244	21:26-31	96
8:4-25	97, 242-44	16:6–19:20	243	21:27–28:31	95
8:14	244n.38	16:9-10	244	21:30-33	98
8:18-24	156, 169	16:15	92	21:38	98, 191
8:20	88	16:16	167-69	22:3-21	139-40
8:26-40	244	16:16-18	156, 169	23	99
9	97	16:18	168	23:13-15	98
9:1-19	139-40	16:19	168	23:29	99
9:1-30	93	16:21–28:31	243	24	99
9:3-6	109	16:33	92	24:5-6	98
9:15-16	97	17	114-15n.39	24:14	243
9:15-17	107-8	17:16	169	25	99
9:27	244n.38	17:16-31	114-15	25:2	98
9:31	93, 243	17:16-34	156	25:7	98
9:31–12:24	243	17:22-24	244n.38	25:11	98
9:32-35	97	18:3	184	25:15-17	98
9:40	97	18:6	97, 164, 164n.11	25:24	98
10	35, 97	18:8	92	25:25	87, 99
10:34-43	114	18:14-15	86	26	99, 114-15
10:36-43	35	18:22	244n.38	26:2	98
10:44-46	244	19:1-7	156, 168	26:4-18	139-41
10:44-48	93	19:3	243	26:27	243
11:2	244n.38	19:4	86	26:27-28	140
11:14	92	19:4-6	210	26:28	87
11:17	87	19:9	97	26:29	168
12	99	19:11-19	97	26:31	99
12:1-19	97	19:13-19	94	26:32	99
12:1-23	93	19:13-20	156, 169	27:21	99
12:23	166	19:17-41	156	27:23	99
12:24	93, 243	19:20	94, 243	27:24	99
12:25–16:5	243	19:23-41	169	27:31-32	99
12:25–21:16	95	19:24-29	169	27:34	99
13:1–20:38	97	20	97	27:35	99
13:2	244	20:22	98	27:42-43	99
13:2-3	93	20:22-23	98	27:43-44	99
13:6-12	169	20:28-30	144	28:1-10	99
13:8-12	156	20:34-35	184	28:4-6	156, 169
13:14-41	114	20:36-37	98	28:11	191
13:19	177, 227	21–28	97, 98	28:15	43

28:16	95	16:23	179	2:14–6:13	203
28:19	95	16:25	53	4:4	86
28:23	99			5:5	51
28:25-28	168	**1 Corinthians**		5:13	54
28:26-28	99	1:10	47	5:14	54
28:28	94, 243	2:8	253	5:14-15	204
28:29	99	2:10-16	279	5:15	54, 204
28:31	243	4:11	201	5:18	204, 205
		5:7	175	5:18-21	37
Romans		5:8	175	5:19-20	205
1–8	111, 132	6:1	87	5:21	203-5
1:5	86	6:4	87	5:29	204
1:16-17	254	7–16	7	6:1-2	204
1:17	264	7:1	220	10:15	63n.19
3:3	55	7:1-2	218	11:6	114
3:21	55	7:1-9	217	11:23-29	201
3:22	54, 55	7:2	219	12:7	86
3:25	55	7:5	183, 218		
3:26	54	7:7	87	**Galatians**	
3:30	55	7:13	87	1:8-9	86
3:31	55	7:17	71n.27	2:10	86
5:1-11	111-12	7:24-25	183	2:16	54, 55
5:11	63n.19	7:25	7	3:2	54
5:15-21	112	8:1	7	3:14-29	37
6:3-7	293	9:8	48-49, 87	4:15	183
6:3-9	59	11:3	260	4:20	88
6:4	59n.16	11:26	87	5:9	175
6:6	276	12:1	7		
8	83	13:4-7	20-22	**Ephesians**	
8:26-27	76n.32	13:8	138	1–3	132
8:28	76-77	13:8-12	138-39	1:1-11	273
9–10	74	13:13	53	1:3-14	23, 116, 127
9:3	88	14:1	139	1:15-23	116-17
9:19	87	14:15	271	1:16-19	124
9:20-21	48-49	14:16	87	1:20	84, 127
11:2	87	15	69n.23	2:6	84, 127
11:13-14	74	15:2	87	2:20	86
12	132	15:20-28	253	3:12	55
12–15	132	15:23	253	3:14-19	115-17, 124-25
12:2	252n.50	15:58	224	3:17	55
12:4	87	16:1	7	4–6	132
12:9-19	63n.19	16:12	7	4:1	84, 127
13	252-54			4:9	86
13:1-7	227	**2 Corinthians**		4:11	277
14:4	87	1:3-7	37	4:12	46-47, 277
14:10	87	2:4	71-72	4:13	46

4:16	47
4:17	52, 84, 127
4:19	52
4:22-24	293
5:2	84, 127
5:8	84, 127
5:15	84, 127
5:18	69-70
5:18-21	117-18
5:21-22	49
5:25	49
5:33	49
6:10-17	293
6:11	84, 127
6:13	84, 127
6:14	84, 127
6:14-17	84

Philippians

1:4-5	50
1:21	50
1:22	51
1:26	50
1:29	47-48
2:1-4	133-34
2:2	50
2:2-4	63n.19
2:6	133
2:6-8	62-63
2:6-11	23
2:9	47-48
2:17	50
2:25	133
2:28	50n.8
3:1	50
3:7-8	133-34
4:1	50
4:4	50

Colossians

1:4-5	53
1:9-11	123-26
1:14	23
1:15-20	22-25
1:21-23	23
2:6	64, 65n.20

2:7	63-65
2:8	64
2:11-12	58-59, 85
2:11-15	293
2:12	55
2:13-15	59-61
2:20–3:4	293
4:9	180
4:16	86

1 Thessalonians

1:3	51-53
2:19	253
3:13	253
4–5	69n.23
4:11	182, 184
4:11-12	183
4:13–5:11	183
4:15	253
4:17	43
4:18	224
5:3	254
5:8	53
5:8-11	224
5:14	182, 183
5:23	253

2 Thessalonians

1:4-6	185
1:11	53, 224
2:1-12	185
2:1-17	183
2:15	224
3:6	182
3:6-15	183, 185
3:7	182
3:8	63n.19, 183
3:10	182
3:11	182, 183

1 Timothy

1:15	56, 57
2:1-2	254
2:13	260
2:14	260
2:15	56, 57

3:1	56-57
3:15	283
3:16	23, 28-29
4:1	53-54
4:3	54
4:9	56, 57
4:10	56
4:12	71n.27
6:17-20	69n.23

2 Timothy

2:10	56, 57
2:11	56
2:11-13	57

Titus

2:13	51
3:1-2	254
3:5-6	56
3:8	56, 57

Philemon

5	181
7	181
8	182
9-10	181
12	181
15-16	180
16	181
18-19	180
19	182

Hebrews

1:1-10	129
1:1–2:18	128
1:5-14	129
1:8-9	79-80
2:1-4	129
3:1–4:13	128
3:7-11	129
3:12–4:13	129
4:14-16	129
4:14–7:28	128
4:20–5:8	196
5:11–6:12	129
6:4-6	66

6:6	66-67	2:1	6	3	69n.23
6:16	87	2:1-13	6	3:8	71n.27
6:17	130	2:3	163		
7:11	87	2:14	6	**1 John**	
8:1-13	129	2:14-26	6	1:5	127
8:1–10:31	128	3:1-12	6	1:6–2:2	2-3
10:11	73	4:13	6	2:2	190
10:12	73	4:13–5:6	6	2:3–5:12	127-28
10:14	73	5:1	6	3:6	44
10:19-20	150	5:7	6	5:13-20	128
10:19-31	129	5:7-11	7		
10:32	87	5:12	6	**2 John**	
10:32-39	121	5:12-18	7	5	201
10:32–12:29	128	5:19	6		
10:36	121	5:19-20	7	**Jude**	
10:37-38	129			2	40
11	121	**1 Peter**		4	40
12:1	121	1:3-12	107, 133	5-7	40
12:1-2	118-21	1:7	44-45	8	40
12:1-29	129	1:13-14	63n.19	11	40
12:2-3	121	1:13–2:3	133	20-21	122-23
13	69n.23	2:4-10	133	22-23	39-41
13:8	73	2:11–3:12	133		
		2:12	63n.19, 87	**Revelation**	
James		2:18	63n.19	1–6	101
1:2	6, 87, 106	3:1	63n.19	1:1	240
1:2-15	6	3:7-9	63n.19	1:3	100, 240
1:3	106	3:13-22	133	2–3	100
1:4	106	3:14	68-69	3:14-22	169-70
1:5	106	4:1-11	133	4–5	101, 254
1:6	106	4:2	87	4:1	240-41
1:7-8	106	4:7	69	4:2-11	100
1:9	106	4:7-11	224	4:6	256
1:10-11	106	4:8-9	63n.19	5:8-14	100
1:11	106	4:10	71-72	6	191
1:13	106	4:11	69	6:1–8:5	100
1:13-15	261	4:12	69	6:8	101
1:14-15	106	4:12-19	133	7:1–8:5	101
1:16	6, 106	4:13	69	7:9-17	100
1:16-18	6	4:14	68-69	8:6–11:14	101
1:18	133	4:18	87	8:6–11:19	100
1:19	6, 106	5:1-14	133	8:7-8	101
1:19-27	6	5:3	87	9:5	289
1:22	106			11:2	163
1:23-24	106	**2 Peter**		11:10	289
1:25	106	2:11-14	224	11:15–12:12	101

11:15-18	100
12–14	100
12:2	289
12:3	255n.55, 256
12:13–13:18	101
13	252-54
13:1	256
13:1-15	100
14–15	101
14:1-5	100
14:13	100
15–16	100
15:2-4	100
16–18	101
16:3-4	101
16:15	100
16:16	226
17–20	100
17:1	256
18:4	86
19:1-8	100
19:1-18	101
19:9	100
19:15	163
19:19–20:10	101
20:6	100
20:7	226
20:11–22:21	101
21:1	191, 255-56
21:4	256
21:22	74-75
22:3	256
22:3-6	88
22:5	256
22:6	240
22:7	88, 100
22:10	240
22:12	88
22:14	100
22:16	173
22:18	240
22:19	240
22:20	88

APOCRYPHA

1 Maccabees

10:63	71n.26
14:9	197
14:11-13	197

2 Maccabees

2:23	103
7:13	289
9–10	165-66
9:5	165-66
14:37-46	167n.15

4 Maccabees

6:5	289

Sirach

50:25-26	161

Wisdom of Solomon

10:7	216
14:1-4	287

OLD TESTAMENT PSEUDEPIGRAPHA

4 Baruch

8:11	161

Joseph and Asenath

21:21	177

Jubilees

6:3-4	78, 189
21:11	78, 189

Psalms of Solomon

16:4	140n.10

Testament of Levi

9:14	189

Testament of Naphtali

6	290

MISHNAH, TALMUD, AND RELATED LITERATURE

Mishnah
Gittin

1:5	162

Kil'ayim

3:2	174n.28

Niddah

4:1	162

Sheqalim

1:5	162

Shev'it

8:10	162

Sotah

3:4	193

Pesaḥim

8:8	212

Ṭohar.

4:5	164

Babylonian Talmud
Berakot

19b	164

Gittin

8a [Bar.]	164

Niddah

13b	206

Sanhedrin

43a	233

Shabbat

16b	162

Yebamot

46a	212

Jerusalem Talmud
Shabbat

3c	162

Sifra on Lev.
26:9   193

Tosephta
Sanhedrin
7:11   111n.30

DEAD SEA SCROLLS

1QS
1:24-26   211
3:8-9   211
4:20-21   215
8:12-16   251n.48
8:13-14   211

4Q246   192

4Q521   192

11QT
46:13   206n.24

EARLY CHRISTIAN
WRITINGS

Augustine
Quaestiones
evangeliorum
2:19   237

Didache
16   69n.23

Eusebius
Historia Ecclesiastica
3:39   104

Martyrdom of Polycarp
2:2   289

Tertullian
On Baptism
12:5   290

OTHER ANCIENT
WRITINGS

Josephus
Antiquities
12:357   165
16:164   192
18:29-30   161
18:117-19   210
19:350   166n.14

Jewish War
2.21.10 §642-45   207n.27
3:459   254
4:618   254
1:656   166
6:345-46   254

Life
34 §169-73   207n.27
35 §177   207n.27

Philo
De Decalogo
87   140n.10

De specialibus legibus
3:169   192

Acts of Augustus
34   254
35   254

Aeschylus
Agamemnon
1642   140n.10

Appian
Civil Wars
1:104-5   166
2.14.99   167n.15

Euripides
Bacchae
794-95   140n.10

Galen
De sanitate tuenda
6:12   170

Plutarch
De defectu oraculorum
9:414E   168n.17

Sulla
36:3   166-67

Pseudo-Aristotle
Mirab. Auscult.
58   170

Suetonius
Vespasian
12   254

Symmachus
Letters
9, 140   182

Terence
Phormio
1.2.27   140n.10

Virgil
Aeneid
1:278-79   254
6:851-53   254